INSIDE THE NYE HAM DEBATE

Is Creation
a viable
model...

Revealing Truths
from the Worldview
Clash of the Century

KEN HAM &
BODIE HODGE

Endorsements

In the never-ending battle for truth, here is a "Gatling gun" for those who are fighting the good fight. This publication is like a "roaring lion" that should help silence the never-ending chattering "chimps of evolutionary believers." I love Ken Ham's love for the truth. He is uncompromising and headstrong — two virtues that are highly commendable when it comes to issues that govern the eternal destiny of this and future generations.

We don't want to win the argument. We want to win the lost to Jesus Christ. This book helps you do that. This publication should put a "smooth stone into your sling" and help you to run toward the enemy, without fear. In a world where evolutionary dreamers stand behind the curtains of true science, Ken Ham and Bodie Hodge pull the curtains away.

> Ray Comfort
> Founder and President/CEO of Living Waters
> Publications. He is a best-selling author and was co-host
> with Kirk Cameron of the award winning television
> program "The Way of the Master."

The Ham/Nye debate, and this follow up book, represents a most vivid illustration of the intellectual and spiritual chasm separating naturalistic materialism and Biblical Christianity as explanations of the origin of everything that exists. In a remarkable moment of candor that night, I remember Mr. Nye being asked," How did matter come to exist?" "I don't know," he replied. Thank you, Mr. Nye, for your honesty. And thank you Ken Ham for giving the answer based on good science AND the divine revelation of the answer to this question in God's Word. What is our authority, is what is at stake in this debate. Is it man's ideas or the truth revealed in the Bible? Thanks, Ken, for not only helping the Church answer the scientific questions at stake in this debate, but doing so completely committed to the authority of Scripture for every question of life.

> Greg Hall
> President of Warner University

First printing: October 2014

Master Books®, P.O. Box 726, Green Forest, AR 72638

Master Books® is a division of the New Leaf Publishing Group, Inc.

ISBN: 978-0-89051-857-1
Library of Congress Number: 2014916985
Cover by Diana Bogardus

Unless otherwise noted, Scripture quotations are from the New King James Version (NKJV) of the Bible. Scriptural passages with fewer than five verses are included as footnotes for easy reference.

Please consider requesting that a copy of this volume be purchased by your local library system.

Printed in the United States of America

Please visit our website for other great titles:
www.masterbooks.net

For information regarding author interviews,
please contact the publicity department at (870) 438-5288

Master
Books®
A Division of New Leaf Publishing Group
www.masterbooks.net

Special Thanks

I would like to acknowledge Ken Ham, Dr. Tommy Mitchell, Roger Patterson, Dr. Danny Faulkner, Dr. Andrew Snelling, Tim Chaffey and the many others who gave me input on the various arguments included within this book, as well as Dr. Stuart Burgess and Dr. Raymond Damadian for each providing a foreword. I would also like to thank Laura Welch of Master Books and Christelle Agboka for their editorial assistance.

Contents

Foreword

Professor Stuart Burgess

The Ham-Nye debate was portrayed in the popular media as "science versus faith," but in reality it was "an atheistic worldview versus a biblical worldview." Evolution is not mainstream science but rather a philosophical view of earth history based on speculation.

As a scientist I know that there is no conflict between true science and the Bible. I have carried out many experiments on biological systems and found them to contain solid evidence of purposeful design. In contrast, I have never seen experimental evidence that one could use to support evolution.

I totally disagree with Bill Nye that denying evolution hinders the development of technology. My belief in creation actually helps me develop technology because my high view of nature encourages me to copy the designs of nature. I believe my successful career has been partly due to my belief in biblical creation.

During the debate, Ken Ham was totally open about his belief in God and the Bible. In contrast, Bill Nye did not acknowledge his atheistic assumptions at any time. It is ironic that Christians are sometimes accused of having a hidden agenda when it is often the evolutionist who has a hidden agenda.

Credit must be given to Bill Nye for actually participating in the debate. Sadly, we live in a society where scientists are often not allowed to question evolution. I sincerely hope that more secular scientists will do what true scientists should do — be open-minded about the evidence.

People ask me who I think won the debate. Of course I think that Ken won the debate, but the most important question is who will win the global war between evolution and God? There is ultimately only one winning side and that is the side of the Creator. It is my hope that all those reading this book will be on that winning side.

Stuart Burgess BSc (Eng) PhD CEng FIMechE is professor of engineering design at the University of Bristol (UK).

His research interests include bio-inspired design, biomechanics, and design in nature. He has worked in industry as a professional designer working on projects for the European Space Agency. He has published over 130 secular papers on the science of design and has been coeditor of the *International Journal of Design & Nature*. He has lectured at both Cambridge University and Bristol University in the UK. He is also a visiting professor at Liberty University, USA. From 2004 to 2011 he was head of the department of mechanical engineering at Bristol University.

Foreword

Dr. Raymond V. Damadian

Regarding evolution: the scientific *evidence* needed to sustain it *does not exist*. In the same way that the abnormal NMR (MRI) signals from cancer tissue together with the pronounced differences of the NMR (MRI) signals among healthy tissues provided the *evidence* paramount to supporting the concept that NMR scanning of the human body (MRI) was feasible and would generate valuable visualizations of the body and its diseased tissues (*Science*, 171: 1151–1153, 1971) the *scientific evidence* paramount to sustaining the concept of evolution *does not exist*.

Specifically, the Intermediate Life Forms (I.L.F.'s) necessary to sustaining the concept of evolution have never been shown to exist. For Darwin's postulate as he proposes it: "therefore I should infer from analogy that probably all organic beings . . . *have descended from some one primordial form*" (C. Darwin, *The Origin of Species by Means of Natural Selection*, 2004, Barnes and Noble Classics, p. 380) the **critical scientific evidence necessary** to sustain his hypothesis that "all organic beings . . . have descended from *some one primordial form*" is proof of the "I.L.F.'s" ("Intermediate Life Forms") that demonstrate the existence of the "natural" transitions from one KIND to the next KIND that would enable successive anatomic and physiologic transitions to progress to higher and higher orders of complexity as required by evolution.

Such I.L.F.'s have never been demonstrated to exist.

Darwin's own evidence was confined to variations *WITHIN* the *KIND* (Genesis 1:25), i.e. beak variations *within* Galapagos finches. Indeed, though he searched for it, he was unable to obtain any evidence demonstrating the existence of transitional forms (I.L.F.'s) *between* *KINDS*. As Darwin himself states, "On the absence or rarity of transitional varieties" — "But, as by this theory *innumerable* transitional forms *must have existed, why do we not find them* embedded in countless numbers in the crust of the earth?" (C. Darwin, *The Origin of Species by Means of Natural Selection*, 2004, Barnes and Noble Classics, p 146). One hundred and fifty-five years later (A.D. 2014) these "innumerable transitional forms" (I.L.F.'s) essential to Darwin's theory of evolution still do not exist, just as Darwin himself found them *not to exist*.

Indeed, in terms of human ancestry, the skulls of our postulated ape "ancestors" differ strikingly from human skulls. The skulls of all the apes house approximately 400 cc of brain in contrast to the human skull which houses 1200 cc of brain. Moreover, the ape skull ceases at the superior orbit of the eye while the human skull extends an additional 2¼ inches of frontal bone above the orbit of the eye to accommodate the threefold increase in cerebral tissue (1200 cc vs. 400 cc) that has to be contained by the skull.

Accordingly, if humans are descended from the apes, where are the fossil remains of the I.L.F.'s necessary to substantiate such a descendancy? Where are the 800 cc fossil skulls or the 1" fossil skull frontal bones needed to contain the I.L.F. 800 cc brain (or any other *intermediate* brain volume)?

Likewise is the evolutionary mystery of the human eye. Proceeding along the optic pathway beginning at the cornea, the eye is an optical chain of nine fundamental structures, the cornea (1), followed by the iris (2), the lens (3), the ciliary processes to contract (or expand) the lens (4), the vitreous (5), the rods and cones of the retina (6), the optic nerve (7), the geniculate bodies of the brain to conduct the optic radiation (8), and the visual cortex of the occipital lobe of the brain to transform the optic radiations into a visual image (9). In the evolutionary model, none of the nine structures is capable of independent function. Each requires the *entire* enumerated 9-entity optical chain to generate vision. Thus the occurrence of any one of the nine structures by evolutionary "chance" achieves no *selective advantage* to accomplish the evolutionary survival by "natural selection" needed for the *evolution* of the eye to proceed. Thus the eye cannot *individually* "evolve" each of the above-mentioned steps in the optic pathway. Accordingly, the eye cannot "evolve" until all nine structures occur simultaneously by "chance" to generate vision. There would, for example, be no opportunity for the iris to occur by "chance" and exercise its *selective advantage* without the completed optic chain and its generated vision.

Accordingly, under the "evolutionary model" all nine structures would have to occur *accidentally* and *simultaneously* to enable the evolutionary genesis of the human eye: a probability of $1/9^9$, a probability of 1 chance in 387,420,489 million.

Darwin himself acknowledged the lack of credibility regarding such an evolutionary genesis of the eye. As he stated in *The Origin of Species* (C. Darwin, *The Origin of Species by Means of Natural Selection*, 2004, Barnes and Noble Classics, p 156), "To suppose that the eye, with all its inimitable contrivances . . . could have been formed by natural selection, seems, I freely confess, *ABSURD* in the highest possible degree." Yet, Darwin openly professed and believed it did!

As the Apostle Paul so profoundly points out to the Colossians more than 1,900 years ago, "In [God and Christ] are hidden all the treasures of wisdom and knowledge [and science]" (Colossians 2:3) which gave us the MRI. Western (Christian) civilization furnishes strong evidence of Paul's affirmation. As Henry Morris has pointed out,[1] knowledge and sciences are synonymous, both being English translations of the Greek *gnosis*.

The Christ-centered Puritan founders of America and the scientists of the Christ-centered nations of the Western world, *following* the appearance and universal availability of the Bible in print by Gutenberg and his printing press in 1455 (and not before), begat the first government in human history structured to secure the *enduring* individual freedom of *all* of its citizens that resulted in its staggering scientific and technological achievements, e.g., the internal combustion engine, electric lighting, the telephone, aircraft, and automobiles, which together with *free government* ushered in the greatest and unprecedented economic explosion and

---

1. H. Morris, *The Bible Is a Textbook of Science* (Dallas, TX: Institute for Creation Research, reprinted from Bibliothea Sacra, December 1964), http://www.icr.org/home/resources/resources_tracts_tbiatos/.

prosperity in human history within the nations that had Jesus Christ, just as the Apostle Paul forecast (Colossians 2:3), none of which occurred in China or India where there are no shortages of smart people.

As Ken Ham asked in a question to Bill Nye that went unanswered by Bill Nye in the Ken Ham–Bill Nye creation-evolution debate, "How does 'life' arise from a collection of inanimate matter?" i.e., How do you get "life" out of nonlife? How does life arise spontaneously from nonliving earth materials when no scientific evidence exists demonstrating the spontaneous generation of "life" from nonliving materials?

Accordingly, the long and short of it is self-evident.
You can't get there without Him!

Dr. Damadian was born in New York and would eventually attend prestigious educational institutions such as University of Wisconsin–Madison (1956) for mathematics, an M.D. degree from the Albert Einstein College of Medicine in New York City (1960), internship and residency in internal medicine at what is now State University of New York Health Science Center at Brooklyn, postdoctoral fellow work at the Washington School of Medicine in St. Louis, MO, transferring to Harvard Medical School, the Air Force's School of Aerospace Medicine in San Antonio, TX, and then returning to State University of New York Health Science Center as a faculty member teaching biophysics to graduate students and being assigned a lab at the facility. He is best known as the pioneering creator of the first working MRI machine.*

He and his wife have been married for over 50 years, and have three children. He currently works at FONAR, a company he started that focuses on development and sales of more affordable MRI machines. He has received numerous awards, including the National Medal of Technology (1988), induction into the National Inventor's Hall of Fame (1989), Lemelson-MIT Lifetime Achievement Award (2001), Honorary Fellow, American Institute for Medical and Biological Engineering (2009). He is also a member of the Biophysical Society, American Association for the Advancement of Science, International Society for Magnetic Resonance in Medicine, and the Society for Medical Innovation and Technology.

*A Brief Note about the Development of the MRI — Advancements in Science

As construction began on the first MRI scanner of the human body, Indomitable, and its "visionary nonsense" commenced, as one of its critics branded it, an economic impasse erupted. Utilizing "Mag Map," an IBM punched-card deck borrowed from the Brookhaven National Laboratory to calculate Indomitable's MRI magnet, the "Mag Map" calculation called for 30 miles of Niobium-Titanium (NbTi) wire, which when estimated at the manufacturer's (Westinghouse) price of $1 per foot required $150,000 to complete construction of the Indomitable MRI magnet. However, the funds available in our bank account were only $15,000. A call made to Westinghouse's Research Sales Director Steve Lane, at the time, for directions on how to make the non-resistive superconducting joints we needed to make between successive lengths of NbTi wire produced the spontaneous unsolicited response from Steve Lane. "Incidentally Dr. Damadian, unknown to anyone at the moment is Westinghouse's decision to cease its manufacture of NbTi superconducting wire and superconducting magnets. In case you have any interest, I have about

30 miles of NbTi wire in our warehouse which I can let you have for 10¢ on the dollar." Steve had no knowledge at the time of the wire length I had calculated with "Mag Map" that was needed for our Helmholtz magnet design. Asking if we would like to have the wire and when we could come for it if we did, I responded that I would send my graduate students, Mike Goldsmith and Larry Minkoff, in a U-Haul truck immediately to come get it.

Stunned by the extraordinary coincidence of Westinghouse's decision to cease making NbTi wire at the very instant I needed it and with their ability to provide, at 10¢ on the dollar, virtually the same length of wire I had computed with "Mag Map" that was needed, I was astonished by the coincidence. Larry and Mike flew immediately to Westinghouse's magnet factory in Baltimore, secured the NbTi wire, loaded it into the rental truck they hired, and brought it directly to our SUNY Brooklyn Downstate Medical Center Research Laboratory so that we could begin construction of our "Indomitable" MRI.

*Commenting a day or so later to my wife's parents, Amy and Bo Terry, both evangelical Christians, on the exceptional **coincidence** of Westinghouse suddenly ceasing the manufacture of NbTi wire at the very instant I needed it and possessing virtually the same length (and not less) of the wire I needed stored in their warehouse and making it available immediately at a 10¢-on-the-dollar price that my budget could achieve, my mother-in-law Amy's response was, "That's no coincidence. Your father and I have been praying continually for the success of your scanner project from the moment we learned of it. This is not a coincidence. This is an answer to prayer!"*

Introduction

Historically, there have been a number of famous debates in the US. One such series of debates — played out in Illinois in 1858 — involved Mr. (and later President) Abraham Lincoln and Mr. (and later Senator) Stephen A. Douglas (who were running against each other for senate), and focused on slavery. These published debates were a focus, on a national scale, for the presidential campaign in 1860. The debates set the stage for the freedom of slaves in the years to come and for the vicious civil war in the US.

Another (world) famous debate that occurred in the US was the Scopes Trial in 1925 in Tennessee. This debate, although technically won by the creationists, set the stage for a takeover of the education system by evolutionists and the removal of Christianity from schools and culture in the years to come. The decline of creationism occurred because the leading Christian defender, Mr. William Jennings Bryan, failed to totally trust the Bible's early pages in Genesis and allowed for secular long-age geology rather than a belief in six literal days of creation to permeate his thinking. He also couldn't answer basic questions like, "Where did Cain get his wife?" This sent shockwaves to the American people, who were predominantly

William Jennings Bryan

Christian at the time. If this leading Christian (Bryan) didn't trust the early pages of the Bible and couldn't adequately defend the Christian faith against the questions of the humanist lawyer, why should anyone trust any of it?

Dr. Duane Gish

Many may recall the series of debates between Dr. Duane Gish and hosts of evolutionists from the 1960s to the 1990s that reignited the creation vs. evolution battles on a scholarly level. The landmark book *The Genesis Flood* by Dr. Henry Morris and Dr. John Whitcomb really began the modern biblical creationist movement that eventually spurred these debates. The overwhelming winner of these debates was Dr. Gish, whose systematic discussion of origins and science from a creation perspective seemed unstoppable. He became known as the world's foremost creationist debater.

Then there was the great debate over the existence of God in 1985. This high-profile debate showcased leading atheist Dr. Gordon Stein and leading Christian philosopher Dr. Greg Bahnsen, who followed Dr. Cornelius Van Til's philosophical groundbreaking work in returning to the Bible to develop a biblical apologetic method. After years of Nietzsche's mantra ("God is dead") that filled philosophical circles, it was this debate that woke America back up to the idea that "God doesn't stay dead"! Dr. Bahnsen's Christlike devastation of the atheistic position and defense of Christian theism was nearly flawless.

Though many other debates could be mentioned here, we will now transition to a debate that stormed the world and is being dubbed "The Debate of the Century," or "Scopes II." In a near reversal of roles, the secular evolutionist's control of the state schools, media, museums, and creation has come under attack. This debate had nearly five million live viewers from over 190 countries around the world (only 195 countries exist today) and as of the publication of this book, it is conservatively estimated that nearly 15 million people have viewed the debate!

The agreed-upon debate topic was:

"Is creation a viable model of origins in today's modern scientific era?"

This debate was essentially on the topic of evolution, creation, science, and origins... The debaters were Mr. Bill Nye, "the science guy," and Mr. Ken Ham, "the observational science man," president and founder of the *Creation Museum* and *Answers in Genesis*. This debate centered on origins (Nye's position: *evolutionary naturalism*, versus Ham's position: *biblical creation*) and authority (Nye's position: *man is the ultimate authority*, versus Ham's position: *God and His Word are the ultimate authority*). The shockwaves from this incredible debate are still being felt.

How the debate became a reality

In brief, Mr. Nye produced a YouTube video with BigThink.com on August 23, 2012, claiming that "teaching creationism was not appropriate for children." Ken Ham and Answers in Genesis scientists Dr. Georgia Purdom and Dr. David Menton responded to his video with their own on YouTube.

As these video debates went viral on the Internet, hosts of people began posting their thoughts in article and video formats. Finally, *Associated Press* reporter Dylan Lovan was talking about the issue with Mark Looy, the chief communications officer at Answers in Genesis. Mr. Looy threw out the option of a formal debate between Bill Nye and Answers in Genesis instead of their going back and forth on YouTube. Dylan Lovan communicated this to Mr. Nye. After much discussion and negotiation, Bill Nye and Answers in Genesis signed a contract with an agreement for a debate between Bill Nye and Ken Ham.

As I understand from the media, Mr. Nye was to be paid an undisclosed amount of money for his appearance. Furthermore, Mr. Nye insisted on metal detectors being set up for the debate. A number of well-known personalities, agreed to by both parties, were considered to be the moderator. Eventually, Tom Foreman of CNN agreed to moderate the event.

Why am I in a position to respond to the debate?

First, I was in a privileged position to be able to see what I believe to be the debate of the century. Yes, I was in Legacy Hall at the Creation

Museum to watch the live debate between Mr. Bill Nye and Mr. Ken Ham as they presented their respective cases.

But I was also in another unique position. I work at Answers in Genesis and the Creation Museum with Mr. Ken Ham as a speaker, writer, and researcher dealing with both scientific, biblical, and historical topics. Furthermore, I'm in the even more peculiar position of being Ken Ham's son-in-law. I met and married Mr. Ham's eldest daughter after coming to work for the ministry over 10 years ago.

In addition, I have a BSc and MSc in mechanical engineering (attaining a level of engineering that is above Mr. Nye in the same field). I developed a new method of production of submicron titanium diboride (yes, real observational science). I've also worked as a test engineer in industry side-by-side with evolutionists and creationists as together we carried out experimental science to help develop technology.

Some might mistakenly think I helped prepare Mr. Ham for the debate and therefore am going to reiterate those discussions in this response. However, unbeknownst to most, I had nothing to do with Mr. Ham's debate preparation. So, like the many viewers (estimated about 5 million live that evening based on web statistics and now almost 15 million and counting), I was awaiting to see not only what Mr. Nye would say but also what Mr. Ham would present.[1]

Accordingly, many have asked me to give my unique perspective as one who is on the inside of AiG and the Ham family, but who also, in this instance, was on the outside looking in on the debate. I then asked Mr. Ham to go carefully through the entire book and add in his own insights, personal thoughts, and other information that would make this a unique appraisal of the debate. So even though it is written from my perspective, it also contains a lot of information to help you, the reader, analyze this historic debate. And as Mr. Ham has added extensively to this publication, it is a powerful inside look at an event that I believe will be an historic event in Christendom in this world.

Lastly, I am in another unique position (besides the fact that I am known to wear a bow tie from time to time like Mr. Nye[2]) to give a response to the specifics of the debate. You see, after the debate, I asked Mr.

---

1. My only involvement consisted of a predebate show for about 30 minutes with *Creation Today*, hosted by Eric Hovind and Paul Taylor.
2. Mr. Bill Nye is famous for his bow ties.

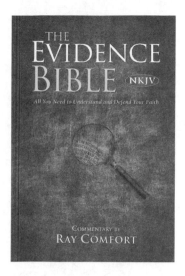
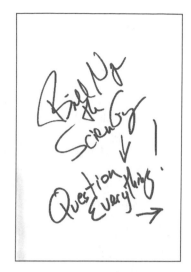

Nye for his signature in a copy of *The Evidence Bible* that I had with me. He opened it, signed it, and wrote "Question Everything." But if I am to question everything, then Mr. Nye is permissively allowing me to question *his claims* in the debate. With this in mind, the bulk of the debate analysis will center on the content of Mr. Nye's claims, though many of Mr. Ham's points will be analyzed and expanded as well.

Neither debater had the time they actually needed to rebut and make a case for all points brought up in the debate. So this is where the analysis in this publication becomes important. I certainly feel privileged to be the one to look into the details of this debate for the purpose of checking and writing about the various claims made.

Am I biased?

The truthful answer is *yes*. But so is everyone else. If someone believes they are not biased, then part of their bias is that they have deceived themselves into thinking they are not biased. People are either for Christ or against Him. People either gather or scatter (e.g., Matthew 12:30,[3] Luke 11:23[4]). There is nothing wrong in admitting one's own bias — in fact, it is only right to do so.

---

3. "He who is not with Me is against Me, and he who does not gather with Me scatters abroad."
4. "He who is not with Me is against Me, and he who does not gather with Me scatters."

Some have asked, "Was your bias for Ken Ham or for Bill Nye"? And my answer is "neither." I pray that my bias is on *God's side,* and I'm sure that Mr. Ham's response would be similar. It is not that *God is on Ken's side*, but rather *Ken is on God's side* (consider Joshua 5:13–15[5]).

My bias, I openly admit, is for the God of the Bible, who is absolute, and therefore, the absolute authority on all things.

Religious bias of the debaters

The debaters also held to a working bias in the debate:

- Ken Ham's operational bias: God and His Word (the Bible) are the supreme authority.

- Bill Nye's operational bias: Man is the supreme authority.

Naturally, Mr. Ham and I share this same allegiance to God and His Word. This is the same bias to which Christians the world over should be adhering.[6]

Mr. Nye holds to a position that demotes or ignores God as any source of authority. This, by default, places *man* in the position of ultimate authority. His stance is inherently the religion of humanism, where man — collectively or individually — is elevated to a position of being greater than God.

Humanism, like Christianity, has various sects, divisions, or denominations…if you will. Christians vary in their doctrinal stances (variations within different aspects of doctrines like modes of baptism, Calvinism/Arminianism, covenant theology versus dispensational theology, eschatology, and so on) — but share the basic beliefs (one God, a triune God [Christ is God], salvation by faith through grace and not works, the Bible as the authority, and so on). Similarly there are variant humanistic "denominations."

---

5. "And it came to pass, when Joshua was by Jericho, that he lifted his eyes and looked, and behold, a Man stood opposite him with His sword drawn in His hand. And Joshua went to Him and said to Him, 'Are You for us or for our adversaries?' So He said, 'No, but as Commander of the army of the Lord I have now come.' And Joshua fell on his face to the earth and worshiped, and said to Him, 'What does my Lord say to His servant?' Then the Commander of the Lord's army said to Joshua, 'Take your sandal off your foot, for the place where you stand is holy.' And Joshua did so."

6. Those Christians who do not view God and His Word as the supreme authority are infusing humanism into their Christianity. They are basically trying to mix two different religions. But this reveals an issue: how can one trust what Christ said if they do not view Christ's Word (the Bible) as that ultimate authority and allow for the changing ideas of man to supersede the Bible? It is a point of inconsistency in regard to authority, not salvation.

Some of these humanistic variants are traditional atheism, new atheism, agnosticism, secularism, "nonreligious," free-thinkers, and so on. They have variant forms where some claim "no God" (atheism), others say "one can't know if God exists" (agnosticism), others are passive (traditional atheism), and some are very aggressive in pushing an agenda (new atheism). But they all adhere to man as the authority, collectively or individually, require evolution and naturalism (no supernatural), or materialism (nothing spiritual).

In many cases, a person invested in this humanistic religion may use several of these terms to denote more of the particulars of their professed beliefs such as naturalist, atheist, materialist, humanist, free-thinker, nonreligious, secular, and others. Christians often do the same thing. We are called Christian, theistic, godly, faithful, or even more specific labels like Lutheran, Presbyterian, Baptist, Reformed, and so on.

Mr. Nye has stated that he is agnostic[7] and received the 2010 Humanist of the Year Award from the *American Humanist Association*.[8] His religion is an open book, just as much as Mr. Ham's religion is an open book. So the debate was an inherently religious one where two individuals adhering to opposing authorities were going to battle. It was God's Word versus man's word, with Mr. Ham representing the godly position and Mr. Nye representing the autonomous human position.

Interestingly, agnostics should be arguing that one cannot know if the God of Bible did create or not, since they argue that one can't know if the God of the Bible exists or not. In the debate, professed agnostic Mr. Nye argued as though he were an *atheist*, and by his aggressive way of trying to silence any opposition, he was actually demonstrating what the new *atheism* constitutes. I found this religious inconsistency glaring.

Basic debate facts and debaters' positions

Mr. Bill Nye

Religion: Humanistic; type: Agnostic

Education: Bachelor of science degree in mechanical engineering, Cornell University

---

7. S. Zaimov, "Bill Nye Reveals He is Agnostic; Shares Expectations for Ken Ham Creationism Debate," *Christian Post*, January 23, 2014, http://www.christianpost.com/news/bill-nye-reveals-he-is-agnostic-shares-expectations-for-ken-ham-creationism-debate-113238/.
8. C. Whitt, "Bill Nye to Be Honored as Humanist of the Year," *American Humanist Association*, April 7, 2010, http://americanhumanist.org/HNN/details/2010-04-bill-nye-to-be-honored-as-humanist-of-the-year.

Believes the age of the earth to be: 4.54 billion years, based on naturalistic and uniformitarian assumptions about rock layers (geologic time scale) and radiometric dating of meteorites (e.g., Patterson, C., "Age of Meteorites and the Earth," *Geochimica et Cosmochimica Acta*, Volume 10, 1956, pp. 230–237)

Believes the age of the universe to be: 13.7 billion years based on naturalistic calculations (e.g., Wright, E., *Age of the Universe*, December, 27, 2012, http://www.astro.ucla.edu/~wright/age.html)

Believes in God? Professes agnostic (i.e., can't know if God exists); in practice and actions, particularly in the debate, Mr. Nye seems to be an atheist (i.e., arguing a position of no God)

Motivation for the debate: "To keep the United States on top technologically"

Ultimate authority: Man

Beliefs:

Astronomical evolution: Big Bang (everything came from nothing)

Geological evolution: millions of years of slow, gradual accumulations of rock layers

Chemical evolution: life came from matter (nonlife), otherwise called abiogenesis

Biological evolution: a single simple life form gave rise to all other life forms down through the ages

Brief biography as given by moderator Tom Foreman

Mr. Nye's website describes him as a scientist, engineer, comedian, author, and inventor. Mr. Nye, as you may know, produced a number of award-winning TV shows, including the program he became so well known for, *Bill Nye the Science Guy*. While working on the *Science Guy* show, Mr. Nye won seven national Emmy awards for writing, performing, and producing the show; [he] won 18 Emmys in five years.

In between creating the shows, he wrote five kids' books about science, including his latest title, *Bill Nye's Great Big Book of Tiny Germs*.

Bill Nye is the host of three television series; his program *The 100 Greatest Discoveries* airs on The Science Channel [and] *The Eyes of Nye* airs on PBS stations across the country.

He frequently appears on interview programs to discuss a variety of science topics. Mr. Nye serves as executive director of the Planetary Society, the world's largest space interest group. He's a graduate of Cornell with a bachelor of science degree in mechanical engineering.

Mr. Ken Ham

Religion: Christian; type: Protestant

Education: Bachelor's degree in applied science with an emphasis in environmental biology from Queensland Institute of Technology; diploma of education from University of Queensland in Brisbane

Believes the age of the earth to be: About 6,000 years, based on six-day creation and the genealogies found in the Bible

Believes the age of the universe to be: About 6,000 years, based on six-day creation and the genealogies found in the Bible

Believes in God? Yes

Motivation for the debate: "The Gospel of Jesus Christ and the authority of the Bible"

Ultimate authority: God, and by extension, the Word of God (Bible)

Beliefs:

Six-day special creation as described in the Bible (origin of matter, time, space, light, and so on)

A literal fall into sin from a perfect creation with Adam and Eve's sin that caused the world to be full of death and suffering, with fallen man needing a Savior

A global flood in Noah's day that was a judgment on sin and laid down the bulk of the rock layers that contain fossils

The Tower of Babel was a real event (after the Flood) that confused the languages and split apart the population. This division resulted in various people groups exhibiting the great genetic variations in humankind. However, all humans are of one race, thus all are related (descended from Adam), and all are sinners in need of the Savior Jesus Christ

Brief biography as given by moderator Tom Foreman

Mr. Ken Ham is the president and cofounder of Answers in Genesis, a Bible-defending organization that upholds the authority of the Scriptures from the very first verse. Mr. Ham is the man behind the popular high-tech Creation Museum where we're holding this debate. The museum has had two million visitors in six years and has attracted much of the world's media.

The Answers in Genesis website is well-trafficked, with two million visitors alone last month. Mr. Ham is also a best-selling author and much-in-demand speaker, [with a] daily radio feature carried on 700-plus stations.

This is his second public debate on evolution and creation. The first was at Harvard in the 1990s.

Mr. Ham is a native of Australia. He earned a bachelor's degree in applied science with an emphasis in environmental biology from the Queensland Institute of Technology as well as a diploma of education at the University of Queensland in Brisbane, Australia.

Specific debate points and tactics

Basic and initial comments

The topic: "Is creation a viable model of origins in today's modern scientific era?"
Date: February 4, 2014
Site: Legacy Hall, Creation Museum, Petersburg, Kentucky, US
Coin toss: Ken Ham wins coin toss and elects to go first
Media: Over 70 media on site from all over the world
Live viewers: Approximately five million worldwide; 900 in Legacy Hall
Moderator: Tom Foreman from CNN

The basic debate format[9]:

Moderator's Introduction
Part 1
    5-minute opening remarks — Ken Ham
    5-minute opening — Bill Nye

---

9. See Appendix A for the complete transcript.

Part 2
    30-minute case — Ken Ham
Part 3
    30-minute case — Bill Nye
Part 4
    First 5-minute rebuttal — Ken Ham
    First 5-minute rebuttal — Bill Nye
    Second 5-minute rebuttal — Ken Ham
    Second 5-minute rebuttal — Bill Nye
Part 5
    Audience Question and Answers
    Moderator's Closing

A few initial comments are warranted to set the stage for the debate. Take note of the title.

The title itself was actually an advantage for Mr. Nye. It placed the emphasis on Mr. Ham to defend the topic of creation and afforded Mr. Nye the luxury of attacking the position of creation. In sports terms, this would be as if Mr. Ham were playing defense for the duration of the debate and Mr. Nye were playing offense. Any sports fan knows that the one playing offense would be in a position to win if they played nothing but offense the entire game.

In reality, due to the nature of the topic, the discussion was not set up as a fair debate. For the debate to be stacked fair from the start, it should have been titled something like: *Creation or Evolution: Which is viable in today's scientific era?*[10] Most viewers likely missed these subtleties. In other words, Mr. Nye was not really required to defend his position but only needed to attack the creationist position to keep to the agreed title.

Mr. Ham was aware of this but told me later that he could still use the debate title to deal with the origins topic in the way it needed to be dealt with — from a worldview philosophical position and an understanding of the real nature of the word "science." Evolutionists, in contrast, do not want to defend their position but are willing to attack the opposition, which gives them an edge.

---

10. Consider if the debate topic had been: *Is Evolution a viable model in this scientific era?* This would have been a debate stacked against an evolutionary worldview that would have made the evolutionist play defense and the creationist play offense.

Mr. Ham likely realized that Mr. Nye would still have to try to defend his position due to the crux of the discussion — origins, which is where creation and evolution converge into natural debate. So Mr. Ham probably agreed to the debate topic knowing it would be skewed against him; that considered, it was very gracious for him to entertain the debate "knowing how the cards were shuffled."

Second, the grace that Mr. Ham showed to Mr. Nye upon winning the coin toss is also noteworthy. In debate, the one who gets the last comment tends to be the one in the best position (Proverbs 18:17[11]). Having time to relax a bit more on stage knowing that about half of the attendees may not be on the opposing side also takes the pressure off the person who goes second. On the other hand, the one who gets to go first can "set the stage" for the demeanor of the debate.

But even so, Mr. Ham opted to go first and give Mr. Nye the final say. Sometime after the debate, I asked Mr. Ham why he did something debaters would rarely do — opt to go first and give his opponent the last say. Mr. Ham said that because so many people have never really listened to the biblical creationist position, he determined to go first so everyone (including Bill Nye) would have a clear understanding of this position. Mr. Ham told me it wasn't so much a debate tactic, but it was most important for him to know that the message God had laid on his heart was heard clearly — even if that meant giving Bill Nye a seeming tactical advantage. And as anyone who watched the debate knows, Mr. Ham presented not only the biblical creationist worldview, but also unashamedly and clearly shared the gospel of Jesus Christ.

Lastly, Mr. Nye, after the debate revealed his ultimate debate tactic. He commented:

> Those of you familiar with creationism and its followers are familiar with the remarkable Duane Gish…His debating technique came to be known as the "Gish Gallop." He was infamous for jumping from one topic to another, introducing one spurious or specious fact or line of reasoning after another. A scientist debating Gish often got bogged down in details and, by all accounts, came across looking like the loser. It quickly occurred to me that I could do the same thing…I did my best to slam Ken

---

11. "The first one to plead his cause seems right, until his neighbor comes and examines him."

Ham with a great many scientific and common sense arguments. I believed he wouldn't have the time or the focus to address many of them.[12]

Of course, this is a great misconception of what Dr. Gish actually did in those famous debates. But this is how it has been misconstrued in the *skeptical method* or *skeptical blitzkrieg*, as I call it, which is actually the method used by many secular humanists. This method is actually quite common on skeptical debate boards. They throw a bunch of information out there and hope that it overwhelms the opponent, whether it is true or false. In many cases, hosts of skeptics team up against a person, like a Christian, to try to "bully that person" with attacks. Many times, even if the Christian refutes a claim, the skeptics bring it up again in hopes of continuing to overwhelm the opponent.

Mr. Nye's tactic in the debate was exactly this. He attempted to throw topics out there fast and quick in hopes of not only distracting the audience but also provoking Mr. Ham into taking this bait and getting bogged down in the details of some of the strange and oftentimes inaccurate points that Mr. Nye brought up (as you will read throughout this response).

In some cases, even though Mr. Ham had already addressed something, Mr. Nye brought it up again as though it had not been dealt with. Mr. Nye knew that Mr. Ham couldn't address everything, as the debate was extremely limited by time constraints. Mr. Ham told me later that he could obviously only choose a few items to comment on but also noted that the answers to many (if not all) of Nye's claims were available on the www.answersingenesis.org website. Mr. Ham also said that he believed he should not use the time allocated during the question time to comment on previous points but to honor the person who submitted the question by responding specifically to what was asked.

So Mr. Nye used the *skeptical method*. But Mr. Ham didn't take the bait and stuck to the debate topic. But by sticking with his debate tactic, Mr. Nye failed to address the many points that Mr. Ham brought up or responded to in the debate. So let's get into the specifics of the debate,

12. B. Nye, "Bill Nye's Take on the Nye-Ham Debate," *Skeptical Enquirer*, vol. 38, no. 3, May/June 2014, http://www.csicop.org/si/show/bill_nyes_take_on_the_nye-ham_debate/.

and keep in mind that I *do* want to address Mr. Nye's many claims, as I am not limited by time constraints in this publication.

Part 1

The 5-minute Opening Statements

Ham opening

In brief, Mr. Ham opened by pointing out that biblical creationists can practice the observational science that enables one to build technology and that an evolutionary worldview is not required to do such a thing. He mentioned some scientists who do this very thing from video clips in their own words (e.g., Dr. Raymond Damadian who invented the MRI scanner).

He then pointed out the terms needing to be defined for the debate. (Mr. Nye did not define terms as Mr. Ham did). The three terms from the debate topic that Mr. Ham defined were: *creation, evolution,* and *science*. He focused on the meaning of the word science, which has the root meaning of "knowledge."

Mr. Ham used this definition of "science":

the state of knowing: knowledge as distinguished from ignorance or misunderstanding.[1]

Mr. Ham then discussed the dual nature of science — the major thrust of his entire presentation. He pointed out that science needs to be broken

---

1. Merriam-Webster Online Dictionary, s.v. "science," http://www.merriam-webster.com/dictionary/science.

into two parts: experimental (observable or operational) science and origins (historical) science. Both creation and evolution involve historical science (beliefs) and observational science (such as the study of genetics, etc.).

Experimental science that builds technology is based on the scientific method. And origins or historical science is the nonrepeatable, nonobservable science (knowledge) dealing with the past, which then enters the realm of beliefs (really, religion).

Mr. Ham used this definition of the scientific method:

> a method of procedure…consisting in systematic observation, measurement, and experiment, and the formulation, testing, and modification of hypotheses.[2]

Mr. Ham summed up with the point that the debate was actually a religious debate over two different worldviews based on two different starting points (God's Word or man's word).

Overall analysis

This was a good opening, considering that the speaker was on the defensive. Mr. Ham started by destroying the idea that creationists cannot be "real" scientists, which is a common claim — and a claim that Mr. Nye had repeatedly made in the media.

Defining terms was also essential because terms have multiple meanings. *Evolution* and *science* are both terms with multiple definitions that can muddy the waters if not clarified up front. Furthermore, it is important to know what the debaters are talking about so they do not "talk past" one another. At least when Mr. Ham gave his presentation, people knew what he meant by words like evolution, science, and creation.

Operational / Experimental / Observable science versus Historical / Origins science

Mr. Ham's main point about the meaning of the word science is crucial. If Mr. Nye admitted that historical science is not observable and repeatable, then he would be opening the door to let the public become aware that evolution is a religion making religious claims about the past and not the type of science that builds technology (i.e., observable and

---

2. Oxford English Dictionary, s.v. "scientific method."

repeatable). Mr. Nye would essentially lose the debate right then and there in the eyes of the public.

But Mr. Nye refused to acknowledge the difference between historical and observational science, as to do so would be to admit he had untestable beliefs concerning his view of origins. Mr. Ham admitted his beliefs based on God's Word, but Mr. Nye refused to admit his beliefs based on man's word until the last question of the Question and Answer time.

Here is why this is so significant. In today's education system, the religion of secular humanism, with its foundation of naturalistic evolution based on man's word or man's beliefs about the past [molecules-to-man], is disguised in textbooks, secular museums, and so on by being called "science." But the same word, "science," is used for experimental science that builds technology. Because students aren't taught the difference between historical and observational science, they are brainwashed into thinking that molecules-to-man evolution is the same science as that which built technology — which it is not. It is a bait and switch fallacy (a fallacy in logic).

Here is how Mr. Ham explained it during the debate:

Public school textbooks are using the same word — science — for observational and historical science. They arbitrarily define science as naturalism and outlaw the supernatural. They present molecules-to-man evolution as fact. They are imposing the religion of naturalism/atheism on generations of students.[3]

He went on to state:

> The word science has been hijacked by secularists in teaching evolution to force the religion of naturalism on generations of kids... The creation/evolution debate is really a conflict between two philosophical worldviews based on two different accounts of origins or historical science beliefs.[4]

Observational science is certainly an observable and experimentally wonderful methodological tool with which to build cars, trains, computers, and the other great technology we use today. Sadly, though, so many people are duped into believing that evolution (molecules-to-man) *is also*

3. See Appendix A.
4. See Appendix A.

science in the same way (bait and switch), and therefore it can remain in the classroom when religion was supposed to be kicked out.

Secularists basically renamed the religious aspect of evolution called "naturalism" as "science," knowing that most people would not understand the bait and switch used to indoctrinate people in the religion of naturalism or atheism.[5] Naturalism is a vital aspect of the religion of secular humanism that teaches that autonomous man is the one who determines truth.

Mr. Ham put it this way in his debate presentation:

> The word evolution has been hijacked using a bait and switch...the word evolution is used for observable changes and then used for unobservable changes such as molecules to man.[6]

Mr. Ham, by delineating between experimental/observational and historical/origins science, placed Mr. Nye on the horns of a dilemma. Either he had to admit that molecules-to-man evolution is a belief (a religion based on naturalism and materialism) when discussing the past, or he would be forced to show molecules-to-man evolution for the audience to observe. The past clearly cannot be repeated or observed. But if Mr. Nye admitted that evolution, naturalism, and materialism were beliefs about the past, then he would be admitting on a very public stage that tax dollars in the US are being used to impose the religion of naturalism on generations of students and on the public as a whole. As Mr. Ham reiterated twice during the debate:

> They [the secularists] present molecules-to-man evolution as fact. They are imposing the religion of naturalism/atheism on generations of students.[7]

Furthermore, Mr. Ham's opening was perfectly consistent since observable science comes out of a Christian worldview that is built on a literal creation.[8] One cannot account for the laws of logic or the laws of nature

---

5. B. Hodge, "Is Science Secular?" Answers in Genesis, May 17, 2013, http://www.answersingenesis.org/articles/2013/05/17/is-science-secular.

6. https://answersingenesis.org/countering-the-culture/bill-nye-debates-ken-ham/.

7. See Appendix A.

8. J. Lisle, "Evolution — The Anti-science?" in K. Ham and B. Hodge, Gen. Eds., *How Do We Know the Bible is True?* Volume 1 (Green Forest, AR: Master Books, 2011), pp. 255–262.

within a naturalistic worldview. Bible-believing Christian Francis Bacon, for example, developed the scientific method. Bacon understood that God set up the laws of logic and nature, and God upholds the world in a particular fashion that makes science possible. We can trust that those same laws won't change and thus can be relied on since the Bible alludes to this in several places (discussed later). Also, Bible-believing Christians developed most fields of science.[9] That is why Mr. Ham publicly asked Bill Nye this question during the debate:

> How do you account for the laws of logic and laws of nature from a naturalistic worldview that excludes the existence of God?

All historical science is wrong, save one

Lastly, I would like to make a *black and white* point: all historical/origins "sciences" are wrong, except one. Only one history really did occur in the past. All the historical sciences (or historical *knowledge*) are wrong, save one. They are all fictional stories but one.

The only one in a position to know the truth about origins is the Creator God who created all things, eyewitnessed it, has always been there, and revealed it to us in His Word as recorded in the Bible. All other forms of historical science are based on man's fallible, imperfect guesses about the past by people who were not there. Therefore, they are arbitrary, next to God's absolute standard.

Nye opening

Ham's story versus mainstream science

Mr. Nye opened with a story about his father that was quite humorous, then transitioned to say that he and Mr. Ham would be debating two stories: one being that of "Mr. Ham's story" and the other of "mainstream science."

Now I would like to comment on the two things positioned here. First, it is not about *Mr. Ham's story*, but rather about *biblical creation* as revealed in God's Word and confirmed by observational science. There have been godly people (numerous biblical authors, including church fathers and reformers) who held to biblical creation long before Mr. Ken

---

9. Answers in Genesis, "Which Scientists of the Past Believed in a Creator?" Answers in Genesis, http://www.answersingenesis.org/home/area/bios/#pastsci.

Ham ever showed up on the scene. Mr. Ham is not teaching anything new when it comes to six-day creation. Rather, he's standing on the shoulders of most Bible-believing Christians, including many who came before him.

So why did Mr. Nye take this tack? The answer is that it is *demanded* by his religion. He is a secular humanist, believing man is the ultimate authority; therefore, he wanted to demote the origins issue from any association with God and place it in the hands of a man. That way it set up the debate for creation as a model established by a man (Ken Ham) as opposed to God. From that perspective, I was actually surprised that he credited it to Mr. Ham rather than to Moses, which would have made much more sense![10] But that is the nature of fallible man. And as we know, even what Moses (or Paul or the other authors) wrote as recorded in God's Word is God-breathed (2 Timothy 3:16[11]).

Second, Mr. Nye inserted a reification fallacy. Instead of trying to play on equal footing (that is, by his own human standard) by then saying the opposing story was "Nye's story," he appealed to what he called "mainstream science's story." The problem is that mainstream science doesn't have stories, conclusions, or ideas. Mainstream science is a methodology. It doesn't speak, nor does it have stories. Instead, *scientists* have stories, conclusions, and so on. In one sense, it is like the methodology of science has been given "life," then has been raised up to an almost "human-like" status; thus, it is a reification fallacy. And of course Mr. Nye included observation and historical science together when he uses the word "science" — but he refused (and still refuses) to acknowledge this.

Really, it was Mr. Nye, representing the ungodly, versus God and His Word. It just so happens that Mr. Ken Ham was representing the position of the godly, which affirms God and His Word.

Changing the topic of the debate by Nye

Mr. Nye then put up a slide that read: *Does Ken Ham's Creation Model hold up? Is it viable?* Of course, this was not the debate topic. But he

---

10. I suggest that the reason Mr. Nye did this was to "divide and conquer." Later in the debate, Mr. Nye tried to separate Mr. Ham's understanding of creation from that of other religious people who were fine with an evolutionary worldview. Had Mr. Nye criticized Moses, he would have lost potential support from Christians who may have been fine with Mr. Nye's evolutionary model, but would not have been fine with his being critical of Moses.

11. "All Scripture is given by inspiration of God, and is profitable for doctrine, for reproof, for correction, for instruction in righteousness."

was trying to change the topic to be pointed to Mr. Ham as opposed to the biblical position that Mr. Ham espoused. This type of *ad hominem* attack (arguing against the man, as opposed to arguing against the issue at hand) is more common in evolutionary literature than one might initially think.

Confusion of historical science with natural law

Next, Mr. Nye, in the context of *CSI* (the television show), said that Mr. Ham's constructs of observational science vs. historical science don't exist on the show. So Mr. Nye concluded that they don't exist elsewhere but only exist in Ham's model. He then countered by saying that natural laws existed in the past and also exist in the present. Though he agreed that *CSI* is fiction, he also agreed that the clues exist in the present and we have to embrace those.

Just because a TV show doesn't acknowledge historical versus observational science (yet) doesn't mean they don't exist. Not once on *CSI* has anyone ever been able to repeat the past or observe the past. They observe things in the present using observational science (e.g., tests for presence of blood) to try to determine what happened in the past using historical science (e.g., who committed the murder).

If historical science works so well in crime labs, why isn't there a 100% conviction rate, and why have there been false convictions? It's because observational science involves experiments that can be observed and repeated in the present, but historical science involves interpretation with regard to past events that can't be repeated or directly observed.

Furthermore, Mr. Nye revealed that he didn't understand the difference between observational science and historical science. He presumed creationists imply that views about unique events in the past like the Flood of Noah's day mean natural law has changed over time! Then he tried to refute his false accusation that creationists believe natural laws have changed.

The historical science of creationists (beliefs concerning creation, the Flood, Tower of Babel, etc.) has nothing to do with natural laws supposedly changing — that was a fabrication by Mr. Nye. Mr. Nye actually set up a straw man, then tried to rebut it. But anyone who has seen the debate can see that this is not the argument Mr. Ham was making but rather was a straw man fallacy committed by Mr. Nye.

Creationists agree that natural laws aren't changing. In fact, in his presentation, Mr. Ham challenged Mr. Nye as to how he could believe the laws of logic and nature from a naturalistic view of origins. Mr. Ham explained to Mr. Nye that from his naturalistic perspective, once there was no logic and then there was logic. So according to Darwinian principles, there must have been a half logic, which is completely illogical.

Mr. Ham explained that the Darwinian view is completely illogical because we might be at the point now of only having half logic, so how could Mr. Nye trust his own arguments? However, this was obviously totally lost on Mr. Nye who falsely claimed Mr. Ham believed the laws of logic changed!

Mr. Ham repeatedly challenged Mr. Nye as to how he could explain the laws of logic and nature from a naturalistic view of origins. Here is the exact text of Ken's question to Bill Nye:

> How do you account for the laws of logic and laws of nature from a naturalistic worldview that excludes the existence of God?[12]

Natural law

Natural laws exist because God created them and is upholding the universe in a particular way (e.g., Hebrews 1:3,[13] Genesis 8:22[14]).[15] We describe these laws, but we don't really know what makes them work. That is God's realm. We can describe gravity, for example, and define these beautiful laws, developed in large part by young earth creationist Isaac Newton. But what *is* gravity? Hypotheses abound…but simply put, gravity is the *name we give* to the way God upholds certain aspects of His creation.

But there is a big difference between clues about the past that you can observe in the present and being able observe the actual past. This is not dependent on natural law.

---

12. See Appendix A.
13. "[Jesus] who being the brightness of His glory and the express image of His person, and upholding all things by the word of His power, when He had by Himself purged our sins, sat down at the right hand of the Majesty on high."
14. "While the earth remains, seedtime and harvest, cold and heat, winter and summer, and day and night shall not cease."
15. J. Lisle, "Don't Creationists Deny the Laws of Nature?" in K. Ham, gen. ed., *The New Answers Book 1* (Green Forest, AR: Master Books, 2006), pp. 39–46.

On a semi-technical note, Mr. Nye is actually borrowing from a biblical worldview to make the claim that natural laws will not change in the future. Let me explain. Christians have a basis for such a thing (natural law being consistent in the future), as previously mentioned. But in a secular view, natural laws have changed from the onset of the Big Bang, and they have no way of knowing that in the future the laws of nature might not change again. Christians know that the laws of nature will not change since God, who is not bound by time and knows the future, reveals that to us. As God's Word states, "Jesus Christ is the same yesterday, today, and forever" (Hebrews 13:8).

It is purely arbitrary for the secularist to know anything about the future, let alone that the laws of nature will not change in the future. If they argue that they can know that the future is like the past by looking at the past, then they merely beg the question since they really never answered the question. In other words, they arbitrarily suggest that they future will be the same, but they can't know it within their worldview.

Global Flood and the animals

Next, Mr. Nye claimed that Mr. Ham and his followers have this remarkable view that there was a worldwide Flood that somehow affected everything we see in nature. He claimed the Ark had 14,000 individual animals on it and that every land plant was underwater for a full year. Mr. Nye then asked if this scenario is even reasonable.

Now, to question some of Mr. Nye's claims here: first, it is not just Mr. Ham and his followers, but the Bible states clearly that there was a Flood (e.g., the basis for this truth claim in the first place), and millions of Mr. Ham's *predecessors* also agreed there was a worldwide Flood.[16]

It has only been in recent times, about the last 200 years, that people really started questioning a global Flood.[17] This happened in the late 18th and early 19th centuries when secular humanists and deists began with the assumption that rock layers, including fossil-bearing layers, were supposedly laid down slowly and gradually without any catastrophic

---

16. We even find over 300 flood legends (most discussing a global or universal destruction of nature) that exist in cultures all around the world, past and present. This is to be expected from a biblical creation perspective as the stories were passed down from Noah's descendants and skewed into what they became; but consider... there should be no global Flood legends in the evolutionary scenario.
17. T. Mortenson, *The Great Turning Point* (Green Forest AR: Master Books, 2004).

processes in the past (i.e., the concept of uniformitarianism). The idea of the past having no significant catastrophes was remarkable, considering the catastrophes we have been able to observe in the last 200 years. Secularists today do realize that there have been catastrophic processes in the past and therefore strict uniformitarianism doesn't work — however, they claim such catastrophic processes happened over millions of years.

Second, Mr. Nye committed a straw man fallacy when he claimed that the Flood affected everything we see in nature. But this is not what any creationist *[that I've ever heard]* claims. It changed the landscape, split continents, affected weather, and judged sin. But laws of nature (e.g., the laws of thermodynamics, gravity, and so on) remained the same, the sun remained, and the moon remained.

I am not sure where Mr. Nye came up with the number of animals allegedly on the Ark. He claimed there were 14,000 animals plus "eight zookeepers," so he arrived at 14,008 total. With any legitimate research into the subject since the 1970s, one would find numbers closer to about 2,000 (Jones)[18] based on a family level of classification more akin to the word "kind" in Genesis (not in every instance of course, but this was an estimation).

Answers in Genesis researchers, in preparation for exhibits in the life-size Noah's Ark project, suggested that there are around 1000 animal kinds at present. This means 2000 + animals (two of each kind, seven of the clean animals) were needed on the Ark. There was plenty of room for the representative animal kinds plus the eight people from Noah's family on the Ark.

Plants and a global Flood

Mr. Nye also committed a straw man fallacy when he claimed that plants remained underwater for an entire year. Mr. Ham has never stated such a thing to my knowledge and research. Perhaps Mr. Nye tried to deduce this because the Flood occurred over the course of a year (370–371 days depending on rounding and assuming a 360-day calendar that many ancient cultures used), and he assumed that plants remained underwater for that entire time. But most fail to realize that the 370–371 days was the time Noah spent in the Ark, not the duration of the waters being at their highest peak.

---

18. A.J. Jones, "How Many Animals in the Ark?" in *Creation Research Society Quarterly*, 10, no. 2 (September, 1973).

But if one neglects the specifics of the Flood, then one might fail to understand that plants were only covered for a short time. The Bible says the "springs of the great deep burst forth," which triggered the Flood (Genesis 7:11[19]). There is no reason to assume the entire earth was covered yet because this does take time, as the account of the Flood proceeds to inform us.

Then the Bible says, "Now the flood was on the earth for forty days. The waters increased and lifted up the ark…" (Genesis 7:17[20]), implying the Ark sat on the ground for 40 days before being lifted up. This means that some land was still exposed during the 40 days. The Ark struck the mountains of Ararat on the 150th day.[21] So again land was likely starting to be exposed from this 150th day onward with a steady decrease of the waters (Genesis 8:3[22]).

This means the whole earth was actually covered by water for a maximum of 110 days. Plants and seeds, in many cases, can survive such conditions (e.g., if not buried to be a candidate for fossilization). Some plants can re-root, others can sprout from seed, and so on.[23] Also, many plants would have survived as part of floating log mats. And we must also understand that there have been 4,300 years of processes like natural selection since the Flood — so some plants or seeds that may not survive underwater today may have been able to do so at the time of the Flood. There are many varying factors that could be considered.

I'm surprised Mr. Nye completely forgot the famous olive leaf. Genesis 8:11[24] discusses the dove's return with a freshly plucked olive leaf. This was on Day 278 of the Flood, showing that plants were growing well before Noah exited the Ark about three months later.[25]

---

19. "In the six hundredth year of Noah's life, in the second month, the seventeenth day of the month, on that day all the fountains of the great deep were broken up, and the windows of heaven were opened."

20. "Now the flood was on the earth forty days. The waters increased and lifted up the ark, and it rose high above the earth."

21. Genesis 8:3–4: "And the waters receded continually from the earth. At the end of the hundred and fifty days the waters decreased. Then the ark rested in the seventh month, the seventeenth day of the month, on the mountains of Ararat."

22. "And the waters receded continually from the earth. At the end of the hundred and fifty days the waters decreased."

23. D. Wright, "How Did Plants Survive the Flood?" Answers in Genesis, October 12, 2012, http://www.answersingenesis.org/articles/aid/v7/n1/how-did-plants-survive-flood.

24. "Then the dove came to him in the evening, and behold, a freshly plucked olive leaf was in her mouth; and Noah knew that the waters had receded from the earth."

25. B. Hodge, "Biblical Overview of the Flood Timeline," Answers in Genesis, August 23, 2010, http://www.answersingenesis.org/articles/2010/08/23/overview-flood-timeline.

Reason in a secular view

Mr. Nye then appealed to the crowd and asked if the version of the Flood that he was describing was "reasonable." This instantly set off red flags to me when I was in the audience. In fact, several times in the debate Mr. Nye asked if things were "reasonable" or stated that he believed certain arguments were "not reasonable."

Now, in one sense, I do understand the sentiment, as a creationist, asking if a belief or argument is reasonable or not. But I want to address something more disturbing about Mr. Nye's use of "reason" by *his own professed worldview.*

Mr. Nye is a secular humanist, thus naturalistic and materialistic in his religion. Naturalism (nature is all that there is) and materialism (everything is material, nothing spiritual or immaterial exists), are crucial parts of the religion of secular humanism. In other words, those who hold to a naturalistic and materialistic worldview say that everything is matter. Materialists and naturalists say that there is nothing spiritual, nothing immaterial, and nothing supernatural. All things that exist must be physical from this religious perspective.

But here is the disturbing part: logic, reason, truth, knowledge, and so on are *not material.* They are not physical. They are conceptual or "nonmaterial." If Mr. Nye (or any other materialist) is consistent in their worldview, then logic, truth, and reason should not exist in their worldview any more than God, who is also nonmaterial (e.g., spiritual; John 4:24,[26] Hebrews 11:3[27]).

So Mr. Nye is actually borrowing from a biblical worldview when he attempts to use logic and reasoning. God is the truth, and logic is a tool. Man was made in the image of a truthful and reasoning God (Genesis 1:26–27,[28] Genesis 9:6,[29] Isaiah 1:18,[30] and so on). So we, as people, are

---

26. "God is Spirit, and those who worship Him must worship in spirit and truth."
27. "By faith we understand that the worlds were framed by the word of God, so that the things which are seen were not made of things which are visible."
28. "Then God said, 'Let Us make man in Our image, according to Our likeness; let them have dominion over the fish of the sea, over the birds of the air, and over the cattle, over all the earth and over every creeping thing that creeps on the earth.' So God created man in His own image; in the image of God He created him; male and female He created them."
29. "Whoever sheds man's blood, by man his blood shall be shed; for in the image of God He made man."
30. " 'Come now, and let us reason together,' says the LORD, 'Though your sins are like scarlet, they shall be as white as snow; though they are red like crimson, They shall be as wool.' "

able to use logic and reasoning because the Bible is true.[31] Mr. Nye obviously does not understand this important point.

The Flood mixture

Mr. Nye, while trying to refute a global Flood, said, "In other words, when there was a big Flood on the earth you would expect drowning animals to swim up to a higher level." Mr. Nye then said, "If you could find evidence of that, my friends, you could change the world."

I must first ask, what evidence would be left behind of animals swimming? I've seen animals swimming quite often, yet they leave no evidence behind.

But the premise of this claim by Mr. Nye assumes that the Floodwaters were rather tranquil, which would allow animals to easily swim upward. But one doesn't get that impression from Genesis 6–8. If anything, precious few creatures would be able to do this, and mere tracks would be left as they tried to get higher and higher with subsequent sediment flows continually being laid down at their feet. For example, if an animal were trying to remain at a breathable position, it would need to get to higher ground even as sediment and water were flowing around it. So its only real hope would be to stay above the sediment level, hence leaving some fossil footprints.

Next, Mr. Nye was making the assumption that animals weren't dead when they were deposited in these layers. Some may have still been alive at the time, but most others were likely dead and transported to where they were buried. By only the 150th day, all the land animals were dead already (Genesis 7:21–23[32]).

The rock layers containing fossils, such as those in the Grand Canyon, are evidence of where the animals were buried, not necessarily where the animals that were preserved in them lived nor where they were perhaps

---

31. People often err when it comes to logic and reason as well, but that is due to the sin in Genesis 3. Due to the fall, men no longer process information properly and are now prone to fallacious thinking; this is why we need to rely on God's Word to correct us, since God in an infallible source.

32. "And all flesh died that moved on the earth: birds and cattle and beasts and every creeping thing that creeps on the earth, and every man. All in whose nostrils was the breath of the spirit of life, all that was on the dry land, died. So He destroyed all living things which were on the face of the ground: both man and cattle, creeping thing and bird of the air. They were destroyed from the earth. Only Noah and those who were with him in the ark remained alive."

trying to survive. Consider the immensity of the Flood — that mechanism would transport and deposit creatures in subsequent layers based on many factors. One of those factors is the natural sorting of water, which we can observe on a smaller scale today.

Another is that the creatures living at lower levels would be buried first (shells, for example, are not going to flee to higher ground). At one stage of the Flood, there was *nothing* higher than sea level (Genesis 7:20[33])! Another factor is that various waves that bring in the sediment could be carrying different things, which are laid down in successive layering that sits aloft previous layers.

But even with this, we *do* still find animals that laid down tracks in the Grand Canyon and are found buried much higher. Some animal tracks are found in the Coconino Sandstone (supposedly laid down 260 million years ago) and yet it is the layers above where such animals were actually buried.[34]

Even the National Park Service website says of these tracks: "Even though no bones have been found, these tracks contain an abundance of information about the animals that made them."[35] This is because the bones are found at higher levels, where secularists are not looking because they have assumed the layers are separated by millions of years. So there is evidence of animals escaping to higher levels, and yet this evidence "did not change the world" as Mr. Nye said it would.

And this brings me to an important point. Mr. Ham knows that interpreting rock layers and fossils in relation to the past involves historical science. He therefore determined that in the debate he would concentrate on ensuring people understood this clearly. He spent time explaining the difference between observational and historical science — and gave examples of different interpretations of evidence based on one's starting point. Mr. Nye rejected this explanation, but it was not lost on the millions who watched it. Mr. Ham told me later, "In many ways, I

---

33. "The waters prevailed fifteen cubits upward, and the mountains were covered."

34. L. Brand, "Field and Laboratory Studies on the Coconino Sandstone (Permian) Vertebrate Footprints and Their Paleoecological Implications," *Palaeogeography, Palaeoclimatology, Palaeoecology,* 28 (1979): pp. 25–38, http://resweb.llu.edu/lbrand/pdf/field_and_laboratory_studies_on_the_coconino_sandstone_(permian)_vertebrate_footprints_and_their_paleoecological_implications.pdf.

35. Fossils, NPS.gov, http://www.nps.gov/grca/naturescience/fossils.htm#CP_JUMP_441243. Accessed February 10, 2014.

Footprints in the Grand Canyon, and yet the creatures are
not buried until a much higher position.

decided I would make sure the media and watching audience understood
the real issues, knowing Mr. Nye would probably not listen."

Religious claims by Mr. Nye: Billions of people do not embrace 6,000-year creation.

There are two points to be made here. First, there are millions of people
who do not embrace the notion of billions of years. So Mr. Nye's arbitrary claim is irrelevant anyway. If Hitler had said that there were millions of people who did not view the Jews as people, would that make it
true? Not at all.

Second, you wouldn't find one person alive before 1956 who said
the age of the earth was 4.5 billion years. The idea of the earth having an
ancient age is radically new. Furthermore, the idea of millions of years of
earth's history is also relatively new, tracing back about 200 years. Prior
to the late 1700s, one would be hard pressed to find any culture that had
the age of the earth older than roughly 6,000–9,000 years old.[36]

---

36. B. Hodge, "How Old Is the Earth?" Answers in Genesis, May 30, 2007, http://www.
answersingenesis.org/articles/2007/05/30/how-old-is-earth.

Keeping the United States ahead

Mr. Nye then said his concern was to keep the United States of America ahead in regard to education and technology. His heartfelt plea was that we would not move forward if we continued to try to eschew "science" (as he defined it), and to divide it into historical and observational science would basically be a detriment. Mr. Nye kept on insisting that the science that built our technology is the same science that, in his mind, proves molecules-to-man evolution!

However, as stated earlier, this is simply not true. Mr. Nye is just not being honest enough to admit he has certain beliefs that determine how he interprets evidence in relation to the past. He doesn't want the world to know that molecules-to-man evolution is a belief. To admit it is a belief is to admit he could be wrong!

If Mr. Nye really believed that his evolutionary views are what keeps the United States of America ahead, then he would be entirely for creation being taught in *all other* countries, as that would supposedly make them fall behind. After all, this would be consistent with the mentality of survival of the fittest. And that seems to be what Mr. Nye wants.

Now, many creationists share Mr. Nye's nationalism but in a different way. I encourage all people to take pride in their countries, regardless of national past wrongs, wars, and so on. But basically, Mr. Nye, in subtle fashion, wants to put other countries down. We as Christians do not share this limited view but want to see other countries *and* the US thrive scientifically for good.

Our motivation as Christians is to help our fellow man — to teach and educate them about all things, including God and His means of salvation though Jesus Christ alone. This is all part of the dominion mandate as given to man in Genesis 1. But why would Mr. Nye have this motivation here? He wants the US to "remain" on top. But I suggest he is practically playing out his evolutionary beliefs, and his motivation is really that of "survival of the fittest." Certainly, to be consistent, he would really have to admit that.

Next, Mr. Ham pre-refuted an idea that Mr. Nye holds crucial. Mr. Nye revealed his hand — i.e., that he believes creationists eschew science. Creationists love science, and Mr. Ham showed video clips of four (of the thousands of) biblical creation scientists who are involved in cutting-edge

CREATIONWISE

Sir Francis Bacon — Established the scientific method
Johannes Kepler — Three laws of planetary motion
Sir Isaac Newton — Co-inventor of calculus
Louis Pasteur — Father of microbiology
James Clerk Maxwell — Laws of electricity and magnetism
Raymond V. Damadian — Inventor of the MRI
BIBLE BELIEVERS CAN'T BE SCIENTISTS!
© AiG 2005 DAN LIETHA

scientific research. I was surprised that Mr. Nye would make this claim (that he had made many times prior to the debate), surely knowing about people like Dr. Raymond Damadian (inventor of the MRI scanner) and Dr. Stuart Burgess (inventor of a gear set for Envisat, the largest, very expensive civilian satellite for the European Space Agency), among many other renowned creation scientists.

But let's conduct a brief history lesson here: Bible-believing Christians developed most fields of science. The US was predominantly Christian and creationist in its thinking in the past, but sadly, that has now shifted. It was the creationists who made this nation great and promoted and increased technology. Even the man whose brilliance masterminded the United States of America to space and to the moon, Werner Von Braun, was a young earth creationist.[37]

Since then, the Bible has been taken out of schools, creation has been taken out of schools, and so on. Maybe one of the reasons the US is falling behind in students' academic scores is because Christianity has by and large been thrown out of public education and replaced with evolutionary humanism! And then we could conduct more of a history lesson and talk about other creationists who were great scientists — such as Isaac Newton, Michael Faraday, James Clerk Maxwell, and many more.

The US is now becoming more "evolutionized," certainly in many ways triggered by the famous Scopes Trial in 1925, but taking more of a full force from 1960 to the present. Now that evolutionists have basically taken over schools, universities, and museums, they have been responsible for educating most of the next generation. This has been happening

37. A. Lamont, "Great Creation Scientists: Werner Von Braun (1912–1977)," *Creation Ex-Nihilo*, March 1, 1994, http://www.answersingenesis.org/articles/cm/v16/n2/von-braun.

for several decades now, and I assert, this is a major reason we are losing the edge we once had as a nation. Now we are seeing the US go from "being on top" in world technology to it transferring elsewhere — and Mr. Nye wants to blame the creationists?

Issue of authority

Mr. Nye claimed at the end of his 5-minute opening:

> So if you ask me if Ken Ham's creation model is viable, *I say no*, it is absolutely not viable [emphasis added].

Mr. Nye appealed to his own authority: "I say no." This is key, and this is what the debate was (and still is) really all about — an issue of authority — God's Word or man's word. Can a fallible human dictate authority over all others or is God the only One in a position to do that as He is the Creator, the absolute authority? If a person can dictate right and wrong, then there is no such thing as absolute right and wrong, for each person could come up with their own moral code. It reminds me of this verse of Scripture:

> In those days there was no king in Israel; everyone did what was right in his own eyes (Judges 21:25).

The more Mr. Nye's naturalistic view of origins permeates the education system, the more I suggest we will see moral relativism pervading the culture — which is exactly what we see happening already. The religion of naturalism will ultimately destroy a culture! Mr. Nye's religion is pernicious for any nation.

Part 2

The Ham 30-minute Case

Ham recap

Mr. Ham began by recapping what he had said in the opening statement, particularly the definitions of observational (or operational) and historical science as well as the words "creation" and "evolution." He reiterated that biblical creationists can be and are great scientists involved in advancing technology.

His major thrust was to explain the difference between how a scientist develops technology and how scientists try to interpret the past in regard to origins. He also gave some specific predictions based on the starting point of biblical creation, and illustrated how observational science can be used to confirm such predictions. He then showed a video clip of astronomer Dr. Danny Faulkner stating, "There is nothing in observational astronomy that contradicts a recent creation."

More creationists than one might expect

Dr. Stuart Burgess, a professor of engineering design at Bristol University in England, was featured in a video clip explaining that many other scientists are sympathetic to creation, but they cannot say anything for "fear of criticism" (such as being fired, ridiculed, and the like).

This is a common trend for creationists across the US. Resources have been devoted to exposing this issue,[1] and it is a common complaint from university students that professors will actively try to remove them, refuse to recommend them, or refuse them degrees in certain fields of science if they find out they are Bible-believing creationists.

Now it is true that creation scientists are in the minority, but there are more than one might think, and there are more coming on board each year as they are emboldened by others who unashamedly take a stand before the world.

Non-Christian scientists are borrowing from a biblical worldview

Mr. Ham made a very powerful and insightful statement that needs to be considered carefully:

> Non-Christian scientists are really borrowing from the Christian worldview anyway to carry out their experimental observational science….When they're doing observational science using the scientific method they have to assume the laws of logic, they have to assume the laws of nature, they have to assume the uniformity of nature.

This is quite powerful, and Mr. Ham knows it. I had briefly written (in the 5-minute segment analyzing Mr. Nye) that Mr. Nye's worldview (secular humanism) doesn't permit anything that is not material. And laws of logic are not material. So the humanistic religion of the unbeliever (agnosticism, atheism, and so on) is inadequate to account for laws of logic by his own professed worldview.[2]

This became one of the hot-button items in the famous Dr. Gordon Stein and Dr. Greg Bahnsen debate regarding the existence of God. Dr. Stein, an ardent atheist (a form of humanism), could not account for the laws of logic in his materialistic religion. So Dr. Bahnsen informed him he was borrowing from the Christian religion to make sense of logic. So for Dr. Stein to make an argument against Christianity, he had to undermine

1. For example: J. Bergmann, *Slaughter of the Dissidents*, Second Edition, Volume 1 (Port Orchard, WA: Leafcutter Press Publishers, 2012); *Expelled* DVD by Ben Stein.
2. J. Lisle, "What Is Wrong with Atheism?" in K. Ham, and B. Hodge, Gen. Eds., *How Do We Know the Bible Is True?* Volume 1 (Green Forest, AR: Master Books, 2011), pp. 263–270.

his own professed worldview and borrow from Christianity to make his case. Naturally, this was self-refuting on Dr. Stein's part.

Mr. Ham actually made a case similar to that of Dr. Bahnsen regarding the laws of logic. He recognized that Mr. Nye ultimately had no foundation for logic, and so Mr. Nye must, like other non-Christians, inadvertently borrow from the Christian religion to make sense of it.

Furthermore, Mr. Ham added another element when he said that non-Christians must borrow from the Christian worldview to actually do the observational science[3] that develops technology. For instance, they are assuming the uniformity of nature (e.g., laws of nature will be the same tomorrow). This is not to be confused with uniformitarianism, which is the belief that the rates and processes that occurred in the past are basically the same as what we observe in the present (e.g., no major catastrophic events like a global Flood). Let me briefly explain.

The laws of nature (which were discussed previously) must be constant in the future for repeatable science to be possible. Christians have a basis for this since God, who knows the future, has revealed that He will uphold things in a consistent way.[4] But in an ever-changing universe as proposed by the secularists, why would the laws of science be constant? Why couldn't they continue to change? The non-Christian must thus borrow from the Bible, though unintentionally.

This powerful form of argumentation is like pulling the rug out from underneath unbelievers to point out that their religion has no foundation, except to borrow from God's Word.[5] Mr. Nye never addressed the secular borrowing of logic and uniformity of nature. Doing so would suffice to destroy the worldview Mr. Nye was professing.

My hope here is to show the readers that at this early stage of the debate, Mr. Nye's worldview was refuted by these points alone. Mr. Nye ignored these powerful arguments and went on to give several supposed examples for evolution that all involved interpretations based on his presupposition of naturalism! Mr. Ham's explanation of historical

3. J. Lisle, "Evolution — the Anti-science?" in K. Ham, and B. Hodge, Gen. Eds., *How Do We Know the Bible Is True?* Volume 1 (Green Forest, AR: Master Books, 2011), pp. 255–262.
4. J. Lisle, *The Ultimate Proof of Creation* (Green Forest, AR: Master Books, 2009), pp. 57–60.
5. B. Hodge, "Is Science Secular?" Answers in Genesis, May 17, 2013, http://www.answersingenesis.org/articles/2013/05/17/is-science-secular.

and observational science as well as his calling Mr. Nye *on the carpet* in regard to the laws of logic and uniformity of nature really undermined Bill Nye's entire attempt at justifying his religion of naturalism.

Expanding on historical science

Mr. Ham took time to expand on explaining historical and observational science using practical examples (Grand Canyon,[6] Hubble telescope,[7] smoke detector and radiometric dating,[8] medicines, and vaccines[9]). In fact, most of the examples Mr. Ham chose were ones that Mr. Nye himself has used quite regularly in various interviews.

Mr. Ham also documented that even secularists recognize the difference between historical and observational science. He quoted from an earth science textbook that did exactly what he was explaining. This text separated out history from the present when discussing geology. Essentially, it was separating observational and historical science; this refuted Mr. Nye's dismissive claim that no one distinguishes these constructs of observable and historical science, as clearly some do.

This is the quote Mr. Ham used:

> In contrast to physical geology, the aim of historical geology is to understand Earth's long history…Historical geology tries to establish a timeline of the vast number of physical and biological changes that have occurred in the past…. We study physical geology before historical geology because we must first understand how Earth works before we try to unravel its past.[10]

Another quote that could be added to confirm this distinction between historical and observational science as understood by some secularists is this one:

6. A. Snelling and T. Vail, "How Did the Grand Canyon Form?" in K. Ham, gen. ed., *The New Answers, Book 3* (Green Forest, AR: Master Books, 2010), pp. 173–186.
7. M. Oard, "Astronomical Problems," *CENTJ*, April 1, 1995, http://www.answersingenesis.org/articles/tj/v9/n1/astronomy.
8. A. Snelling, "Radioactive Dating of Rocks?" in K. Ham and B. Hodge, *How Do We Know the Bible Is True?* Volume 2 (Green Forest, AR: Master Books, 2012), pp. 145–160.
9. A. Gillen and F. Sherwin, "Louis Pasteur's Views on Creation, Evolution and the Genesis of Germs," *Answers Research Journal*, 1 (2008): 43–52, http://www.answersingenesis.org/articles/arj/v1/n1/louis-pasteurs-views.
10. E. Tarbuck and F. Lutgens, *Earth Science*, Indiana Teacher's Edition (Upper Saddle River, NJ: Pearson Prentice Hall, 2006), pp. 2–3.

Paleontologists and other geoscientists often deal with phenomena that occurred millions of years ago, which makes paleontology and geology different from most other sciences, so they are sometimes labeled **historical sciences** [bold theirs]. These scientists will never be able to conduct experiments on fossil subjects as living organisms or study directly the environments they lived in.[11]

Again this shows that the world does recognize these clear distinctions, contrary to Mr. Nye's assertion as he dismissed, without any basis, one of the most powerful arguments of the evening. Mr. Ham told me he was sure Mr. Nye would reject this argument, as he had already heard him do so in interviews, but he knew it was vital for the watching audience to hear it explained clearly.

The same evidence

Mr. Ham proceeded to make the point that creationists and evolutionists really have the same evidence when discussing the topic of origins. We have the same Grand Canyon, same fossils, same dinosaurs, same humans, same radioactivity, and so on.

So the issue is not about evidence, but is rather an argument about how the evidence is *interpreted* in relation to the past. This then actually becomes a worldview/religious debate, which Mr. Ham pointed out very clearly. It is our worldview, based on our starting point (God's Word or man's word) that drives the interpretation of evidence. This is particularly relevant to the discussion of origins.

Mr. Ham admitted he started with God and His Word (the revelation as given in the Bible, beginning with Genesis) as his ultimate authority, whereas Mr. Nye, by rejecting God's authority, must, by default, appeal to man (and thus the religion of naturalism) as his authority (i.e., his own authority or the collective authority of those he appeals to). This is humanism. As Mr. Ham said: "And that's really the difference when it comes down to it."

I heartily concur! The issue is between God and man. God speaks to this issue:

---

11. A.J. Martin, *Introduction to the Study of Dinosaurs* (Atlanta, GA: Blackwell Publishing, 2006), p. 88.

It is better to trust in the LORD than to put confidence in man (Psalm 118:8).

Stop regarding man in whose nostrils is breath, for of what account is he? (Isaiah 2:22 ESV).

But the natural man does not receive the things of the Spirit of God, for they are foolishness to him; nor can he know them, because they are spiritually discerned (1 Corinthians 2:14).

In whom [Christ] are hidden all the treasures of wisdom and knowledge (Colossians 2:3).

These are really "faith statements." Mr. Nye holds unswervingly to man's opinions as the absolute truth, and Mr. Ham holds unswervingly to God's Word as the absolute truth.

Using observational science to confirm biblical model predictions

Mr. Ham then proceeded to explain that observable evidence is a confirmation of predictions based on the biblical creation model.[12] Actually, Mr. Ham showed a slide with the heading "Predictions Based on the Bible" twice, yet Mr. Nye said he needed to make predictions! Mr. Ham listed these predictions:

- evidence confirming an INTELLIGENCE produced life
- evidence confirming AFTER THEIR KIND
- evidence confirming a GLOBAL FLOOD
- evidence confirming ONE RACE
- evidence confirming the TOWER OF BABEL
- evidence confirming a YOUNG UNIVERSE

Because of time restraints, Mr. Ham then discussed only three of these in more detail (e.g., after their kind, information/intelligence, and one race). However, I have included discussion on all six.

12. Confirmations of a biblical worldview are not a test of the truth of the Bible. Instead, the Bible is the absolute standard for truth, and truth only makes sense in light of God's Word being the absolute standard! God (and by extension His Word) is the precondition for truth to exist. Such observational confirmations are used to show the bankruptcy of false worldviews by revealing that all things are predicated on the Word of God, even scientific observations.

Intelligence

Because the Bible is true, we expect to see evidence that life was created by an intelligence. The DNA of living things encapsulates a brilliant code system. Based on a complete set of the DNA of a creature from just one cell, an entire copy of that creature could be built. That is how much information is in the DNA. There are about three billion base pairs in our DNA that code for the physical body of a human. The information in a human is estimated (I believe conservatively) to be equivalent to about 1,000 books of about 500 pages each (500,000 pages total!) — that is a lot of information![13] And that information needs a code to translate and read it.

Consider: in a secular viewpoint, it was predicted that a simple cell was simply that — simple. When we were finally able to look into a cell, Darwin's "black box" was opened. It was not simple, but was like a little biological factory with extreme precision. Therefore, that prediction failed. At an even smaller scale, we find that the DNA and its information is used to build that cell! Interestingly, single-celled amoebas actually have a DNA strand that dwarfs the human strand — more than 100 times bigger![14]

But here is the point. Where did the information come from? Information must have a source. Information is not confined to DNA. DNA is merely the substrate that holds it (like a hard drive or memory in a computer) — and DNA needs a language to decode and read the information. DNA itself contains the information to construct the code and translate it!

If you (the creative source), wrote an article and saved it on your hard drive, the information came from you, from your fingers to a keyboard, through a processor, and finally resided on the hard drive. Then you could send that article to someone via email, they could open it on another computer, and an eavesdropper could hear someone read that paper aloud from another room. The information traveled to that eavesdropper and they could use smoke signals in Morse code to send it to far-off friends who could see it from a distance! But the information is not material and

---

13. M. Johansen, "The Living Database," *Creation Ex Nihilo*, September 1, 2000, http://www.answersingenesis.org/articles/cm/v22/n4/living-database.
14. E.R. Winstead, "Sizing up Genomes: *Amoeba* is King," *Genome News Network*, February 12, 2001, http://www.genomenewsnetwork.org/articles/02_01/Sizing_genomes.shtml.

it didn't come from matter, but from a creative source — even though it travelled through a multitude of mediums.

In the secular view, nothing immaterial is supposed to exist, so a confirmation of information is a confirmation in a creation model, but not in an evolution model.[15]

We could also discuss the *law of biogenesis* (attributed to Professor Louis Pasteur). This law that is accepted by secular scientists states that living things only come from other living things! But naturalistic evolution as Mr. Nye holds to it must account for living things coming from non-living matter!

After their kind

According to the Bible, creatures were created "after their kind" or "according to their kind" in Genesis 1 (10 times this occurred). Then they were told to multiply.[16] This is a natural, created-order boundary. The implication from this statement in Genesis is that each was created after its kind and would reproduce its own kind.

Creation scientists believe that in most instances, the word "kind" used in Genesis 1 would be at the Family level in the modern classification system.

There is a dog kind, a cat kind, sheep/goat kind, dove/pigeon kind, and an elephant kind, for example.[17] Yes, there are variations (even different species) within dogs, and we denote these dogs with various names like poodles, dingoes, wolves, and so on. But these dogs are not changing into a totally different kind. This is exactly what we observe — dogs breed with dogs and you get dogs. Cats breed with cats and you get cats. Now different species of dogs and cats can develop because of the great genetic variability within a kind, but dogs are still dogs and cats are still cats.

We do not observe single-celled organisms changing into dogs, cats, or cows. This simply does have observational or repeatable support. But we do observe dogs changing into dogs. So this prediction in biology based on the Bible is confirmed.

---

15. M. Riddle, "Information: Evidence for a Creator?" in K. Ham, gen. ed., *The New Answers Book 2* (Tenth Printing) (Green Forest AR: Master Books, 2008), pp. 195–206.
16. B. Hodge, "A Biblically Based Taxonomy?" Answers in Genesis, June 25, 2010, http://www.answersingenesis.org/articles/2010/06/25/feedback-a-biblically-based-taxonomy.
17. G. Purdom and B. Hodge, "What Are the 'Kinds' in Genesis?" in K. Ham, gen. ed., *The New Answers Book 3* (Green Forest, AR: Master Books, 2010), pp. 39–48.

Furthermore, we expect changes in living creatures as well (e.g., Genesis 30:32[18]) — variations within the dog kind or variations within the cat kind. Mr. Ham denoted this as the famous "creationist orchard"; this dispels the often-promoted myth that creationists believe God created all the animals exactly the way they are today.

Mr. Ham also featured a video clip of Dr. Andrew Fabich, who earned a BSc in molecular genetics from Ohio State University, and a PhD in microbiology from the University of Oklahoma. He did his dissertation on *E. coli* and continues his research in this area. In the video clip, Dr. Fabich debunked a commonly held claim that new evolutionary changes are supposedly occurring in *E. coli*. His research documents that such changes have nothing to do with molecules-to-man evolution! Again, this confirms the biblical expectation in regards to separate kinds.

Global Flood

Clearly, the Bible talks of the global Flood (Genesis 6–8)[19] of Noah's day around 4,300 years ago. Most cultures around the world have a Flood legend (over 300 of them)[20] that contains similar elements to that in Genesis. Flood stories permeate most cultures (even in arid and mountainous regions), which is actually what we'd expect based on the Bible's account of the Flood. As people spread about the globe from Babel after the Flood, they took this account with them. Naturally it skewed and lost information or was embellished — this is common in a sin-cursed and broken world.[21] However, elements of the original account (as given in the Bible) can easily be seen, attesting to the truth of what is recorded in Genesis.

In an evolutionary model, there shouldn't be any global Flood legends, since such an event would not have occurred in the past by their reckoning, and people would have had to totally invent the idea without any basis. Of course, some secularists, to explain the plethora of Flood

---

18. "Let me pass through all your flock today, removing from there all the speckled and spotted sheep, and all the brown ones among the lambs, and the spotted and speckled among the goats; and these shall be my wages."

19. K. Ham and A. Snelling, "Was the Flood of Noah Global or Local in Extent?" in K. Ham, gen. ed., *The New Answers Book 3* (Green Forest, AR: Master Books, 2010), pp. 39-48.

20. Many of these are documented in C. Martin, *Flood Legends* (Green Forest, AR: Master Books, 2009), and B. Hodge and L. Welch, *The Flood of Noah: Legends and Lore of Survival* (Green Forest, AR: Master Books, 2014).

21. The Bible records the true account by Moses through the Holy Spirit.

legends, will claim all these people experienced some sort of local flood. However, this does not account for the many similarities (including names) to the account in the Bible. This is confirming evidence for the Bible's account of origins.

The bulk of the rock layers that contain fossils *are* also a confirmation of the biblical Flood. Producing the enormous fossil-bearing layers across the world would require massive amounts of water-borne sediment involving the quick burial of organisms. Even a world-famous evolutionary textbook of the past agrees:

> Burial is of course the first prerequisite for fossilization and it should be as to exclude the air so as to prevent oxidation of the organism. This burial is most often effected by water-borne sediment, which in turn is derived from the degradation of older rocks.[22]

Fossils do not form by slow and gradual processes, which is where the idea of millions of years came from — the supposedly slow and gradual formation of rock layers. Fossils and rock layers form as the result of catastrophes like a flood. In the case of the bulk of the rock layers with fossils, we believe the global Flood[23] of Noah's day was responsible — and there is much evidence confirming that.

The idea of vast geological time (e.g., the secular *Geologic Time Scale*) is based on the presumption of the slow accumulation of these rock layers *without* catastrophes. This is called "uniformitarianism." Many secularists today disagree with this concept of "no catastrophes" and recognize that a significant portion of the rock layers had to be formed by catastrophes (e.g., floods, volcanoes, and so on), otherwise you would not get fossils. This is due to observations that fossils do not form on lake bottoms or ocean floors. The creature must be buried quickly to be a candidate for forming a fossil. So now the secular side appeals to immense numbers of local floods throughout their "millions of years" of proposed time to account for these rock layers and the fossils in them.

Years ago, secularists would essentially say fossil layers were formed by slow processes over millions of years. Now they are really saying fossil

---

22. R. Lull, *Organic Evolution, A Text-Book* (New York, NY: The MacMillan Company, 1917), p. 415.

23. Rock layers with fossils have occurred since the time of the Flood via local floods and volcanoes, but these occur in small volume compared to the Flood. So it is better to say *the bulk of* the rock layers with fossils came from the Flood.

layers were formed by quick processes that occurred in brief segments over millions of years!

But this notion introduces a devastating problem for the secularists. If the rock layers with fossils were laid down by catastrophes, like local floods, then the rock layers no longer represent eons of time. These rock layers would not be evidence for millions of years of slow gradual process, so millions and billions of years of geological time would be refuted. The secularists now say that these local floods laid down the rock layers quickly, but there were vast eons of time *in between these rock layers* that were laid down by the occasional local floods.

But this puts the concept of *millions of years* in an even more devastating position. If the millions of years are actually between the rock layers, then there is no evidence for millions of years whatsoever, as there is nothing between these rock layers. This is exactly what Mr. Ham brought up when discussing the interpretation of the rock layers. He pointed out that the Coconino Sandstone and the Hermit Shale in the Grand Canyon sit directly one atop the other.

In the secular view, there are 50 million years between those two rock layers. Mr. Nye never mentioned such missing years or even tried to address it — as he can't give an adequate answer.

So the rock layers and fossils are exactly what creationists expect from a global Flood, including the order of burial.[24]

Let's now look at the big picture. Can anyone observe and repeat the formation of these rock layers that cover continents? No. It is not observable or repeatable. But in the creation model, based on the Bible, we expected to find fossiliferous rock layers all over the world, which cover continents and even mountaintops (that were pushed up during the Flood).[25] This is exactly what has been found. The prediction based on the Bible's account of the Flood is confirmed.

Was there enough water to cover the earth with water at the time of the global Flood? Yes. If one brings the mountains and ocean basins to

24. Creatures living at lower places (e.g., sea creatures) or lack of mobility (e.g., sea shells) buried first and so on: A. Snelling, "Doesn't the Order of Fossils in the Rock Record Favor Long Ages?" in K. Ham, gen. ed., *The New Answers Book 2*, Tenth Printing (Green Forest, AR: Master Books, 2008), pp. 341–354.

25. A. Snelling, "Could the Flood Cataclysm Deposit Uniform Sedimentary Rock Layers?" in K. Ham, gen. ed., *The New Answers Book 4* (Green Forest, AR: Master Books, 2013), pp. 173–186; B. Hodge, "Did Noah Need Oxygen on the Ark?" in K. Ham, gen. ed., *The New Answers Book 4* (Green Forest, AR: Master Books, 2013), pp. 375–382.

the same level, then there is enough water to the cover the earth to nearly two miles deep.[26]

The mountains were rising and the valleys sinking during that Flood year (e.g., Genesis 8:4[27]). Psalm 104 seems to confirm this. This Psalm begins with creation, transitions to the Flood, and then to a post-Flood situation. Specifically, verses 8–9[28] discuss the rising of the mountains and the sinking of the valleys (ocean basins) to something close to what we observe today.

Now we still have some residual effects of past catastrophic events, like the slight movement of the continents. But this ongoing tectonic activity has considerably slowed.[29] God said (e.g., Genesis 9:11[30]) that the waters would not return to cover the earth, and Psalm 104:9 reflects this promise. We have certain seen plenty of local floods since Noah's day — but never another global Flood.

It is sad that many of the secularists who criticize the Bible for the idea of a global Flood by saying there is not enough water on earth for such an occurrence are the same people who have claimed there were was a massive Flood on Mars — a planet that has no liquid water! Mr. Ham pointed this out in the debate as well.[31]

One race

Evolutionists predicted that there would be multiple races of mankind — some closer to the supposed ape-like ancestor than others. Such ideas were promoted by Charles Darwin in *The Descent of Man*, Ernst Haeckel (who popularized evolution in Germany), and many others. Mr. Ham quoted from one of the main biology textbooks being used in the public

---

26. B. Hodge, "Did Noah Need Oxygen on the Ark?" Answers in Genesis, July 6, 2009, http://www.answersingenesis.org/articles/2009/07/06/did-noah-need-oxygen.
27. "Then the ark rested in the seventh month, the seventeenth day of the month, on the mountains of Ararat."
28. "The mountains rose; the valleys sank down to the place which You established for them. You set a boundary that they may not pass over, so that they will not return to cover the earth" (NASB).
29. A. Snelling, "Can Catastrophic Plate Tectonics Explain Flood Geology?" in K. Ham, gen. ed., *The New Answers Book 1* (Green Forest, AR: Master Books, 2006), pp. 186–197.
30. "Thus I establish My covenant with you: Never again shall all flesh be cut off by the waters of the flood; never again shall there be a flood to destroy the earth."
31. Though the alleged Martian flood was supposedly very large, it was not necessarily global, see J. Kluger, "The Great (and Recent) Martian Flood," *Time (Science & Space)*, March 11, 2013, http://science.time.com/2013/03/11/the-great-and-recent-martian-flood/.

school science classes in the US at the time of the Scopes Trial. Students were really being taught racist ideas based on Darwinian evolution. In the textbook we read:

> At the present time there exists upon earth five races or varieties of man...and finally the highest type of all, the Caucasians, represented by the civilized white inhabitants of Europe and America.[32]

Imagine if such statements were made in public school textbooks today — and yet that statement reflects accurately what Darwinian evolution actually teaches. Of course Mr. Nye didn't say a word about such a quote! If he disagreed with it, then he would be disagreeing with Mr. Darwin — but on the other hand, he couldn't agree with it as that would be political suicide!

Now Professor Ernst Haeckel, said to be "Darwin's bulldog" in Germany, said in his book:

> At the lowest stage of human mental development are the Australians, some tribes of the Polynesians, and the Bushmen, Hottentots, and some of the Negro tribes.[33]

Furthermore, "Haeckel divided humans into twelve different species, which are in their turn divided into 36 different races."[34] Haeckel set the stage in Germany for popularizing racism to a degree that ultimately led to Hitler and Nazis.

According to the Bible, there can only be one human race because all people are the descendants of Adam and Eve (1 Corinthians 15:45,[35] Genesis 3:20[36]).[37] Even though they wouldn't admit it, the *Human Genome Project* confirmed the Bible's account of human history when they

32. George William Hunter, *A Civic Biology: Presented in Problems* (New York: American Book Company, 1914), p. 196.
33. E. Haeckel, *The History of Creation* (New York: D. Appleton and Co., 1880), pp. 362–363.
34. E. Van Neiker, "Ernst Haeckel: A Hostile Witness to the Truth of the Bible," Creation website, March 3, 2011, http://creation.com/haeckel-hostile-witness-bible-truth.
35. "And so it is written, 'The first man Adam became a living being.' The last Adam became a life-giving spirit."
36. "And Adam called his wife's name Eve, because she was the mother of all living."
37. K. Ham, "Are There Really Different Races?" in K. Ham, gen. ed., *The New Answers Book 1* (Green Forest, AR: Master Books, 2006), pp. 220–236.

announced their findings to the world. Back in 2000, we read in the *New York Times*:

> Dr. Venter [head of the Celera Genomics Corporation, Rockville, MD] and scientists at the National Institutes of Health recently announced that they had put together a draft of the entire sequence of the human genome, and the researchers had unanimously declared, there is only one race — the human race.[38]

Thus, the biblical model was confirmed in its prediction of one race as a result of this research that involved observational science. The corollary of this is that the evolutionary models were patently false.

Tower of Babel: Languages

Mr. Ham mentioned languages but didn't have the time to expound on this. In a biblical framework, there was originally one language for man to communicate with God. Adam and Eve were preprogrammed with that language to talk and fellowship with God and each other. This same language survived until after the Flood, where only eight people survived.

But after the rebellion at Babel, God confused the language of the whole world, giving distinct languages to different groups (Genesis 10, 11). There was a minimum of about 78 language families listed in Genesis 10 as coming out of Babel that were unique and separate (different grammar, different words, some pictorial, some sounded out, some more tonal or less tonal, some that write left to right and some that write right to left, or top down and so on). Since then (over 4,000 years ago), these languages have been shifting and changing to what we have today.[39]

In an evolutionary framework, however, language slowly developed among evolving humans and originated with a "proto-language" or ancestor to all languages. This language was supposedly "primitive" (think "primate-like"). It was surely based on grunts and other basic animal sounds, since people were supposed to be animals evolving into humankind.

---

38. N. Angier, "Do Races Differ? Not Really, Genes Show," *New York Times* web, August 22, 2000, http://www.nytimes.com/2000/08/22/science/do-races-differ-not-really-genes-show.html.
39. For more, see B. Hodge, *The Tower of Babel* (Green Forest, AR: Master Books, 2013).

The claim is that the first proto-language emerged nearly two million years ago with *Homo erectus*.[40] For the reader, *Homo erectus* is a name evolutionists have given to a group of humans (based on fossil finds) that, from a Christian worldview, were buried in post-Flood sediments. Therefore, Noah was alive before these fossils were even laid down!

Now secular researchers are trying to find commonalities in language, especially with grammar, and have produced various models. One such popular model is called "universal grammar" or UG. It is but one attempt that still falls short, as many researchers rightly recognize that with the diversity of language and without massive exceptions, UG may not only be improbable but perhaps impossible.[41]

One must understand that the secular humanistic community *must* have a story in place to make sense of languages (speech, written, and sign). This was the case with the old Greek mythologies; they needed to have stories to explain why the sun took a particular path in the sky. In the same way, evolutionary storytelling is a necessity when looking at real issues like language.

We can speak simply because the Creator made us in His image to communicate with Him.[42] We can think, reason, and be creative in ways that animals never can. But an unbelieving secular community has refused to allow God in the door. So they must come up with stories to try to explain language naturalistically. And they look to animals — because they believe we are simply animals — for answers.

Evolutionists presuppose that man evolved from ape-like ancestors, so apes today should be the closest animals to us and hence closest to being able to develop human language. This brings us to studies on apes like Koko, who was able to learn certain signs. Koko is a fascinating gorilla but is far from being human. Koko has learned nearly 1000 signs in American Sign Language and knows quite a number of voice commands. It has taken Koko nearly 32 years to learn all this.[43] And other

---

40. W.T. Fitch, "The Evolution of Language," *NewScientist*, December 4, 2010, pp. ii–viii; available online at http://www.newscientist.com/data/doc/article/dn19554/instant_expert_6_-_the_evolution_of_language.pdf.

41. C. Kenneally, "Talking Heads," *NewScientist*, May 29, 2010, pp. 32–35.

42. C. Abney, "The Image of God," in K. Ham, gen. ed., *The New Answers Book 4* (Green Forest, AR: Master Books, 2013), pp. 383–390; B. Hodge, *The Fall of Satan* (Green Forest, AR: Master Books, 2011), pp. 112–115.

43. For facts about Koko, visit http://www.koko.org/friends/meet_koko.html.

animals, like the bonobo named Kanzi, have also been trained to hear commands.[44]

These trained responses are similar to those of dogs and many other animals. They can be trained to respond to certain sounds or motions and even give a response in return. For example, Chanda-Leah, the world's smartest dog according to the *Guinness Book of World Records*, could recognize over 1,022 commands and respond to each accordingly — some were even math problems! Many of these commands were vocal or hand signals, much like the commands Koko is given.[45]

Yet Chanda-Leah, being only 10 years old, was much younger than Koko, and many dogs have this capability; therefore, dogs seem to be far superior to the apes that are alleged to be our closest relatives. Trained response, however, is much different than the ability to use reasoning in the same manner as humans.

Man is made in the image of God, whereas animals are not.[46] This is an extreme difference and is why looking to animal behavior for answers will simply never get one to the truth about human origins or human language. When we study languages today, we find incredibly diverse families of languages, each unique and fascinating in their own respects.[47] This is what is expected in a biblical framework encompassing the Tower of Babel. But the origins of languages are impossible to explain using and evolutionary framework. This would severely challenge the evolutionary prediction.

Young universe

Mr. Ham showed a video clip of Mr. Nye trying to combine observational science and historical science when Mr. Nye said:

> You can show the earth is not flat. You can show the earth is not 10,000 years old.

But there are two issues brought up here. First is the concept of a flat earth and the second is the age of the earth, which is a significant key to

---

44. Fitch, "The Evolution of Language," *New Scientist*, http://www.newscientist.com/data/doc/article/dn19554/instant_expert_6_-_the_evolution_of_language.pdf.
45. For facts about Chanda-Leah, visit http://www.pethall.com/chanda_leah-tricks.htm and http://www.pethall.com/chanda_leah_doorway.htm.
46. B. Hodge, *The Fall of Satan* (Green Forest, AR: Master Books, 2011), pp. 112–115.
47. Of course, languages are constantly changing, as we would expect since Babel.

the whole debate. This first issue (flat earth) needs to be addressed right from the start for the sake of the reader.

Flat earth

There is a false claim that many secularists often promote accusing creationists of being flat earthers.[48] As far as I'm aware, no biblical creationists believe this. The Bible doesn't teach a flat earth nor does historical or modern scholarship indicate that this belief was widespread.[49] Conversely, the Bible makes it clear that the earth isn't flat, in plain language, so it shouldn't be an issue:

> It is He who sits above the circle of the earth, and its inhabitants are like grasshoppers, Who stretches out the heavens like a curtain and spreads them out like a tent to dwell in. (Isaiah 40:22)

Another verse that teaches a circular or round earth is Job 26:10:

> He has inscribed a circle on the surface of the waters at the boundary of light and darkness. (Job 26:10, NASB)

Believers in a flat earth were found in ancient Greece before 500 BC, though many Greeks held to a round earth. This belief resurfaced as a rare view held by Lactantius in the early A.D. 300s and only a few others throughout history. Humanists later revived this strange belief of a flat earth during the Renaissance and tried to indicate that Christians, for the most part, believed this view. However, this was simply not true. A fictional novel promoted the idea that Christians believed in a flat earth — and this myth was taken up by atheists and spread through the public.[50]

Taking some biblical passages out of context further propagated this misunderstanding. One such example is Revelation 7:1,[51] which prophetically and allegorically refers to the four corners of the earth. The

---

48. D. Faulkner, "Creation and the Flat Earth: Columbus and Modern Historians," *Creation Matters*, 2, no. 6 (1997): p.1.
49. Editors, "Who Invented a Flat Earth?" *Creation* 16, no. 2 (March 1994): p. 48–49, http://www.answersingenesis.org/creation/v16/i2/flatearth.asp.
50. Ibid.
51. "After these things I saw four angels standing at the four corners of the earth, holding the four winds of the earth, that the wind should not blow on the earth, on the sea, or on any tree."

verse is taken out of context by making the verse a strict literal sense meaning and ignoring any figurative speech. Expositor John Gill comments on this verse, saying:

> Four angels are mentioned, in allusion to the four spirits of the heavens, in Zec. 6:5; and though the earth is not a plain square with angles, but round and globular, yet it is said to have four corners, with respect to the four points of the heavens; and though there is but one wind, which blows sometimes one way, and sometimes another, yet four are named with regard to the above points, east, west, north, and south, from whence it blows.[52]

It was obviously referring to the directions of north, south, east, and west. Poetic passages such as Psalms 75:3, which refers to the "pillars" of the earth, were also used to derive the false view of a flat earth. Commentators such as John Gill,[53] Matthew Henry,[54] and others rightly point out that this is figurative for a firm foundation set by Christ.

By using observational science, we have been able to study the earth, as Mr. Ham denotes, and see that it is indeed round, circular, or spherical, thus confirming the passages in Isaiah and Job. And the rehashed mythos of a flat earth down through the ages is pure fiction.

Age of the earth

In returning to Mr. Nye's claim that the age of the earth *can be shown* not to be 10,000 years, we are driven into the issue of the age of the earth. Both Mr. Nye and Mr. Ham are in complete disagreement with each other on this point. Recall:

> Mr. Nye holds to about 4.5 billion years for the age of the earth.
> Mr. Ham holds to about 6,000 years for the age of the earth.

There will be much more discussed on this issue in the section on Mr. Nye's 30-minute presentation. But for now, I wish to explain the basis

---

52. *Exposition of the Old Testament*, Commentary by John Gill, Expositor, Notes on Revelation 7:1, 1748–1763.
53. *Exposition of the Old Testament*, Commentary by John Gill, Expositor, Notes on Psalm 75:3, 1748–1763.
54. *Matthew Henry Bible Complete Commentary*; Matthew Henry, notes on Psalms 75:3.

of the 6,000 years to which Mr. Ham appeals (not 10,000 as some creationists allow for).

Simply put, it came from the Bible. Of course, the Bible doesn't explicitly say anywhere: "the earth is 6,000 years old." Good thing it doesn't; otherwise it would be out of date the following year (and the Bible was completed nearly 2,000 years ago — so if the Bible said the earth was 6,000 years old 2,000 years ago, the Bible would obviously be in error). But we wouldn't expect an all-knowing God to make that kind of mistake.

God gave us something better. In essence, He gave us a "birth certificate." For example, using a personal birth certificate, a person can calculate how old he is at any point in time. It is similar with the earth. Genesis 1 says that the earth was formed on the first day of creation (Genesis 1:1–5). From there, we can begin to calculate the age of the earth.

Let's do a rough calculation to show how this works. The age of the earth can be estimated by taking the first five days of creation (from earth's creation to Adam since Adam was made on Day 6), by following the genealogies from Adam to Abraham in Genesis 5 and 11, then by adding in the time from Abraham to today.

Adam was created on Day 6, so there were five days before him. If we add up the dates from Adam to Abraham, we get about 2,000 years, using the Masoretic Hebrew text of Genesis 5 and 11.[55] Whether Christian or secular, most scholars would agree that Abraham lived about 2,000 BC (that is, 4,000 years ago).

So a simple calculation is:

$$
\begin{array}{r}
5 \text{ days} \\
+ \sim 2000 \text{ years} \\
+ \sim 4000 \text{ years} \\
\hline
\sim 6000 \text{ years}
\end{array}
$$

Quite a few people have done this calculation using the Masoretic Hebrew text (which is what most English translations have been based on since the 1500s), and with careful attention to the biblical details, have arrived at the same time frame of about 6,000 years, or roughly 4,000

---

55. B. Hodge, "Ancient Patriarchs in Genesis," Answers in Genesis, January 20, 2009, http://www.answersingenesis.org/articles/2009/01/20/ancient-patriarchs-in-genesis.

Table 1 — Jones and Ussher

Name	Age calculated	Reference and date
Archbishop James Ussher	4004 BC	*The Annals of the World*, AD 1658
Dr. Floyd Nolan Jones	4004 BC	*The Chronology of the Old Testament*, AD 1993

BC. Two of the most popular, and perhaps best, studies of this nature are a recent work by Dr. Floyd Jones[56] and a much earlier book by Archbishop James Ussher[57] (1581–1656). See table 1.

The misconception exists that Ussher and Jones were the only ones to arrive at a date of about 4,000 BC; however, this is not the case at all. Jones[58] lists several chronologists who have undertaken the task of calculating the age of the earth based on the Bible, and their calculations range from 5501 to 3836 BC, but they hover on each side of 4,000 BC. A few are listed in table 2.

As you will likely note from table 2, the dates are not all 4,004 BC. There are several reasons chronologists have different dates,[59] but following are two primary reasons:

1. Some used the Septuagint or another early translation instead of the Hebrew Masoretic text. The Septuagint is a Greek translation of the Hebrew Old Testament, done about 250 BC by about 70 Jewish scholars (hence it is often cited as the LXX which is Roman numerals for 70). It is good in most places, but appears to have a number of inaccuracies in the translation. For example, one relates to the Genesis chronologies where the tallies in the LXX indicates that Methuselah would have lived past the Flood, without being on the Ark!

56. Floyd Nolan Jones, *Chronology of the Old Testament* (Green Forest, AR: Master Books, 2005).
57. James Ussher, *The Annals of the World* (Green Forest, AR: Master Books, 2003), translated by Larry and Marion Pierce.
58. Jones, *Chronology of the Old Testament*, p. 26
59. Others would include gaps in the chronology based on the presence of an extra Cainan in Luke 3:36. But there are good reasons this should be left out, which will not be discussed here. See T. Chaffey and J. Lisle, *Old-Earth Creationism on Trial* (Green Forest, AR: Master Books, 2008), Appendix C, pp. 179–183, http://www.answersingenesis.org/articles/oect/gaps-genesis-genealogies.

Table 2 — Chronologists' calculations according to Dr. Jones

	Chronologist	When calculated?	Date BC
1	**Julius Africanus**	c. 240	5501
2	**George Syncellus**	c. 810	5492
3	**John Jackson**	1752	5426
4	**Dr. William Hales**	c. 1830	5411
5	Eusebius	c. 330	5199
6	Marianus Scotus	c. 1070	4192
7	L. Condomanus	n/a	4141
8	Thomas Lydiat	c. 1600	4103
9	M. Michael Maestlinus	c. 1600	4079
10	J. Ricciolus	n/a	4062
11	Jacob Salianus	c. 1600	4053
12	H. Spondanus	c. 1600	4051
13	Martin Anstey	1913	4042
14	W. Lange	n/a	4041
15	E. Reinholt	n/a	4021
16	J. Cappellus	c. 1600	4005
17	E. Greswell	1830	4004
18	E. Faulstich	1986	4001
19	D. Petavius	c. 1627	3983
20	Frank Klassen	1975	3975
21	Becke	n/a	3974
22	Krentzeim	n/a	3971
23	W. Dolen	2003	3971
24	E. Reusnerus	n/a	3970
25	J. Claverius	n/a	3968
26	C. Longomontanus	c. 1600	3966
27	P. Melanchthon	c. 1550	3964
28	J. Haynlinus	n/a	3963
29	A. Salmeron	d. 1585	3958
30	J. Scaliger	d. 1609	3949
31	M. Beroaldus	c. 1575	3927
32	A. Helwigius	c. 1630	3836

ourselves to every man's conscience in the sight of God. (2 Corinthians 4:2)

All the utterances of my mouth are in righteousness; There is nothing crooked or perverted in them. They are all straightforward to him who understands, and right to those who find knowledge. (Proverbs 8:8–9)

In other words, we are to read and understand the Bible in a *plain* or *straightforward* manner. This is usually what people mean when they say "literal interpretation of the Bible" (this phrase is common among those not well-versed in hermeneutics). I try to use the term "plainly" so I don't confuse people. In the question time, Mr. Ham explained that by literally, he meant "naturally"; that is, taking God's Word as it is written, according to the grammar and the type of literature — whether poetry, historical narrative, or apocalyptic etc.

Reading the Bible "plainly" means understanding that literal history is literal history, metaphors are metaphors, poetry is poetry, and so on. The Bible is written in many different literary styles and should be read accordingly. We can understand that Genesis records actual historical events as it is written in typical historical narrative.

Reading the Bible plainly/in a straightforward manner (taking into account literary style, context, authorship, etc.) is the basis for what is called the *historical-grammatical* method of interpretation, which has been used by theologians since the church fathers.[64] This method helps to eliminate improper interpretations of the Bible.

For example, I once had someone (who was not a Christian) say to me, "the Bible clearly says, 'there is no God' in Psalms 14:1." When you look up the verse and read it in context, it says:

The fool says in his heart, "There is no God." They are corrupt, their deeds are vile; there is no one who does good. (Psalm 14:1)

So the context helps determine the proper interpretation — that a *fool* was saying this.

---

64. This is the methodology of interpreting Scripture with Scripture since God is His own authority on interpretation. Furthermore, this method even predates church fathers as New Testament authors and Old Testament prophets interpreted Scripture via this method as well.

I also once had someone tell me, "To interpret the days in Genesis, you need to read 2 Peter 3:8, which indicates the days are each a thousand years." 2 Peter 3:8–9, in context, says:

> But do not forget this one thing, dear friends: With the Lord a day is like a thousand years, and a thousand years are like a day. The Lord is not slow in keeping his promise, as some understand slowness. He is patient with you, not wanting anyone to perish, but everyone to come to repentance. (2 Peter 3:8–9)

This passage employs a literary device called a *simile*. Here, God compares a day to a thousand years in order to make the point that time doesn't bind Him, in this case regarding His patience. God is not limited to the time that He created — that would be illogical. And the context is in regard to the second coming of Christ ("Where is the promise of his coming…").

Also, this verse (originally written in Greek) gives no reference to the days in Genesis (originally written in Hebrew), so it is not warranted to apply to the days in Genesis 1. When read plainly, these verses indicate that God is patient when keeping His promises.

Defining creation

Mr. Ham then moved to define creation. He explained creation as defined by the Bible or, as many have put it, "biblical creation." Creation basically entails taking Genesis as straightforward history, which is the style that it is written in.

Thus, God would have created in six normal-length days, then rested for a day (which is a pattern for our work week). Everything was very good (Genesis 1:31[65]) and perfect (Deuteronomy 32:4[66]), which is what we would expect from a perfectly good God. Then death,

---

65. "Then God saw everything that He had made, and indeed it was very good. So the evening and the morning were the sixth day."
66. "He [*God*] is the Rock, His work is perfect; for all His ways are justice, a God of truth and without injustice; righteous and upright is He."

bloodshed, and suffering came in as a result of sin by Adam (and Eve) in Genesis 3 (see also Romans 5, Romans 8). This is why we need a Savior in Jesus Christ who saves us from sin and death. And this, as Mr. Ham pointed out, is why the supposed millions of years of rock layers that contain death and evidence of diseases like cancer, couldn't have occurred until *after* Adam and Eve sinned.[67]

As time progressed, violence and evil increased because of sin, so God sent a Flood to judge this wickedness. Since man had dominion over the whole earth, the whole earth was judged with a global Flood (Genesis 1:26–28[68]). The text makes it clear that it was a global Flood (e.g., Genesis 7:19–22[69]). This event would have rearranged continents and formed the high mountains and deep ocean basins we have today (Psalm 104:8–9[70]). Those who were on the Ark were saved from this judgment via entrance into Noah's Ark. The Lord had it prepared and even sent Noah as a preacher of righteousness to warn the pre-Flood world. Sadly, only Noah was seen as righteous in that generation, so only he and his family (whom he represented) were saved.

In many cases, biblical creation also entails the events of Genesis 10–11, specifically the Tower of Babel, which explains why the gene pool was split apart so that various people groups were dominated by limited numbers of genes. In other words, it explains why we look a little different in different parts of the world. But it also explains the various languages (which we already discussed). And finally, the division at Babel

---

67. The Flood of Noah's day accounts for most of the rock layers that contain fossils. Of course, there have been some rock layer that record death sin the Flood, but either way, these are post-sin.

68. "Then God said, 'Let Us make man in Our image, according to Our likeness; let them have dominion over the fish of the sea, over the birds of the air, and over the cattle, over all the earth and over every creeping thing that creeps on the earth.' So God created man in His own image; in the image of God He created him; male and female He created them. Then God blessed them, and God said to them, 'Be fruitful and multiply; fill the earth and subdue it; have dominion over the fish of the sea, over the birds of the air, and over every living thing that moves on the earth.'"

69. "And the waters prevailed exceedingly on the earth, and all the high hills under the whole heaven were covered. The waters prevailed fifteen cubits upward, and the mountains were covered. And all flesh died that moved on the earth: birds and cattle and beasts and every creeping thing that creeps on the earth, and every man. All in whose nostrils was the breath of the spirit of life, all that was on the dry land, died."

70. "They went up over the mountains; they went down into the valleys, to the place which You founded for them. You have set a boundary that they may not pass over, that they may not return to cover the earth."

also explains that we are all related and all in need of Jesus Christ no matter what we look like or sound like.

Mr. Ham briefly discussed that these creation elements (Genesis 1-11) are presented in the Creation Museum *and* covered how they relate to geology, anthropology, astronomy, biology, and so on. I am still saddened that Mr. Nye has stopped by the Creation Museum twice now (once to take a picture and the other for the debate) yet has refused to go through the museum. Mr. Ham offered to give Mr. Nye a personal tour through the Creation Museum before the debate, but this offer was not taken up.

Origin of many doctrines

Mr. Ham then explained why biblical creation is vitally important as a foundation to the Gospel and the worldview of Christianity. Genesis is so important that, as Mr. Ham, denoted: "Ultimately every single biblical doctrine of theology, directly or indirectly, is founded in Genesis." Mr. Ham also explained that taking Genesis as written is an authority issue. If one uses man's beliefs about the past (such as evolution and/or millions of years) to interpret Genesis, then man becomes the authority, not God. Let's look more closely at some of these doctrines and explain them so they are not missed.

Marriage

God created a man and a woman, so marriage is between a man and a woman in a covenant with God. Jesus affirmed it is between male and female in Matthew 19:4–6[71] and Mark 10:6[72]. Interestingly, the world borrows this doctrine from God.

In many cases, the secularists skew it and redefine it so that the doctrine can hardly be recognized. God is replaced with the government… or sometimes no one or nothing. Sometimes it is skewed to be man and man or woman and woman or multiple women and one man, and the list continues. But even with this warping of marriage, there is no basis for the doctrine outside of a literal/that is "plain" reading, of Genesis.

---

71. "And He answered and said to them, 'Have you not read that He who made them at the beginning "made them male and female," and said, "For this reason a man shall leave his father and mother and be joined to his wife, and the two shall become one flesh"? So then, they are no longer two but one flesh. Therefore what God has joined together, let not man separate.'"
72. "But from the beginning of the creation, God 'made them male and female.'"

Sin and death

Genesis explains why there is sin and death in the world and even explains the relationship between sin and death. Death is the result of sin. It is a judgment by God upon sin (Genesis 2:16–17,[73] 3:19,[74] Romans 5:12[75]). We all sin, so we all die. We are all under that judgment. Even you (reading this) are under the judgment of death, and one day this judgment is coming for you.

Christ, who is God, became a man and stepped into history to die on our behalf. The God-man took on flesh to offer Himself as a tribute to take the infinite punishment (this is how long death would last) upon Himself. This is how much Christ loved us. That is why salvation in Jesus Christ is a free gift. The infinite Son took the infinite punishment on our behalf, so the debt was fully paid and the wrath upon our sin was completely satisfied. Therefore, those saved in Jesus Christ have no fear of death, for the sting of death (eternal separation from God) has been taken away.

Those who are not in Christ still have the sting of death waiting for them. This eternally enduring punishment is called the second death or "Hell," where the wrath of God will abide on them for their sin forever (Matthew 25:46;[76] Revelation 20:14;[77] Matthew 10:28[78]). And there will be no escape.

But note the flip side in a secular view. Death is the wonderful stepping-stone in an evolutionary worldview. Death and suffering are elements that supposedly drive evolution. So in a biblical view, death is an enemy that needs to be destroyed (1 Corinthians 15:26[79]), and in the humanistic view, death is the ultimate hero.

Now Mr. Ham at one stage did challenge Mr. Nye concerning the topic of death. He asked Mr. Nye why he talked about the joy of discovery

---

73. "And the Lord God commanded the man, saying, 'Of every tree of the garden you may freely eat; but of the tree of the knowledge of good and evil you shall not eat, for in the day that you eat of it you shall surely die.'"
74. "In the sweat of your face you shall eat bread till you return to the ground, for out of it you were taken; for dust you are, and to dust you shall return."
75. "Therefore, just as through one man sin entered the world, and death through sin, and thus death spread to all men, because all sinned."
76. "And these will go away into everlasting punishment, but the righteous into eternal life."
77. "Then Death and Hades were cast into the lake of fire. This is the second death."
78. "And do not fear those who kill the body but cannot kill the soul. But rather fear Him who is able to destroy both soul and body in hell."
79. "The last enemy that will be destroyed is death."

when one day he would die, and from his secular perspective, he would cease to exist. So, if Mr. Nye was going to cease to exist, what was the point of anything he did? Mr. Nye did not respond to this challenge from Mr. Ham.

Clothes

Clothing is a biblical doctrine. Originally, man had no shame (Genesis 2:25[80]) in a perfect created order. After Adam and Eve sinned, things changed and they now experienced shame; subsequently, so do we (Genesis 3:7,[81] see also many others such as: Exodus 28:42[82] and Revelation 16:15[83]). We wear clothes to cover that shame. Actually the giving of clothes involved the first blood sacrifice, thus pointing toward the One who would be the ultimate sacrifice — the Lord Jesus Christ.

After sin, Adam and Eve made coverings for themselves from fig leaves (Genesis 3:7[84]). But that was not good enough. The punishment for sin was death, so the solution had to involve death. The Lord made garments of skin for Adam and His wife (Genesis 3:21[85]). This was the first record of death in the Bible. An animal "helped" lead Eve, and subsequently Adam, into sin, so it is almost fitting that an animal be involved in the solution to sin and death by becoming the very clothes to cover the shame of that first sin.

But we wear clothes to cover our nakedness. All over the world, cultures borrow this from God where the descendants of Adam and Eve have taken this doctrine to various parts of the world after the Flood through the Tower of Babel.

Death of Christ

The reason for Christ stepping into history to become a man and die on a cross goes back to the very first sin and the resulting judgment of death.

---

80. "And they were both naked, the man and his wife, and were not ashamed."
81. "Then the eyes of both of them were opened, and they knew that they were naked; and they sewed fig leaves together and made themselves coverings."
82. "And you shall make for them linen trousers to cover their nakedness; they shall reach from the waist to the thighs."
83. "Behold, I am coming as a thief. Blessed is he who watches, and keeps his garments, lest he walk naked and they see his shame."
84. "Then the eyes of both of them were opened, and they knew that they were naked; and they sewed fig leaves together and made themselves coverings."
85. "Also for Adam and his wife the LORD God made tunics of skin, and clothed them."

Part 3

The Nye 30-minute Case

After thanking Mr. Ham for teaching him some things, Mr. Nye immediately changed the agreed topic of the debate (*Is creation a viable model of origins in today's modern scientific era?*) to something else (*Does Ken Ham's creation model hold up? Is it viable?*).

This is a common debate tactic. Mr. Nye once again deviated from the debate topic of creation (a well-established view for thousands of years) to make it sound as though creation is a new Ken Ham idea. In a subtle sense, he used this tactic to devalue creation as being from God by trying to give ownership of it to a man — Mr. Ham.

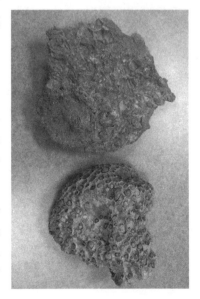

Fossils in Kentucky

Mr. Nye proceeded to discuss some fossils found in the general vicinity of the debate at the Creation Museum, particularly zooxanthellae coral. He said:

> And when you look at it closely you can see that they live their entire lives, they lived typically 20 years, sometimes more than that if the water

conditions are correct. And so we are standing on millions of layers of ancient life.

To the untrained listener, Mr. Nye just presented a devastating argument. But this was a fallacious means of arguing. Mr. Nye was assuming naturalism to prove naturalism. He assumed there were no catastrophes in the past and that rates and processes have always been identical (this is called "uniformitarianism" and is based on naturalism) to make the claims at hand. Then he proceeded to use these assumptions to definitively state the naturalistic position of millions of years.

This fallacy is called *affirming the consequent* and is arguably the most common fallacy evolutionists commit. Therefore, Mr. Nye proved nothing but merely assumed what he was trying to prove, an arbitrary and self-refuting argument.

Mr. Nye then demonstrated his misunderstanding of a basic tenant of creation, saying:

> How could those animals have lived their entire life and formed these layers in just 4,000 years? There isn't enough time since Mr. Ham's flood for this limestone that we're standing on to have come into existence.

Besides the fact that it was "Noah's Flood,"[1] not Mr. Ham's flood, it was the Flood that produced the bulk of the fossil layers including the corals in question. Mr. Nye failed to understand that a catastrophe like the Flood explains the massive burial of plants, animals, and so on to trigger the fossilization process by rapid sediment burial that seals out the oxygen.

Mr. Nye essentially assumed that the Flood was meaningless in regard to fossil formation. He then presumed to apply a naturalistic mechanism to fossil formation since the time of the Flood (about 4,000 years ago or 4,350 years to be a little closer) to account for the fossils we see today.

Creationists, such as Mr. Ham, do not adhere to naturalism from the time of the Flood to make the fossils in question. I was actually surprised at Mr. Nye's assertion, as most evolutionists have been fully aware that from a biblical perspective, the Flood *was the mechanism* that formed the bulk of the fossils.

---

1. More properly, it would be the global Flood that occurred in Noah's day.

Ice Cores

Mr. Nye then discussed ice cores. They are simply cores of ice that have been drilled out of ice sheets such as those on Greenland or Antarctica. These compacted ice layers were built up from previous storms of ice and snow.

Mr. Nye pointed out that there are some cores with upwards of 680,000 layers in them — and they allegedly took long ages to be laid down. Now I (and most creationists I know) actually agree that there are a lot of these ice layers. Of course, due to compression, the layers toward the bottom have molecular diffusion, so it has to be *estimated* as to how many layers might have been there (it is true that there is long age assumption here too, of which one needs to be careful). But generally, we agree with evolutionists on this point. But remember, the ice layers don't come with labels on them telling us their age!

But then, Mr. Nye made an interpretation of these observable *and* estimated ice layers that I want to call into question. He said:

> And we find certain of these cylinders to have 680,000 layers. 680,000 snow winter-summer cycles.

He assumed these layers were divided by winter-summer cycles. Apparently, there miraculously becomes an observable division between ice layers where all the ice and snow from storms in one year get compacted into one single layer, and all the ice and snow from storms the next year get compacted into the next layer, and so on! Obviously this is problematic.

I have personally seen multiple ice layers in *one winter* in Kentucky! These layers simply resulted from several ice storms and snow storms piled one on top of the other. Sometimes they were merely due to various phases within the same storm (such as ice-snow-ice). The lower layers sometimes became more compact from the layers on top of them, and yet, this was only *one winter*.

Many people around the world could concur that multiple storms will produce multiple layers of snow and ice, which they can — and have — observed every winter. In places like Kentucky, these ice layers melt off each year, but in places where ice sheets are growing (some places in Antarctica and Greenland, for example), they do not melt off but continue to accumulate.

The point is that multiple storms can be observed to produce multiple ice layers. So why assume each of these layers develop in winter-summer cycles? That would go against scientific observation, to say the least. Such abundant ice layers are not dependent upon a winter-summer cycle. Mr. Nye has made a fallible assumption — one that does not fit with what we observe. That should settle it.

But let's discuss this further. While working with the Institute for Creation Research, Dr. Larry Vardiman (PhD in atmospheric science from Colorado State University) and Mike Oard, an expert meteorologist (MSc in atmospheric science from the University of Washington), board member of the Creation Research Society and former National Weather Service meteorologist, are both weather scientists who have dealt with this issue extensively. Neither would yield to the argument that ice cores are evidence for long ages or winter-summer cycles.

Dr. Vardiman has pointed out that WWII planes buried just 50 years ago in Greenland were already under 250 feet of ice when found![2] Mr. Ham referred to this specific example during the debate. Dr. Vardiman has asserted that if uniformitarian rates were to be assumed from this data alone, it would take less than 1,000 years to form the entire Greenland ice sheet! Dr. Vardiman did further calculations and found that a few thousand years were all that would be required for the entire sheet.[3]

Mr. Oard has also addressed the ice cores in great detail from a technical perspective, touching on the oxygen content that is to be expected since climate and atmospheric changes do occur and have occurred since the time of the Flood.[4] Such things are actually perfectly anticipated in a biblical creationist's framework.

Bristlecone Pines

Mr. Nye brought up bristlecone pines and arbitrarily asserted that some of them are over 6,000 years old. He made another such statement that a particular tree (Old Tjikko) is 9,550 years old. During the debate, Mr.

2. Editors, "Deep Layers," Answers in Genesis, October 26, 2002, https://answersingenesis.org/evidence-against-evolution/deep-layers/.
3. Larry Vardiman, PhD, 1992, "Ice Cores and the Age of the Earth," *Acts & Facts*, 21 (4), http://www.icr.org/article/ice-cores-age-earth/.
4. M. Oard, "Do Greenland Ice Cores Show over One Hundred Thousand Years of Annual Layers?" December 1, 2001, http://www.answersingenesis.org/articles/tj/v15/n3/greenland.

Ham said that many of the examples Mr. Nye used were already answered on the www.answersingenesis.org website. I urge people to use the website to find these answers.

Please note that Mr. Nye did not make any argument as to how he arrived at that date. An arbitrary claim is simply that — *arbitrary* — and carries no weight in an argument or debate. Bill Nye spouted off a number of items like this, and as he admitted later, it was a strategy hoping to overpower Mr. Ham. However, Mr. Ham didn't get dragged into this rabbit trail. He stayed focused on what he had prepared to do. Are we to simply believe something because Mr. Nye says it or believes it? He did not provide any reason for anyone to believe him except his own authority. Mr. Nye had been wrong before, so why would we trust him now (John 3:12[5])?

Let me explain where the "dates" for these trees come from. They come from tree rings. In simple form, people add up tree rings (this involves assumptions too) as there can be thousands of them. Then one has try to cross-match them with others to determine an "unbroken" chronology. Of course, there is a large degree of guesswork here.

So what is the big deal? Simple: there is the hypothesis that each tree ring is a yearly cycle and that it would be impossible to have more than one per year. It would be like every March 1st all these trees decided to make a new ring.

But the answer is rather easy: the tree rings are actually from *growth* cycles, not necessarily from *yearly* cycles. Many types of trees are observed to have multiple growth cycles even in one year with favorable conditions. So depending on previous wet-dry cycles (or otherwise good or bad growth periods within a year), there could be multiple growth cycles, thus multiple rings.[6]

Bristlecone pines are no exception. The ones that tend to have more rings and live longer are those in arid, higher altitudes where little rain occurs each year. Let me explain: in the dry, arid areas growth stops until the next rain or watering, then the trees can yet again begin to grow. But when they become dry and arid, the trees cease to grow once more.

---

5. "If I have told you earthly things and you do not believe, how will you believe if I tell you heavenly things?"
6. M. Matthews, "Evidence for Multiple Ring Growth Per Year in Bristlecone Pines," *Journal of Creation*, 20, no. 3 (December 2006): pp. 95–103.

So growth is dependent upon getting water, not upon a (yearly) calendar date. Thus a tree having great numbers of rings simply means there were greater numbers of growth cycles in the past. To say that each ring is a yearly ring would require Mr. Nye to prove that each year in the past, there was only one rainfall per year — a truly bold and unprovable assumption on his part. Such a situation is in the realm of historical science, involving hypotheses/beliefs about the past. But Mr. Nye refuses to accept this very obvious fact. The point to take here is that when someone says the bristlecone pines are of a certain age, it is *not* due to direct observation, but by interpretation based on unprovable assumptions. Mark Matthews, writing about bristlecone pines (BCPs), says:

> Perhaps the best evidence that some BCPs can grow multiple rings per year is the fact that it has already been demonstrated. Lammerts, a creationist, induced multiple ring growth in sapling BCPs by simply simulating a two week drought. [Lammerts, W.E., Are the Bristle-cone Pine trees really so old? *Creation Research Society Quarterly* 20, no. 2 (1983): pp. 108–115] Some dismiss this evidence, saying that while multiplicity has been demonstrated in young BCPs, it hasn't been demonstrated in mature BCPs and therefore may not occur in mature BCPs. [LaMarche Jr, V.C. and Harlan, T.P., Accuracy of tree ring dating of Bristlecone Pine for calibration of the radiocarbon time scale, *Journal of Geophysical Research* 78, no. 36 (1973): pp. 8849–8858] While this hypothesis could be true, surely the burden of proof should be on those who propose that what happens in immature trees doesn't happen in mature trees.
>
> An expert in the genus *Pinus* didn't seem to have any problem believing that White Mountain BCPs grew multiple rings per year. In his book, *The Genus* Pinus, Mirov states, 'Apparently a semblance of annual rings is formed after every rather infrequent cloudburst.' [LaMarche Jr, V.C. and Harlan, T.P., Accuracy of tree ring dating of Bristlecone Pine for calibration of the radiocarbon time scale, *Journal of Geophysical Research* 78, no. 36 (1973): pp. 8849–8858] If an expert like Mirov readily accepted multiplicity in these BCPs, then perhaps the

doubters of this notion should at least give the evidence a serious examination.[7]

The bristlecone pines, with its dry climate, doesn't readily afford multiple tree rings, but to assume the climate has always been identical to that of today is without warrant, even by Mr. Nye's standards. Again, it's Mr. Nye's interpretation based on fallible assumptions — man's historical science. However, using God's historical science (the Bible), then, the weather patterns would have been greatly different after the Flood of Noah's day for quite some time, permitting more watering in the past.

But in short, trees with high numbers of tree rings are not a problem for an earth age of about 6,000 years. Such tree rings are thus not proof of long ages but illustrate once again the battle between God's historical science and man's historical science. At least biblical creationists (like Mr. Ham) admit their beliefs/assumptions concerning their interpretation of the past — it's a shame Mr. Nye will not be that honest.

Seeds, saplings, and trees

Mr. Nye continued:

> You can try this yourself, everybody, get — I mean, I don't mean to be mean to trees, but get a sapling and put it under water for a year. It will not survive in general nor will its seeds, they just won't make it. So how could these trees be that old if the earth is only 4,000 years old?

There are a couple of problems here. First, the earth is not 4,000 years old according to any creationist using the Bible as a basis for chronology. Usually dates hover around 6,000 years when adding up the chronological data in the Bible to arrive at the age of the earth.[8] However, we will give Mr. Nye the benefit of the doubt that perhaps this was a slip of the tongue and will not pursue comment on this statement of about 4,000 years (although he has said this on other occasions).

---

7. Ibid.
8. That is by using the Hebrew-based Old Testaments like most English translations use. The Greek translation called the LXX (Septuagint) has dates that tally in an extra 1,000 years or so, but there are problems with this translation when dealing with the genealogies — such as Methuselah living a decade after the Flood without being on the Ark! Therefore, it should not be used to supersede the Hebrew text, which is consistent regarding the chrono-genealogies.

Next, when Christians say the Flood occurred *over the course of about a year*, that was the time that Noah was onboard the Ark (Genesis 7:11,[9] Genesis 8:14[10]). It does not pertain to the actual amount of time water covered the entire earth. The Bible gives us some information on water levels. The *maximum* time that the water would have covered the entire earth is about 110 days — from the day the Ark lifted up to the day it struck the mountains of Ararat that had been rising up (Genesis 7:17,[11] Genesis 8:4[12]). So Mr. Nye was exaggerating the length of time plants and seeds would have to deal with water. It really does show Mr. Nye did not study creationist literature (or the Bible) on this matter very carefully.

Experiments have been done to show that some seeds are able to survive in water after being soaked for 140 days.[13] Furthermore, saplings or seeds could also survive on driftwood too. In fact, the Bible records the famous scene where a dove returns with an olive leaf by the 278th day of the Flood (Genesis 8:11[14]), which shows that vegetation can *and did* survive well before the end of the year-long Flood while Noah remained aboard the Ark.[15]

Settling rock layers

Mr. Nye brought up the issue of settling in the context of rock layers from the Flood. He took issue with sediments settling out in an "extraordinarily short amount of time" as being "for me, not satisfactory." Of course, he didn't give a specified amount of time. So if sediment settling out in an unspecified amount of time is not satisfactory to Mr. Nye, then perhaps he should check his math.

9. "In the six hundredth year of Noah's life, in the second month, the seventeenth day of the month, on that day all the fountains of the great deep were broken up, and the windows of heaven were opened."
10. "And in the second month, on the twenty-seventh day of the month, the earth was dried."
11. "Now the flood was on the earth forty days. The waters increased and lifted up the ark, and it rose high above the earth."
12. "Then the ark rested in the seventh month, the seventeenth day of the month, on the mountains of Ararat."
13. G. Howe, "Seed Germination, Sea Water, and Plant Survival in the Great Flood," *Creation Research Society Quarterly*, 5(1968):105–112; J. Woodmorappe, *Noah's Ark: A Feasibility Study* (Dallas, TX: Institute for Creation Research, 2003), p. 155.
14. "Then the dove came to him in the evening, and behold, a freshly plucked olive leaf was in her mouth; and Noah knew that the waters had receded from the earth."
15. D. Wright, "How Did Plants Survive the Flood?" Answers in Genesis, October 10, 2012, http://www.answersingenesis.org/articles/aid/v7/n1/how-did-plants-survive-flood.

But I want the reader to note something here. Mr. Nye again appealed to *his own authority* to say something couldn't happen. But Mr. Nye is not the authority on the past, God is. God specified in the Bible that the time from when the Ark struck the mountains of Ararat on the 150th day until Noah was called off the Ark was over seven months.[16] So I'm not sure why Mr. Nye thinks it is outrageous for the floodwaters to allow sediment to settle at the bottom, then to recede, with much of the compressed, layered, and drying sediment formed into rock by the time Noah exited the Ark! I've seen concrete (which is in reality artificial rock) solidify into solid rock in days, so to say it is impossible is weak.

Mr. Nye then said:

> This is what geologists on the outside do, study the rate at which soil is deposited at the end of rivers and deltas, and we can see it takes a long, long time for sediments to turn to stone.

There are a couple of problems here. First, Mr. Nye was trying to make it sound as though geologists who work with Mr. Ham and are somehow restricted, and only secular geologists conduct such studies. Perhaps Mr. Nye doesn't realize that the Answers in Genesis staff geologist, Dr. Andrew Snelling, and many others we work with (Dr. John Baumgartner, Dr. John Whitmore, and so on) are highly qualified geologists who have (and continue to) carry out field research in geology, so his debate tactic of trying to demote creation geologists is nothing but a red herring fallacy.

Next, trying to compare rock formation in deltas to continents drying at the end stages of the Flood is like apples to oranges. For example, deltas remain wet, where the Bible says the earth was dried (Genesis 8:13–14[17]). Furthermore, a delta doesn't have the intense pressure that would have been exerted on the settled layers from sediments and water above from the global Flood.

Continuing, Mr. Nye said:

---

16. B. Hodge, "Biblical Overview of the Flood Timeline," Answers in Genesis, August 23, 2010, http://www.answersingenesis.org/articles/2010/08/23/overview-flood-timeline.

17. "And it came to pass in the six hundred and first year, in the first month, the first day of the month, that the waters were dried up from the earth; and Noah removed the covering of the ark and looked, and indeed the surface of the ground was dry. And in the second month, on the twenty-seventh day of the month, the earth was dried."

Also, in this picture you can see where one type of sediment has intruded on another type. Now, if that was uniform wouldn't we expect it all to be even without intrusion?...Furthermore you can find places in the Grand Canyon where you see an ancient riverbed on that side going to an ancient riverbed on that side and Colorado River has cut through it.

He showed a picture of an intrusion of rock into another rock layer and then what was interpreted as a riverbed in the Grand Canyon. I have been to the Grand Canyon and have seen such things. Here is a picture I took in the Grand Canyon of such "river beds"

Grand Canyon, supposed dual riverbeds that have been filled in.

that have been filled in (as told by our Grand Canyon guide).

Now intrusions are actually expected in the Global Flood model. There is a misconception that the Flood was rather tranquil and that everything was calm and uniform. But this was certainly not the case. There would be pockets of uniformity at times, and other times changes would occur depending on the circumstances.

Again, Mr. Nye was imposing a particular interpretation of these sedimentary layers based on certain assumptions. He was presenting his view of historical science as fact — but it's one particular interpretation. Mr. Nye wasn't there to see these sediments deposited.

Creation geologists disagree with his interpretation. You see, his riverbed interpretation could simply be the result of smaller runoff areas during the recessional phases within the Flood (or some drainage "rivers" that occurred at the near final recession as well). These are to be expected.

When drainage tributaries would run their course during a particular phase in the Flood year, they would look identical to a riverbed.

Furthermore, *filling in the riverbed* would take quite a bit of sudden sediment deposition from subsequent phases in the Flood so it wouldn't get washed down with the river flow; if it were just a river over long periods of time, then it would simply take the sediment downstream.

In a global Flood model, we expect these sorts of features *and* we can even explain why they are filled in with sedimentation from later phases in the Flood! We admit we can't prove that this is so, but creationists can propose a model to explain such evidence. In other words, creationists have a different way of interpreting the same evidence. So as Mr. Ham pointed out in his presentation, the battle is not over evidence so much as it is over how one interprets evidence in regard to the past. It's a battle between two different accounts of historical science — it's that battle between God's Word and man's word.

Fossil order

In the context of fossil order, Mr. Nye claimed, "You never ever find a higher animal mixed in with a lower one. You never find a lower one trying to swim its way to the higher one."

Now creationists have the same rock layers and the same fossils as the evolutionist — we all have the same evidence in the present. However, we admit we just don't buy into their evolutionary assumptions since we believe what God says in His Word about both creation and the Flood.

However, we don't expect clams (and other sea life), algae, and trees to flee to higher ground! From a Flood point of view, we expect sea creatures to be buried first, then land plants and creatures to be buried higher up. Land creatures that float will have the lowest possibilities of being rapidly buried by the sediment at the bottom of the floodwaters. A number of factors such as buoyancy, natural sorting of water, elevation, and amount of sediment being deposited in an area are all factors affecting the order of burial.[18]

As for Mr. Nye's claim that "you never find a higher animal mixed with a lower one," this is blatantly absurd. Dr. John Morris, president of the Institute for Creation Research and co-author of *The Fossil Record,*

---

18. For more geological details on the order of burial from the Flood, I suggest, A. Snelling, "Doesn't the Order of Fossils in the Rock Record Favor Long Ages?" in K. Ham, gen. ed., *The New Answers Book 2* (Green Forest, AR: Master Books, 2008), pp. 341–354; J. Morris, "Does the Geologic Column Prove Evolution?" *Acts & Facts*, 23, no. 7(1994), http://www.icr.org/article/does-geologic-column-prove-evolution/.

has stated in this treatise, "For instance, clams are found in the bottom layer, the top layer, and every layer in between."[19]

Dr. Morris and biological colleague Mr. Frank Sherwin state:

> If evolution were true, one would expect the record to start with one type of animal life, then increase to two, and so on. Yet fossil studies have shown that essentially all phyla were present at the start, each distinct from the others and each fully equipped to function and survive. Even vertebrate fish were present in the lower Cambrian.[20]

The underlying assumption from Mr. Nye is that certain creatures he would call "less evolved" should (according to his evolutionary assumptions) have lived prior to creatures that are "more evolved." But even today we have clams and sea creatures that Mr. Nye would say are rudimentary as well as creatures he believes are "higher," all living at the same time! Yet if there was a massive fossilization event today, Mr. Nye's assumption would be that only higher animals should be fossilized! How absurd! The fossil record actually, in many ways, represents what we see in the world today — all sorts of creatures and plants together at one time.

Furthermore, there are fossils that would shock Mr. Nye. The Smithsonian documented both bear and human (simian-like as they proclaimed) footprints in New Mexican Permian strata that were purported to be more than 250 million years old![21] According to evolutionists, we find feathers in rock layers prior to the time dinosaurs existed.[22] Strangely, the article tries to put these feathers on a reptile, in an anatomically impossible position no less, buried elsewhere in the same rock layer without warrant! This is equivalent to taking a clamshell found in a rock layer and trying to put it on a horse because the fossil was found in the same rock layer!

When I went to the Grand Canyon, we found fossil footprints of vertebrate quadrupeds. However, we never found any fossils of these creatures. Instead these creatures were buried much higher up.

19. J. Morris, "Does the Geologic Column Prove Evolution?" *Acts & Facts*, 23(7), 1994, http://www.icr.org/article/does-geologic-column-prove-evolution/.
20. J. Morris and F. Sherwin, "The Fossil Record," Institute for Creation Research, Dallas, TX, 2010, p. 124.
21. D. Stewart, "Petrified Footprints: A Puzzling Parade of Permian Beasts," *The Smithsonian*, 23, no. 4 (July 1992): pp. 70–79.
22. *NewScientist*, 213, no. 2857 (March 24–30, 2012): p. 8.

These vertebrates were not found buried there but instead were found in rock layers much higher up. They fended for their life as the Flood waters rose — since their footprints were left in waterborne sand — and then finally were themselves buried in sediment higher up.[23] I could go on, but this should be sufficient to disprove Mr. Nye's claim on this point.

In the debate, Mr. Ham actually used (in his first rebuttal time) an example of an out-of-place fossil. Referencing dating methods Mr. Nye has accepted as giving accurate dates, he gave the example of wood that was estimated by carbon dating to be about 45 thousand years old (carbon dating) in basalt rock supposedly 45 million years old (K/AR dating[24]). Mr. Nye attempted an explanation, but Mr. Ham pointed out that Mr. Nye had misunderstood the example and so clarified the point he was making. Mr. Nye then ignored this example. I'm not sure if he had never heard of examples like this (though such examples are replete in creationist literature) or he just didn't want to acknowledge that what he'd said was wrong.

Missing links: skulls

Mr. Nye claimed:

> Now here's an interesting thing. These are fossil skulls that people have found all around the world. It's by no means representative of all of the fossil skulls that have been found, but these are all over the place. Now, if you were to look at these I can assure you not any of them is a gorilla. Right? If, as Mr. Ham and his associates claim, there was just man and then everybody else, there were just humans and all other species, where would you put modern humans among these skulls?

Mr. Nye then showed a slide with hosts of human and ape skulls that had been found. The slide was really hard to read, was obviously meant for effect, and was only up for viewing for a very short time. There was

---

23. A. Snelling and S. Austin, "Startling Evidence for Noah's Flood," December 1, 1992, https://answersingenesis.org/geology/grand-canyon-facts/startling-evidence-for-noahs-flood/.

24. K/AR dating is "potassium-argon" dating that is used to give long age dates like millions and billions of years to rock — particularly rock that had solidified from lava. In the secular world, this method is assumed to be one of the more accurate dating methods. This is not so of course, and will be discussed later in this book as well in Appendix B.

no way Mr. Ham could respond to a slide like this without being able to read the name given to each skull and then where it was found, etc. One of our researchers has since gone through the slide in detail. Actually most of these skulls are simply skulls of humans and a few are of apes. Perhaps Mr. Nye wanted us to interpret them as missing links, but they are not missing links at all. There are two significant reasons.

First, expert human anatomist Dr. David Menton has pointed out three easily "spottable" features that distinguish humans and apes.[25] There are more, of course, but these should suffice for the sake of this argument. By applying these recognizable features to the skulls in question one can readily identify what is human and what is ape:

A. From the side view, one can spot a vertical face in humans versus a forward sloping face in apes.

B. From the side view, one can easily see into the eye socket (orbit) where the ape's skull obscures the eye socket.

C. The nose bone in humans can hold a pair of glasses, but in apes there are no significant protruding nasal bones to hold any glasses.

Clearly, the skulls Mr. Nye displayed did not show "missing links" but rather apes or humans, not a blend of intermediate forms.

Second, let's look at these ape and human skulls that Mr. Nye put up as an image. Did you know that each of these skulls of apes and humans is found in what creationists would call post-Flood sediment?[26] Let me explain.

They are found in rock layers that were made after the Flood of Noah ended. These rock layers were made from post-Flood events like volcanoes. Why is this significant? Noah and 10 generations of people were living *prior* to when these people and apes died in the post-Flood world. In other words, the specific human skulls that Mr. Nye was pointing out couldn't have existed until Noah came off the Ark and his descendants began to populate the earth. The apes that Mr. Nye had on the slide couldn't have existed until

---

25. D. Menton, "Did Humans Really Evolve from Apelike Creatures?" in K. Ham, gen. ed., *The New Answers Book 2* (Green Forest, AR: Master Books, 2008), pp. 83–94.

26. We find them in Pleistocene rock layers (lower, middle, and upper) and above. This sediment is universally accepted as post-Flood sediment among researchers. For a listing of human and ape fossils found and their associated rock layer see: M. Lubenow, *Bones of Contention* (Revised and Updated) (Grand Rapids, MI: Baker Books, 2004), pp. 338–353.

the land animals came off the Ark and the ape kind began to populate. The point is that man was around long before these skulls ever existed.

Really, this was a very poor attempt by Mr. Nye to intimidate people into believing his evolutionary view. Anyone can quickly show a slide depicting lots of skulls, claim this is evidence of evolution, and move on! That was a very unfair tactic by Mr. Nye, and not becoming of someone truly wanting to debate the issue of origins in a carefully thought-out way.

How did animals get to Australia?

Mr. Nye proceeded to attack the idea that animals could get from the Middle East to Australia in 4,000 years.[27] He said:

> And so places like Australia are populated, then, by animals who somehow managed to get from the Middle East all the way to Australia in the last 4,000 years. Now that to me is an extraordinary claim.

Now remember, Mr. Nye said earlier that creationists believe the earth is 4,000 years old. Either that was a slip of the tongue or Mr. Nye truly doesn't understand the timeline of events from creation through the Flood, then from the Tower of Babel to the present. The more I listened to Mr. Nye, the more I suspected he just has not carefully studied the teachings and research from creation scientists or the Bible.

I'm not sure why Mr. Nye would state that such migration of animals (from the Middle East to Australia) is an extraordinary claim. Ancient people built boats and obviously traveled extensively (ancient maps show this to be the case). Since the time of the Flood, people have been taking animals (boar, deer, pheasants, rats, etc.) and dropping them off at different places all over the world. During the Age of Exploration, rats were taken all over the world on boats by accident!

Birds can fly long distance, and land bridges exposed land to the Americas, Japan, and England during the Ice Age that followed the Flood. So many creatures could have walked to these places. Even evolutionists believe there were land bridges in different parts of the world — they just have a very different timeline because of their belief in millions of years.

---

27. Prior to this Mr. Nye does think that it is an extraordinary claim that a large wooden ship went aground on a mountain in the Middle East. This was not worthy of comment in the main body since any said mountain would have been at sea, and I hardly think it worth debate to refute Mr. Nye's errant claim that a boat can't run aground at sea level.

Evolutionists propose models of how they believe events occurred in the past, so why can't creationists propose models based on their beliefs?

In fact, creationist literature (if Bill Nye had researched it) has articles specifically dealing with a model to explain how marsupials, for instance, traveled to Australia. Marsupials can travel with their young in a pouch, whereas oth-

Kangaroo in Australia

er mammals have to wait until the young have grown strong enough to travel. It's possible that when marsupials and other mammals were competing for territory, some marsupials moved away — eventually, via a land bridge, moving to Australia.

If the land bridge was then cut off by waters covering it (as the Ice Age receded, or due to tectonic activity), then such animals would have become isolated in Australia before a lot of other mammals were able to travel there. This is a very plausible scenario. But Mr. Nye would mock at such a model because he totally rejects the possibility that the creationist timeline of events based on the Bible could be true! He rejects the creationists' historical science but insists his historical science is fact!

Tectonic activity since the time of the Flood is still rampant in the Oceana region (recall the 2004 tsunami caused by ocean floor shifting); this activity could have potentially connected Australia and Southeast Asia and their islands in the area. The fact that certain areas continue to be geologically tectonic could be the main reason the ocean is deeper in some of those areas today.

Some animals are also caught in storms and raft to certain places on driftwood — we have even observed this in the present world. However, there is no reason to belabor this point since there has been much published on how animals made it to places like Australia.[28]

---

28. P. Taylor, "How Did Animals Spread All Over the World from Where the Ark Landed?" In K. Ham, gen. ed., *The New Answers Book 1* (Green Forest, AR: Master Books, 2006), pp. 141–148; B. Hodge, "Feedback: Animal Migrations," Answers in Genesis website, June 8, 2012, http://www. answersingenesis.org/articles/2012/06/08/feedback-animal-migrations.

Mr. Nye, in continuing with this argument, though, then claimed we should find the fossils of kangaroos between the Middle East and Australia within this approximately 4,000-year period since the Flood. First of all, fossilization is a catastrophic event requiring special circumstances. Just because one doesn't find the fossils of animals in an area doesn't mean those animals didn't live there. Think of the millions of buffalo killed on the prairies in the US — where are all their fossils? Most just decayed and turned to dust.

In the Los Angeles area, there is a museum near the Le Brea Tar Pits. One would have never known mastodons and wolves lived in this area except for the unique circumstances of these tar pits and the preservation of the remains of these creatures found in the tar. Let's consider this argument much further.

First, the kangaroos didn't show up in Australia in the past hundred years or so. They already filled the continent, so it is likely they existed on this continent for quite some time. But let's just assume 4,000 years and apply this expectation to *his* worldview.

Mr. Nye expects to finds fossils (that is, *plural*), so that is a minimum of two fossils in 4,000 years just on this *one route* from the region of Ararat to Australia. Let's apply this to *T. rex* fossils in Mr. Nye's worldview. If at least two fossils are expected per 4,000 years, then if Mr. Nye's assessment of kangaroo fossils is consistent, he should affirm that there should also be 2,500 *T. rex* fossils per route. Here is why:

A. *T. rex* supposedly lived for ~5 million years (70–65 million years ago)

B. Divide this by 4,000 to arrive at how many 4,000-year segments we have: 1,250

C. Multiply this by two since we expect at least two fossils per 4,000-year segment according to Mr. Nye: 2,500 *T. rex* fossils should be found on each travelled route (that would be the same length of Ararat to Australia as a *minimum* number according to Mr. Nye if he were consistent)

So how many *T. rex* fossils are there? Between 50–60 (according to the latest count) in total. Furthermore, there are great distances between some fossils of *T. rex* in North America and Asia, and there is even one on the Iberian Peninsula (think of Spain and Portugal)! Some of these distances (i.e., routes without fossils) rival or beat the distances that kangaroos apparently traveled to get to Australia! Where are all the fossils between those deposits?

Mr. Nye's assumptions are simply not reasonable. Fossilization is quite rare. Unless there was a significant catastrophe (flood, volcano, and so on) while kangaroos were en route through Southeast Asia, there is no reason to assume any fossils should exist. Now, we have cattle all over the world today, and yet rarely are they ever fossilized… So not finding fossils someplace is not a good indication that they never existed there, especially if they were merely migrating through.

Nye's gross confusion of species and kinds

Mr. Nye then transitioned by saying:

> So, let's see, if there are 4,000 years since Ken Ham's flood. And let's say, as he said many times, there are 7,000 kinds, today the very, very lowest estimate is that there are about 8.7 million species, but a much more reasonable estimate is it is 50 million or even a 100 million when you start counting the viruses and the bacteria and all the beetles that must be extant in the tropical rainforest that we haven't found.
>
> So we'll take a number which I think is pretty reasonable, 16 million species today. Okay? If these came from 7,000 kinds, that's let's say we have 7,000 subtracted from 15 million, that's 15,993, we have 4,000 years, we 365 and a quarter days a year. We would expect to find 11 new species every day.

Again, it was not Mr. Ken Ham's flood; Mr. Ham was not even born until about 4,300 years later. So, this needs to be corrected to *Noah's Flood* or perhaps, more properly the *Flood in Noah's day*. Again, Mr. Nye is using a tactic to try to convince his audience that the belief in a global Flood is Mr. Ham's idea! Anyone who has read the Bible knows this is patently absurd! Millions of people in the world today believe as Mr. Ham does, as they take the book of Genesis in the Bible as God's revelation to man concerning our origins.

Number of kinds

Next, Mr. Ham has never said there were 7,000 kinds. I've tried to search out where this number came from and I can't find anything. So this number was pulled out of the air and applied to Mr. Ham; hence, it is a straw man fallacy. Now Mr. Ham has quoted a researcher who suggested what he believed to be the maximum number of land-dwelling, air-breathing animal kinds — but Mr. Ham also quotes researchers stating the number was much less than this (see below). Mr. Nye either didn't research this number at all, or at best, his research was very sloppy.

But look at the numbers for kinds that Mr. Ham has given:

> Scripture clearly says that Noah took animals aboard according to their "kinds" (Genesis 7:14)….Researcher John Woodmorappe, in Noah's Ark: A Feasibility Study (Dallas, TX: ICR Publications, 2009) found that, at most, there were approximately 8,000 animal kinds (or 16,000 individuals) on board. Researcher Arthur J. Jones, in "How Many Animals in the Ark?" (*Creation Research Society Quarterly* 10, no. 2, September 1973) found that, at minimum, there were 1,000 animal kinds (or 2,000–3000 individuals — there were seven of some kinds) on board the Ark. Remember, Noah did not need to bring insects or any of the water-dwelling creatures on board either, so that would significantly reduce the amount of required animals the skeptic usually mentions.

Here Mr. Ham relates the work of John Woodmorappe, whose goal was to show that the *maximum* figures of land-dwelling, air-breathing animals that needed to be on the Ark (using a genus level of classification[29]) would have been about 8,000 kinds or 16,000 individuals. Then Woodmorappe used the smaller cubit[30] of about 18 inches and hence, used a smaller Ark to see if these maximum animals would fit.

Indeed they would. His calculations included water (which may not have been necessary since it could have been harvested) and food (Genesis 6:21[31]) for this *maximum* number of animals. Only 85% of this smaller Ark (based on the small cubit) would be required to hold animals, cages, food, and water.

---

29. Woodmorappe understood that most kinds were at a family level but did genus level to specially have maximum numbers.
30. The Ark's dimensions were given in "cubits." It was 300 by 50 by 30. There are two cubits listed in Scripture: an older or longer cubit and common or short cubit. The shorter cubit was likely about 18 inches and the longer cubit likely about 20–21 inches. Understandably, these numbers varied in ancient cultures.
31. "And you shall take for yourself of all food that is eaten, and you shall gather it to yourself; and it shall be food for you and for them."

But again, these are maximum figures. Dr. Arthur Jones did more realistic numbers in the journal for the Creation Research Society called the *Creation Research Society Quarterly*. In it, Dr. Jones found that most (but not all) kinds are likely at a family level of classification, and for those land-dwelling, air-breathing animals, the number of actual kinds would closer to 1,000 kinds or around 2,000 individuals. In both cases, these researchers included the small list of clean animals that came in by seven.

Actual numbers — currently being ascertained by a group of animal experts — are being published in the *Answers Research Journal*. These numbers are much closer to those of Dr. Jones — the prediction from these researchers currently is around 1,000 actual land animal kinds. So the number of 7,000 kinds is blatantly arbitrary and significantly high and should not be used.

Kinds are not species

But kinds are not species, which Mr. Nye (along with most evolutionists) seems to mistakenly equate.[32] Such an equivocation fallacy should be avoided. I almost chuckled in the audience when Mr. Nye started to subtract the invented 7,000 kinds from his presumed 16 million species. Subtracting kinds from species is like comparing apples to oranges or pounds to dollars. What ran though my head was, *what would happen if a banker did this while trying to convert funds? They would be fired!*

Now, assume that in the majority of instances (and there has been detailed research done on this and published in the *Answers Research Journal*[33]), the Hebrew word translated "kind" in Genesis is actually the "family" level of classification (as we said there are a few exceptions to this).. We have a dog kind, elephant kind, bear kind, cat kind, chicken kind, owl kind, horse kind, and so on. Interestingly, there are dozens of cat species, dozens of dog species, eight bear species, etc.

"Species" is a bit of an arbitrary dividing line and becomes a paradox, hence the famous "Species Problem" when trying to define it. Some claim that if creatures can interbreed, then they are the same "species"; but clearly that is not always the case since various species of dogs can

---

32. G. Purdom and B. Hodge, "What Are the 'Kinds' in Genesis?" in K. Ham, gen. ed., *The New Answers Book 3* (Green Forest, AR: Master Books, 2010), pp. 39–48.
33. For example see T. Hennigan, B. Hodge, G. Purdom, and J. Lightner, "Determining Ark Kinds," *Answers Research Journal* 4 (2011): pp. 195–201, November 16, 2011, https://answersingenesis.org/noahs-ark/determining-the-ark-kinds/.

DOG VARIATIONS

Dog kind

CHICKEN VARIATIONS

Chicken kind

HORSE VARIATIONS

Orlov Trotter   Timor   Dale   Lipizzaner

Tarpan   Arab   Fjord Pony   Normandy Cob

Pinto   Falabella   Belgian Heavy Draught   Shetland

Horse kind

and do interbreed — yet they are still considered different species. The same is true of cats (blinx, ligers, tigons, etc.).

As stated, most kinds are closer to a family level, but in some cases they could be genus, species, or in the event of the elephant kind, are likely at the level of order (including the extinct families of elephants such as mammoths and mastodons, for example).

So each time that Mr. Nye was subtracting out one of those kinds, he needed to subtract out all the species that are part of that kind. Again, if Mr. Nye had researched creationist literature, he would have understood this as there are a numerous articles on this topic.

The more I listened to the debate, the more I realized that Mr. Ham's understanding of the nature of science and the origins issue was way above that of Mr. Nye. It was evident that Mr. Ham had carefully researched the origins issue (both sides), understood the difference between historical and observational science, and had thoughtfully prepared his slides so everyone could see clearly what he was referring to.

Furthermore, Mr. Nye failed to understand the account in Genesis surrounding the animals that were needed on the Ark — only land-dwelling, air-breathing animal kinds (Genesis 6:20[34]; Genesis 7:21–23[35]). These were *fleshly* creatures that breathed through their *nostrils* and lived on *land*. Water creatures could live in the water, and insects could lay eggs on driftwood (and easily survive in pupal or larvae forms — or survive in their adult forms on floating vegetation, etc.). This limitation for creatures on the Ark massively reduces the host of species Mr. Nye claimed had to be on the Ark. He was simply wrong on this issue! In fact, Mr. Ham alluded to this matter when he discussed the speciation in dogs. Only two of the dog kind were needed on the Ark — not all the different dog species.

Mr. Bill Nye and I actually agree on something!

Mr. Nye then discussed some aspects of the engineering on the Boeing 747 that he used to work on. He also discussed the Lake Missoula Flood where something like an ice dam at some time in the past broke open and drained this Ice Age lake.

We actually agree here. We both believe that the Lake Missoula Flood really did occur. This is expected from post-Flood Ice Age events, where such accumulation of ice and subsequent melting could occur. In fact, creation researcher Mike Oard ("Mr. Ice Age") has researched this Lake Missoula Flood extensively and concurs. He wrote a technical treatise on this subject as well (*The Missoula Flood Controversy and the Genesis Flood*[36]), which I recommend to technical readers.

Creationists and evolutionists do agree on some things, believe it or not! However, even though we agree on these events, we don't agree on the timeline of when they occurred!

Cobbles and boulder rocks

Mr. Nye then wanted to discuss large, rounded rocks in the Washington State and Oregon State areas. He assumed such rocks would sink to the

---

34. "Of the birds after their kind, of animals after their kind, and of every creeping thing of the earth after its kind, two of every kind will come to you to keep them alive."
35. "And all flesh died that moved on the earth: birds and cattle and beasts and every creeping thing that creeps on the earth, and every man. All in whose nostrils was the breath of the spirit of life, all that was on the dry land, died. So He destroyed all living things which were on the face of the ground: both man and cattle, creeping thing and bird of the air. They were destroyed from the earth. Only Noah and those who were with him in the ark remained alive."
36. M. Oard, *The Missoula Flood Controversy and the Genesis Flood* (Chino Valley, AZ: CRS Books, 2004).

bottom of the Flood event and not be where they are found. However, there are two things he needs to remember.

First, the Flood was not just a tranquil event. Water can be a catastrophic force to move large objects (as we've seen even with local floods), and sedimentation was occurring significantly as a result of the worldwide catastrophe. We expected planation surfaces, water gaps, buttes, and even rounded stones of virtually every size. These cobbles and boulders should be expected, as they were rolled by water currents and rounded off.

These rocks are much better explained in light of the Flood than by the secularists. They do not just appear in these two states but are in Canada and on each side of the Rocky Mountains. Researchers have been able to trace these cobbles and boulders to sources within the Rocky Mountains. They have been transported by water (hence their roundedness), in some cases 800 miles.[37] In the secular view then, as a result of rain and wind, why would they form into rounded boulders and cobbles?

Second, Washington State and Oregon State *were* under water at one time (the floodwaters). These stones rolled around *at the bottom* of the floodwaters, and as the mountains were rising during the Flood, to be deposited where they exist today. Now because Mr. Nye does not believe in the global Flood of Noah's day, he will not accept the possibility of such an explanation. But it also seems to me that Mr. Nye doesn't understand the enormous force water can be, as demonstrated by local events (observable science).

Could Noah build an Ark?

Mr. Nye then moved to attack that a wooden ship with the dimensions of Noah's Ark (which was 300 cubits long; that is about 450 feet or 510 feet depending on the short or long cubit) could survive the Flood.[38] He compared it to a wooden ship called the *Wyoming*, which was one the biggest wooden sailing ships built with the technology of the 1800s.

The *Wyoming*, unlike the Ark, was a sailing ship, not a floater; but interestingly, it was about the same length as Noah's Ark if you use the shorter cubit (18 inch cubit as opposed to the 20.4 inch cubit). It was

37. M. Oard, *Flood by Design* (Green Forest, AR: Master Books, 2008), pp. 55–61.
38. T. Chaffey, "Bill Nye the Straw Man Guy and Noah's Ark," Answers in Genesis website, February 28, 2014, http://www.answersingenesis.org/articles/2014/02/28/bill-nye-straw-man-guy-noahs-ark.

450 feet long if you count the jib-boom. Mr. Nye pointed out that it was not a great sea-worthy vessel, and it twisted and sank, killing all 14 on board. Ergo, Noah's Ark was basically an impossibility.

I beg to differ. The *Wyoming* was a great example to show that the Ark was indeed legitimate. Besides, using one example of a wooden ship (when there is much historic information about massive wooden ships built in the past) to claim Noah's Ark couldn't have been built to survive the Flood is a very poor argument indeed.

Now the *Wyoming* was used and sailed for *14 years* before it sank. Noah's Ark only needed a maximum of about 110 days of floating time.[39] Furthermore, the *Wyoming* used 1800s technology. By then, mankind had lost a great deal of technology about boat building. Ark researcher and mechanical engineer Tim Lovett writes:

> Ancient shipbuilders usually began with a shell of planks (strakes) and then built internal framing (ribs) to fit inside. This is the complete reverse of the familiar European method where planking was added to the frame. In shell-first construction, the planks must be attached to each other somehow. Some used overlapping (clinker) planks that were dowelled or nailed, while others used rope to sew the planks together. The ancient Greeks used a sophisticated system where the planks were interlocked with thousands of precise mortise and tenon joints. The resulting hull was strong enough to ram another ship, yet light enough to be hauled onto a beach by the crew.[40]

It makes sense that this ancient technology was passed down through the Flood to the coastline/maritime peoples (Genesis 10:5[41]) but had been lost by the Age of Exploration.

I suspect Mr. Nye has never read about such research in regard to ancient ships — but again, this information was available on the Answers in Genesis website and the Worldwide Flood website (worldwideflood.org) had he conducted careful research.

39. B. Hodge, "Biblical Overview of the Flood Timeline," Answers in Genesis website, August 23, 2010, http://www.answersingenesis.org/articles/2010/08/23/overview-flood-timeline.
40. T. Lovett (with B. Hodge) "What Did Noah's Ark Look Like?" in K. Ham, gen. ed., *The New Answers Book 3* (Green Forest, AR: Master Books, 2010), pp. 17–28.
41. "From these the coastland peoples of the Gentiles were separated into their lands, everyone according to his language, according to his families, into their nations."

Unskilled and alone?

Then Mr. Nye made a bold claim: *"Is that reasonable? Is that possible that the best ship builders in the world couldn't do what 8 unskilled people, men and their wives, were able to do?"*

First, how does Mr. Nye know that Noah and his family were unskilled? Mr. Ham quite rightly told Mr. Nye that he wasn't there to know what they were like. The Bible reveals that Noah had 500 years under his belt before he was given the instruction to build the Ark. So it is possible Noah could have had many years of shipbuilding experience before the Lord instructed him to build an Ark. I doubt you will find anyone from the 1400s until today with such a resume.

Then Noah had 50–75 years (estimated) to research and build the Ark.[42] I trust that few people in the past 500 years would ask someone to build them a ship and give them upwards of 75 years to do it. The point is, if Noah wasn't an expert already, then he would easily have had the time to become one. It is the same with his family.

Second, how does Mr. Nye know that God didn't give Noah specific instructions on how to build the Ark? The Bible simply doesn't say, but it is a possibility. The Bible does tell us that God gave Noah the dimensions and wood to use. It would be outrageous to say that that an all-knowing God wouldn't know how to design an Ark to survive a Flood.

Next, why does Mr. Nye assume Noah had no help? He could easily have contracted with people who may have been experts on certain things. Furthermore, other family and friends could have been helping until they died, such as Methuselah, Lamech, or others (Genesis 5:30,[43] 6:11[44]). We don't know. What we do know is that Noah and his family were the only ones left who were worthy of being saved by God by the time of the Flood itself.

Lastly, Mr. Nye again appealed to autonomous human reason for his arguments. As I've said before, he has a major problem that he refuses to acknowledge. In his humanistic, materialistic worldview, logic, which is abstract and not material, does not exist anymore than God, who is spirit

42. B. Hodge, "How Long Did it Take for Noah to Build the Ark?" Answers in Genesis website, June 1, 2010, http://www.answersingenesis.org/articles/2010/06/01/long-to-build-the-ark.

43. "After he begot Noah, Lamech lived five hundred and ninety-five years, and had sons and daughters."

44. "The earth also was corrupt before God, and the earth was filled with violence."

(John 4:24[45]), would exist in his religion. Logic exists because God exists, and God's creation is subject to logic because a logical God upholds and sustains everything (Hebrews 1:3[46]).

We as humanity and descendants of Adam have God's image stamped on us, so we too can reason and use logic and seek truth. A belief in the God of the Bible is a prerequisite for logic, reason, truth, and other such abstractions to exist.

Now I have reiterated this before, and will do so again later in this treatise, to reveal a major inconsistency in Mr. Bill Nye's worldview and debate tactic: that is, he needed to borrow from God and His Word (the Bible) just to make an argument against God and His Word. By doing so, Mr. Nye had already lost the debate.

As a consistent materialist and self-proclaimed agnostic, Mr. Nye should have answered, "I don't know if logic and reason really exist, and I don't know if God really exists. I'm open to the possibility but just not sure." Furthermore, this is how a *consistent* agnostic, who really believes in agnosticism, should answer most of the issues brought up in the debate.

Sciences

Mr. Nye, while moving to more issues about Noah's Ark, made a comment that needs to be addressed. He said:

> By the way, this picture that you're seeing was taken by spacecraft in space orbiting the earth. If you told my grandfather, let alone my father, that we had that capability they would have been amazed. That capability comes from our fundamental understanding of gravity, of material science, of physics, and life science, where you go look looking.

Now the implication by Mr. Nye throughout the debate was that creationists cannot be "real scientists." Of course, this is a "no true Scotsman" fallacy. But Mr. Nye obviously failed to realize the error of his implication here: most fields of science were developed by Bible-believing

---

45. "God is Spirit, and those who worship Him must worship in spirit and truth."
46. "Who [Jesus] being the brightness of His glory and the express image of His person, and upholding all things by the word of His power, when He had by Himself purged our sins, sat down at the right hand of the Majesty on high."

Christians, which includes the fields he referred to! Where would we be without Mr. Isaac Newton's laws of gravity? Even Dr. Albert Einstein's relativity was built on Newton's work! Furthermore, physics, life science, chemistry, astronomy, and so on are a result of people who believed the Bible is true and that God upholds the world in a consistent fashion (e.g., Genesis 8:22[47]).

Here are just a few[48] of the great Bible-believing scientists of the past (even though they were fallible people with whom we would not necessarily agree on all theological aspects):

- Francis Bacon
- Galileo Galilei
- Johannes Kepler
- Blaise Pascal
- Robert Boyle
- Isaac Newton
- Carolus Linneaus
- Michael Faraday
- Samuel Morse
- Henry Rogers
- James Joule
- Louis Pasteur
- Gregor Mendel
- James Clerk Maxwell

Can Noah's Ark, a "rescue vessel," be compared to a modern zoo?

I was shocked to see Mr. Nye try to compare the Ark to the National Zoo in Washington, D.C.:

> This place is often, as any zoo, is deeply concerned and criticized for how it treats its animals. They have 400 species on 163 acres, 66 hectares. Is it reasonable that Noah and his colleagues, his family, were able to main 14,000 animals and themselves, and feed them aboard a ship that was bigger than anyone has ever been able to build?

47. "While the earth remains, seedtime and harvest, cold and heat, winter and summer, and day and night shall not cease."
48. For more, please see: http://www.answersingenesis.org/home/area/bios/#pastsci.

I have already discussed the inaccurate number of animals Mr. Nye tried to put on the Ark. But Noah's Ark was not a zoo — it was a rescue ship. Keep in mind that all animals were originally vegetarian (Genesis 1:30[49]) in the perfect world (Deuteronomy 32:4[50] and Genesis 1:31[51]) God created. Now animals live in a sin-cursed and broken world today due to sin. Furthermore, the world's original environments were demolished and reset by a global Flood (Genesis 6–8), so the animals on the Ark were going to have to readjust to the post-Flood environments.[52] So any environment they are in *today* is simply not an ideal one but a broken one.

Also, human arguments against animal treatment (in a fallen world) are second rate next to God's righteous judgments on said creatures due to the effects of sin. Animals are not without repercussions for their actions as the Bible reveals (e.g., Genesis 3:14;[53] Leviticus 20:15–16[54]). And Scripture tells us that all flesh (which included animals) had corrupted itself on the land at the time of Noah (Genesis 6:12–13[55]). So animals that died in the Flood were judged righteously if we could use such terminology. But the Ark was unique in that it was a rescue vessel designed by God to save representatives of each land-dwelling, air-breathing animal's kind — and Noah's family of eight.

Surely no one would complain today if a rescue vessel were sent to a sinking ship and piled creatures in that were about to drown. It would be crazy to complain that the rescue vessel wasn't a zoo and needed the proper environments to take the animals to safety. Besides, I still assert that there was plenty of room for the around 2,000 animals (bear in

---

49. " 'Also, to every beast of the earth, to every bird of the air, and to everything that creeps on the earth, in which there is life, I have given every green herb for food'; and it was so."

50. "He [God] is the Rock, His work is perfect; for all His ways are justice, a God of truth and without injustice; righteous and upright is He."

51. "Then God saw everything that He had made, and indeed it was very good. So the evening and the morning were the sixth day."

52. G. Parker, "Is Speciation Evidence for Creation or Evolution?" in K. Ham, gen. ed., *The New Answers Book 4* (Green Forest, AR: Master Books, 2013), pp. 335–342.

53. "So the LORD God said to the serpent: 'Because you have done this, you are cursed more than all cattle, and more than every beast of the field; on your belly you shall go, and you shall eat dust all the days of your life.' "

54. "If a man mates with an animal, he shall surely be put to death, and you shall kill the animal. If a woman approaches any animal and mates with it, you shall kill the woman and the animal. They shall surely be put to death. Their blood is upon them."

55. "So God looked upon the earth, and indeed it was corrupt; for all flesh had corrupted their way on the earth. And God said to Noah, 'The end of all flesh has come before Me, for the earth is filled with violence through them; and behold, I will destroy them with the earth.' "

mind, the average size of a land animal is not that big) needed on the Ark for a comfortable journey during the Flood.

I want the reader to understand that Mr. Nye's accusation implying bad treatment of animals is one tactic used by skeptics against those who believe the account of Noah's Ark in the Bible. But the Bible actually makes it clear that Noah and his family were to care for the animals:

> And of every living thing of all flesh, you shall bring two of every sort into the ark, to keep them alive with you; they shall be male and female. Of the birds after their kind, of animals after their kind, and of every creeping thing of the earth after its kind, two of every kind will come to you to keep them alive. And you shall take for yourself of all food that is eaten, and you shall gather it to yourself; and it shall be food for you and for them (Genesis 6:19–21).

There would be no land-dwelling, air-breathing animals today if God hadn't provided Noah with the information to save his family and the animals.

Furthermore, Mr. Nye assumed that large numbers of people were required to service animals on the Ark in the same way that large numbers of people are required to service a zoo. However, there were no grounds, no electricity, no computers, no security force, no shows, no public, and no extravagant animal housing, simply food, water, and a prepared cage to handle waste.

Automatic feeding and watering systems would make the task easier as well. And straw or false bottom cages make the job of waste rather simple. There are many examples today where, due to climate and other factors, farmers look after animals inside buildings with ingenious methods for feeding, watering, and waste removal, etc.[56]

Science, predictability, and natural law

The next topic for discussion was the predictability of scientific law and methodology. Mr. Nye claimed:

> Now here is the thing, what we want in science, science as practiced on the outside, is an ability to predict. We want to have

---

56. For technical details, see J. Woodmorappe, *Noah's Ark: A Feasibility Study* (El Cajon, CA: ICR, 1996).

a natural law that is so obvious and clear, so well understood that we can make predictions about what will happen.

According to Mr. Nye, this would mean that scientific *observation* is not science since observations have no predictability.[57] For example, when a plane crashes, one can do scientific investigations (observations) of the wreckage and document them in a scientific way or make observations about rock layers or animals. These observations have little to do with predictability.

To be more accurate, Mr. Nye should have claimed that *some aspects* of science have predictable merit. And we agree. But predictability is predicated on the laws of nature remaining the same; this is of course predicated on God who makes the claim that He will sustain things in a consistent fashion. This is what makes science possible in the first place. Predictive science actually comes out of a biblical worldview.

But in a secular worldview, such as Mr. Nye's, how can one know the future? I wrote about this already, so let me briefly reiterate. From a secular perspective, the laws of nature changed at the Big Bang and could change again someday (or be changing even now); but unless one knows the future, they can't know when or how. So why even try to do predictable science in a secular worldview? The laws of nature may change tomorrow! Again, this assumption of predictability is being borrowed from a Christian viewpoint.

Now consider this from a big picture. Creationists have a basis to do predictable science because God promised to uphold things in a consistent fashion. But the secularists have no basis for this. So in answering the debate topic, "Is creation a viable model of origins in today's modern scientific era?" the creationists are the only ones who have a *logical basis* that makes science possible; all others must borrow (many times inadvertently) from a biblical understanding just to have reasons to do science.

But let's test a couple of predictions on the secular side. Mr. Charles Darwin (father of the modern forms of evolution) predicted [1] that civilized

---

57. Predictability in a scientific model is not necessarily saying what will happen in the future but what is expected based on the model. For example, in the biblical model we expect to find rock layers all over the world formed of waterborne sediment, massive graveyards, sea creatures on mountains, and so on. These are successful predictions of the creation model that has a global Flood.

Caucasians would exterminate darker-skinned, less-evolved people like the Australian Aborigines (less-evolved in his view, that is). He said this would occur shortly, not measured by centuries. Darwin stated:

> At some future period, not very distant as measured by centuries, the civilized races of man will almost certainly exterminate and replace the savage races throughout the world. At the same time the anthropomorphous apes . . . will no doubt be exterminated. The break between man and his nearest allies will then be wider, for it will intervene between man in a more civilized state, as we may hope, even than the Caucasian, and some ape as low as a baboon, instead of as now between the negro or Australian [Aborigine] and the gorilla.[58]

So we have gone one and a half centuries and this is not the case. In fact, what Mr. Darwin considered lesser-evolved "races" of man includes the Chinese and Indians (from India), who constitute well over $2/7^{th}$ of the world's population today! Such a belief by Mr. Darwin and his followers has fed eugenics, abortion, and racist ideas as well.[59]

Darwin also predicted [2] that the most basic cells would be "simple" when he said:

> Looking to the first dawn of life, when all organic beings, as we may believe, presented the simplest structure, how, it has been asked, could the first step in the advancement or differentiation of parts have arisen? Mr. Herbert Spencer would probably answer that, as soon as simple unicellular organisms came by growth or division to be compounded ofseveral cells,...[60]

However, even the so-called "simple cells" have been examined and are much more complex than ever realized. They are like many little factories all rolled into one! Even the single-celled ameba (amoeba) has at least 100 times the DNA information of humans! As the *Genomics News Network* published:

---

58. C. Darwin, *The Descent of Man*, Second Edition (New York, NY: A. L. Burt, 1874), p. 178.
59. R.J. Guliuzza, "Darwinian Medicine: A Prescription for Failure," *Acts & Facts*, 38, no. 2(2009): p. 32.
60. C. Darwin, "On the Origin of Species by Means of Natural Selection for the Preservation of Favored Races," 1859, in R. Hutchins, Editor in Chief, *Great Books of the Western World*, Volume 49 (Chicago, IL: William Benton Publisher, 1952), p. 61.

As reported this week, the human genome contains about 3 billion chemical units of DNA, or base pairs. "In the animal kingdom, the relationship between genome size and evolutionary status is not clear. One of the largest genomes belongs to a very small creature, Amoeba dubia. This protozoan genome has 670 billion units of DNA, or base pairs. The genome of a cousin, Amoeba proteus, has a mere 290 billion base pairs, making it 100 times larger than the human genome.[61]

But let's now answer the question, "Do creationists do predictable science?" Yes. Dr. Russell Humphrey correctly predicted the magnetic fields of Uranus and Neptune based on creation principles, whereas the evolutionary predictions were falsified.[62] I correctly predicted in my research that cracking carbon to form an intimate coating around titanium dioxide powders would set off a gas phase reaction to form titanium diboride faster, cheaper, and of a higher quality than a typical carbothermal process.[63] Dr. Stuart Burgess predicted that his new mechanism would work properly in space for the Envisat satellite for the ESA (featured in the debate by Mr. Ham). These and others are just a few.[64] But there is no reason to belabor the point.

Note some of the debate tactics

Let us pause for a moment and look at the big picture of what was occurring in the debate. Mr. Nye threw out many alleged claims in an attempt to overwhelm his opponent. Recall that this was the tactic Mr. Nye was planning to use in the debate (the *skeptical method*). He actually admitted to this in an NCSE fundraising letter. We read in that letter:

A particularly delicious strategy emerged. As Genie Scott observed, creationist debaters tend to engage in what she calls "the Gish Gallop" [editor's note: a misrepresentation of what the

61. E. Winstead, "Sizing up Genomes: Amoeba Is King," *Genome News Network*, February 12, 2001, http://www.genomenewsnetwork.org/articles/02_01/Sizing_genomes. shtml.

62. R. Humphreys, "Beyond Neptune: Voyager II Supports Creation," *Impact* 203, May 1990, www.icr.org/pubs/imp/imp-203.htm; and Humphreys, R., "The Creation of Planetary Magnetic Fields," *Creation Research Society Quarterly*, 21, no. 3(December 1984): pp. 140–149, December 1984, www.creationresearch.org/crsq/articles/21/21_3/21_3.html.

63. D.B. Hodge, *New Method for Production of Submicrometer Titanium Diboride* (Carbondale, IL: Southern Illinois University at Carbondale, 1998).

64. Editors, "Successful Predictions by Creation Scientists," Answers in Genesis, download date: 4/23/2014, http://www.answersingenesis.org/get-answers/features/successful-predictions.

famous creationist Dr. Duane Gish did] — a recitation of supposed problems with evolution delivered so rapidly that there's no way to rebut all of them.[65]

To the untrained listener, it may seem like an opponent, like Mr. Ham, cannot respond and hence loses the debate. There was no way Mr. Ham could address all these quick claims in the short time they had available, though I was impressed at how many claims Mr. Ham did respond to within the short debate time that he was allotted to speak.

What Mr. Nye did is called an "elephant hurl" in philosophy. Think of it like this: you throw a lot of mud and hope some of it sticks. But as one can see, his claims can easily be refuted. But I also want to commend Mr. Ham for not being distracted by these little things, sticking to the debate topic at hand, and focusing on the big picture. Each debater has precious little time, so it needs to be used properly. It was good that Mr. Ham did not get caught up in all these "bunny trails" during the debate and instead stuck to the topic, whereas Mr. Nye deviated from the debate topic to use his elephant hurl tactic.

Furthermore, throughout the debate, Mr. Nye used several epithet fallacies; that is, biased language or language meant to be emotive. Let's review just some of these epithet fallacies. Mr. Nye said, for example:

- "...science as practiced on the outside..." that evolutionary based-science is the only true science
- "...traditional science..." suggesting creationists don't do traditional science
- "...8 unskilled people..." referring to Noah's family to undermine their abilities
- "...8 people and these people were unskilled..." referring to Noah's family again to undermine them
- "Now out there in regular academic pursuits..." implying creationists are not academic
- "...regular geology people..." implying that creationists are not real geologists

---

65. NCSE Fundraising Letter, May, 2014; see also K. Ham, "Secularists Use Ham-Nye Debate for Fundraising," July 28, 2014, https://answersingenesis.org/ministry-news/core-ministry/secularists-use-ham-nye-debate-for-fundraising/.

- "...the scientists of the world challenge you..." implying creationists aren't real scientists

- "This is what geologists on the outside do..." implying that creationist geologists don't work on the outside and aren't real geologists.

- "... computed by traditional scientists,..." implying that creationists aren't real scientists

- "...this is something that we in science want..." implying that he speaks for science and that people who actually believe the Bible from its opening pages, are to be omitted as scientists.

And of course, as I stated, before his use of "Ken Ham's Flood," and "Ken Ham's facility" is really an attempt to demonize Mr. Ken Ham.

A position should stand or fall on the arguments; epithet fallacies should not be used in debate and are a sign that the debater had little else on which to stand. Epithets like name-calling and degrading comments just make Mr. Nye look bad.

Sequence of animals in the rock layers

Returning to the specifics of the debate, Mr. Nye began discussion on the fossil layers. He said:

> ...we find a sequence of animals in what generally is called the "fossil record." This would be to say when we look at the layers that you would find in Kentucky, you look at them carefully, you find a sequence of animals, a succession.

This statement in context implies that the animals are found in an evolutionary sequence. However, this is not the case. What we find in fossil layers is simply fossils at particular positions in the fossil record. Creationists and evolutionists actually agree on the rock layers and the fossils found in them. There is no dispute here.[66]

Mr. Nye actually held up a piece of fossil-containing rock that he'd obtained from the Cincinnati series as if this was evidence of evolution. But the rock didn't come with any labels about age or theoretical evolutionary history. Mr. Nye, on the basis of the assumptions/beliefs he has about

---

66. We agree with mapping rock layers with index fossils (and the like), though we disagree with the connotations of evolution surrounding the index fossils.

Plaster casts of victims of the 79 A.D. eruption of the Vesuvius, found in the so-called "Garden of the Fugitives" in Pompeii.

the past, was imposing his interpretation of these fossils on the viewing audience.

When evolutionists line up a series of fossils and propose them as a sequence of one kind of creature turning into another kind of creature, they are simply telling their evolutionary story — in accord with their worldview based on the religion of naturalism. We creationists look at identical fossils, and through the lens of our worldview based on the Bible (our religion of Christianity), we interpret them differently. We view the bulk of the fossil record as evidence consistent with a global catastrophe that occurred over the course of about one year in Noah's day.[67]

Looking at the same fossils in that alleged series, we view them as dying in the same catastrophe about 4,300 years ago; therefore, they cannot be evidence in a series of one kind of creature changing into a different kind. It would be like going to investigate the remains of Pompeii (which was destroyed by Mt. Vesuvius in A.D. 79) and making the claim that the peoples whose remains are found there actually lived tens of thousands of years apart from each other! That would be absurd since they died in the same catastrophe.

Mr. Bill Nye and Mr. Ken Ham were looking at the same fossil evidence, but they had two different interpretations to explain the fossils

67. Naturally, we have had fossils laid down *since* the time of the Flood with local volcanoes or other smaller scale catastrophes.

in the context of origins. They had the same rock layers and fossils but contrasting perspectives according to their worldview. The real difference between Mr. Nye and Mr. Ham is that they had dissimilar accounts of historical science — one based on God's Word and one based on man's word (apart from God). They didn't disagree on the type of rock the fossils were in or the classification of the fossils — they disagreed on the *timing* by which the fossil layers were laid down and how they were interpreted in regard to the question of the origin of living things.

Mr. Nye sees the fossils as being laid down millions of years ago in the evolutionary story. Mr. Ham believes they were laid down during the Flood of Noah's day and represent distinct kinds of creatures descended from those God originally created.

Mr. Nye accepts the "Geologic Time Scale" (see following page) produced by evolutionists — a theoretical evolutionary scale illustrating when they believe the various fossil-bearing layers were laid down. Mr. Ham believes most of the same fossil record was actually laid down during the approximately year-long catastrophic processes associated with the global Flood of Noah's day.

Let us raise a point of consistency for those Christians who accept the belief of millions of years concerning the history of the fossil record. Because this idea came out of naturalism, it was believed that the fossil layers were laid down slowly over millions of years. To be consistent, if a Christian accepts the millions of years idea, they can't accept Noah's Flood as a global event — if it was such, it would have destroyed the fossil layers that supposedly represent millions of years' worth of history.

So it was either a global Flood or just some local event. God's Word affirms clearly that it was a global Flood (e.g., Genesis 7:19–20[68]). Those Christians who accept the millions of years have to reject the clear teaching of Scripture in order to reconcile the secularist belief with the Bible. This undermines the authority of God's Word and is essentially trying to mix aspects of two different religions.

Mosaics

But back to the debate. Mr. Nye then transitioned to say that evolutionists expect to find some animals with characteristics that could be found

---

68. "And the waters prevailed exceedingly on the earth, and all the high hills under the whole heaven were covered. The waters prevailed fifteen cubits upward, and the mountains were covered."

GEOLOGIC TIMESCALE

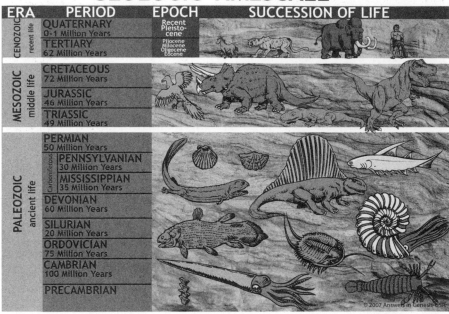

Slow gradual process with no significant catastrophes in the past

GEOLOGIC TIMESCALE

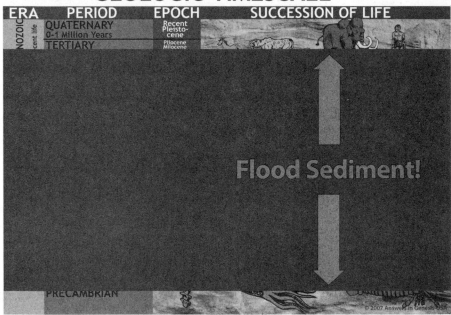

Rock layers in view of a global Flood

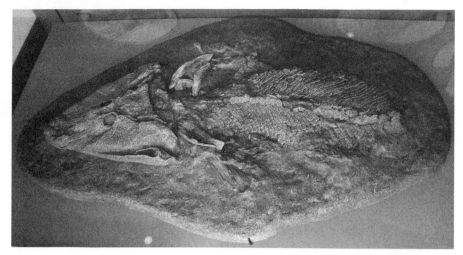

Tiktaalik fossil

in two different creatures. Ergo, these would be the intermediate links between two kinds as evidence of evolution. He then used an example of a so-called missing link that Answers in Genesis has refuted on its website for many years. Again, he obviously had not researched creationist literature to understand what this creature really was. He used the example of *Tiktaalik*, which was a lobe-finned fish.[69]

Now creationists do expect to find animals with common design features because all living things were fashioned by one designer — the Creator God of the Bible. Just like engineers use the same or similar designs in multiple applications, we would expect God, with His perfectly masterful engineering talents, to follow certain patterns — which is exactly what we find.

We find duck-billed dinosaurs, the duck-goose kind, and the platypus with a duckbill. We also find all sorts of animals with four legs. Common design is expected because God created them all.[70] In fact, the platypus is a great example. It has fur like a mammal, lays eggs like a reptile, has

---

69. Anatomist Dr. David Menton comments that, "Whatever else we might say about *Tiktaalik*, it is a fish. Like nearly all bony fishes, these fish have small pelvic fins, retain fin rays in their paired appendages and have well-developed gills — all consistent with an entirely aquatic life style." D. Menton, "*Tiktaalik* and the Fishy Story of Walking Fish," Answers-in-Depth, March 7, 2007, http://www.answersingenesis.org/articles/aid/v1/n1/story-walking-fish.

70. Since we are living in a sin-cursed and broken world since Genesis 3, we expect to see mutations and flaws cropping up in these designs.

webbed feet like a duck, yet suckles its young (it is a type of mammal), is poisonous, and has a beaver-like tail! Creatures like this are called a "mosaic." Mosaics have characteristics we observe in other distinct creatures. But the platypus is clearly not a missing link and lives today.

Now *Tiktaalik* has some mosaic features. In particular, it seems to have features similar to a tetrapod (tetrapod means "four feet"). But just because it has some features akin to a four-footed creature doesn't mean it is related to it! *Tiktaalik* was a fish with features we call mosaic (just as we explained for the platypus). Finding *Tiktaalik* was not a big deal for creationists since we expect to find creatures with mosaic features. So what of *Tiktaalik* — did it evolve into tetrapods? Expert anatomist Dr. David Menton[71] comments:

> Shubin et al. make much of the claim that *Tiktaalik*'s bony fins show a reduction in dermal bone and an increase in endochondral bone. This is important to them because the limb bones of tetrapods are entirely endochondral. They further claim that the *cleithrum* (a dermal bone to which the pectoral fin is attached in fish) is detached from the skull, resembling the position of the scapula (shoulder blade) of a tetrapod. They also claim that the endochondral bones of the fin are more similar to those of a tetrapod in terms of structure and range of motion. However, none of this, if true, proves that *Tiktaalik*'s fins supported its weight out of water, or that it was capable of a true walking motion. (It certainly doesn't prove that these fish evolved into tetrapods.)[72]

No, *Tiktaalik* is not a missing link, nor is it anything other than an aquatic fish that people hoped with "unfounded notions" (per Dr. Menton) to be a missing link.

Interestingly, Mr. Nye made a prejudicial conjecture that our worldview doesn't have predictable power when he said, "So far, Mr. Ham and his worldview, the Ken Ham creation model, does not have this capability. It cannot make predictions and show results." And yet, all this time, we creationists expected to find creatures buried in Flood sediment with

---

71. Biography of Dr. David Menton, Answers in Genesis, https://answersingenesis.org/outreach/speakers/david-menton/bio/.

72. D. Menton, "*Tiktaalik* and the Fishy Story of Walking Fish, Part 2," Answers-in-Depth, May 23, 2007, http://www.answersingenesis.org/articles/aid/v2/n1/tiktaalik-fishy-fish.

some mosaic features. So is finding *Tiktaalik* a fulfillment of creationist predictions as well? I would suggest it is.

And just as an aside — in the debate Mr. Ham twice put up a list entitled "Predictions Based on the Bible," and yet, Mr. Nye kept implying that creationists can't offer predictions. Mr. Ham proceeded, even in the short time he had, to give more detailed evidence in support of two predictions — 1) that we would find animals reproducing after their kind and 2) that humans belong to one biological race. Mr. Bill Nye never acknowledged that Mr. Ham clearly illustrated the point that creationists make predictions confirmed by observational science.

But let's not miss the power of predictions. Why is predictive power seen as "good"? That goes back to God's Word! Consider prophecy. Predictive prophecy is predicated on God knowing the future and being 100% accurate in His prophecy.

Scientists, meteorologists for example, pride themselves if they get an accurate prediction about the weather. But how often are they wrong? Rather often in the Midwest of the US where I come from.

When it comes to predictions, one should be careful not to fall into the trap of being a false prophet. The Bible has strict warnings against such things, especially in ancient Israel (Deuteronomy 13:1–5, 18:18–22). Accurate prophecy was a sign of being a prophet of God. This is why predictive power is good; the concept is a biblical one.

But when it comes to fallible man making predictions about a scientific model from the perspective of naturalism, we need to understand that such predictions are most likely an interpretation being forced on the evidence in order to support the religion of the one making the prediction. So in scientific models, they should still be held tentatively.

Origin of sex

Mr. Nye brought up a topic that actually made much of the audience wonder what he was doing. He began to talk about *sex*.

Now the origin of sex is a huge problem for the secular evolutionary worldview, so I'm surprised Mr. Nye even brought it up. Think about it. How do we get male and female evolving at the same time so they are totally compatible for reproducing the next generation?

Mr. Nye talked about asexual reproduction (e.g., a cell splitting into two cells), which purportedly is what happened first in the evolutionary story. The first life that allegedly came together by random chemicals billions of years ago just happened to have all the information required to procreate by asexual reproduction — in other words, this "simple" first cell was complex enough to be able to split itself in half and make two of itself.

Now to be perfectly frank, I'm not sure what that first cell ate (single-celled amoebas eat things like algae, bacteria, or particulates of plants and animals, but none of that was available when first life supposedly came about by naturalistic means!), or how it excreted waste with its simple structure. But this single-celled organism was apparently complex enough to have been accidently formed with those abilities too! I would encourage a study of the complexities of a cell to see that it is in no way simple.

Claiming a cell is "simple" is a gross misconception. No, even a so-called "simple" cell is more like a well-designed miniature biological factory. But let's return to the discussion of asexual and sexual reproduction (male and female, as opposed to asexual), which is another insurmountable problem for evolutionists.

Mr. Nye then implicitly asked, why does [anything] bother with sexual reproduction? He said it is due to germs and parasites. Then he alluded to animals that use sexual reproduction because they have different mixtures of genes to help them fight off these enemies (germs and parasites). His prime example was the red queen fish, which can reproduce sexually or asexually.

Mr. Nye rightly pointed out that fish reproducing asexually lack the variability to fight off infections. Now creationists do not disagree with Mr. Nye here in the least. We agree that sexual reproduction can be quite beneficial for fighting off germs and parasites and keeping an organism from infection.

But Mr. Nye made a strange claim when he said, "In other words, the explanation provided by evolution made a prediction, and the prediction's extraordinary and subtle, but there it is. How else would you explain it?"

First, there was no prediction made by "evolution." Evolution doesn't have a mind, nor does it speak. Evolution does not predict anything. Rather, humans make predictions concerning origins, based on their beliefs. And really, Mr. Nye's evolutionary belief is nothing but a human fairy tale about origins similar to the Greek myths such as the one about why the sun went around the earth. It is a story attempting to explain life without God and nothing more.

Furthermore, there was no prediction anyway. Mr. Nye, using his naturalistic religious worldview, presumed that evolution was true in the past, and then presumed that it was responsible for sexual reproduction. Finally, he presumed that seeing sexual reproduction was a confirmation of that prediction! But in reality, he only assumed the very thing he was trying to prove! So this was nothing but a circular argument.

Allow me to explain this fallacy further using the Greek myth about Helios. Helios was the Greek "god" that allegedly drove the sun across the sky in a chariot. Let's say a Greek mythologist said, "there was predictive power" in Greek mythology, then proceeded to explain that in Greek mythology, the sun rising, setting, and going across the sky is good. Since we see the sun rising, setting, and going across the sky, the explanation provided by Greek mythology is proof of a Greek mythology's predictive power. After all, how else would you explain it? Do you note the absurdity in this similar analogy?

Of course there is a much easier way to explain why sexual reproduction exists: God created things that were asexual as well as sexual; there were male and female from the beginning (e.g., Genesis 1:27;[73] see also Genesis 7:2–3[74]). To an infinite all-knowing God, such a task was quite easy to accomplish. But there is more. In the Christian worldview, we have a reason for *why* death and suffering have entered into the creation, and why some bacteria and viruses cause infections and are parasitic. We have an explanation for why things are "enemies." It is due to sin and the curse in Genesis 3:14–17[75] (see also Revelation 22:3[76]). We are now subject to a world that has a *taste* of what life is like without God

---

73. "So God created man in His own image; in the image of God He created him; male and female He created them."
74. "You shall take with you seven each of every clean animal, a male and his female; two each of animals that are unclean, a male and his female; also seven each of birds of the air, male and female, to keep the species alive on the face of all the earth."
75. "So the LORD God said to the serpent: 'Because you have done this, you are cursed more than all cattle, and more than every beast of the field; on your belly you shall go, and you shall eat dust all the days of your life. And I will put enmity between you and the woman, and between your seed and her Seed; He shall bruise your head, and you shall bruise His heel.' To the woman He said: 'I will greatly multiply your sorrow and your conception; in pain you shall bring forth children; your desire shall be for your husband, and he shall rule over you.' Then to Adam He said, 'Because you have heeded the voice of your wife, and have eaten from the tree of which I commanded you, saying, "You shall not eat of it": Cursed is the ground for your sake; in toil you shall eat of it all the days of your life.'"
76. "And there shall be no more curse, but the throne of God and of the Lamb shall be in it, and His servants shall serve Him."

— it's a fallen world, not an evolutionary one. But it would not escape an all-knowing God that sexual reproduction would also help creatures survive in a sin-cursed and broken world.

To the evolutionist, though, why are germs and parasites bad? There is no such thing as "bad" in an evolutionary worldview because there is no God to set what is right and wrong. So what is deemed good and bad would simply be arbitrary.

Perhaps parasites or germs that cause infection are what leads to the next phase of evolution — so it might be important to protect them! They might be an important selection pressure for evolution in the future! As I've heard Mr. Ham say at times, "If evolutionists were consistent, they would start a 'save the tapeworm' society or 'save the polio virus' society." Mr. Nye cannot claim that such organisms are really enemies but would have to allow the possibility that they could be a good thing in the evolutionary scenario for the future for a while as the ultimate future of evolution promises nothing but death and extinction, a future of grim hopelessness and meaninglessness.

But let's step back and look at the big picture of this argument. Mr. Nye is basically saying that sexual reproduction works well; therefore, evolution is true. Consider this same hypothetical argument with a refrigerator [Bill argues for a designer for the system and John argues for random process]:

Bill: "How did refrigeration come about?"

John: "Refrigeration works really well to cool things off!"

Bill: "But who first came up with the idea of compressors and refrigerant and designed these first models; and how did they first build them?"

John: "Look how well these refrigerators and freezers make ice cubes and keep things cool. Refrigeration preserves food from rotting and getting bacterial growth."

Bill: "But who was the first one to design this system?"

John: "By cooling things it helps preserve food against enemies, so this prediction is what I would expect if refrigeration came about by random processes."

Did you notice that John never addressed the issue of the origin of the refrigerator but tried to play off of the fact that refrigeration works well as though this were some sort of support for his argument? This is what Mr. Nye *tried* to do with his sexual reproduction argument. He didn't talk about the origin of sex (in a debate about origins no less), but proceeded to discuss the benefits of sexual reproduction, then made a wild jump to say it was support for his view.

Prediction: a biblical or secular concept?

Mr. Nye then claimed:

> And to Mr. Ham and his followers, I say this is something that we in science want, we want the ability to predict.

First, it is not *Ken Ham and his followers*, but rather "Mr. Ham and fellow followers of the Bible." And note once again, his wording implying that if you are not an evolutionist, you can't do science or be a scientist. This was a common theme throughout Mr. Nye's debate presentation, and it is a common theme in what he has been stating publicly concerning science and technology.

Now Mr. Nye seems to think predictability is a good thing. But *why* is this so in his worldview? Why would his religion with the teaching that nothing is immaterial include a concept like predictability, which is not material? This is self-refuting for the materialistic worldview that Mr. Nye has been professing. I mention this again because I want you to see that the non-Christian who believes in naturalism has to borrow from the Christian worldview — it is inevitable, and we need to point it out as they can't (or don't want to) see it!

But the concepts of predictability are twofold biblical concepts. First, it is God alone who can tell the end from the beginning (e.g., Isaiah 46:10;[77] Deuteronomy 18:18–22). In the Bible this is often called "prophecy" or "predictions." I find it fascinating that most evolutionists reject the fulfilled prophecy in the Bible (of their own accord), all the while relying on failed "prophecies" or "predictions" by secular scientists (e.g., dropped transitional forms, changing evolutionary ideas), and yet keep coming back for more! Ultimately, I suggest to you that it is a spiritual issue —

---

77. "Declaring the end from the beginning, and from ancient times things that are not yet done, saying, 'My counsel shall stand, and I will do all My pleasure,'"

one of the *heart*. It is an issue of man's sin and his rebellion against the truth of His Creator.

Second, the knowledge of the future (that it will operate consistently in accord with the laws of nature) is actually a biblical one predicated on God upholding the world in a consistent fashion. God promised to do so (as you should recall at this point) in Genesis 8:22.[78] But in a secular view, where everything may change tomorrow (like the laws of nature), why assume any form of predictability would be possible? Secularists, like Mr. Nye, must borrow these concepts from the Bible to make sense of predictability, whether they realize and acknowledge it or not.

Have natural laws changed?

Mr. Nye proceeded to make a false claim about us when he said:

> And your assertion that there's some difference between the natural laws that I use to observe the world today and the natural laws that existed 4,000 years ago is extraordinary and unsettling.

This is false. Creationists do not say that natural laws have ever changed. Mr. Ham never said this. In fact, when I was speaking with Mr. Ham later, he couldn't understand what Mr. Nye was really saying here, as it didn't make sense. Mr. Ham guessed that perhaps because creationists believe there was a global Flood in the past, Mr. Nye somehow thought Mr. Ham was saying that natural laws change.

In fact, Mr. Ham clearly said at one stage that he didn't believe the laws of nature had changed! Mr. Nye's argument here was — yet again — a straw man fallacy. He set up something that wasn't true and then proceeded to say it was wrong! Perhaps Mr. Nye confused uniformity with uniformitarianism. Let me explain:

> **Uniformity:** God upholds laws in a consistent fashion (e.g., gravity will always be the same [so long as the earth endures — Genesis 8:22]; so there are no worries that the earth will suddenly fall out of its orbit).

> **Uniformitarianism:** Rates of process today are the same as they were in the past (e.g., the assumption that the Mississippi

---

78. "While the earth remains, seedtime and harvest, cold and heat, winter and summer, and day and night shall not cease."

River has always had the same sedimentary deposit rates in the past, or mountains have always grown at the same rates by presuming there were no major catastrophes in the past like the global Flood in Noah's day.)

The difference is that the laws of nature deal with the uniformity, which has not changed, but we disagree that there have been no major catastrophes in the past. But even evolutionists believe in past catastrophes — at least they have been shifting in that direction recently. For instance, some evolutionists believe an asteroid impact wiped out the dinosaurs! I must admit, creationists still are perplexed at Mr. Nye's accusation at this part of the debate.

God in His Word has revealed that the earth was once (in the days of Noah) subjected to a global Flood, but this has nothing to do with Mr. Nye's accusation that creationists believe natural laws were different in the past. That's just nonsense!

Big Bang

There was a brief period where Mr. Nye discussed the history of the idea of the Big Bang. The presumption was that if stars are moving away from each other then, as Mr. Nye said:

> …it's very reasonable that at one time they were all together, and there's a place from whence, or rather, whence these things expanded.

Now is this a reasonable explanation? I've watched a phenomenon where several objects were all moving away from each other. However, I'm confident (since I was an eyewitness to the events) that they did not all originate from one place and expand from that point.

The phenomenon: baseball warm-ups (think "cricket" for the international crowd) when all the balls were being thrown from the center of the field to its outer edges during a warm-up. If I were to have leaned over to a pal sitting next to me and said, "It is reasonable to deduce that all the baseballs were originally at the exact same point, were all together at once, and spontaneously flew out from each other," my pal would have thought I was loony!

The point is that the idea of the Big Bang is nothing but an unprovable assumption. But I would go so far as to say it is a *disprovable* assumption. Provability is predicated on God, as I have written before, and turning to the pages of the Bible we have an entirely different account of origins that disproves the Big Bang. God, being an eyewitness to His creation, has the intimate knowledge that Mr. Nye, Sir Fred Holyle (who coined the term Big Bang but was actually a critic of it), and Dr. Ed Hubble didn't have. They relied on just a few pieces of information, and they let their false religion of naturalism influence their observations to arrive at an incorrect conclusion about origins.

These next three subsections might be a little technical, but they are useful to the discussion at hand. If it seems a bit too much for you, don't let it bother you as these sections are not crucial to the rest of the debate analysis, and you can skip past them.

Different Big Bang models

Let's talk about the Big Bang for a moment to explain it in more detail. There are three different popular models of the Big Bang:

1. Closed model: Spherical
2. Open model: Flat
3. Open model: Saddle-shaped

I'm always curious as to which one someone believes when they say they believe in the Big Bang and why (according to them) the others are wrong in their view. Interestingly, Mr. Nye never said which camp he was in or why he chose one particular model over another.

But for the readers, the Big Bang models are models proposing that the universe came into existence by itself. Basically there was no time or space or anything in existence; then something (infinitely dense and hot) popped into existence and rapidly exploded or expanded (massive inflation quickly). This allegedly happened about 13–14 billion years ago.[79]

But as a loud and clear point, there is no God or "gods" required in Big Bang models. It was always meant to explain the origin of the universe from a totally naturalistic, materialistic viewpoint. So Christians who might consider the option that God could have *used* the Big Bang are essentially adding God to a view that was formulated to explain the universe without God!

---

79. There are calculations that place the Big Bang all over the place. Some go as far back as about 20–30 billion and other calculations have it as close to 8 billion. Most secularists generally assume that it is about 13.6–13.7 billion at this stage, but that may change again due to the nature of this unstable calculation.

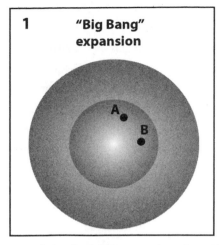
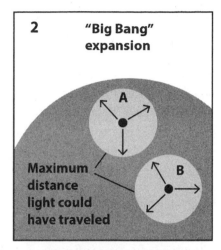

1. Early in the Big Bang, points A and B start out with different temperatures.
2. Today, points A and B have the same temperature, yet there has not been enough time for them to exchange light.

But trying to mix Big Bang with the Bible creates hosts of problems besides the fact that they are opposing religions.[80] God's Word states clearly that the earth (consisting of water that was without form or void on Day 1 — Genesis 1:2[81]) was created before the sun (which was created on Day 4).

In the Big Bang idea, the sun actually comes before the earth, and then the earth is a hot molten blob that cools down before water forms on the surface. These two accounts are totally opposite to each other. If Christians attempt to force Big Bang into the Bible, they have to say that God's Word in Genesis in regard to the creation of the earth and the sun is totally wrong!

Horizon Problem (Semi-technical)

Now in the Big Bang models, we have what is called the "Horizon Problem," a variant of the light-travel time problem.[82] This is based on the

80. J. Lisle, "Does the Big Bang Fit with the Bible?" in K. Ham, gen. ed., *The New Answers Book 2* (Green Forest, AR: Master Books, 2008), pp. 103–110, https://answersingenesis.org/big-bang/does-the-big-bang-fit-with-the-bible/.

81. "The earth was without form, and void; and darkness was on the face of the deep. And the Spirit of God was hovering over the face of the waters."

82. Robert Newton, "Light-Travel Time: A Problem for the Big Bang," *Creation*, September–November 2003, p. 48-49, http://www.answersingenesis.org/articles/cm/v25/n4/light-travel-time.

exchange of starlight/electromagnetic radiation to make the universe a constant temperature.

In the Big Bang, the light could not have been exchanged throughout the universe in the approximately 14 billion years of time. Also, the universe was expected to have many variations of temperature in the background radiation (for instance, hot spots). However, this was not the case when it was measured. Such problems cause many (including secularists and Christians who have mixed Big Bang with the Bible) to struggle with the Big Bang model, and rightly so.

Inflation problems

How did secularists try to solve the Horizon Problem? In laymen's terms, they appealed to an "inflation of the universe" in the Big Bang models as an *ad hoc* explanation. In other words, very quickly after the Big Bang, the fabric of space in the universe expanded very quickly (faster than the speed of light), then instantly slowed to the rate we see today. But what caused all that? And what evidence do they cite for this idea?

They suggest that a field existed that caused inflation. But there is no direct evidence for inflation or that field; that is, there is no independent evidence. Inflation was invented to solve the Horizon Problem and another problem (the Flatness Problem, but that will not be addressed here). People need to understand that there are many unsolvable problems with the Big Bang idea — and that's what it is, an idea or belief attempting to give a purely naturalistic origin of the universe.

Now researchers recognize that there are problems with inflation and the Big Bang. Some secular physicists and astronomers have been "jumping ship" from the Big Bang model in recent times. This movement has continually gained steam since an open letter with respected signatories against the Big Bang idea was published in the magazine *New Scientist* in 2004.[83] However, the majority of secular old universe believers still adhere to the Big Bang because nothing else has been proposed to take its place! And of course, like Mr. Nye, they have already ruled out the possibility that God created, as it states in the Bible — because no matter what evidence they find, they have deemed God's Word concerning origins unacceptable.

---

83. Eric Lerner, "Bucking the Big Bang," *New Scientist*, May 22, 2004, p. 20. To view the signers of this statement, visit http://www.cosmologystatement.org.

The hope of many who opposed the Big Bang was to revise it and the inflation hypothesis to avoid the many problems they fostered. More recently, *New Scientist* ran an article called "Bang Goes the Theory."[84] The article quotes two leading cosmologists, Drs. Paul Steinhardt and Max Tegmark:

> We thought that inflation predicted a smooth, flat universe . . . Instead, it predicts every possibility an infinite number of times. We're back to square one.[85]

> Inflation has destroyed itself. It logically self-destructed.[86]

To boil it down, some researchers recognize there are problems with inflation and the Big Bang, and they are questioning aspects of these ideas, such as:

1. The Big Bang and its type
2. Nothing to something
3. What started and stopped inflation
4. The starlight problem and recognizing how bad it is

Inflation and the Big Bang certainly have their failings, and honest scientists fully admit this. Many scientists now openly reject the Big Bang idea. This has occurred so much so that there is a public statement (cosmologystatement.org) of dissent from the Big Bang idea, with hundreds of scientific signers (most of whom are not Christian). It is called "An Open Letter to the Scientific Community" and was originally published in the *NewScientist*, May 22, 2004, and people continually add their names to this letter. So there is growing concern — even within the secular scientific ranks — that Big Bang is simply not true.

Biblical explanation for why the stars are expanding

Do those who believe the Bible have any reason to have expected that the heavens are expanding? Yes, for example:

God stretched out the heavens[87]

- Isaiah 42:5: Thus says God the LORD, who created the heavens and stretched them out, who spread out the earth and its offspring,

84. Amanda Gefter, "Bang Goes the Theory," *New Scientist*, June 30, 2012, pp. 32–37.
85. Ibid., p. 5.
86. Ibid., p. 35.
87. All passages in this section are NASB; some translations still use "firmament."

who gives breath to the people on it, and spirit to those who walk in it.

- Isaiah 45:12: It is I who made the earth, and created man upon it. I stretched out the heavens with My hands, and I ordained all their host.

- Isaiah 48:13: Surely My hand founded the earth, and My right hand spread out the heavens; when I call to them, they stand together.

- Isaiah 51:13: That you have forgotten the LORD your Maker, who stretched out the heavens and laid the foundations of the earth, That you fear continually all day long because of the fury of the oppressor, as he makes ready to destroy? But where is the fury of the oppressor?

- Jeremiah 51:15: It is He who made the earth by His power, who established the world by His wisdom, and by His understanding He stretched out the heavens.

- Jeremiah 10:12: It is He who made the earth by His power, who established the world by His wisdom; and by His understanding He has stretched out the heavens.

God stretches out the heavens

- Isaiah 40:22: It is He who sits above the circle of the earth, and its inhabitants are like grasshoppers, who stretches out the heavens like a curtain and spreads them out like a tent to dwell in.

- Isaiah 44:24: Thus says the LORD, your Redeemer, and the one who formed you from the womb, "I, the LORD, am the maker of all things, stretching out the heavens by Myself and spreading out the earth all alone."

- Zechariah 12:1: The burden of the word of the LORD concerning Israel. Thus declares the LORD who stretches out the heavens, lays the foundation of the earth, and forms the spirit of man within him.

Expanse of the heavens

- Genesis 1:6: Then God said, "Let there be an expanse in the midst of the waters, and let it separate the waters from the waters."

- Genesis 1:7: God made the expanse, and separated the waters which were below the expanse from the waters which were above the expanse; and it was so.

- Genesis 1:8: God called the expanse heaven. And there was evening and there was morning, a second day.

- Genesis 1:14: Then God said, "Let there be lights in the expanse of the heavens to separate the day from the night, and let them be for signs and for seasons and for days and years."

- Genesis 1:15: "and let them be for lights in the expanse of the heavens to give light on the earth"; and it was so.

- Genesis 1:17: God placed them in the expanse of the heavens to give light on the earth.

Yes. On the basis of God's Word, Christians would expect to find the heavens stretching as well as evidence of it having been stretched. This stretching is a great confirmation of what was predicted based on the Bible.

Now it's important to understand that there is a mistaken assumption about the expansion of the universe to arrive at a Big Bang explanation. It is assumed (on the basis of what they themselves have proposed) that if all of the heavens were wound backwards, the universe would arrive at an almost infinitely dense singularity that popped into existence. However, the secularists have assumed the very thing they are trying to prove. They are assuming naturalism (no God) to argue for proof of naturalism. Therefore, they are begging the question once again.

CMB and COBE

Mr. Nye made comments about the CMB (*cosmic microwave background radiation*), which was part of the research conducted by the COBE spacecraft mission (using the Cosmic Background Explorer). But his statements were not entirely accurate. Dr. Danny Faulkner, an astronomer, comments:

> In discussing the CMB, Nye showed a plot of the temperature curve from the COBE satellite and commented on its purpose:

"We built the Cosmic Observatory for Background Emissions, the COBE Spacecraft, and it matched exactly, exactly the astronomer's predictions."

Actually, COBE is an acronym for Cosmic Background Explorer, but that is a minor point. While the COBE project more precisely determined the temperature of the CMB, the temperature was known with reasonably good precision as far back as its 1965 discovery. However, the Big Bang model does not predict the *temperature* of the CMB, but merely the *existence* of the CMB. Pre-discovery predictions of the temperature had a wide range, because the model was not well constrained.

Nye appears not to grasp what the purpose of the COBE mission was, which was to detect spatial temperature fluctuations in the CMB. The Big Bang model predicts that there must have been irregularities in density in the early universe and that those irregularities produced slight differences in temperature in the CMB. The COBE satellite was designed specifically to detect the temperature fluctuations in the CMB predicted by the Big Bang theory.

The prediction was that spatial temperature fluctuations on the order of one part in 10,000 must exist in the CMB. But the COBE data showed a perfectly smooth CMB with regard to temperature. It was not until the application of a very sophisticated statistical analysis by George Smoot and his team that they were able to tweak out of the COBE data temperature fluctuations an order of magnitude lower, at one part in 100,000.

These fluctuations were at a level below the capability of the COBE mission, but they eventually were confirmed by later experiments. However, the important fact is that the data and predictions did not agree. In response to this problem, the model was altered to fit the data. Hence, to claim that the data and predictions "matched exactly" is to rewrite history.[88]

---

88. D. Faulkner, "Is Bill Nye an Expert in Astronomy?" Answers in Genesis, February, 13, 2014, https://answersingenesis.org/creation-vs-evolution/is-bill-nye-an-expert-in-astronomy/.

Does general agreement equal truth?

Mr. Nye claimed, "Now, along that line is some interest in the age of the earth. Right now it's generally agreed that the Big Bang happened 13.7 billion years ago."

When I first heard this, what I immediately saw through was Mr. Nye's *appeal to the masses* fallacy. If people generally agree on something...does that make it true? Mr. Nye assumes that if the masses agree on something, then it must be so.

Mr. Ham actually commented during the debate (in the Question and Answers time) that the majority of doctors (in Europe, England, and the US) once believed people didn't need to wash their hands to help stop the spread of disease. Those who advocated this were even met with hostility when told they had to wash their hands. There are many examples in history where the majority of scientists believed something that was later found to be wrong — e.g., the appendix supposedly not having a function and therefore being claimed to be a vestigial organ when in fact it is a very important properly functioning organ!

There was a time when many in Germany (when the Nazis reigned) thought that Jews (as well as anyone else who was not of purely Germanic blood) were a blight on the world. But it was not just Germany. Many places in Europe and the United States had very similar thoughts that the civilized people of Europe and America were superior and all others were thus inferior. At one stage in this country (the US), the majority of individuals thought people with dark skin were property, could not be citizens of the US, and should be deprived of freedom. The US Supreme Court in the *Dred Scott Decision in 1857* upheld this. But just because so many believed these things, did that make them true? Of course not.

As Darwin once stated:

> At some future period, not very distant as measured by centuries, the civilized races of man will almost certainly exterminate and replace the savage races throughout the world. At the same time the anthropomorphous apes . . . will no doubt be exterminated. The break between man and his nearest allies will then be wider, for it will intervene between man in a more civilized state, as we may hope, even than the Caucasian, and some ape as low

as a baboon, instead of as now between the negro or Australian [Aborigine] and the gorilla.[89]

When Darwin's evolutionary ideas became dominant (that the "civilized races" would exterminate the others), people like Jews, Poles, Slav, and many others paid the price in the Holocaust and WWII at the hands of Nazi Germany, and faced oppression by the Communistic Soviets as well.

In the US, there was even a general consensus that people of African descent were to be seen as property. Again, this made it as far as the world-famous *Dred Scott Decision* by the US Supreme Court in 1857, which, sadly, upheld such a view. Do you realize what it took to change the consensus view in the United States or Germany from these false beliefs? You see, if the masses agree on something, that doesn't necessarily make it true. Truth is dependent upon God and His Word because God is the truth and the standard of truth.

Mr. Nye makes an outrageous claim

Mr. Nye professed:

> What we can do on earth, these elements that we all know on the periodic table of chemicals, even ones we don't know, are created when stars explode. And I look like nobody, but I attended a lecture by Hans Bethe who won a Nobel Prize for discovering the process by which stars create all of these elements.

Mr. Nye stated matter-of-factly that elements are created when stars explode. Then he appealed to a lecture he heard by Hans Bethe that stated they know the process by which this occurs. Has anyone observed this? No. Has anyone repeated this? No. So at best, this is mere wishful thinking to try to tell a story about how they believe elements came about.

But let me explain what is happening regarding the secular Big Bang. *Once upon a time*, something basically popped into existence and rapidly exploded. By calculations, this explosion gave off hydrogen, helium, and lithium, which are the three lightest elements of the periodic table. Naturally, this is an arbitrary story since no one today was alive watching this occur (recall the secularists refuse to acknowledge God's account of creation).

89. C. Darwin, *The Descent of Man* (New York: A.L. Burt, 1874), 2nd ed., p. 178.

So the secularists have a problem — where did all the stars and galaxies come from? So they appeal to more storytelling. *Once upon a later time*, these three elements over billions of years coalesced together and made stars and galaxies. Interestingly in the secular model, secularists need stars to propose how stars were made!

But this still doesn't answer the question of where heavier elements came from. So in comes more storytelling. *Once upon an even later time*, these stars became the furnaces to form heavier elements inside them.

So how did the heavier elements get to places like earth? More story telling: *Once upon an even much later time*, stars exploded and the elements rushed out from them, sending them to various places in the universe.

But how did planets form with all these heavier elements? Well, in come more stories with the proposed nebular hypothesis. This is basically another *once upon a time* story that all the planets in the solar system (and the sun) were formed by coalescing material from nebula material that may include leftover star explosion material.

Did you notice that none of what they claim has been observed? In rare instances, we have seen stars explode, like the Supernova 1987a, but we have not measured any heavy elements that came from it. Mr. Nye revealed at the end of his 5-minute opening segment that his intention was to keep operational and origins science as one and the same. So where are the observation and repeatability here?

There is an estimated 10^{22} to 10^{24} stars in the universe.[90] If the universe is really 13–15 billion years, then where are all the new stars being formed that we should be able to see? We should be seeing billions of stars form every year! Where are these observations? The predictions by secularists is disproved.

Mr. Nye's claim is simply fiction. It is stories, on top of stories, on top of stories. He is deliberately mixing historical science and observational science together and calling them one word — *science*. This is exactly what Mr. Ham said is happening in the state education system through the textbooks and through many of the teachers. It reminds me of the way Greek mythologists kept coming up with stories to explain things, regardless of how ridiculous the stories were.

---

90. This is the estimate from the European Space Agency here: http://www.esa.int/Our_Activities/Space_Science/Herschel/How_many_stars_are_there_in_the_Universe.

So whose arbitrary stories should be trusted — those of the Greek mythologists or the modern humanistic mythologists? The answer: neither. One should trust God, Who being in the position of ultimate authority is not arbitrary when He speaks. His account is the one to trust when it comes to explaining matter like heavy elements.

During the question time, Mr. Nye was asked where matter came from in the first place and admitted he didn't know. Mr. Ham responded to Mr. Nye with the statement, "Well, Bill, there is a Book" — a Book that does explain where matter came from. Mr. Ham then held up the Bible. "There is a Book" has become the most quoted phrase from the debate.

Let's read what *The Book* states:

> Nehemiah 9:6: "You alone are the LORD; You have made heavens, the heaven of heavens, with all their host, the earth and everything on it, the seas and all that is in them, and You preserve them all. The host of heaven worships You."

> Colossians 1:16: For by Him all things were created that are in heaven and that are on earth, visible and invisible, whether thrones or dominions or principalities or powers. All things were created through Him and for Him.

Radiometric dating (semi-technical)

How accurate is radiometric dating? Let's take a look. Mr. Nye discussed one method called rubidium-strontium when he said:

> Rubidium become strontium spontaneously. It's an interesting thing to me, a neutron becomes a proton and it goes up the periodic table.
>
> When lava comes out of the ground, molten lava, and it freezes, it turns to rock, when the melt solidifies or crystallizes, it locks the rubidium and strontium in place. And so by careful assay, by careful — by being diligent you can tell how — when the rock froze. You can tell how old the rubidium and strontium are and you can get an age for the earth.

For the reader, radiometric dating methods are one particular form of uniformitarian dating methods. Uniformitarian dating methods simply assume something has been uniform in past — that is, unchanging. For example, if we wanted to estimate how old the earth was by one of the many uniformitarian methods, we might select sodium influx into the oceans. Here is how it works:

A. We assume there was no sodium (e.g., salt) in the oceans to begin with.

B. We measure how much sodium is eroding into the oceans today by rivers, volcanoes, and so on.

C. We measure how much sodium is leaving the oceans (like sea spray from ocean storms that come inland and leave some sodium inland).

D. We assume that there have never been any *significant* catastrophes in the past to make major changes to sodium influx into the oceans (in other words, we assume these rates have always been the same).

E. Then we calculate how long it would take for the ocean to arrive at their sodium level today (i. e., how salty the ocean has become).

In this example, we really made some wild assumptions, didn't we? First, we assumed there were no catastrophes in the past. Next, we assumed that the ocean had no salt to begin with. Of course, these are fallible assumptions. When God gathered the seas on Day 3 and let dry land appear (Genesis 1:9–10[91]), He could well have made sure they had a certain degree of sodium or saltiness. If so, that would upset this dating method.

Furthermore, we can read about the global Flood in Genesis 6–8 that was a significant catastrophe that surely increased the sodium influx tremendously. Let's also not forget about famines and droughts that plagued the Old Testament world, which certainly played a role as well by reducing influx of sodium. The point is that catastrophes that throw a "monkey wrench" into any uniformitarian dating method have been an important part of our past.

---

91. "Then God said, 'Let the waters under the heavens be gathered together into one place, and let the dry land appear'; and it was so. And God called the dry land Earth, and the gathering together of the waters He called Seas. And God saw that it was good."

In his rebuttal time, Mr. Ham actually discussed these false assumptions behind dating methods and gave specific examples to illustrate how untrustworthy such methods are. But Mr. Nye refused to even acknowledge that the dating methods he refers to do have fallible assumptions. Mr. Nye didn't want people to know such methods aren't reliable!

By the way, the age of the oceans, according to the uniformitarian calculation of sodium influx, turns out to be a *maximum* of only 62 million years.[92] Not that this figure is accurate by any means, but do you realize that it is far less than the age of the oceans that Mr. Nye is proposing?[93]

Now radiometric dating is one specific form of uniformitarian dating method. Although most uniformitarian dating methods give ages of the earth that are far less than billions of years (many only thousands of years maximum), a few *radiometric* dating methods do yield estimates in the billions.

The late Dr. Henry Morris compiled a list of 68 uniformitarian estimates for the age of the earth from Christian and secular sources.[94] The current accepted age of the earth by secularists is about 4.54 billion years based on the radiometric dating of a group of meteorites.[95] Keep this in mind when viewing table 3.

As you can see from the table, uniformitarian *maximum* ages for the earth obtained from methods other than a few long-age radiometric dates are nowhere near the 4.5 billion years of the other methods. Only two calculated dates were as high as 500 million years.

Radiometric dating is based on a radioactive material decaying into another material. For example, uranium will decay in a series all the way down to a certain form of lead. A radioactive form of potassium will decay

---

92. Steven A. Austin and D. Russell Humphreys, "The Sea's Missing Salt: A Dilemma for Evolutionists," in *Proceedings of the Second International Conference on Creationism*, R.E. Walsh and C.L. Brooks, ed., Volume 2 (Pittsburgh, PA: Creation Science Fellowship, 1990), pp. 17–33.

93. Even if *just the oceans* existed three billion years ago as many evolutionists propose, then this would be about 48 times less than what was expected; this shows the inaccuracy of uniformitarian estimates either way.

94. H. Morris, *The New Defender's Study Bible* (Nashville, TN: World Publishing, 2006), pp. 2076–2079.

95. C. Patterson, "Age of Meteorites and the Age of the Earth," *Geochemica et Cosmochemica Acta*, 10(1956): pp. 230–237.

Table 3 — Uniformitarian Estimates Other than Radiometric Dating Estimates for Earth's Age Compiled by Morris

	0 – 10,000 years	>10,000 – 100,000 years	>100,000 – 1 million years	>1 million – 500 million years	>500 million – 4 billion years	>4 billion – 5 billion years
Number of uniformitarian methods*	23	10	11	23	0	0

*When a range of ages is given, the maximum age was used to be generous to the evolutionists. In one case, the date was uncertain, so it was not used in this tally. The total estimates used were 67. A few on the list had reference to Saturn, the sun, etc., but since biblically the earth is older than these, dates related to them were used.

into argon, carbon 14 (radiocarbon) will decay into nitrogen, and so on. The time it takes for half the parent element to decay into its daughter elements is called the half-life.

As an aside note, carbon 14, because of its short half-life, can only give dates of thousands of years up to a theoretical maximum of 50,000 to 100,000 years — not that these are all that accurate either. Therefore carbon-14 cannot give dates of millions of years. So if you find something that is allegedly millions of years old, and it has carbon-14 in it, it can only be thousands of years old — maximum. There are many examples in the literature of fossils, etc., that are supposed to be millions of years old, yielding carbon dates; thus they can't be millions of years in age!

But the method that Mr. Nye brought up is rubidium-strontium, where a radioactive element (rubidium; Rb) changes into another element (strontium; Sr).[96] More specifically, it is a specific isotope of ^{87}Rb and ^{87}Sr or ^{86}Sr. For the lay reader, don't let this terminology scare you — it is simply rubidium (the parent element) that changes into strontium (the daughter element).

It is claimed that the half-life of this change from Rb to Sr is about 48–49 billion years. In other words, for half of the Rb to change into Sr, it would take roughly 49 billion years. Yes, you read this correctly; this is what is claimed by Mr. Nye's camp: it would take about three times

---

96. Strontium is named for a village in Scotland, where it was first discovered.

the estimated age of the universe to change half of the Rb in the universe to Sr. (So it is curious where all the strontium in the universe came from since only minute amounts could have been generated from Rb if the universe is only 13–15 billion years. Strontium is, after all, the 15th most common element on earth, yet rubidium is the 23rd most common element.[97]) But this problem is not an issue for a God who created the universe element rich.

Obviously, an experiment cannot be observed or repeated to verify this half-life in its fullness, so where did this *guess* come from? After all, there are other isotopes of Rb like ^{83}Rb or ^{86}Rb; and in total there are about 32 isotopes, though only two are naturally occurring. But these other isotopes decay in days — that is, a few have observable half-lives of less than 90 days, sometimes less than 35 days, and in many cases less than one day. So why is it assumed that the half-life of ^{87}Rb is about 48–49 billion years?

Simple — scientists observe in a lab how much ^{87}Rb there is one day, measure how much ^{87}Rb there is another day, and then calculate the half-life by extrapolating. For the technical person, that is $[t_{1/2} = t * \ln(2)/\ln(N_0/N_t)]$; where t is time between observations, N_0 is how much was there originally, and N_t is the amount of the substance after this amount of time.

But the problem here is simple: how do we know that the half-life really is this long (48–49 billion years)? We really should not detect many decay changes (alpha and beta particle discharges, for example) over days, weeks, and a few years by observation. And yet this is extrapolated from tens to the power of 8! This would not be acceptable in other disciplines. Allow me to use a layman example. If I polled five people on a question, then extrapolated that to say all 6–7 billion people on earth agree, would that be acceptable? Not at all! Even if we had a few years of observations, this is still far too short a time to give us a reasonable sampling of N_t, let alone allow us to calculate a proper rate — let alone possible rate decay changes by other factors.

But when it comes to *any* radiometric date, there are assumptions involved... a lot of them. For instance:

---

97. K.K. Turekian and K.H. Wedepohl, "Distribution of the Elements in Some Major Units of the Earth's Crust," *Geological Society of America Bulletin*, 72, no. 2 (1961): pp. 175–192; W.C. Butterman and R.G. Reese, "Mineral Commodity Profiles: Rubidium," accessed June 23, 2014, http://pubs.usgs.gov/of/2003/of03-045/of03-045.pdf.

1. Initial amounts?
2. Was any parent amount added?
3. Was any daughter amount added?
4. Was any parent amount removed?
5. Was any daughter amount removed?
6. How has the rate changed due to the environmental effects?

Now here is where it gets interesting. If radiometric dating methods were accurate, then we would expect them to line up across the board when using various methods on the same samples. But this is simply not the case, even with Rb-Sr. Dr. Andrew Snelling, after a seven-year radioisotopes study with RATE,[98] showed that dates of Rb-Sr (isochron) did not match the dates given by other radiometric dating methods like potassium-argon, samarium-neodymium, or lead-lead dating. In fact, they were not even close, even being off by millions and millions of years.[99]

Dr. Snelling further states about the Grand Canyon:

> We find places on the North Rim where volcanoes erupted after the Canyon was formed, sending lavas cascading over the walls and down into the Canyon. Obviously, these eruptions took place very recently, after the Canyon's layers were deposited. These basalts yield ages of up to 1 million years based on the amounts of potassium and argon isotopes in the rocks. But when we date the rocks using the rubidium and strontium isotopes, we get an age of 1.143 billion years.... To make matters even worse for the claimed reliability of these radiometric dating methods, these same basalts that flowed from the top of the Canyon yield a samarium-neodymium age of about 916 million years, and a uranium-lead age of about 2.6 billion years![100]

Even the solidified lava of a modern volcano, which erupted in New Zealand (Mt. Ngauruhoe) in 1977, was dated at millions of years

---

98. RATE was a research initiative between the Institute for Creation Research and the Creation Research Society studying *radioisotopes and the age of the earth* (i.e., RATE).

99. L. Vardiman, A.A. Snelling, and E.F. Chaffin, Eds., *Radioisotopes and the Age of the Earth: Results of a Young-Earth Creationist Research Initiative* (El Cajon, CA: Institute for Creation Research, and Chino Valley, AZ: Creation Research Society, 2005), pp. 393–524.

100. A. Snelling, "Radiometric Dating: Problems with the Assumptions," September 2, 2009, (originally published in *Answers* magazine) https://answersingenesis.org/geology/radiometric-dating/radiometric-dating-problems-with-the-assumptions/.

old![101] If we can't get dates correct on volcano flows where we know exactly when they formed, how can we trust dates on things we don't know? The obvious point is that we can't trust the Rb-Sr method or any radiometric dating method due to the many assumptions behind the calculations and estimates.

Besides, God's Word is the ultimate authority since only God knows all things, so only God is in a position to know the age of the earth and universe. Why not trust Him? God commands all people everywhere to repent and believe His Word and the Gospel.

Mr. Nye agrees with catastrophic events

Mr. Nye then moved to mention two catastrophes: Ash Falls State Park, in conjunction with Yellowstone National Park, and Mt. St. Helens. He discussed ever-so-briefly how the Yellowstone catastrophe made fossils, playing off of his experience with Mt. St. Helens.

Now this brief comment was hardly worth mentioning since there is nothing that we creationists would necessarily disagree with here. But here is why I wanted to comment: the Flood was a catastrophe that laid down immense numbers of fossils, yet this catastrophe was sorely neglected by Mr. Nye as a possible serious source for fossils.

Mr. Nye has such a religious adherence to millions of years (supposedly from the fossil layers) that he refuses to even consider the possibility of a global Flood catastrophe causing the majority of rock layers with fossils. I note a serious inconsistency on the part of Mr. Nye over this very point.

Nuclear medicine

Mr. Nye then began to denigrate the state of Kentucky. He brought up nuclear medicine (which has been done since the 1950s) with regard to rubidium being used in heart medicine. Even though Mr. Nye made it sound like this is new medicine, radiopharmaceuticals for myocardial perfusion imaging has actually been around since the 1980s. Then Mr. Nye said:

---

101. A.A. Snelling, "The Relevance of Rb-Sr, Sm-Nd and Pb-Pb Isotope Systematics to Elucidation of the Genesis and History of Recent Andesite Flows at Mt. Ngauruhoe, New Zealand, and the Implications for Radioisotopic Dating," in *Proceedings of the Fifth International Conference on Creationism*, R.L. Ivey Jr., ed. (Pittsburgh, PA: Creation Science Fellowship, 2003), pp. 285–303; Ref. 4, 2005.

Now, my Kentucky friends, I want you to consider this. Right now there is no place in the Commonwealth of Kentucky to get a degree in this kind of nuclear medicine, this kind of drugs associated with that. I hope you find that troubling. I hope you're concerned about that.

This is called a "crackers in the pantry" fallacy. Allow me to explain. If two people are arguing over whether or not there are crackers in the panty (one affirming and one denying), the easy way to solve the argument is by opening the pantry to see if there are crackers.

In this instance, Mr. Nye claimed there are no crackers in the pantry. So let's look at this more closely.[102] There have been two nuclear medicine programs at Kentucky colleges (Jefferson Community College and Bluegrass Community and Technical College). One of the two programs is still current, so Mr. Nye was wrong in his assertion. I haven't heard him publicly admit this yet, though!

But again, I must ask, why Mr. Nye (and the evolutionary crowd) care about medicine. That would be going against the evolutionary mantra of "survival of the fittest." Shouldn't death, which is the hero for an evolutionary worldview, be their guidepost, as opposed to helping people (which is a biblical concept)? Consider what Mr. Nye claims:

> You want scientifically literate students in your commonwealth for a better tomorrow for everybody.

In Mr. Nye's religion…why? From an agnostic or atheistic perspective… who cares? Who cares about what happens tomorrow after you are dead, or why try to make things "better" as though there were some universal and absolute God who sets what is better? Such things are meaningless in the evolutionary worldview but make sense in a Christian worldview. So Mr. Nye was inadvertently borrowing Christian principles to try to promote his religion. This relates to Mr. Nye's comment about joy. At one stage, Mr. Ham commented on Mr. Nye's statement about his "joy of discovery." Mr. Ham asked him what the purpose of his joy of discovery was if ultimately he believes that when he dies, he will cease to exist. What is the point of

---

102. K. Ham, Blog: "Answering Bill Nye-Rebutting Nye's Argument That Kentucky Is Backward Technologically," Feb. 8, 2014, http://blogs.answersingenesis. org/blogs/kenham/2014/02/08/answering-bill-nye-rebutting-nyes-argument-that-kentucky-is-backward-technologically/.

the joy of discovery then? Yes, good point, Mr. Ham! Again, Mr. Nye was borrowing the biblical concept of joy.

Distant starlight (semi-technical)[103]

Distant starlight is seen as one of the biggest obstacles to trusting God's Word about a young universe and earth. When adding up genealogies back to the Creation Week, there are about 4,000 years from Christ to Adam.[104] Assuming six normal-length days in Creation Week (and the Hebrew word for day in context in Genesis 1 clearly means an ordinary day), there is no room for the idea of billions of years (Exodus 20:11[105])! Mr. Nye said:

> Now as far as the distance to stars, understand this is very well understood. We — it's February. We look at a star in February, we measure an angle to it, we wait six months, we look at that same star again and we measure that angle. And so by measuring the distance to a star you can figure out how far away it is, that star, and then the stars beyond it and the stars beyond that.

This is called parallax. But this works for stars that are closer. When the angle gets too small for very distant stars and galaxies, then parallax cannot work, so another method is used to determinate the distance: Hubble Relation. This is based on red shifted starlight. Without getting caught up in the details here, creationists and evolutionists — for the most part — agree on the distances. So this really isn't the big issue anyway. Mr. Nye continued:

> There are billions of stars, billions of stars, more than 6,000 light years from here. A light year is a unit of distance, not a unit of time. There are billions of stars. Mr. Ham, how could there be billions of stars, more distant than 6,000 years, if the world's only 6,000 years old?

Mr. Nye had it right when he said a light year is a unit of distance, not a unit of time. It is fascinating that he then treated it like a unit of time!

103. Thanks to Dr. Danny Faulkner for his help on this section. We co-authored a chapter on these models in *The New Answers Book 4*.
104. B. Hodge, "How Old Is the Earth?" in *The New Answers Book 2*, Ken Ham, gen. ed. (Green Forest, AR: Master Books, 2008), pp. 41–52.
105. "For in six days the LORD made the heavens and the earth, the sea, and all that is in them, and rested the seventh day. Therefore the LORD blessed the Sabbath day and hallowed it."

Allow me to explain. Dr. Albert Einstein asserted that time is not constant in the universe; but the speed of light is. This may well be the key to solving the distant starlight issue according to some creationists.

Regardless, let's look at this issue in more detail because of what the evolutionists, like Mr. Nye, fail to mention. You see, they have the same problem. It is called the *Horizon Problem* in physics. This was briefly discussed in a previous section called "Horizon Problem." But the point is that they have a distant starlight problem as well; the difference is that theirs is purely unsolved.

The issue is even more difficult than many may think. We are not just trying to get light billions of light-years away to earth in only 6,000 years as Mr. Nye proposes, but we are also trying to get light to earth in only two days. Why? The stars were created on Day 4, and Adam was created on Day 6. Starlight needed to arrive for Adam to be able to use the stars to mark the passage of time, which is one of the purposes of stars listed in Genesis 1:14.[106]

Interestingly, biblical creationists have known about the distant starlight problem for a while and have been working on solutions. The popular ideas to solve this include:

1. Light in transit (or mature creation)
2. Speed of light decay (cdk[107])
3. Relativistic models
4. Alternate Synchrony Conventions
5. *Dasha* Solution

Let's take a look at each of these in brief.

Light in transit

Light in transit: This is the idea that God created the universe mature, or fully functioning. The functions of the stars (Genesis 1:14–17;[108] Psalm

---

106. "Then God said, 'Let there be lights in the firmament of the heavens to divide the day from the night; and let them be for signs and seasons, and for days and years.'"
107. cdk = c decay, where c is the symbol that physicists use for the speed of light.
108. "Then God said, 'Let there be lights in the firmament of the heavens to divide the day from the night; and let them be for signs and seasons, and for days and years; and let them be for lights in the firmament of the heavens to give light on the earth'; and it was so. Then God made two great lights: the greater light to rule the day, and the lesser light to rule the night. He made the stars also. God set them in the firmament of the heavens to give light on the earth."

$19:1-2^{109}$) required that Adam see them right away. Therefore, God created starlight in transit when He created the stars. Many reject this particular model today.

The reason many do not accept the light-in-transit idea is because starlight contains a tremendous amount of detailed information about stars. For instance, stars have been known to blow up into supernovas like *SN 1987a*. Had this merely been starlight in transit, then what we saw would *not* have represented a star or a supernova, but instead would merely have been light arriving at our eye to *appear* as a star and then a supernova. In other words, the star that was observed before the supernova could not have come from the actual star. If the light-in-transit idea is correct, then the light was encoded on the way to earth to make it look like an actual star. In that case, the supernova itself did not really happen but amounted to an illusion, sort of like a movie.

Many have suggested that if this were the case, most stars are not stars. The implication is that God would be leading us to believe they were stars, when in fact they were illusions of stars. The idea of light in transit was widely popular among creationists for some time, but now many reject this idea because it seems far too deceptive.

Speed of light decay (cdk)

Speed of light decay (spearheaded by Mr. Barry Setterfield): This is the idea that the speed of light was much faster in the past and has been slowing down primarily in a uniform fashion (but possibly in steps) to what we observe today.

Many creationists reject this idea, but we encourage researchers to keep working on it. In the end, it appears to have problems with other constants in the universe that are tied to it. If the speed of light were to change, then these constants would change too. Those constants would govern the structure of matter so that matter would drastically change as the speed of light changed.

Evidence for a reduced speed of light decay is also lacking, and in centuries past, the accuracy of such measuring devices has been limited. Furthermore, as people really researched the speed of light over the past three

---

109. "The heavens declare the glory of God; and the firmament shows His handiwork. Day unto day utters speech, and night unto night reveals knowledge."

centuries, they discovered it was not changing as previously thought, but has remained largely the same.[110]

In recent times, secularists such as Drs. John Moffat, Andreas Albrecht, and Joao Magueijo have appealed to the speed of light decay (VSL or Variable Speed of Light) as a possible solution to the secular starlight problem.[111] Perhaps as secular scientists do further research, they will see that there are some problems with this model. Either way, creation scientists are "light years" ahead of them in the research (pun intended).

Relativistic model: White Hole Cosmology[112]

Dr. Russell Humphreys has a model dubbed the "White Hole" cosmology. A white hole is like a black hole, except that matter flies outward from a white hole whereas matter falls into a black hole. Near the boundary of a black hole or a white hole, space and time are distorted. According to Einstein's theory of general relativity, this distortion can be described as stretching the fabric of space, and time progresses at different rates depending upon where you are.

So this theory plays off of general relativity to solve the distant starlight problem with gravitational time dilation. From an overview perspective, Dr. Humphreys challenges the commonly held assumption that the universe has no boundary. Running a bounded cosmos through general relativity results in a model that is not at all like the Big Bang and is consistent with biblical creation.

Essentially, in the White Hole cosmology, all the matter in the universe flew out of this "white hole." This would have occurred during Creation Week, and the white hole would have vanished some time during that week. As matter left the white hole, gravitational time dilation occurred. The earth was near the center of the white hole, so time on earth passed much more slowly than time near the boundary of the white hole.

Though there are still problems with this issue, such as blue shifts and red shifts not matching what they should be,[113] this model also holds some promise, and so we encourage further research into it.

---

110. Gerald A. Aardsma, "Has the Speed of Light Decayed?" Institute for Creation Research, http://www.icr. org/article/has-speed-light-decayed/ (accessed June 17, 2013).

111. Andrew Sibley, "Variable Speed of Light Research Gets a Boost," *Journal of Creation*, 20, No. 1(2006): pp. 16–18, http://creation.com/images/pdfs/tj/j20_1/j20_1_16-18.pdf.

112. D. Russell Humphreys, *Starlight and Time* (Green Forest, AR: Master Books, 1994).

113. John G. Hartnett, "Look-back Time in Our Galactic Neighbourhood Leads to a New Cosmogony," *Technical Journal*, 17, no. 1 (2003): pp. 73–79.

Relativistic model: Hartnett Model (Carmelian Physics)[114]

A solution utilizing Carmelian physics (named for Dr. Moshe Carmeli) was proposed by physicist Dr. John Hartnett. In a different approach to Humphrey's White Hole cosmology where the bounded universe was in four dimensions, this has assumed five dimensions (utilizing Dr. Carmeli's approach), which were still bounded.

Like the Humphreys model, the Hartnett model also relies on time dilation — a massive amount on earth. He postulates that most of this occurred on Day 4 of Creation Week, resulting from space expansion as God was creating galaxies. So time was running at different rates with six days passing on earth but more time passing elsewhere. Much of this dilation of time would have occurred during Creation Week, as opposed to Humphrey's model where it occurred all along at a steadier rate. Hartnett has produced some interesting results. Both the Humphreys and the Hartnett models are still being developed.

Alternate Synchrony Convention: Lisle-Einstein Convention[115]

This model derives passages like Genesis 1:17,[116] which states that the stars were to "give light on the earth." For a God who created all things, having distant stars give light on earth is no problem. Astrophysicist Dr. Jason Lisle (also writing under the pen name of Robert Newton) led the research on this model.

From the concept of light being given from stars to light the earth, Dr. Lisle derived the Lisle-Einstein Synchrony Convention, otherwise known as the Anisotropic Synchrony Convention (ASC), which is based on an alternative convention — that is, *position-based* physics as opposed

---

114. Hartnett, "A New Cosmology: Solution to the Starlight Travel Time Problem," *Technical Journal* 17, no. 2 (August 2003): pp. 98–102; Hartnett, "Starlight, Time, and the New Physics," in *Proceedings of the Sixth International Conference on Creationism*, Andrew A. Snelling, ed. (Pittsburg, PA: Creation Science Fellowship, Inc. and Institute for Creation Research, 2008), pp. 193–204.

115. For more, see Robert Newton, "Distant Starlight and Genesis: Conventions of Time Measurement," *Technical Journal*, 15, no. 1 (April 2001): pp. 80-85, http://www. answersingenesis.org/articles/tj/v15/n1/starlight; Jason Lisle, "Anisotropic Synchrony Convention — A Solution to the Distant Starlight Problem," *Answers Research Journal* 3 (2010): pp. 191–207, http://www.answersingenesis.org/articles/arj/v3/n1/anisotropic-synchrony-convention; Lisle, "Distant Starlight — Anisotropic Synchrony Convention," *Answers*, January–March 2011, pp. 68–71. http://www. answersingenesis.org/articles/am/v6/n1/distant-starlight.

116. "God set them in the firmament of the heavens to give light on the earth."

to *velocity-based* physics. Einstein left both options open, but did most of his work on velocity-based physics; so have most physicists since him.

Einstein pointed out that time is not constant in the universe, so our simple equation [Distance = Speed x Time] is not so simple anymore. But this starlight model is based on something quite "simple." Dr. Jason Lisle built on this position-based physics and the *one* direction speed of light (which cannot be known); his model thus solves distant starlight.

In laymen's terms, think of it like this: You leave on a jet in New York at 1 p.m. and you land in L.A. at 1 p.m. But you might say, "The flight took about five hours on the jet." Here is the difference: according to Einstein, when you approach the speed of light, time goes to zero. So if you rode on top of a light beam from a star that was billions of light years away to earth, it took *no time* for you to get here. So that five-hour flight was a "no hour" flight for light; it was an instantaneous trip.

Based on this convention-based model, light left distant stars and arrived on earth in no time. This fulfills God's statement that these lights were to give light on the earth in Genesis 1:14–15.[117] Of course, the physics is more complicated than this, but this analogy should give you an idea of how this model might work. However, it does not appear that we could perform an experiment to see if the ASC solution is true, since it is impossible to test the one direction of the speed of light; only round trips can be tested. Regardless, this model does solve distant starlight.

Dasha Solution

We would leave open miraculous options (as this was Creation Week). One particular form is by Dr. Danny Faulkner (astronomer), dubbed the *Dasha Solution*.[118] *Dasha* is the Hebrew word for "sprout" as found in Genesis 1:11. Many processes during Creation Week were done at rates uncommon today.

While some things were created *ex nihilo* (out of nothing) during Creation Week (Genesis 1:1[119]), many things during that week probably

---

117. "Then God said, 'Let there be lights in the firmament of the heavens to divide the day from the night; and let them be for signs and seasons, and for days and years; and let them be for lights in the firmament of the heavens to give light on the earth'; and it was so."

118. Danny Faulkner, "Astronomical Distance Determination Methods and the Light Travel Time Problem," *Answers Research Journal*, 6 (2013): pp. 211–229, http://www.answersin-genesis.org/articles/arj/v6/n1/astronomical-distance-light-travel-problem.

119. "In the beginning God created the heavens and the earth."

were made of material created earlier in the week. For instance, the Day Three account tells us something about how God made plants (Genesis 1:11–12[120]). The words used there suggest that the plants shot up out of the ground very quickly, sort of like a time-lapse movie. That is, there may have been normal growth accomplished abnormally quickly. The result was that plants bore fruit that the animals 2–3 days later required for food. The plants had to mature rapidly in order to fulfill their function.

God made stars on Day Four, but to fulfill their functions the stars had to be visible by Day Six when Adam was on the scene. As the normal process of plant development may have been sped up on Day Three, the normal travel of starlight may then have been sped up on Day Four. If so, this rapid thrusting of light toward earth could be likened to the stretching of the heavens already mentioned.

Some people may want to equate this stretching of starlight with some physical mechanism such as cdk or relativistic time effects, but this would not explain the abnormally fast development of plants on Day Three. It would also overlook the fact that much about the Creation Week was miraculous, hence untestable today. If one were to attempt to explain the light-travel-time problem in terms of a physical mechanism, one might as well look for a physical mechanism for the Virgin Birth or Resurrection.

The Dasha Solution would solve starlight for Creation Week, but it still leaves open the problem of getting starlight here after Creation Week, which is one of the shortcomings of this model.

Concluding Distant Starlight

This alleged problem of distant starlight does not seem as problematic for the biblical creationist as some think. Researchers have several options that can possibly solve this problem. But from a big-picture standpoint, no one outside of God completely understands all the aspects of *light* (or *time* for that matter). It acts as a particle and in other instances acts as a wave, but we simply cannot test both at the same time. This dual

---

120. "Then God said, 'Let the earth bring forth grass, the herb that yields seed, and the fruit tree that yields fruit according to its kind, whose seed is in itself, on the earth'; and it was so. And the earth brought forth grass, the herb that yields seed according to its kind, and the tree that yields fruit, whose seed is in itself according to its kind. And God saw that it was good."

behavior is still an underlying mystery in science that is simply accepted in practice. The more light is studied, the more questions we have, rather than finding answers.

But the point is, Mr. Nye was pointing the finger at the creationists, claiming they have a problem, when secularists have the same type of problem to explain within their model. Most people don't seem to understand that this is the case.

Light is truly unique in its makeup and properties; and with further study perhaps we can be "enlightened" to understand this issue in more detail. Regarding the distant starlight issue, there are plenty of models that have some promising elements to solve this alleged problem, and we would leave open future models that have not been developed yet (and we would also leave open the miraculous).

But as creationists, this really isn't a problem in the least. Here is why: God created these lights in the heaven to *give light on the earth*, and *it was so*. This is not a problem for an all-powerful Creator.

Mr. Nye's brief 30-minute conclusion

Mr. Nye then moved to summarize a few of his many points that he threw out quickly like ice cores, tree rings, and radiometric dating, and then reiterated a brief attack on the Ark as well as a political push by denigrating not only Kentucky, but also Texas, Tennessee, Oklahoma, and Kansas. Then he quoted the Christian[121] Constitution of the United States of America and tried to get away with a bait and switch fallacy. Mr. Nye said:

> . . . to promote the progress of science and useful arts.

Of course, science doesn't mean "evolution and/or millions of years of naturalism, but refers to operational, repeatable, and experimental science. So we are baited with science, then Mr. Nye is switching this to an evolutionary and naturalistic religion. But science doesn't mean the humanistic religion that Mr. Nye is defending in this debate.

---

121. Yes, the US Constitution is a Christian-based document. Please see: Miller, D., "Christianity is in the Constitution," Apologetics Press, 2008, http://www. apologeticspress. org/apcontent. aspx?category=7&article=2556; In fact, all four *Organic Laws of the United States* are completely Christian in their readings: The Declaration of Independence, The Constitution of the United States, The Northwest Ordinance, and The Articles of Confederation.

Of course, Mr. Nye moved to say that "Ken Ham's creation model" is not viable. Once again, this debate is not over Mr. Ham's creation model, but biblical "creation" being viable scientifically.

Although Mr. Nye brought up hosts of points, he really didn't present anything that would be construed as remotely devastating to creation. Most of his assertions were fraught with assumptions, in some cases evidenced poor research, and in some cases were simply wrong. In each case, his allegations were easily answerable.

Perhaps Mr. Nye knew this, so it is possible that this was one reason he used the *Skeptical Method* when he threw a lot of things out quickly (fallacy of elephant hurling) in the hopes that some of it would help convince the audience. However, a careful check of his claims uncovers that he was not able to poke holes in the creation model built on God's revealed Word.

Let me use a brief analogy to summarize Mr. Nye's 30-minute segment. He basically took a gun and shot a lot of shots, but in the end they turned out to be blanks; so it made a lot of noise, but didn't do any damage to creation, which is where he was aiming.

It was wise of Mr. Ham to ignore this blast and instead concentrate on teaching the true nature of science and relating the worldview conflict that was being acted out before the eyes of the worldwide viewing audience.

Part 4

Rebuttals:
Ken Ham and Bill Nye

In a debate, rebuttals allow the debaters a chance to respond to certain claims in the debate that they have just heard. In the case of Mr. Nye and Mr. Ham, they were given two opportunities to rebut, but these were very limited with an agreed time constraint of only five minutes for each of their two rebuttals. So the debaters had to be very selective when choosing which points to hit. Let's now turn and evaluate these four rebuttals, while keeping in mind that each claim has already been discussed more extensively in the analysis of the 30-minute cases.

Ken Ham: first rebuttal

Mr. Ham told me that as Mr. Nye had referred to the age of the earth many times in his public comments before the debate, he rightly assumed this would be in Mr. Nye's debate presentation and had a number of slides ready to deal with this issue.

It's interesting that after the debate some secularists and Christians claimed that Mr. Ham had focused his arguments on the age of the earth. But if you watch the debate carefully, while he did briefly mention the age of the earth as an example of historical science, he did not focus on this issue at all until the first 5-minute rebuttal. On the other hand, Mr.

Nye certainly did bring up the age of the earth/universe in his main debate presentation.

Mr. Ham's rebuttal points focused on these key issues:

- The age of the earth cannot be observed, and thus is historical science

Early in the debate, Mr. Nye chose to take the route that there is no division between operational and historical science. And of course, this placed him in the predicament of trying to marry historical science to *observations* and *repeatability*. In other words, Mr. Nye seemed to believe that things in past can be repeated and observed. Of course, this is illogical to anyone who knows anything about the past.

For example, one simply cannot observe and repeat the actual Roman Empire. But of course we have a lot of written records from people who were witnesses of this empire. Even then, there is much we don't know. When one discusses the issue of origins, this is a much greater problem for evolutionists who don't have human witnesses recording what happened to form the universe and life and supposedly evolve the different kinds of creatures.

However, creationists point to a witness — the infinite God of creation. And whether people believe it or not, God's Word is the record of One who knows everything, who has always been there, and who has had what we need to know about this history written down for us. Creationists then use observational science (which exists because God upholds as He said He would) to confirm this history — as we discussed in the previous chapters.

Mr. Ham's first point of response was actually cutting to the heart of that debate issue. Regarding the age of the earth, he made the point clearly that it is *not* observable or repeatable but is an interpretation. Mr. Ham then made a statement that needs to be clarified. He said:

> Now just to understand, just so you understand where I'm coming from, yes, we admit we build our origins from historical science on the Bible.

Mr. Ham was pointing out that because the *origins models* biblical creationists use are built on the Bible, creationists employ a degree of historical science; Mr. Ham is open about that and admits it publicly. However, to clarify, origins (as opposed to the scientific models built on the Bible) as stated in the Bible are the truth since God's Word is true by virtue of coming from the God *who is truth*. Models built upon the Bible's origins account, however, are subject to change!

- The biblical age of the earth based on the days[1] and genealogies in the Bible

Mr. Ham rightly ascertains the biblical age of the earth as about 6,000 years, which is what most biblical chronologists have also arrived at by meticulously studying the Scriptures. See Appendix B for more detail on the age of the earth.

- Inaccuracy of radiometric dating methods (which Mr. Nye held to with a God-like devotion)

Mr. Ham pointed out that radiometric dating methods have a problem, and we discussed this in detail in Nye's 30-minute segment analysis. Mr. Ham used an example of wood that was found encased in a lava flow. The lava flow dated to 45 million years by the potassium-argon method (by the way, potassium-argon has been revered by many adherents of long ages as one of the most accurate methods even though it isn't).

However, the wood that was encased in the lava was sent to a lab to date using the carbon dating method. They concluded that it was 45,000 years old. How could a 45,000-year-old rock be encased in a 45-million-year-old rock? It means there is a problem with these dating methods. This research, conducted by geologist Dr. Andrew Snelling, powerfully reveals that radiometric dating methods are not as accurate as one might have been led to believe.[2]

Next Mr. Ham discussed the Mt. St. Helens lava dome that solidified in 1986. Dr. Steven Austin, whose research on Mt. St. Helens is a must-read, again using the potassium-argon dating method, found dates ranging from as low as 0.35 million years to upwards of 2.8 million years for

1. J. Stambaugh, "The Days of Creation: A Semantic Approach," *TJ*, 5 no. 1 (April 1991): pp. 70–78. Editorial note: This paper has a subsequent expanded edition that was published at the Evangelical Theological Society.
2. A. Snelling, "Radioactive 'Dating' in Conflict!" Answers in Genesis, December 1, 1997, https://answersingenesis.org/geology/radiometric-dating/radioactive-dating-in-conflict/.

the same rock sample![3] This illustrates yet again that there is something very wrong with such dating methods, as the dates varied widely within the same rock and also differed markedly from the true age.

Mr. Ham then went on to discuss the basic assumptions behind all radiometric dating methods. This was already discussed in detail in the response on the rubidium-strontium dating method used in the 30-minute presentation by Mr. Nye. In the end, Mr. Ham's point that radioactive dating methods are simply not trustworthy was well made, and we need to admit to the fallible assumptions underlying these methods.

- The mistake of Christians buying into millions of years

Mr. Ham knew that many Christians had tried to mix their religion (God's Word) with the secular humanistic religion (man's word). They were taking aspects of the false religion and mixing it with their Christianity. In most cases, this is done by taking the secular beliefs about origins (particularly "millions of years") and reinterpreting God's Word in an attempt to fit them in. Sadly, many Christians accept man's views of geological evolution and try to mix it with Scripture.

Let me clarify something here. Most people, when they hear the word "evolution," really think of the "general theory of evolution (GTE)" or in laymen's terms "molecules-to-man," "electron-to-engineer," or "goo-to-you." But there are really four types of evolution that make up that word:

Astronomical (Cosmological) evolution: Big Bang (everything came from nothing)

Geological evolution: millions of years of slow, gradual accumulations of rock layers

Chemical evolution: life came from matter (nonlife), otherwise called abiogenesis

Biological evolution: a single, simple life form gave rise to all other life forms down through the ages

Within the church, there are those who try to fit either astronomical evolution, geological evolution, chemical evolution, or biological evolution into the Bible. Some Christians accept one, some, or all of these in their

---

3. S. Austin, "Excess Argon within Mineral Concentrates from the New Dacite Lava Dome at Mount St. Helens Volcano," Institute for Creation Research, 1996, http://www.icr.org/research/index/researchp_sa_r01/.

attempts to accommodate the secular beliefs with God's Word. As Mr. Ham pointed out, this acceptance undermines the authority of the Word of God. This is ultimately undermining the Gospel, as it undercuts the WORD from which the Gospel comes.

Let me explain this further, as it is quite important to know. Virtually all Christians who have bought into an old earth (that is millions and billions of years or long ages) place the millions of years *prior* to Adam.

We have genealogical lists that connect Adam to Christ (e.g., Luke 3). For the old-earth Christians, it would be blatantly absurd to try to insert millions and billions of years into these genealogies and say that Adam and Eve were made at the beginning of creation.[4]

Instead, old-earth creationists (as they are often denoted[5]) take these long ages and insert them somewhere prior to Adam; hence creation week has been a divisive point in Christianity ever since the idea of long ages such as millions of years became popular in the 1800s (see Appendix B). Here are some of the differing positions within the church — but all having one common factor — endeavoring to somehow fit geological evolution into the Bible:

Gap Theories (each adhere to geological and astronomical evolution)

1. **Pre-time gap.** This view adds long ages prior to God creating in Genesis 1:1.[6] The pre-time gap falls short for a number of reasons such as death before sin, allowance of man's ideas about millions of years to supersede God's Word, and the like. As another example, how can one have millions of years of time prior to the creation of time? It is quite illogical.

2. **Ruin-reconstruction gap.** This is the most popular gap idea, which adds long ages between Genesis 1:1[7] and Genesis 1:2.[8]

---

4. In Mark 10:6 Jesus says: "But from the beginning of the creation, God 'made them male and female.'"
5. In many other cases, those Christians who adhere to long ages are called "compromised Christians" since they are compromising by mixing these two religions' origins accounts (humanism and Christianity).
6. "In the beginning God created the heavens and the earth."
7. Ibid.
8. "The earth was without form, and void; and darkness was on the face of the deep. And the Spirit of God was hovering over the face of the waters."

Scottish pastor Thomas Chalmers popularized it in the early 1800s. This idea is promoted in the Scofield and Dake Study Bibles and is often associated with a Luciferian fall and flood — but that would make Lucifer (Satan) in his sinful state very good and perfect, as after God created Adam, God said everything He made was "very good" (Deuteronomy 32:4;[9] Genesis 1:31).[10]

3. **Modified gap/precreation chaos gap.** This view adds long ages between Genesis 1:2[11] and 1:3,[12] and it is primarily addressed in the International Conference on Creation article listed in this reference.[13]

4. **Soft gap.** This also includes a gap between Genesis 1:2[14] and 1:3,[15] but unlike previous views, it has no catastrophic events or destruction of a previous state. Furthermore, it merely proposes that God created the world this way and left it for long periods of time in an effort to get starlight here. In essence, this view has a young earth and an old universe. The problem is that stars were created after the proposed gap (Day Four), and it is unnecessary to make accommodations for long ages to solve the so-called starlight problem.

5. **Late gap.** This view has a gap between chapters 2 and 3 of Genesis. In other words, some believe that Adam and Eve lived in the Garden for long ages before sin. This view has problems too. For example, Adam and Eve were told by God to be "fruitful and

---

9. "He is the Rock, His work is perfect; for all His ways are justice, a God of truth and without injustice; righteous and upright is He."

10. K. Ham, "What About the Gap & Ruin-Reconstruction Theories?" in *The New Answers Book*, K. Ham, gen. ed. (Green Forest, AR: Master Books, 2006; for a technical response see also W. Fields, *Unformed and Unfilled* (Franktown, CO: Burgener Enterprises, 1997).

11. "The earth was without form, and void; and darkness was on the face of the deep. And the Spirit of God was hovering over the face of the waters."

12. "Then God said, 'Let there be light'; and there was light."

13. One refutation of this view is in *Proceedings of the Sixth International Conference on Creationism*, Andrew Snelling, ed., "A Critique of the Precreation Chaos Gap Theory," by John Zoschke (Pittsburgh, Pa: Creation Science Fellowship, Dallas, TX: Institute for Creation Research, 2008).

14. "The earth was without form, and void; and darkness was on the face of the deep. And the Spirit of God was hovering over the face of the waters."

15. "Then God said, 'Let there be light'; and there was light."

multiply" in Genesis 1:28,[16] and waiting long ages to do so would have been disobeying God's Word. This doesn't make sense. In addition, there is the problem of Adam only living 930 years as recorded in Genesis (Genesis 5:5[17]).[18]

When someone tries to put a large gap of time in the Scriptures when it is not warranted by the text, this should throw up a red flag to any Christian.

Day-Age Models (each adhere to geological and astronomical evolution)

1. **Day-Age.** This idea was popularized by Hugh Miller in the early 1800s after walking away from Thomas Chalmers' idea of the gap theory, and prior to his suicide. This model basically stretched the days of creation out to be millions of years long. Of course, lengthening the days in Genesis to accommodate the secular evolutionist view of history simply doesn't match up with what is stated in Genesis 1.[19]

2. **Progressive Creation.** This is a modified form of the Day-Age idea (really in many ways it's similar to Theistic Evolution) led by Dr. Hugh Ross, head of an organization called Reasons to Believe. He appeals to nature (actually the secular interpretations of nature) as the supposed 67th book of the Bible, and then uses these interpretations to supersede what the Bible says, thus reinterpreting Genesis to force these ideas into Scripture. Dr. John Ankerberg is also a leading supporter of this viewpoint.[20] This view proposes that living creatures go extinct repeatedly over millions of years, but God, from time to time, makes new kinds and

---

16. "Then God blessed them, and God said to them, 'Be fruitful and multiply; fill the earth and subdue it; have dominion over the fish of the sea, over the birds of the air, and over every living thing that moves on the earth.'"

17. "So all the days that Adam lived were nine hundred and thirty years; and he died."

18. B. Hodge, *The Fall of Satan* (Green Forest, AR: Master Books, 2011), pp. 23–26, https://answersingenesis.org/bible-characters/adam-and-eve/when-did-adam-and-eve-rebel/.

19. T. Mortenson, "Evolution vs. Creation: The Order of Events Matters!" Answers in Genesis, April 4, 2006, https://answersingenesis.org/why-does-creation-matter/evolution-vs-creation-the-order-of-events-matters/.

20. J. Seegert, "Responding to the Compromise Views of John Ankerberg," Answers in Genesis, March 2, 2005, https://answersingenesis.org/reviews/tv/responding-to-the-compromise-views-of-john-ankerberg/.

new species all fitting with a (geologically and cosmological/astronomically) evolutionary view of history.[21]

Theistic Evolutionary Models (each basically adhere to geological, astronomical, and biological evolution)

1. **Theistic Evolution (Evolutionary Creation).** Basically the idea of Genesis 1–11 is thrown out or heavily reinterpreted to allow for evolutionary ideas to supersede the Scriptures. This view is heavily promoted by a group called Biologos. Basically, they accept the prevailing evolutionist history including the Big Bang and then add God to it. Biologos writers have different ways of wildly reinterpreting Genesis to accommodate evolution into Scripture.

2. **Framework Hypothesis.** Dr. Meredith Kline (1922–2007), who accepted some evolutionary ideas, popularized this view in America.[22] It is very common in many seminaries today. Those who hold this view treat Genesis 1 as being like poetry or semi-poetic, with the first three days paralleling the last three days of creation. These days are not seen as 24-hour days but are taken as metaphorical or allegorical to allow for ideas like evolution/millions of years to be entertained. Hence, Genesis 1 is treated as merely being a literary device to teach that God created everything.[23] However, Genesis 1 is not written as poetry but as literal history.[24]

---

21. K. Ham and T. Mortenson, "What's Wrong with Progressive Creation?" in K. Ham, gen. ed., *The New Answers Book 2* (Green Forest, AR: Master Book, 2008), pp. 123–134.
22. It was originally developed in 1924 by Professor Arnie Noordtzij in Europe, which was a couple of decades before Dr. Kline jumped on board with Framework Hypothesis.
23. T. Chaffey and B. McCabe, "What is Wrong with Framework Hypothesis?" Answers in Genesis, June 11, 2011, https://answersingenesis.org/creationism/old-earth/whats-wrong-with-the-framework-hypothesis/.
24. Hebrew expert Dr. Steven Boyd writes: "For Genesis 1:1–2:3, this probability is between 0.999942 and 0.999987 at a 99.5% confidence level. Thus, we conclude with statistical certainty that this text is narrative, not poetry. It is therefore statistically indefensible to argue that it is poetry. The hermeneutical implication of this finding is that this text should be read as other historical narratives ..." Dr. Steven Boyd, Associate Professor of Bible, The Master's College, *Radioisotopes and the Age of the Earth*, Volume II, editors Larry Vardiman, Andrew Snelling, and Eugene Chaffin (El Cajon, CA: Institute for Creation Research; St. Joseph, MO: Creation Research Society, 2005), p. 632. I would go one step further than Dr. Boyd, who left open the slim possibility of Genesis not being historical narrative, and say it *is* historical narrative and all doctrines of theology, directly or indirectly, are founded in the early pages of Genesis — though I appreciated Dr. Boyd's research.

Each old-earth Christian worldview has no choice but to demote a global Flood to a local flood in order to accommodate the alleged millions of years (geological evolution) of rock layers (a global Flood would have destroyed these layers and laid down new ones).[25]

Also, the compromise views that accept the Big Bang idea have accepted a view that contradicts Scripture. They have adopted a model to explain the universe without God. So if God is added to the Big Bang idea, then really…God didn't do anything because the Big Bang dictates that the universe really created itself.[26]

Each view also has an insurmountable problem in regard to the issue of death before sin that undermines both the authority of God's Word and the Gospel.[27] For the readers, allow me to briefly explain. The idea of millions of years came out of naturalism — the belief that the fossil-bearing rock layers were laid down slowly and gradually over millions of years before man.

This idea was meant to do away with the belief that Noah's Flood was responsible for most of the fossil-bearing sedimentary layers. Now in the fossil remains in these rock layers, there is evidence of death, suffering, thorns, carnivory, cancer, and other diseases like arthritis.

So *all* old-earth worldviews have to then accept death, suffering, bloodshed, thorns, carnivory, and diseases like cancer before Adam's sin. Now after God created Adam, He said everything He made was "very good" (Genesis 1:31[28]). This is confirmed as a *perfect* creation by the God of life in Deuteronomy 32:4[29] since every work of God is perfect.

But if one has accepted the millions of years idea to explain the fossil record, then millions of years of death, bloodshed, disease, thorns, suffering, and carnivory existed before man. But as the Bible makes clear,

25. J. Lisle and T. Chaffey, "Defense — A Local Flood?" in *Old Earth Creation on Trial* (Green Forest, AR: Master Books, 2008), 93–106, https://answersingenesis.org/the-flood/global/defensea-local-flood/.
26. J. Lisle, "Does the Big Bang Fit with the Bible?" in K. Ham, gen. ed., *The New Answers Book 2* (Green Forest, AR: Master Books, , 2008), pp. 103–110, https://answersingenesis.org/big-bang/does-the-big-bang-fit-with-the-bible/.
27. B. Hodge, *The Fall of Satan* (Green Forest, AR: Master Books, 2011), pp. 68–76.
28. "Then God saw everything that He had made, and indeed it was very good. So the evening and the morning were the sixth day."
29. "He is the Rock, His work is perfect; for all His ways are justice, a God of truth and without injustice; righteous and upright is He."

it was Adam's sin that caused death (Genesis 2:16–17,[30] Genesis 3:19[31]), suffering (e.g., Genesis 3:16–17[32]), thorns, (Genesis 3:18[33]), and the whole reason why we need a new heavens and a new earth (e.g., Isaiah 66:22;[34] 2 Peter 3:13;[35] Revelation 21:1[36]) — because what we have now are now cursed and broken (Romans 8:22[37]).

Also, originally, the Bible makes it clear in Genesis 1:29–30[38] that man and animals were vegetarian — however, the fossil record has many evidences of animals eating animals. Genesis 1:30 is verified as a strictly vegetarian diet since man was not permitted to eat meat until after the Flood in Genesis 9:3,[39] which was directly contrasted to the command in Genesis 1:29.[40]

To accept millions of years also means God called diseases like cancer (of which there is evidence in the fossil record) "very good." And because "…without shedding of blood there is no remission" (Hebrews 9:22[41]),

30. "And the Lord God commanded the man, saying, 'Of every tree of the garden you may freely eat; but of the tree of the knowledge of good and evil you shall not eat, for in the day that you eat of it you shall surely die.'"
31. "In the sweat of your face you shall eat bread till you return to the ground, for out of it you were taken; for dust you are, and to dust you shall return."
32. "To the woman He said: 'I will greatly multiply your sorrow and your conception; in pain you shall bring forth children; your desire shall be for your husband, and he shall rule over you.' Then to Adam He said, 'Because you have heeded the voice of your wife, and have eaten from the tree of which I commanded you, saying, "You shall not eat of it": Cursed is the ground for your sake; in toil you shall eat of it all the days of your life'" [emphasis added].
33. "Both thorns and thistles it shall bring forth for you, and you shall eat the herb of the field."
34. "'For just as the new heavens and the new earth which I will make shall remain before Me,' declares the Lord, 'so your offspring and your name will endure.'"
35. "Nevertheless we, according to His promise, look for new heavens and a new earth in which righteousness dwells."
36. "Then I saw a new heaven and a new earth, for the first heaven and the first earth had passed away. Also there was no more sea."
37. "For we know that the whole creation groans and labors with birth pangs together until now."
38. "And God said, 'See, I have given you every herb that yields seed which is on the face of all the earth, and every tree whose fruit yields seed; to you it shall be for food. Also, to every beast of the earth, to every bird of the air, and to everything that creeps on the earth, in which there is life, I have given every green herb for food'; and it was so."
39. "Every moving thing that lives shall be food for you. I have given you all things, even as the green herbs."
40. "And God said, 'See, I have given you every herb that yields seed which is on the face of all the earth, and every tree whose fruit yields seed; to you it shall be for food.'"
41. "And according to the law almost all things are purified with blood, and without shedding of blood there is no remission."

then allowing the shedding of blood millions of years before sin would *undermine* the atonement. Really, believing in millions of years blames God for death and disease instead of blaming our sin from which Christ came to rescue us.

Some compromised Christians have objected and said, "But that just means the death of humans now entered (Romans 5:12[42]), but animals could have died for billions of years." But this neglects that the first recorded death of animals (to replace fig leaf clothing with animal skins — the first blood sacrifice) in the Bible came as a direct result of human sin in the Garden of Eden (Genesis 3:21[43]).

One cannot deny biblically that there is a relationship between human sin and animal death. Just briefly look at the sacrifices of animals required for human sin throughout the Old Testament. This sacrifice began in the Garden of Eden (the first blood sacrifice as a covering for their sin, a picture of what was to come in the lamb of God who takes away the sin of the world), that points to Jesus Christ, the ultimate and final sacrifice:

> ...for this He did once for all when He offered up Himself (Hebrews 7:27).

Dealing with the sin and death issue, Mr. Ham's response led straight to a presentation of the Gospel. My hope is that these Christians (who have bought into an old earth), will return to the plain teachings in the Bible and stop mixing God's Word with secular beliefs that clearly contradict God's revelation and undermine the Gospel by blaming God for death instead of our sin.

Even those Christians who disagree with Mr. Ham's uncompromising stand on Genesis would have to admit that he clearly presented the Gospel message concerning our sin and need for a Savior, and the solution in a resurrected Christ. When you watch the debate, you will see that Mr. Ham presented the Gospel by starting in Genesis with the origin of sin and then moved to the message of the cross. As I've heard Mr. Ham say many times, "We need to present the Gospel the way God does in the Bible, by starting at the beginning!"

---

42. "Therefore, just as through one man sin entered the world, and death through sin, and thus death spread to all men, because all sinned."
43. "Also for Adam and his wife the Lord God made tunics of skin, and clothed them."

- Most dating methods yield a younger age of the earth.

Mr. Ham then pointed out what I discussed previously — that most age-dating methods actually yield an age of the earth far less than the billions of years that many secularists propose. As we discussed earlier, all these methods have their shortcomings and assumptions that make them untrustworthy. But I concur with Mr. Ham when he says:

> And I claim there's only one infallible dating method, it's the Witness who was there, who knows everything, who told us, and that's from the Word of God.

Overall, given the short time frame agreed to, Mr. Ham covered quite a lot of information in this rebuttal. Naturally, you have to pick and choose what you are going to rebut since you can't rebut everything. Mr. Ham kept to the main issues that he was debating and decided to select a few points about which to give some detail rather than cover more points without adequate explanatory information. He told me that he also selected topics that would help him in presenting the Gospel. Actually, he did present the Gospel clearly three times during this debate.

Now Mr. Nye, just to try to make his case, had to borrow from the Christian worldview to make sense of science, logic, and morality. Mr. Ham rightly pointed this out in his 30-minute case and reasserted it in the second 5-minute rebuttal. But Mr. Nye never addressed it. This argument by Mr. Ham, that Mr. Nye must borrow from the Bible to make a case against it, was quite powerful.

Mr. Nye's worldview, in which everything is material, cannot even make a case without logic, truth, or knowledge — as they are immaterial. He is arguing for things to be "right" or "wrong" or "good" or "bad," and yet his naturalistic religion cannot make sense of those things since everything — in his view — is merely undergoing predetermined chemical reactions and there is no absolute authority. The consequences of such a view really remind me of Judges 21:25:

> In those days there was no king in Israel; everyone did what was right in his own eyes.

Mr. Nye also assumed his senses and memory are basically reliable (a biblical assumption by the way), and that science is possible because the laws of nature are not going to change in the future (uniformity). But how does he really know this? Only *Someone* who knows all things (including the future) would be in a position to reveal this to us (Colossians 2:3[44]). That *Someone* is the all-knowing God of the Bible.

These things that Mr. Bill Nye required just to debate are predicated on the Bible being true, not on any variant of humanistic thought such as atheism or agnosticism. In other words, for Mr. Nye to be debating in the first place meant that he had already lost the debate as he had to give up his religion and (inadvertently) borrow from the biblical religion that Mr. Ham was defending.

Bill Nye: first rebuttal

Mr. Nye began his first rebuttal with "Thank you very much. Let me start with the beginning." But Mr. Nye didn't start with the beginning; instead he started with the wood being encased in lava.

- Wood encased in lava

Mr. Nye said:

> If you find 45-million-year-old rock on top of 45,000-year-old trees, maybe the rock slid on top. Maybe that's it. That seems a much more reasonable explanation than it's impossible. Then as far as dating goes, actually the methods are very reliable.

But Mr. Nye failed to understand the argument. Mr. Ham, when he had opportunity, explained this problem for Mr. Nye once again. It was not that "45-million-year-old rock" was found "on top of 45,000-year-old trees." The lava had encased the wood *inside* of the lava flow. There was no intrusion; there was no rock falling on top of later wood. The lava flow encased the wood. When the lava flow solidified, it was supposed to start the radiometric clock for the newly formed rock.

Now the rock, according to potassium-argon dating, was 45 million years old. The wood, according to carbon dating, was 45,000 years old. So obviously something about these dates is wrong. Actually, from an evolutionist perspective, it is an example of a fossil being in a rock it shouldn't be found in. Mr. Nye either misunderstood the problem or was

---

44. "In whom are hidden all the treasures of wisdom and knowledge." [This is in reference to God, both of the Father and of Christ, see Colossians 2:2.]

trying to come up with an explanation — in any case, his explanation certainly didn't work.

From here, Mr. Nye revealed his allegiance to his "god." He appeals to this god for his authority for all issues, including the age of the earth. Mr. Nye will not challenge this god of his. Who is his god? It is man — that autonomous man (man *apart* from God) can determine the truth about origins. His god is not to be questioned and must be taken as the authority even when proven incorrect.

Now Mr. Ham clearly showed that the dating methods have been proven to be inaccurate. Instead of questioning the accuracy of the dating methods in the face of the empirical evidence, Mr. Nye merely affirmed his allegiance to them.

- Asteroid ages (semi-technical)

Mr. Nye proposed that:

> One of the mysteries or interesting things that people in my business, especially at the Planetary Society, are interested in, is why all the asteroids seem to be so close to the same date in age, 4.5–4.6 billion years. It's a remarkable thing.

First, all the asteroids have not been dated. There is an entire asteroid belt that hasn't been touched. But I'll be forgiving here since I presume Mr. Nye meant to say meteorites, not asteroids.

But meteorites are only dated by long-lived radioactive dating methods. The USGS (United States Geological Survey) said:

> The ages of Earth and Moon rocks and of meteorites are measured by the decay of long-lived radioactive isotopes of elements that occur naturally in rocks and minerals and that decay with half lives of 700 million to more than 100 billion years to stable isotopes of other elements.[45]

As has been stated earlier, such dating methods are based on a number of fallible assumptions, including extrapolating the observed decay rates back hundreds of millions of years.

---

45. USGS Editors, "The Age of the Earth," United States Geological Survey Website, accessed July 3, 2014, http://pubs.usgs.gov/gip/geotime/age.html.

One of the popular forms used on meteorites is Mr. Nye's old friend Rb-Sr (rubidium-strontium; at least 10–30 years ago). Of course, we've seen how inaccurate that method is in dating samples we already know the age of.[46] And since we cannot trust it on dates we know, why would we trust it on dates we don't know (see the section on rubidium-strontium dating in

iron meteorite

the response on Mr. Nye's 30-minute case[47])?

This whole idea of the earth being the age of the rest of the solar system is another assumption based on the secular viewpoint anyway. For all they know, the earth could have been separated from the solar system and later captured. But due to stories on top of stories on top of stories, they assume with religious fervor that the earth formed at the same time as the rest of the solar system.

Interestingly, the Christian knows (based on God's written revelation) that the earth and solar system formed at about the same time because God made the earth on Day 1, then began forming and filling it; while on Day 4, the rest of the solar system (sun, moon, other planets) formed (as well as the rest of the astronomical objects and stars). The creation of all things occurred in one week. Perhaps the secular understanding (the earth and solar system formed at essentially the same time) has really been borrowed from the biblical record. Regardless, the same USGS article is open about the foundational assumptions that the earth was formed at the same time as the rest of the solar system:

---

46. See also J. Woodmorappe, *Studies in Flood Geology*, 2nd ed. (El Cajon, CA: Institute for Creation Research, 1999); J. Woodmorappe, *The Mythology of Modern Dating Methods* (El Cajon, CA: Institute for Creation Research, 1999); J. Woodmorappe, "Contra Rb-Sr Dating," Answers in Genesis, April 1, 2001, https://answersingenesis.org/geology/radiometric-dating/contra-rb-sr-dating/.

47. See also A. Snelling, "Determination of the Radioisotope Decay Constants and Half-Lives: Rubidium-87 (^{87}Rb)," Answers Research Journal, 7 (2014): pp. 311–322, https://answersingenesis.org/geology/radiometric-dating/determination-radioisotope-decay-constants-and-half-lives-rubidium-87-87rb/.

Nevertheless, scientists have been able to determine the probable age of the Solar System and to calculate an age for the Earth by assuming that the Earth and the rest of the solid bodies in the Solar System formed at the same time and are, therefore, of the same age.[48]

At least they put the word "assuming" in the quote! So because they assume the earth and solar system formed at the same time, when they date a meteorite, the date will be the same as the age of the earth because they already assumed this would be so!

Let me put this into simpler terms. In Hinduism, there is a story that the earth and the sea are being upheld by a tortoise named Akupara. So based on this story, we just need to find a piece of tortoise shell that washed up on the ocean or river and then date it. We can get the age of the earth since the tortoise had to be in place to hold up the earth in the first place. Only someone who was *shell-shocked* would believe the age of the earth based on that date and story! Yes, pun intended.

The point is that Mr. Nye holds religiously that dating methods are accurate and doesn't acknowledge any of the many fallible assumptions involved. He refuses to question the dates arrived at even when they have been shown to be inaccurate — instead he ignores these dates. Why?

• Bible has been translated

Mr. Nye finally moved to attack the Bible (his underlying agenda through the entire debate), but he did so with an *ignorant conjecture* (as it is called in philosophy) regarding translations. Mr. Nye said:

> So I understand that you take the Bible as written in English, translated countless — oh, not countless, but many, many times over the last three millennia, as to be a more accurate, more reasonable assessment of the natural laws we see around us than what I and everybody in here can observe. That to me is unsettling, troubling.

Mr. Nye later said:

> I give you the lion's teeth, you give me verses as translated into English over, what, 30 centuries? So, that is not enough evidence

---

48. USGS Editors, "The Age of the Earth," United States Geological Survey Website, accessed July 3, 2014, http://pubs.usgs.gov/gip/geotime/age.html.

for me. If you've ever played telephone, I did I remember very well in kindergarten, where you have a secret and you whisper it to the next person, to the next person, to the next person. Things often go wrong.

Does this sound like an agnostic who doesn't know if the Bible is true or not? Mr. Nye professes to be an agnostic, yet his attack on God's Word is more in tune with that of an atheist.

Having the Bible translated many times is not a problem. But Mr. Nye, as is common with many secularists (as evidenced from their writings), misunderstands what this entails. They have wrongly assumed that the Bible was translated into English like the game of "telephone."

For those who do not know the game of telephone, let me explain. Get about ten kids in a room and have them sit in a circle. Then whisper a sentence to one of the children, and have them whisper it in the ear of the next child, and then the next, until the last child. By the time the message gets back to the person who started it, it is usually quite mangled and not too close to the original message. This is the same type of situation the secularists commonly claim occurred with the transmission of the Bible. In the debate, it sounded as though Mr. Nye was repeating this same old canard brought up in secularist literature that attacks the Bible.

But the Bible wasn't translated into one language, then into another from that translation, then into another from that translation and so on, until it finally made its way into English. It was not oral history that was passed along for generations until someone wrote it down. Even remedial research on this subject would prove otherwise. But the main English Bibles today (and for hundreds of years) have been translated from original language texts.

The Bible was originally written in Hebrew and Greek, with a few passages in Aramaic). We have original language texts such as the Masoretic text or Samaritan Pentateuch (books of Moses), and even an early translation of the Hebrew into Greek called the Septuagint or LXX. We have also had access to the Dead Sea Scrolls, which were around prior to New Testament times that were discovered in our modern era.

For the Greek New Testament, we have more than 5,000 copies and fragments! And we have over 24,000 copies and fragments of the New

Testament if you include the early Latin versions. Translation into English from the original language texts began in the 1500s with Tyndale — and we have had a host of translations since. There is only one English translation I am aware of that came from another translation: Wycliffe in the 1300s. He translated the Bible from the Latin Vulgate, which was all he had available to him at that time.[49]

Bible translation from ancient texts is done for various reasons. For instance, the English language has changed. Read a few translations from the 1500s (e.g., Tyndale, Geneva Bible, Matthews Bible, Bishops' Bible, Coverdale Bible, Great Bible) to understand this. There are also several translations today that focus on different aspects. For example, there are forms that emphasize *dynamic equivalence* (thought-for-thought) while others emphasize *formal equivalence* (word-for-word). In other instances, it could be a mixture to one degree or another of thought-for-thought versus word-for-word. There is considerable scholarship involved in ensuring the most accurate translation of the Scriptures.

In other cases, there are translations that are meant for different reading levels, whether a 5th grade reading level or a 12th grade one. Naturally, all translations need to be judged by their accuracy against original language texts. But it has little to do with the "telephone game" mentality that Mr. Nye was using.

But notice Mr. Nye's underlying assumption. He has assumed that the God of the Bible — that is, the Holy Spirit — could not have guided the authors to produce the inspired text (2 Peter 1:21[50]). He has also presumed that an all-powerful God couldn't keep His promise to preserve the text of Scriptures (e.g., Psalm 12:6–7[51]).

Mr. Nye has already assumed and argued that God isn't God, and therefore God couldn't have had any involvement in the Bible. Mr. Nye is essentially demoting God to the level of an incompetent human and trying

49. For more on these topics in this paragraph, see J. McDowell, *A Ready Defense* (Nashville, TN: Thomas Nelson Publishers, 1993); B. Edwards, *Nothing But the Truth* (Faverdale North, Darlington, England: Evangelical Press, 2006).
50. "For prophecy never came by the will of man, but holy men of God spoke as they were moved by the Holy Spirit."
51. "The words of the LORD are pure words, like silver tried in a furnace of earth, purified seven times. You shall keep them, O LORD, You shall preserve them from this generation forever."

to apply human standards to God's Word (Isaiah 55:9[52]). In other words, Mr. Nye has an atheistic starting point as the basis for his worldview. Mr. Ham was right in making sure people understood that this was a battle between two different worldviews based on two different starting points — God's Word versus man's word.

Mr. Nye set up the debate as "the Bible versus observation" when he said, "as to be a more accurate, more reasonable assessment of the natural laws we see around us than what I and everybody in here can observe." There is a mistake here.

Observations made today are not in discord with what the Bible says. Nor are the laws of nature in any conflict with Scripture, but Scripture must be true to make sense of the laws of nature in the first place. The mistake is that it is Mr. Nye's interpretations, based on his religion of naturalism, that are in conflict with the Bible — not observations or the laws of nature. So in essence, Mr. Nye is assuming his religion is true to say that the Bible is not true. But his religion cannot make sense of truth in the first place, so he must borrow from the truth of the Bible to argue against it.

Take note, though, that Mr. Nye never did even try to answer Mr. Ham's devastating challenge in asking:

> How do you account for the laws of logic and laws of nature from a naturalistic worldview that excludes the existence of God?

- Disease

Mr. Nye said in defense:

> And then about the disease thing were the — are the fish sinners? Have they done something wrong to get diseases? That's sort of an extraordinary claim that takes me just a little past what I'm comfortable with.

This can easily be refuted. Mr. Nye essentially believes that there is no relationship between human actions and animal death. But this is absurd.

---

52. "For as the heavens are higher than the earth, so are My ways higher than your ways, and My thoughts than your thoughts."

Man had dominion over the animals, so when man fell, the whole dominion fell and this affected the animals. For example, animals died under Führer Adolf Hitler's dominion due to his actions that affected his dominion (e.g., horses and so on). Would Mr. Nye deny that WWII took place because he is uncomfortable with animals dying in that event? Would Mr. Nye argue:

> And then about the DEATH thing were the — are the HORSES sinners? Have they done something wrong to DIE? That's sort of an extraordinary claim that takes me just a little past what I'm comfortable with.

In WWII, the horses, though being replaced by war machines, were still in active use, and it is true that many died as a result. Should it be so difficult to believe that, due to the repercussions of war, animals caught in the middle of the conflict suffered and died? These animals were merely vessels used by warring dominions. [Such wars today occur because of man's sin — that man rebelled against God.] Should someone deny that WWII happened or that Adolf Hitler existed because they can't believe horses died as a result of that incident? In essence, this is what Mr. Nye's argument leads to. But it's all because he rejects a Holy God and the notion of sin and its relationship to animal death!

The reason animal disease and death exist is unfathomable to Mr. Nye because he doesn't understand what happened from a Christian worldview. Man (that is Adam and Eve) was given dominion over the world (e.g., Genesis 1:28[53]). When Adam sinned, all under his dominion fell also, with the consequences of death and suffering (Genesis 3:14–19, Romans 8:22[54]). This is why we need a Savior and a new heavens and a new earth — this one is cursed and broken.

But let's not forget that an animal was used as a vessel for Satan in that first sin and as a result this animal suffered a curse as well (e.g., Genesis 3:14;[55]

---

53. "Then God blessed them, and God said to them, 'Be fruitful and multiply; fill the earth and subdue it; have dominion over the fish of the sea, over the birds of the air, and over every living thing that moves on the earth.'"

54. "For we know that the whole creation groans and labors with birth pangs together until now."

55. "So the LORD God said to the serpent: 'Because you have done this, You are cursed more than all cattle, and more than every beast of the field; on your belly you shall go, and you shall eat dust all the days of your life.'"

Revelation 12:9[56]). Animals are corrupt and they also suffer judgment (e.g., Genesis 6:12;[57] Leviticus 20:15–16[58]).

But here is what Mr. Nye fails to tell you. When he looks at disease (or death) from an allegedly Christian viewpoint, he sees it as bad and is thus uncomfortable with it. But when he looks at disease and death from his religious viewpoint of humanism, it is the hero and is perfectly natural. In essence, it must be "worshipped" for evolution to take place…note the double standard.

- Observing the past

Mr. Nye claimed that we do observe the past when we look at astronomy. He said:

> And then as far as you can't observe the past, I just have to stop you right there. That's what we do in astronomy. All we can do in astronomy is look at the past.

So according to Mr. Nye, if you look at the stars in the present, then that is not the present but the past. But if it is the past, then it is not the present and hence we are stuck in a catch-22. One would think the concept of past, present, and future would be easy to grasp.

Anything we observe in real time is in the *present*. Mr. Nye has observed the past through his telescope, but that would have been done in the days, weeks, and years before. But Mr. Nye saw nothing that was older than he is. If Mr. Nye goes and looks through a telescope tonight, he is not seeing the past, but instead he is seeing the *present*. Of course he has an assumption that the light he is viewing takes millions of years to reach his eyes — so that's why he claims he's viewing the past. In other words, once again, his worldview is built on assumptions — and if his assumptions aren't true, then his worldview fails.

---

56. "So the great dragon was cast out, that serpent of old, called the Devil and Satan, who deceives the whole world; he was cast to the earth, and his angels were cast out with him."
57. All flesh (including animals) had corrupted itself and were thus destroyed in the Flood; see Genesis 6:12 that says: "God looked upon the earth, and indeed it was corrupt; for all flesh had corrupted their way on the earth."
58. "If a man mates with an animal, he shall surely be put to death, and you shall kill the animal. If a woman approaches any animal and mates with it, you shall kill the woman and the animal. They shall surely be put to death. Their blood is upon them."

Here is the presumption (semi-technical). [Though I have already discussed distant starlight in detail in Mr. Nye's 30-minute case (and refer you to that), allow me to use just one of the models to examine Mr. Nye's point here.] Mr. Nye assumed that the distant starlight he saw today was something that left a long time ago (perhaps billions of years ago). He presumed that light can only go the speed of its *round-trip* while travelling in *one direction*. Dr. Albert Einstein disagreed.[59] He argued that the one-direction speed of light was impossible to ascertain. We simply do not know all the properties of light.

If the one-direction speed of light toward earth is near instantaneous (Einstein synchronization), then we are not seeing distant starlight from many years in the past (just now arriving) but are seeing things like starlight close to real time. Consider that God created the lights in the heavens to "give light on the earth and it was so" — Genesis 1:15.[60]

- Mr. Nye's crux of the issue is a fallacy.

During the debate, Mr. Ham pointed out that he and Mr. Nye have the same Grand Canyon layers such as the Coconino Sandstone and Hermit Shale. Mr. Ham explained that both he and Mr. Nye could agree on the fact that these layers were sandstone and shale — that is observational science. But they disagreed on *when* they were formed.

When we see the layers, we are only looking at the present — not the past. Mr. Nye claims he is looking at layers that are millions of years old. Mr. Ham states that we are only looking at layers in the present, and there are no labels on them to tell their age. When one is discussing the age of these layers, then one has stepped into the realm of historical science, involving interpretation in regard to the past. Sadly, Mr. Nye would never admit the difference between observations in the present versus interpretations about the past.

Mr. Nye proclaimed:

> So this idea that you can separate the natural laws of the past from the natural laws that we have now I think at the heart of our

59. A. Einstein, *Relativity: The Special and General Theory*, authorized translation by R.W. Lawson (New York: Crown Publishers Inc., 1961), p. 23.
60. "And let them be for lights in the firmament of the heavens to give light on the earth"; and it was so.

disagreement. I don't see how we're ever going to agree with that if you insist that natural laws have changed.

But creationists don't believe this. It is that simple. Mr. Nye has set up a straw man fallacy here. Creationists don't believe that the laws of nature in the past have changed. Either Mr. Nye is trying to deliberately misrepresent what Mr. Ham was teaching the audience, or he truly misunderstands that when Mr. Ham was referring to unique events like the Flood of Noah's day, this had nothing to do with natural laws supposedly changing. It would seem that Mr. Nye was equating unique events like the global Flood, which we don't observe today, as somehow meaning creationists believe natural laws have changed. This is preposterous.

Furthermore, Christians have a basis for the laws of nature to remain the same (uniformity of nature) since God promised this (as discussed previously). But in a secular understanding, the laws of nature might change tomorrow. The only way to know they will not change in the future is if someone who knows the future revealed this to us. And this is exactly what God did. So it is actually Mr. Nye's religion that cannot account for the laws of nature to remain the same. If anyone should believe the laws of nature can change, it is Mr. Nye! If he were consistent, then he would give up his naturalistic religion. And we invite Mr. Nye to do so.

I'm still surprised that Mr. Nye's "heart of our disagreement" was actually a fallacy about something creationists don't believe. Mr. Ham said he pondered why Mr. Nye was claiming this about the laws of nature and could only conclude that somehow Mr. Nye thought that the historical science based on the Bible (e.g., Creation, Flood, Tower of Babel) meant that because those events aren't happening today, creationists believe the laws of nature have changed.

Mr. Ham told me that he thinks a lot of the confusion is because Mr. Nye, being thoroughly indoctrinated by the secularists, doesn't grasp the difference between historical science and observational science. However, after the debate, Mr. Ham found that overwhelmingly, young people saw this issue and understood it. And again, Mr. Ham said he realized that Mr. Nye might not "hear" anything he said, so he worked hard to communicate to the watching audience.

- Another fallacy by Mr. Nye: Lions on the Ark

Mr. Nye falsely claimed:

> So, your assertion that all of the animals were vegetarians before they got on the Ark, that's really remarkable. I have not been — spent a lot of time with lions, but I can tell they have got teeth that really aren't set up for broccoli. That these animals were vegetarians until this flood is something that I would ask you to provide a little more proof for. I give you the lion's teeth, you give me verses as translated into English over, what, 30 centuries?

This is another straw man fallacy. Creationists, including Mr. Ham, do not claim that animals were vegetarian prior to the Flood. They were vegetarian prior to *the Fall into sin* (Genesis 1:30[61]). And this is logical. A God of life made a world full of life, not a world full of death. The *punishment* for sin was death, which is why death entered into the creation as a result of sin. This is why we needed a Savior in Jesus Christ to save us from sin and death.

Mr. Ham said that such false accusations like this from Mr. Nye showed he clearly did not understand what biblical creationists believe. Mr. Nye really had not conducted good research to understand the biblical creation position. I believe that in this debate, Mr. Ham understood Mr. Nye's position clearly, which is why he could carefully point out the issues of evidence, interpretation, and worldviews.

However, Mr. Nye obviously was quite blinded as to what biblical creationists believe and teach. In that way, it was sort of a one-sided debate. Mr. Ham had a big-picture understanding of the two clashing worldviews, whereas Mr. Nye did not even understand it was a worldview clash!

But note Mr. Nye's other fallacy. The cat kind was created in Genesis 1, but lions didn't exist until after the Flood when the two cats on Noah's Ark came off the Ark. All cats today are the descendants of those two cats — including lions! Just an aside here — in the debate, Mr. Ham used the example of dogs in discussing speciation, but the same concepts apply to cats. The formation of different species of cats within the cat kind had

---

61. "'Also, to every beast of the earth, to every bird of the air, and to everything that creeps on the earth, in which there is life, I have given every green herb for food'; and it was so."

nothing to do with molecules-to-man evolution. And such speciation occurred after the Flood.

However, this example used by Mr. Nye also illustrates that he does not understand the biblical creationist position. Think about it! Mr. Nye was using a post-Flood example to discuss the pre-Flood proposal that he made. Of course, the Flood was not the point of change to meat eating anyway; instead, this happened post-Fall. Now creationists do believe that various animals were eating flesh by the time of the Flood, though man was not specifically told he could eat animals until after the Flood (Genesis 9:3[62]).

Mr. Nye, though, did not do his homework. Sharp teeth simply do not mean that something is a meat eater but that it has sharp teeth. There

are many animals that have sharp teeth but do not eat meat and furthermore, there are examples of lions (and other meat eaters) that have refused to eat meat.[63] As Christians, we also can't ignore that a supernatural God brought specific animals to Noah (e.g., Genesis 6:20[64]).

Mr. Nye then concluded his section on lions as:

> So it's very reasonable to me that instead of lions being vegetarians on the Ark, lions are lions, and the information that you use to create your worldview is not consistent with what I as a reasonable man would expect.

Of course, lions (a post-Flood species of cats) weren't on the Ark, but two representatives of the cat kind were. And none of us know exactly what

---

62. "Every moving thing that lives shall be food for you. I have given you all things, even as the green herbs."

63. B. Hodge and A. McIntosh, "How Did Defense/Attack Structures Come About?" in *The New Answers Book 1*, K. Ham, gen. ed. (Green Forest, AR: Master Books, 2006), pp. 259–270, https://answersingenesis.org/evidence-for-creation/design-in-nature/how-did-defense-attack-structures-come-about/; see also DVD: *Dragons, Dinosaurs, and the Bible*, B. Hodge, Answers in Genesis, 2014.

64. "Of the birds after their kind, of animals after their kind, and of every creeping thing of the earth after its kind, two of every kind will come to you to keep them alive.

these cats looked like or how they behaved. None of us were there. At least Mr. Ham admitted that the debate of such topics was in the realm of historical science. Mr. Nye, on the other hand, used fallacious arguments to mock the account of Noah's Ark.

But here Mr. Nye missed a significant point. It seems he misunderstood what creationists believe at a very basic level. He assumed that our worldview comes from man, not from the pages of the Scriptures. He assumed that we are humanistic in our outlook when he claimed we "create" our "worldview."

We do not *create* our worldview, however. Our worldview comes from the pages of Scripture. That is God's worldview, which we try to echo. Of course, due to sin, we tend to fall short of having a perfect understanding of the true worldview that God has presented to us; we thus rely upon the Holy Spirit to correct us.

We are simply trying to discover God's true worldview, not create our own. If Mr. Nye had conducted some research, he would surely have understood that biblical creationists use the history revealed in Genesis concerning creation, the Fall, the Flood, the Tower of Babel, etc., and then build a worldview based on this so they can look at the evidence in the present to interpret such things in accord with their worldview. Mr. Ham actually explained this in his presentation, but it seems Mr. Nye neglected it.

But Mr. Nye's "human-created" worldview, where everything is material, posed a major problem for Mr. Nye, as was pointed out earlier in this book. He continually claimed that he is a reasonable man, and that reason exists. But reason has no mass. This reminds me of someone who says that ghosts don't exist, then proceeds to talk about the ghosts who told him they don't exist. In philosophical circles, this is called *intellectual schizophrenia*. The reason we can have reason and be reasonable in the first place is because we are created in the image of a reasoning God (Isaiah 1:18;[65] Genesis 9:6[66]).

- The Bible as a science textbook?

---

65. " 'Come now, and let us reason together,' says the LORD, 'Though your sins are as scarlet, they will be as white as snow; though they are red like crimson, they will be like wool.' "
66. "Whoever sheds man's blood, by man his blood shall be shed; for in the image of God He made man."

Mr. Nye then reiterated a false claim that often pops up in secular sources. He said:

> If we accept Mr. Ham's point of view, that — Mr. Ham's point of view that the Bible as translated into American English serves as a science text...

Now let's be realistic. When Bill Nye used the words "science text," I believe everyone hearing this would conclude (as Mr. Nye wanted them to), that he was referring to the common understanding of "science text." People would be thinking of a constantly changing biology, physics, or geology text as used in schools or universities. But Mr. Ham holds to no such position. In fact, I'm not aware of any creationist who holds to such a bogus position. Again, this is a straw man fallacy. Mr. Ham is actually famous for popularizing the phrase: "We don't take the Bible as [a] science textbook, and that is good because science textbooks change every year!"

I'm surprised when I hear someone who tries to attribute this claim that "the Bible is a science textbook" to Mr. Ham, as it shows that they have not done their research. It would be like saying the Japanese dropped an atomic bomb on the US in WWII when the truth is that it was the other way around. Mr. Ham is famous for his response to this alleged claim, not the claim itself.

Now I have heard Mr. Ham say that once you understand the difference between historical and observational science, you could call the Bible "God's historical science textbook" — because the Bible is primarily a book of history. And Mr. Ham made this very clear during the debate. So Mr. Nye's accusation here flies in the face of what Mr. Ham clearly stated. Again, it seems obvious that Mr. Nye either didn't understand the biblical creation position or was deliberately misleading the audience to believe something that's not true!

• Interpretation versus observation

Mr. Nye continued his attack on creationists by setting up a false dilemma (bifurcation fallacy) for the audience. He claimed in reference to the Bible:

> It means that Mr. Ham's word, or his interpretation of these other words, is somehow to be more respected than what you can observe in nature...

First, it has nothing to do with Mr. Ham's interpretation, but instead is about letting God interpret His own Word. As Genesis is written as a historical narrative, Mr. Ham reads it as history, just like Mr. Nye would read a history book outlining the events of, say, World War I. If Mr. Ham and Mr. Nye both read a history book about the war and just read the account as written, would Mr. Nye claim that was Mr. Ham's interpretation?

Now there is no conflict here between the Bible and "what you can observe in nature." Both the Bible's plain interpretation (Scripture interpreting Scripture) and observations of the world are not in conflict. They are not mutually exclusive (bifurcated), as Mr. Nye would have you believe. In fact, creation scientists have illustrated over and over again (as Mr. Ham did in the debate with predictions concerning "kinds" and "one race") that observational science confirms the statements in the Bible.

But actually, having a proper understanding of the observations is predicated on the Bible being true. For example, why would our senses be reliable in the secular worldview if we are just rearranged chemicals doing what chemicals do…perhaps for a survival advantage? How do we know that our memory is reliable in such a secular naturalistic evolutionary understanding? Such things really can't be ultimately known in a secular worldview.

These must be borrowed from the Christian worldview based on the Bible, where God created us with our senses to be reliable and not "nascent" or "vestigial" (that is, in process of evolving into something else that will work differently or devolving from something else that used to work). Our memory is generally reliable because we are made in the image of a God who remembers (Genesis 8:1[67]) since He knows all things (1 John 3:20[68]). Of course, our memory can fail us due to sin and the curse, but the Bible's truth explains that as well.

- Troubling, uncomfortable, unsettling,

Numerous times, Mr. Nye proclaimed that things were troubling or uncomfortable or unsettling. But why, in his professed worldview, would this be the case? There is no right or wrong in his naturalistic religion. It is

---

67. "Then God remembered Noah, and every living thing, and all the animals that were with him in the ark. And God made a wind to pass over the earth, and the waters subsided."
68. "For if our heart condemns us, God is greater than our heart, and knows all things."

purely subjective and relative since there is no God who sets an absolute standard. Since people come up with what is right and wrong in this humanistic religion, such things are only subjective and ultimately, utterly meaningless. And if Mr. Nye were consistent with this relativism, he should say, "Well that is true for you, Mr. Ham, and that is great that you think that way — but I have a different truth that I have decided for myself."

Yet what is strikingly obvious is the fact that Mr. Nye doesn't think that way but acts and speaks as though there is absolute morality. But his religion demands that there is no absolute morality. It would be manmade if anything, and might perhaps have a survival advantage, but then again, it might not! And how does one decide whether or not such a survival advantage is best overall for the evolutionary process for the future anyway?

But there is absolute morality, and Mr. Nye can't escape it, even though within his worldview of agnosticism and humanism he really professes that it doesn't exist. For the law of God is written on Mr. Nye's heart whether he wants to believe it or not (Romans 2:15[69]).

Mr. Nye's actions, if he were consistent, would be to say that anyone can do and believe whatever they want because we are all just chemicals acting in a particular way that cannot be stopped. You act and believe certain things because that is what the chemicals are doing. So why did Mr. Nye even show up to the debate? On what basis did Mr. Nye think that his chemical processes that are interpreted as morality were better than Mr. Ham's?

- The five "races" of man

Mr. Nye's evolutionary religion is well known for its racism throughout the past. Mr. Charles Darwin's writings certainly fueled racism and prejudice. For instance, Mr. Darwin, in his book *The Descent of Man*, even promoted the idea of Caucasians as a superior race, exterminating what he called the "lower races."[70] Darwin's first book's title even mentions "favored races" (*On the Origin of Species by Means of Natural Selection, or the Preservation of Favored Races*). Now even though this book was primarily about animals, at the end of the book, Darwin made it clear he would apply the

---

69. "...who show the work of the law written in their hearts, their conscience also bearing witness, and between themselves their thoughts accusing or else excusing them."
70. Charles Darwin, *The Descent of Man,* 2nd ed. (New York: A.L. Burt, 1874), p. 178.

same ideas to humans when he stated, "In the distant future...Light will be thrown on the origin of man and his history."[71]

Charles Darwin

Mr. Darwin's book *The Descent of Man, and Selection in Relation to Sex* also promoted higher and lower races of mankind with an entire chapter on it (Chapter 7, *On the Races of Man*, 1871). As previously discussed, Professor Ernest Haeckel, an early evolutionist who endorsed this Darwinian religious viewpoint in Germany in the late 1800s (that opened the door for Nazi policies), was openly racist and placed people of darker skin at the lowest level of humanity. Adolf Hitler, leader of the Nazi regime, was a well-known evolutionist and racist.

The list goes on even into modern times with Dr. James Watson, co-discoverer of DNA, leading evolutionist, and Nobel Prize winner having recently promoted the idea that African peoples are lesser in intelligence than "whites."[72] Sadly, the Darwinian ideas of race still persist on the streets in much of the Western world, but political correctness (which in this case, follows the biblical position) has tried to snuff this out a bit (finally).

And so it makes sense why Mr. Nye's response was one in line with political correctness, opposing what his fellow evolutionists have been promoting for 150 years. He said:

> The five races were claimed by people who were of European descent, and they said, "Hey, we're the best. Check us out." And that turns out to be if you've ever traveled anywhere or done anything, not to be that way. People are much more alike than they are different.

But it is a biblical viewpoint that people are of one race — the human race, going back to Adam and Eve. Thus, all humans are equal before God. It

---

71. Charles Darwin, *On the Origin of Species by Means of Natural Selection, or the Preservation of Favored Races,* 1st edition (1,250 copies; November 23, 1859), 2nd edition (3,000 copies; January 1860), chapter 14.
72. S. Adams, "Nobel Scientist Snubbed After Racism Claims," *The Telegraph*, October 7, 2007, http://www.telegraph.co.uk/news/uknews/1566468/Nobel-scientist-snubbed-after-racism-claims.html.

also means all humans are sinners in need of salvation, which is why missionaries take the Gospel message to every tribe and nation. So it was nice to see Mr. Nye oppose Darwinian evolution on this point and actually side with biblical creationists who have been promoting one race against the Darwinians for years. Pray this happens with more evolutionists.

In his debate presentation, Mr. Ham quoted from an article about the results of the Human Genome Project back in 2000:

> Dr. Venter (head of the Celera Genomics Corporation, Rockville, MD) and scientists at the National Institutes of Health recently announced that they had put together a draft of the entire sequence of the human genome, and the researchers… unanimously declared, there is only one race — the human race.[73]

Mr. Ham also (as quoted earlier in the book) used a quote from a biology textbook used in American schools in the early 20th century that promoted racism based on Darwinian evolution:

> The Races of Man — At the present time there exist upon the earth five races or varieties of man…and finally, the highest type of all, the Caucasians, represented by the civilized white inhabitants of Europe and America.[74]

If only the state schools in the US had taught the correct anthropology founded on the historical science in the Bible, they would never have taught students such erroneous and damaging ideas as light-skinned people being a higher race!

- Attacking God's Word one more time

Mr. Nye finished with:

> So, are we supposed to take your word for English words translated over the last 30 centuries instead of what we can observe in the universe around us?

---

73. N. Angier, "Do Races Differ? Not Really, DNA Shows," *New York Times*, Aug. 22, 2000, http://partners.nytimes.com/library/national/science/082200sci-genetics-race.html.
74. G. Hunter, *A Civic Biology: Presented in Problems* (New York: American Book Company, 1914), p. 196.

Again Mr. Nye's comment was in the context of the Bible. This attack was based on Mr. Nye's false telephone belief about how we obtained the Bible in English; here he was also falsely saying that observations are a good reason to dismiss the Bible. And once again, he was confused in regard to the difference between a history book (historical science) and observations made in the present (observational science).

In a way, it was almost fitting for Mr. Nye to lash out one last time at God in this first rebuttal of his. After all, this is the *real* crux of the debate. It is a man (Mr. Nye) versus God and His Word. The Word of God comes with the authority of God Himself. And it is God's Word that will judge Mr. Nye, which is why it is so important for Mr. Nye to repent before that time of judgment (John 12:48;[75] Hebrews 4:12;[76] Acts 17:30[77]).

But this is the debate: man's word versus God's Word, and here Mr. Nye really affirmed his religious belief in man being the ultimate authority over God. But there is nothing greater than God (e.g., Job 40:2;[78] Hebrews 6:13[79]) so Mr. Nye has it back-to-front. Actually, Mr. Nye here demonstrated what the devil, through the use of a serpent,[80] offered Eve in the Garden:

> …you will be like God… (Genesis 3:5[81])

Because Adam sinned, our very nature is that we want to be our own "god"! We want to be "god"! And that's the heart of Mr. Nye, as demonstrated clearly in this and other statements he made, including his signa-

---

75. "He who rejects Me, and does not receive My words, has that which judges him — the word that I have spoken will judge him in the last day."
76. "For the word of God is living and powerful, and sharper than any two-edged sword, piercing even to the division of soul and spirit, and of joints and marrow, and is a discerner of the thoughts and intents of the heart."
77. "Truly, these times of ignorance God overlooked, but now commands all men everywhere to repent."
78. "Shall the one who contends with the Almighty correct Him? He who rebukes God, let him answer it."
79. "For when God made a promise to Abraham, because He could swear by no one greater, He swore by Himself."
80. B. Hodge, "Was Satan the Actual Serpent in the Garden of Eden?" Answers in Genesis, February 9, 2010, https://answersingenesis.org/angels-and-demons/satan/was-satan-the-actual-serpent-in-the-garden/; also found in B. Hodge, *The Fall of Satan* (Green Forest, AR: Master Books, 2011).
81. "For God knows that in the day you eat of it your eyes will be opened, and you will be like God, knowing good and evil."

tory in a copy of the Bible indicating that we should question everything specifically directed at the contents of the Bible! This same attack was used on Eve, and we are not to be led into sin by cleverly deceptive arguments (2 Corinthians 11:3,[82] 2:11[83]).

Ken Ham: second rebuttal

- Clarifications

Mr. Ham immediately clarified Mr. Nye's misconceptions about the wood encased in lava and that natural laws haven't changed — both of which were previously discussed in detail in this volume. So it was nice that Mr. Ham pointed this out publically at the debate.

Mr. Ham also clarified Mr. Nye's misstatements that what had been stated was "Ken Ham's model" or "Ken Ham's view." Mr. Ham pointed out that many scientists also hold to such a view. I would go further and say people have believed God's creation account for thousands of years, whether scientists, theologians, farmers, shepherds, kings, presidents, and so on. It is God's creation account as found in the pages of Scripture, not Mr. Ham's model. But Mr. Ham is standing on the shoulders of giants to repeat their same profession in biblical creation as revealed to us by the Creator Himself.

But take note of this. Mr. Nye still hadn't really dealt with the debate topic. He changed it to attack "Ken Ham's view," but never really addressed creation as a whole to see if it is a viable model of origins in today's scientific era. So with the major portion of the debate completed, Mr. Nye still hadn't bothered to deal with the debate topic. Sadly, he'd been more persistent at *ad hominem* arguments against Mr. Ham (attacking the personal position as opposed to the model).

- The Ultimate Proof

Then Mr. Ham stated:

> As I talked about, you know, I said we have the laws of logic, the uniformity of nature and that only makes sense within a biblical worldview anyway, of a creator God who set up

---

82. "But I fear, lest somehow, as the serpent deceived Eve by his craftiness, so your minds may be corrupted from the simplicity that is in Christ."
83. "Lest Satan should take advantage of us; for we are not ignorant of his devices."

those laws. And that's why we can do good experimental science because we assume those laws are true and that will be true tomorrow.

I've harped on this previously in the book, and Mr. Ham pointed this out for the second time. Mr. Nye must borrow from the Bible to make sense of logic, uniformity of science, and morality — but this undercuts his whole premise of debate. Mr. Ham recognized this, but Mr. Nye never addressed this point — either because he didn't want to address it, or he didn't really understand it. From this I echo that Mr. Nye lost the debate at this juncture because to even begin to make an argument against God and His Word, Mr. Nye must borrow from God and His Word! This is likened to a person arguing that books don't exist and then pointing to a book to make his case.

- Species and Kinds

Mr. Ham then moved to point out the error of Mr. Nye who made the same mistake that we find on secular websites — that species and kinds are the same thing. Mr. Ham said:

> I believe you're confusing terms in regard to species and kinds. Because we're not saying God created all those species, we're saying God created kinds, and we're not saying species got on the Ark; we're saying kinds. In fact we've had researchers working on what is a kind. For instance, there's a number of papers published on our website and elsewhere in the literature where, for instance, they look at dogs and they say, "Well, this dog breeds with this dog." And then another paper points out that this other dog breeds with this one; and this one dog over here breeds with this one and with this one, on down the line. And you can look at all the papers around the world and you can connect them all together and say, "That obviously represents one kind." In fact, as they have been doing that research they have predicted probably less than actually a thousand kinds were on Noah's Ark, which means just over 2,000 animals. And the average size of a land animal is not that big, so you know there was plenty of room on the Ark.

All I have to say is…amen. You can find out more information about this ongoing research into kinds in the *Answers Research Journal.*[84]

- One can't observe the past

Mr. Ham then spoke about tree rings, ice layers, and kangaroos' travel routes and pointed out the simple fact that events concerning them can't be observed as they involved happenings in the past. Now we have already discussed this in detail, outlining how Mr. Nye's misconception about these uniformitarian rates (growth layers, not yearly layers; storm layers as opposed to yearly layers, etc.) have led him to the wrong conclusion. Mr. Ham even pointed out the lost squadron example, thus documenting that ice layers can form quickly, which thoroughly debunks the "one layer of ice per year" model in Greenland (previously discussed).[85]

- Sharp teeth mean sharp teeth

Mr. Ham thoroughly rebutted Mr. Nye's claim that sharp teeth means meat eater, which Mr. Nye was concluding when he was discussing lions on the Ark (lions were actually a post-Flood species within the cat kind). After discussing a few creatures that have sharp teeth and yet have primarily or purely vegetarian diets (bears, fruit bats, and pandas), Mr. Ham said:

> So just because an animal has sharp teeth doesn't mean it is a meat eater; it means it has sharp teeth.

---

84. For example, the first article in the research can be found here: T. Hennigan, B. Hodge, G. Purdom, J. Lightner, "Determining Ark Kinds," *Answers Research Journal*, 4 (2011), pp. 195–201, https://answersingenesis.org/noahs-ark/determining-the-ark-kinds/.

85. Editors, "Deep Layers," Answers in Genesis, October 26, 2002, https://answersingenesis.org/evidence-against-evolution/deep-layers/.

This is exactly right. There are a lot of people with dull teeth, and they eat meat too! Even fish like the Pacu (likely part of the "Piranha kind") and *Tometes camunani,* a specific type of piranha, are vegetarian.[86] As pointed out previously to devastate Mr. Nye's case, there are also vegetarian lions.[87]

• Mr. Ham and Mr. Nye agree?

Yes, it is true. Mr. Ham acknowledged the catastrophism that caused Lake Missoula. Mr. Ham pointed this out, as it was worth commenting on! For more detail, I addressed this in Mr. Nye's 30-minute case.

•Brilliant technology in the past

Mr. Ham said:

> And again, in regard to historical science, why would you say Noah was unskilled? I mean, I didn't meet Noah, and neither did you. And you know, really, it's an evolutionary view of origins, I believe, because you're thinking in terms of people before us aren't as good as us. Hey, there are civilizations that existed in the past and we look at their technology and we can't even understand today how they did some of the things that they did.

I was glad that Mr. Ham took the time to comment on Mr. Nye's assertion that Noah was unskilled. This prejudicial conjecture may have gone unnoticed by many viewers of the debate.

But Mr. Ham put this together. It was based on the evolutionary assumption that many in the past were "primate-like" or "primitive"… that is, less intelligent. But Mr. Ham nailed the response here regarding Mr. Nye's false evolutionary assumptions being imposed on the Bible's historical people like Noah.

Mr. Ham then continued to discuss the incredible intelligence required for ancient technology and ships. There is a lot written on such

---

86. E. Mitchell, "Vegetarian Piranha's Teeth Point to Pre-Fall Perfection," News to Know, Answers in Genesis, October 31, 2013, https://answersingenesis.org/aquatic-animals/fish/vegetarian-piranhas-teeth-point-to-pre-fall-perfection/.
87. G. Purdom, "No Taste for Meat?" Answers in Genesis, March 30, 2009, https://answersingenesis.org/animal-behavior/what-animals-eat/no-taste-for-meat/.

technology of ancient cultures that time would not allow Mr. Ham to detail but that can be easily found through further research.[88]

- Distant Starlight

The final issue Mr. Ham got to selectively rebut was the issue of distant starlight. Having completed the extensive response to distant starlight in Mr. Nye's 30-minute case, Mr. Ham would not be afforded such time due to the constraints of the debate. Though his response was succinct, it got the point across. He rebutted with:

> And one last thing, concerning the speed of light, and that is, I'm sure you're aware of the horizon problem, and that is, from a Big Bang perspective, even the secularists have a problem of getting light and radiation out to the universe to be able to exchange with the rest of the universe to get that even microwave background radiation. On their model, 15 billion years or so, they can only get it about halfway, and that's why they have inflation theories. Which means everyone has a problem regarding the light issue, there's things people don't understand. And we have some models on our website by some of our scientists to help explain those sorts of things.

The *Horizon problem* (a light-travel time problem for Big Bang) is enough to "put out the fire" of attacks on a young universe by long agers trying to use distant starlight as an excuse. They basically have the same problem — but most people don't know this as the secularists by and large don't want them to know. But their problem, in my opinion, is much worse than that of the creationists since there is a God who can easily get light from created stars to earth just like He commanded in Genesis 1:15[89] — secularists have no answer except to make up a hypothesis by telling stories to attempt to overcome the issue.

Furthermore, we have models that suggest valid solutions to this problem, and Mr. Ham referred people to the *Answers in Genesis* website for details. But these models are also found in numerous books. For a concise

---

88. For the reader, there is a book that deals with some of this ancient technology called *The Genius of Ancient Man*, D. Landis, editor (Green Forest, AR: Master Books, 2012).
89. " 'And let them be for lights in the firmament of the heavens to give light on the earth'; and it was so."

summary of these models, see my response to Mr. Nye's 30-minute section on distant starlight earlier in this book.

Mr. Ham's rebuttal was concise and accurate, covering as many points as he could in the time allowed to respond to Mr. Nye's statements. This is what a rebuttal should be.

Bill Nye: second rebuttal

• Fundamental issues?

Mr. Nye began:

> Thank you, Mr. Ham, but I'm completely unsatisfied. You did not, in my view, address the fundamental questions.

I'm not sure what fundamental means to Mr. Nye, but first, Mr. Ham completely undercut the very reason Mr. Nye was on the stage. Mr. Nye had no reason to assume laws of logic, which are predicated on the Bible's truth — which makes debate possible — yet make no sense in the materialistic worldview of Mr. Nye. Regardless, Mr. Nye continued to use them without addressing this fundamental issue.

Not only that — Mr. Ham dealt very carefully with the debate topic and then made an affirmative statement concerning the debate question at the end of his presentation. Mr. Nye did not do this — he didn't specifically deal with the debate topic in a formal manner.

So what were the "fundamental questions" Mr. Nye claimed weren't addressed?

> 680,000 years of snow ice layers which require winter-summer cycle

But this isn't fundamental. Furthermore, this is merely an interpretation based on various assumptions on Mr. Nye's part. In truth, the layers are separated by different types of storm precipitations, not years (summer-winter cycles). I addressed this in detail earlier in the book.

But Mr. Ham addressed this issue in two ways. Mr. Nye obviously rejected what Mr. Ham stated and in this rebuttal, claimed such "fundamental questions" weren't addressed.

1. Mr. Ham clearly taught the difference between historical and ob-servational science, thus helping people understand that to say hundreds of thousands of years were required for ice layers to be laid down is an interpretation based on certain assumptions. Mr. Nye claims to be the "science guy," but it is Mr. Ham who truly understands the meaning of the word "science." Mr. Ham taught the audience how to think about this issue correctly.

2. Mr. Ham's use of the *Lost Squadron* (Mr. Ham didn't use the name but referred to the example) was sufficient to refute Mr. Nye's claim about these layers being winter-summer cycles. Mr. Ham clearly pointed out that ice layers have been observed to form fairly quickly. If Mr. Nye was unsatisfied, then he was going against an example where observa-tional science contradicted his statement that ice layers take a very long time to form.

What was another fundamental issue for Mr. Nye?

> Let's say you have 2,000 kinds instead of 7, that makes the problem even more extraordinary. Multiplying 11 by what's — by 3 and a half? We get to 35, 40 species every day that we don't see.

For the reader, when Mr. Nye said 7, he meant 7,000 kinds to contrast with the 2,000, so we can be forgiving here. Again Mr. Nye failed to un-derstand the issue of species versus kinds and the animals that needed to be on the Ark. And he was confusing what we observe (re: species) in the post-Flood world versus the kinds that existed in the pre-Flood world. Again, Mr. Nye's misunderstanding (or non-understanding) of the bibli-cal creation model caused him to make very erroneous statements.

It is not 35–40 species of land-dwelling, air-breathing animals per day. Mr. Nye failed to realize the limits of the animals that needed to be on the Ark by the biblical constraints — it was only two of each KIND (seven of the clean). As stated earlier, research is predicting that probably only around 1,000 animal kinds were needed on the Ark.

But interestingly, we have 36 wild species of cats still living today.[90] This doesn't include domestic or extinct cat species. We also have 34 species of dog (Canidae). But Mr. Nye won't understand this at all until

---

90. Editors, "Feline Species Information," The Cat House, Exotic Feline Breeding Com-pound's Feline Conservation Center, http://www.cathouse-fcc.org/species.html, accessed July 6, 2014.

he understands that only kinds were represented on the Ark and species (variations within that kind) of those kinds formed after the Flood.

- Noah had superpowers?

Mr. Nye then went on to be critical of Noah by saying:

> Then as far as Noah being an extraordinary shipwright, I'm very skeptical. The shipwrights, my ancestors, the Nye family in New England, spent their whole life learning to make ships. I mean, it's very reasonable perhaps to you that Noah had super-powers and was able to build this extraordinary craft with seven family members. But to me it's just not reasonable.

Interestingly, my ancestors were shipwrights as well. They built a wooden boat that was 300 by 50 by 30 cubits, and it survived a global Flood. So I'm skeptical of Mr. Nye's skepticism. To deny that Noah was an extraordinary shipwright, Mr. Nye needs a better answer than his opinion.

I find it fascinating that Mr. Nye would appeal to people who spent *decades* learning to make ships and thinks this is a legitimate comparison to someone who may have known about ship making for *centuries*. What was Noah doing for the first 500 years of his life? How does Mr. Nye know he wasn't involved in ship making? Mr. Nye's conjecture is thus meaningless.

The fact is that Noah could have been learning about ship making, at the very least, for the amount of time that modern ship builders live their entire lives. And as Mr. Ham pointed out, Noah could have been highly intelligent — much more intelligent than us today. In fact, I marvel at the intelligence of those who built the pyramids [or the stonework of Cusco by the Incas (e.g., Saksaywaman)]. Could Mr. Nye design and build a pyramid as the Egyptians did? I don't think anyone completely understands how they accomplished this!

- Not reasonable?

Just because Mr. Nye thinks something is "not reasonable" means nothing. It is a *mere opinion,* and *mere opinions* carry no weight in a debate or argumentation in general. I'm not sure if the readers fully understand this in today's culture, so allow me to elaborate.

In philosophy, an opinion isn't worth two cents. But in our culture, which has become very much a *humanistic* enterprise, where man's opinions are seen as "god-like," people mistakenly think that their opinions mean something. But in debate and argumentation they mean *nil or nada.*

Sadly, many people entertain debates and throw out their opinions as though they are "the end" of the argument — that their word is the absolute authority. But this is actually quite embarrassing to the trained debater as well as to someone who has learned a little logic and philosophy. Let me give you a hypothetical example of someone trying to use his or her "opinion" as though it means something.

> Math teacher: "2 + 2 = 4."
>
> Bobby Joe: "But that is simply not reasonable."
>
> Math teacher: "Why would you say that?"
>
> Bobby Joe: "Well, my ancestors were math teachers, and they studied math all their lives, so I know that '2 + 2 = 4' is an outrageous claim."
>
> Math teacher: "But there have been hosts of people over the years going back to ancient cultures that wrote that '2 + 2 = 4.' We even find it in books today."
>
> Bobby Joe: "I simply don't have that kind of blind faith to think that someone made up this claim that '2 + 2 = 4' years ago, and after years of oral tradition and translations, how could this possibly be accurate? It's like the game of telephone."
>
> Math teacher: "But we use this principle today and it makes sense."
>
> Bobby Joe: "I'm still not convinced and will remain skeptical."

Opinions and conjectures like this are meaningless in a debate and only "muddy the waters." An opinion is a result of someone stating what they believe, but that's all it is — their belief. We already know that Mr. Nye doesn't believe God's Word. So having him tell us he doesn't think the Bible is reasonable didn't help his case. He was merely appealing to his own authority to say something couldn't be the case, simply because he believed it couldn't be the case.

• Provability

Mr. Nye said:

> Then, by the way, the fundamental thing we disagree on, Mr.
> Ham, is this nature of what you can prove to yourself.

This was a very revealing statement by Mr. Nye. If Mr. Nye really believes that the issue is the "nature of what you can prove to yourself," then it doesn't matter what anyone else says or believes, *including* Mr. Nye. By citing this philosophy, Mr. Nye just destroyed everything he had been trying to argue for (on the basis of what he believes) because it doesn't matter — and that's by his own admission.

What matters, as Mr. Nye said, is one's own provability to oneself. Therefore Mr. Ham need not use anything from Mr. Nye to prove something to himself if he doesn't want to; for that matter, no one else needs to bother with anything Mr. Nye says because those things need not play a factor for one's own provability to oneself — by Mr. Nye's own profession.

The point is that Mr. Nye is being contradictory. Yet strangely in the context of proving, Mr. Nye openly appeals to assumptions (guesses) about issues he has already made declaratory statements about:

1. Radiometric dating
2. The origin of the universe
3. Rates of change in the past in genetics
4. Previous experience

Assumptions are not proof. But "provability" and "proving" something is not tangible or material. So again, Mr. Nye's naturalistic religion doesn't really allow for provability! Christians have a basis for such things since we are made in the image of a God who can prove and reprove (e.g., Proverb 30:6[91]).

-   Natural law changes…again?

I was surprised to hear Mr. Nye reiterate a claim that Mr. Ham had just refuted in the debate. It was as if he hadn't paid any attention to the rebuttal that he was supposed to disprove. It is possible that he cleverly tried to sneak this past the audience, but it needs to be called out. The claim was that Mr. Ham believed that natural laws changed. Mr. Ham

---

91. "Do not add to His words, lest He rebuke you, and you will be found a liar."

made clear he did not believe this, yet Mr. Nye again reiterated his false position:

> So next time you have a chance to speak, I encourage you to explain to us why we should accept your word for it, that natural law changed just 4,000 years ago, completely, and there's no record of it.... And it's just not reasonable to me that everything changed 4,000 years ago. By everything I mean the species, the surface of the earth, the stars in the sky, and the relationship of all the other living things on earth to humans. It's just not reasonable to me that everything changed like that.

A point of clarification: The event of creation, according to Biblical chronology, was around 6,000 years ago. The Flood in Noah's day was around 4,300 years ago.

Mr. Ham had stated:

> And I would also say that natural law hasn't changed.

Yet, Mr. Nye persisted. Mr. Nye continued to believe this straw man fallacy that he had set up. Furthermore, Mr. Ham had already addressed it, but strangely, Mr. Nye seemed to believe he hadn't. I also addressed this in this book, specifically in Mr. Nye's opening, 30-minute case, and again in the first 5-minute rebuttal.

Natural law was put into place during creation week. It is God who upholds the laws of nature in a particular fashion, and yet God is not bound to these laws by any means since He is the Lord over them.[92]

Mr. Ham has no problem with laws of nature remaining constant as God set up, but he also recognizes that God is above His own laws so can perform miracles[93] (such as raising Lazarus from the dead). Mr. Nye seems fixed on believing that the event of a global Flood equates to the natural law being changed.

Now when God created, He also created the laws that enable this universe to function — and those laws continue. Mr. Nye can't account

92. B. Hodge, "A Rock So Big…," Answers in Genesis, September 26, 2008, https://answersingenesis.org/who-is-god/a-rock-so-big/.
93. Some miracles may clearly defy the laws of nature but some miracles are due to timing and some may well be *within* the laws of nature that God knew how to operate within. We simply do not know all the laws of nature.

for those laws in his naturalistic religion, as stated many times in this book.

Now we don't know how God initiated the Flood, but believing in a global Flood and all the consequences that flow from that, is (except for the extent of it) no different in a sense than believing in a local flood and seeing the consequences of such a local catastrophe.

Now maybe God supernaturally causing the Flood to occur is what Mr. Nye was referring to in regard to natural law supposedly changing. But God can (and does at times) override the natural laws He set up — but that doesn't mean natural law has changed! The laws continue (the uniformity of nature) unchanged even if God has intervened (as He can do because He set up those laws) to accomplish His purposes!

So Mr. Nye set up a false belief that Mr. Ham doesn't believe and then tried to tear that false belief down. This type of fallacy (straw man fallacy) is very common with skeptics.

- Pyramids and human populations before 4,000 years ago?

Mr. Nye, when discussing his errant understanding of the creationists' view of natural law (changing 4,000 years ago), asserted:

> You know, there are pyramids that are older than that. There are — there are human populations that are far older than that with traditions that go back farther than that.

We do need to acknowledge that dates not based on the chronology in the Bible are fallible (e.g., Mesopotamian dating or the unrevised Egyptian dating). Archeologists use a variety of methods to try to date ancient cultures — but all those methods are based on fallible assumptions, as is true of any dating method.

There are secular dates for civilizations that date back beyond the 2,350 BC date (4,350 years go) of the Flood (Babel occurred about 4,250 years ago). Just because man's fallible dating methods date civilizations back beyond the date of the Flood doesn't mean the Bible is wrong. Biblical creationists would say the secular dates are wrong because the assumptions used for the calculations are fallible.[94] Once

---

94. For more detail on these subjects, I suggest these books: B. Hodge, *The Tower of Babel* (Green Forest, AR: Master Books, 2013); D. Down and J. Ashton, *Unwrapping the Pharaohs* (Green Forest, AR: Master Books, 2006).

again, Bill Nye was not recognizing historical science when it comes to dating methods.

When I hear someone claim that the pyramids are older than the Flood, I often chuckle to myself. Here is why. The pyramids are Egyptian — built by order of the Egyptians. The Hebrew word for Egypt is *Mizraim,* and we translate it as "Egypt" (e.g., Genesis 12:10[95]). Egypt comes from the Greek form Ægyptus/Aegyptus (that is, *Aiguptos*; e.g., Matthew 2:13[96]). The point is that for the pyramids to exist, Egypt had to exist.

Here is where it gets interesting! Mizraim (Ægyptus/Aegyptus) was Noah's grandson (Genesis 10:6[97]). The nation of Egypt, or Mizraim, couldn't have existed until Noah's grandson was born and old enough to have a family, and after Babel when he was scattered from Babel to his new homeland that became known as Mizraim or Egypt. *Then* the pyramids were built.

So when someone says they dated the pyramids to be older than the Flood, the dating method is significantly off. To relate this to a modern example — if someone said they dated the Constitution of the United States to well before the first settlers came to the Americas from Europe...would you believe the dating method? Surely not!

• Deeply religious people

Mr. Nye began:

> And another thing I would very much appreciate you addressing: There are billions of people in the world who are deeply religious, and I respect that. People get tremendous community and comfort and nurture and support from their religious fellows in their communities, in their faiths...

It was necessary for me to cut Mr. Nye off to reveal something that is so obvious, I couldn't help but comment. Mr. Nye is deeply religious. Let me repeat that. Mr. Nye is *deeply religious.*

---

95. "Now there was a famine in the land, and Abram went down to Egypt [Mizraim] to dwell there, for the famine was severe in the land."
96. "Now when they had departed, behold, an angel of the Lord appeared to Joseph in a dream, saying, 'Arise, take the young Child and His mother, flee to Egypt [Ægyptus], and stay there until I bring you word; for Herod will seek the young Child to destroy Him.'"
97. "The sons of Ham were Cush, Mizraim, Put, and Canaan."

He too gets comfort from his humanistic religious convictions. He too has other people within his community of humanistic believers who comfort and nurture and support him. He is not without religion. This book should have made that clear. But it sounds as though Mr. Nye doesn't want people to know that his materialistic worldview is in that category (i.e., trying to act like an outside neutral observer); nonetheless, it should be obvious to people from all that he has stated.

- What about Christians who give up the Bible's origins account and side with humanism?

Mr. Nye made the point that there are Christians who do not side with biblical creation, a point Mr. Ham also discussed. Mr. Nye claimed:

> …yet they don't accept your point of view. There are Christians who don't accept that the earth could somehow be this extraordinarily young age because of all of the evidence around them. And so, what is to become of them in your view?

Let me reiterate something. Just because someone has the *opinion* that God is wrong in Genesis 1–11 and requires reinterpretation, that doesn't make it so. There are certain people who deny the holocaust (like some neo-Nazis), but does that mean that this should be a legitimate view among all people? By no means. There are a lot of evolutionists who are racist, but does that mean that Mr. Nye must say that racism is a legitimate position? By no means!

The fact is that if Christians have reinterpreted or denied Genesis to allow man's ideas to supersede the Word as written, then they are acting like humanists on this point. They are mixing two different religions — man's word and God's Word. How did God view the Israelites when they mixed their godly worship with the Baal worship in the Old Testament? The Lord was not pleased and often judged them severely (e.g., 2 Kings 22:17[98]).

The issue is between God and these people who deny what God plainly said. As Mr. Ham has stated in his lectures over and over again, it's an issue of authority. Who is the ultimate authority — God or man? If one takes man's beliefs about the past (man's historical science) and

---

98. "Because they have forsaken Me and have burned incense to other gods, that they might provoke Me to anger with all the work of their hands. Therefore My wrath shall be aroused against this place and shall not be quenched."

uses them to reinterpret God's record about the past (God's historical science), then that means God's Word is fallible — but man's word is infallible! The truth is, it's the other way around!

Sadly, such undermining of biblical authority, beginning in Genesis, is what has greatly weakened the church in this era of history and been a major contributing factor to many young people leaving the church by the time they reach college age. I would urge you to read Mr. Ham's two books that cover this topic in detail: *The Lie*[99] and *Already Gone.*[100]

Our hope is that they would repent of such beliefs, return to the clear teachings in the book of Genesis, and believe them as many other authors of the Bible certainly did.[101] Even I was influenced by long ages at one time, and I needed to get back to what God said instead of putting the fallible ideas of sinful men above the infallible Word of God. I discussed this earlier in the analysis of Mr. Ham's first 5-minute rebuttal.

In Mr. Ham's second rebuttal, he actually dealt with the situation in a bit more detail in discussing the issue of death (which I detailed earlier). As Mr. Ham explained, for those Christians who allow for evolution and/or millions of years, they are forcing a position on Scripture that necessitates death, bloodshed, carnivory, disease, and thorns being in existence millions of years before man — before sin! Such compromise blames God for death and suffering and undermines the Gospel and the authority of God's Word.

- Should the Old Testament be disconnected from the New Testament?

Now, Mr. Nye is not a theologian, and he admitted this. But he went on to say something peculiar:

> And by the way, this thing started, as I understand it, Ken Ham's creation model is based on the Old Testament. So when you bring in — I'm not a theologian — when you bring in the New Testament, isn't that a little out of the box?

99. K. Ham, *The Lie: Evolution/Millions of Years*, 25th Anniversary Edition (Green Forest, AR: Master Books, 2012).

100. K. Ham, B. Beemer, with T. Hillard, *Already Gone* (Green Forest, AR: Master Books, 2009).

101. T. Mortenson, "Did Bible Authors Believe in a Literal Genesis?" in K. Ham, *The New Answers Book 3* (Green Forest, AR: Master Books, 2010), pp. 81–90.

From this, I can tell Mr. Nye knows little of the Bible — and he's right in saying he is not a theologian. From Genesis to Revelation, the Bible, for those who do not know, is about Christ and the saving Gospel. The Bible is God's revelation to tell us who we are, where we came from, what our problem is, and what the solution to our problem is in Jesus Christ. God's Son became a man (Jesus Christ the God-man), to save us from our own sin and the consequences of eternal separation from God's goodness where we would have the wrath of God upon us for all eternity (Hell). He died in our place and rose again. Furthermore, Christ is the Creator. He is the One who created all things in six days as recorded in His Word (see Appendix C).

The Old Testament and the New Testament are about Christ, who is the second member of the one Triune God (Father, Son, and Holy Spirit). There are not multiple gods, but one God eternally existing in three persons. As an analogy, think of an equilateral triangle, which has three identical points; each point makes up the other two points and yet there is one triangle. Or for the science buffs, think of the triple point of water being solid, liquid, and gas all at the same time at a particular temperature and pressure. Of course, no analogy is perfect, but these should give you an idea. See Appendix C for more on the triune God as derived *from* the Bible.

The point is that the message of salvation in the Bible begins in Genesis, with the whole of Scripture (Old and New Testament) giving details so we can understand who God is, who we are, the meaning of sin, and the means by which we can be saved. And the whole Bible is about the Creator, Jesus Christ, our Lord ("For by Him all things were created that are in heaven and that are on earth, visible and invisible, whether thrones or dominions or principalities or powers. All things were created through Him and for Him" Colossians 1:16). The Old and New Testaments are inextricably linked together.

Consider this powerful New Testament passage about creation in the context of the first marriage between Adam and Eve:

> But from the beginning of the creation, God "made them male and female." (Mark 10:6)

Jesus Christ, who made this statement, affirms that man and woman came at the beginning of creation, not billions of years later. Day 6 of creation week is clearly the beginning, considering that Jesus made this statement about 2,000 years ago (about 4,000 years after day 6 of Creation).[102]

In Matthew 19, Jesus quotes from Genesis chapters 1 and 2 to give the foundation for marriage (one man for one woman for life). In actual fact, every single doctrine of theology is directly or indirectly founded in Genesis. Now many secularists (and I highly suspect this is true of Mr. Bill Nye) misunderstand the nature of the civil laws, sacrificial laws, ceremonial laws, etc. given to the Israelites as a nation in regard to how Christians should act today.

We certainly don't sacrifice animals today for sin because this was a foreshadowing of what was to come in Christ. Embodied in many of the laws given to the Israelites was the importance of keeping separate from the pagan nations so they wouldn't compromise God's Word. All of this is another topic, but let me say here that most secularists just do not understand the nature of the Old Testament, the nation of Israel, and the church — and I do recognize there are differences in the way Christians approach these topics.[103] Nonetheless, we would all agree that there was much foreshadowing of Christ in the Old Testament that many secularists fail to understand.

- Science is "guesses" per Mr. Nye?

Mr. Nye elaborated on the nature of science in a way that surprised me. He asserted:

> I'm looking for explanations of the creation of the world as we know it based on what I'm going to call science, not historical science, not observational science — science. Things that each of us can do, akin to what we do, we're trying to outguess the characters on murder mystery shows, on crime scene investigation, especially....For us in the scientific community I remind you that when we find an idea that's not tenable, that doesn't work,

102. T. Mortenson, "But from the Beginning of...the Institution of Marriage?" Answers in Genesis, November, 1, 2004, https://answersingenesis.org/family/marriage/but-from-the-beginning-of-the-institution-of-marriage/.

103. For a brief understanding of how Christians vary on these subjects (for example Old Testament Law) please see B. Hodge, "Why Don't Christians Follow all the Old Testament Laws?" in *Demolishing Supposed Bible Contradictions*, Volume 2, K. Ham, B. Hodge, T. Chaffey, eds. (Green Forest, AR: Master Books, 2012), pp. 161–165.

that doesn't fly, doesn't hold water, whatever idiom you'd like to embrace, we throw it away, we're delighted.

There are a few glaring issue here.

I submit that Mr. Nye's statement, "What I'm going to call science, not historical science, not observational science — science," is really an admission that he is using the one word, "science," for both observational and historical science. This is exactly what Mr. Ham said secularists are doing (in the state schools, for instance) to indoctrinate generations of people in the evolutionary belief system.

Now Mr. Nye seemed to be implying that science is based on "out-guessing." First, I'm surprised he used the example of a murder mystery to discuss "science." For starters, investigating a murder involves both historical and observational science. Actually, it's akin to the origins issue. Something happened in the past, and yet we have evidence we observe in the present (not having actually observed the event of the past). Thus, we are trying to interpret the past.

Now if we had someone who was there who saw it happen and who doesn't tell a lie, then we would know what happened. We could then test our observations of the present to see if they confirmed the account of the past. Now creationists have a revelation from Someone who doesn't tell a lie (Titus 1:2[104]) and who has told us the big events of history (Creation, Fall, Flood, Tower of Babel, etc.). Our observations in the present confirm God's account of history.

Now evolutionists have a story about the past to try to explain the evidence — but observations in the present do not confirm their story about the past. They weren't there and have no authority who was, so they have to guess what happened. What Mr. Nye believes is such a guess. He has already ruled out God's Word as a possible explanation and God as a witness — so he is left with fallible man's stories about the past. As a forensic investigator, Mr. Nye has already decided that God did not do it (God did not create, for instance), and he sets out to try to prove the conclusion he started with.

You see, ultimately, all evidence is circumstantial and must be interpreted. And one's interpretation depends upon one's starting point — God's Word or man's word.

---

104. "In hope of eternal life which God, who cannot lie, promised before time began."

It is true that Mr. Nye is involved in attempts at "outguessing," — but biblical creationists are not because they don't have to guess! They already have a revelation from the One in whom are "all the treasures of wisdom and knowledge" (Colossians 2:3[105]).

Now with a murder mystery, all you have to do is watch the show and find out who the murderer was (or read the end of the book and you'll find out) because the author of the show or book knew it all along.

Yet Mr. Nye refused to even acknowledge the Book by God, the Author of creation. He already assumed no God to argue for a no-God scenario, which is begging the question.

But take note of Mr. Nye's statement closely, "I'm looking for explanations of the ***creation of the world***" (emphasis added). Rarely do we hear an evolutionist say things were created! Even in an evolutionary scenario, they do believe things were created. They just claim that it created itself (e.g., the Big Bang, where no God is required) or that somehow matter simply came into existence on its own, etc. So in reality they could be dubbed *atheistic creationists*, if we wanted to use that term. Mr. Nye seemed to be saying the universe was *created* by natural processes!

But Mr. Nye then proclaimed something that is simply not true. He said, "We find an idea that's not tenable, that doesn't work, that doesn't fly, doesn't hold water, whatever idiom you'd like to embrace, we throw it away, we're delighted." But Mr. Nye's own words prove him guilty of not doing what he said he would do! For example, science is observable and repeatable and yet, these things are not observable and repeatable:

1. No one has been able to observe or repeat the making of life from nonlife (matter giving rise to life or chemical evolution). Yet Mr. Nye still claims that somehow life came from nonlife even though we all accept the law of biogenesis that states that life can only come from life.

2. No one has been able to observe or repeat the changing of a single-celled life-form like an amoeba into a cow or goat over billions of years (biological evolution). Now Mr. Nye does try (unsuccessfully) to fit various fossil finds into his biological evolutionary story — but he has never demonstrated how one

---

105. "In whom are hidden all the treasures of wisdom and knowledge."

kind of creature can change into a different kind! Yes, he can document that different species can form — but they are only variant species[106] within a particular kind. Yet he continues to hold that biological evolution is true.

3. No one has been able to observe or repeat the Big Bang (astronomical evolution). Now he (like other evolutionists) points to supposed evidence of the Big Bang — but no one has actually observed it. More and more secular scientists reject the Big Bang — yet Mr. Nye continues to adhere to it.

4. No one has observed millions of years of time progressing in geological layers (geological evolution). Mr. Nye did not observe the layers of sedimentary rock being deposited at the Grand Canyon. He did not observe labels on them stating their age as millions of years old. Yet he continues to hold onto the belief that they were laid down over millions of years — the same could be said of ice layers too!

Are evolutionists delighted to throw these unscientific concepts away? By no means — these tenets are crucial to their denial of God and His Word. So there is a double standard in Mr. Nye's viewpoint here.

And once again, as I keep emphasizing (and need to, as this is a major point the secularists just don't want to admit), it all involves understanding the difference between what one actually observes in the present (observational science) compared to one's interpretation of the past in regard to origins (which dives into historical science). This is the difference between observing the layers of sedimentary rock at the Grand Canyon and interpreting them in regard to how and when they formed.

If the secularists were to clearly teach the difference between observation and interpretation like this to students in schools, they would quickly realize that evolution (whether biological, geological, astronomical, or anthropological) is a belief — really, a religion to explain life and the universe without God. The secularists don't want students to know this, so to indoctrinate them in their religion of humanism with its aspects of naturalism (materialism), they brainwash and intimidate using the word "science."

---

106. Species within a kind is somewhat arbitrary, but this goes back to the whole species problem that we already discussed.

- Is Mr. Nye willing to give up his naturalistic religion?

Mr. Nye challenged:

> That's why I say, if you can find a fossil that has swum between the layers, bring it on. You would change the world. If could you show that somehow the microwave background radiation is not a result of the Big Bang, come on, write your paper, tear it up.

There are plenty of fossils found in a layer in the geologic record, then not seen again until a higher layer. For example, simply look at the fragmentary nature of the dinosaur record. I mentioned some specific instances that are referenced in the 30-minute case by Mr. Nye.

But I'm shocked that Mr. Nye doesn't know the standard evolutionary responses to these *out-of-place* fossils such as "the fossil record is just fragmentary" or "the creature was living all through those periods but we just don't have a record of it."

But *out-of-place* fossils are actually quite common. The Smithsonian documented a bear and human (they couched it as "simian") print in Permian rock that supposedly predates dinosaurs.[107] There are footprints of land creatures before Mr. Nye's beloved Tiktaalik (mentioned earlier in the debate), which is interpreted by evolutionists to be the first walker.[108] In fact, books have been written about such out-of-place fossils — including the "living fossils" (plants or animals living today that are found in the fossil record purportedly existing millions of years ago).[109]

And again, regarding the cosmic microwave background (CMB), creationists have discussed this extensively in the past, but here is the reference to the latest by astronomer Dr. Danny Faulkner (see Faulkner, D., "Comments on the Cosmic Microwave Background," *Answers Research Journal*, 7 (March 19, 2014) pp. 83–90, https://

---

107. D. Stewart, "Petrified Footprints: A Puzzle Parade of Permian Beasts," *Smithsonian Magazine*, 23, no. 4 (July 1992): pp. 71–79.

108. J. Bryner, "Four-legged Creature's Footprints Force Evolution Rethink," Live Science Website, January 6, 2010, www.livescience.com/animals/100106-tetrapod-footprints.html.

109. C. Werner, *Evolution: The Grand Experiment*, Volume 2, Living Fossils (Green Forest, AR: New Leaf Press, 2008); J. Whitmore, "What about Living Fossils?" in K. Ham, gen. ed. *The New Answers, Book 4* (Green Forest, AR: Master Books, 2013), pp. 143–150.

answersingenesis.org/astronomy/cosmology/comments-on-the-cosmic-microwave-background/). Would Mr. Nye be willing to give these two things up? His answer would be no — but to understand his answer, one has to understand that anything involving historical science (beliefs about the past), means one can't absolutely in an empirical sense prove those things!

When it involves historical science, one can always come up with a story (no matter how complex or unrealistic) to try to give a different explanation. You see, when it comes to origins, we can't prove to Mr. Nye via empirical observations the verity of God's Word concerning creation, the Fall, the Flood, or the Tower of Babel — just like we can't prove by empirical observation the verity of the resurrection.

When it comes to origins, there is a faith aspect. And only one faith (biblical Christianity) makes provability possible. Furthermore, biblical creationists would say Mr. Nye has a blind faith (a subjective faith) because observational science does not confirm his worldview, nor would provability be possible in his religion — this must be borrowed from a Christian worldview. But creationists have a basis for truth and provability in God's Word and our objective faith is repeatedly confirmed by observational science — as Mr. Ham stated clearly.

> But without faith it is impossible to please Him, for he who comes to God must believe that He is, and that He is a rewarder of those who diligently seek Him (Hebrews 11:6).

> For by grace you have been saved through faith, and that not of yourselves; it is the gift of God (Ephesians 2:8).

• Again attacking the Bible

For being a professed agnostic, Mr. Nye sure doesn't act like it. Agnostics, by the very nature of their religion, *can't know* if the Bible is true or not. Yet Mr. Nye seemed to attack it like a *new atheist* (*new atheists* are very aggressive in trying to impose their view on others!) when he, once again, remarked:

> So your view that we're supposed to take your word for this book written centuries ago, translated into American English, is

somehow more important than what I can see with my own eyes is an extraordinary claim.

But Mr. Ham, or any other creationist, isn't asking anyone to take *our word for it* that God's Word is true. We recognize that that would simply be an opinion, and random opinions carry no weight in a debate.

Instead, God is the one commanding all people to repent and return to Him and His Word (e.g., Acts 3:17–19,[110] Acts 17:30;[111] 2 Peter 3:9[112]). So the issue has nothing to do with us or Mr. Ham but is an issue between all people and God. God's Word itself claims that it is the God-breathed (2 Timothy 3:16–17[113]) Word of God.

Since the Bible really is the infallible Word of God, it would behoove Mr. Nye to check it out carefully as Mr. Ham challenged him to. But Mr. Nye's many erroneous statements show that he has not checked it out carefully at all! Mr. Nye is at this time totally committed to his belief that the Bible is not true and God does not exist. We pray that God, through His Word, will open Mr. Nye's heart to the truth of His Word and the saving Gospel:

> So then faith *comes* by hearing, and hearing by the word of God (Romans 10:17).

> That if you confess with your mouth the Lord Jesus and believe in your heart that God has raised Him from the dead, you will be saved (Romans 10:9).

Mr. Nye really believes that what he can see with his own finite eyes is better than what God sees. Yet many things that Mr. Nye professes to believe in, he cannot see. For example, Mr. Nye has not observed the changing of a single-celled organism like an amoeba into a multicelled

---

110. "Yet now, brethren, I know that you did it in ignorance, as did also your rulers. But those things which God foretold by the mouth of all His prophets, that the Christ would suffer, He has thus fulfilled. Repent therefore and be converted, that your sins may be blotted out, so that times of refreshing may come from the presence of the Lord."

111. "Truly, these times of ignorance God overlooked, but now commands all men everywhere to repent."

112. "The Lord is not slack concerning His promise, as some count slackness, but is longsuffering toward us, not willing that any should perish but that all should come to repentance."

113. "All Scripture is given by inspiration of God, and is profitable for doctrine, for reproof, for correction, for instruction in righteousness, that the man of God may be complete, thoroughly equipped for every good work."

creature and eventually into fish, amphibians, reptiles, mammals, and then humans. Mr. Nye has not observed millions of years — he did not observe the layers of the Grand Canyon being laid down. Mr. Nye has not observed life from nonlife by natural processes millions of years ago. Mr. Nye has not observed the Big Bang.

But there is a Book (the Bible)…that Mr. Nye *can* see with his own eyes, but he doesn't believe that. This is a double standard. By the way, the "most quoted from" or "referred-to phrase" from the debate from what I've seen and heard is when Mr. Ham challenged Mr. Nye in regard to the origin of matter by saying to him that "there is a Book" referring to the Bible of course.

- Why should Mr. Nye care about the future?

The hero in an evolutionary worldview is death. In fact, an evolutionary understanding of all things can be summed up as: *we accidentally exist after we evolved from nothing that exploded, and one day soon, we are all going to be dead and won't know we ever existed — we will cease to be.* This is evolution in a nutshell. It's depressing, isn't it? That's why Mr. Ham asked Bill why he loved the "joy of discovery" when one day he won't even know he thought about it after he dies. From his perspective, he will just cease to exist! So what is the point of Bill Nye debating these issues anyway — from his perspective, why care about it? Ultimately, why does it matter at all?

An evolutionist who really believes this should eat, drink, and be merry, for tomorrow he will die, and his consciousness will go into nothingness. In an evolutionary frame of belief, there should be no cares about tomorrow. After all, it is not like there would be a "god" out there who cares, so why should anyone else? And yet, Mr. Nye summed up the rebuttal time with an appeal to the online viewers about caring about the future. He said:

> And for those watching online especially, I want to remind you that we need scientists and especially engineers for the future. Engineers use science to solve problems and make things. We need these people so that the United States can continue to innovate and continue to be a world leader. We need innovation and that needs science education.

This is inconsistent with his religion's basic understanding of existence. It is as if Mr. Nye cares about the future and specifically cares that a particular group of people be dominant on the earth — that is the US. Perhaps he is applying "survival of the fittest" to nations, which is what Adolf Hitler tried to do with his extreme evolutionary nationalism.

But why does one need to innovate in a religion that doesn't care? Why care about scientific investigation if tomorrow you will die? Why care about the US being a world leader if you are rotting in your grave and no longer exist as a consciousness? These things make no sense in Mr. Nye's professed humanistic and materialistic religion.

But caring is a biblical principle from the early pages of the Bible where we are told that we were made in the image of God. People have value because they are not just creatures to be exterminated like mosquitoes but beings made in the image of God. It is good to innovate and be a leader in scientific technology in an effort to help one another (Christ's Golden Rule). Actually, it's all a part of the dominion mandate given to man through Adam in Genesis. So in one sense it is nice that Mr. Nye cares on these points, but by his own religion, it is purely inconsistent.

In reality, the reason Mr. Nye does care demonstrates that this comes down to a spiritual issue. Romans 1 makes it clear that those who reject creation are indeed without excuse. We are also told in this passage that those in rebellion against God will "suppress the truth in unrighteousness." Because God has made it obvious to everyone that He exists (Romans 1:19–20[114]) and because God's law is written on our hearts (Romans 2:15[115]), those in rebellion against God will do their best to suppress the truth.

Yes, Romans 1 is being demonstrated as we observe Mr. Nye (as other non-Christians) in his failed attempt to suppress the truth of God's Word and the Gospel of Jesus Christ. In summary, Mr. Nye's second rebuttal was a rebuttal of his own failed position.

---

114. "Because what may be known of God is manifest in them, for God has shown it to them. For since the creation of the world His invisible attributes are clearly seen, being understood by the things that are made, even His eternal power and Godhead, so that they are without excuse."

115. "Who show the work of the law written in their hearts, their conscience also bearing witness, and between themselves their thoughts accusing or else excusing them."

Part 5

Audience Questions
and Answers

Introduction

To recap, the debate entailed a 5-minute opening from both Mr. Ham and Mr. Nye. Then each debater had a 30-minute case and finished off with two 5-minute rebuttal times. In each case, Mr. Ham went first and Mr. Nye had the last word.

At this stage of the debate, things "shifted gears," so to speak. It was time for the moderator to take written questions from the audience. Each question was filled out on a card and turned in prior to the debate (so some of the questions may have been addressed in the debate itself). These cards were passed along to Mr. Tom Foreman, a well-respected and award-winning journalist for CNN who was the moderator of the event. He separated the questions into those to be addressed to the particular presenter. Then he selected the questions to be used in the debate. The moderator would ask a question of either Mr. Nye or Mr. Ham, giving them a 2-minute time limit to answer. The other presenter would then be given a 1-minute response.

Even though this section encompassed 45 minutes in total, it did go quickly in the live arena.

213

Question: How does creationism account for the celestial bodies — planets, stars, moons — moving further and further apart, and what function does that serve in the grand design?

Mr. Ham, 2-minute response:

Mr. Ham's response was excellent (see the transcript in Appendix A); he even used this response to share the Gospel of our Lord. Mr. Ham acknowledged that the universe is expanding and creationists have recognized this for quite some time. This is in no way a problem. Mr. Ham even mentioned that the Bible says God stretches out the heavens. Here are some passages affirming this:

- Job 9:8: He alone spreads out the heavens, and treads on the waves of the sea.

- Isaiah 40:22: It is He who sits above the circle of the earth, and its inhabitants are like grasshoppers, who stretches out the heavens like a curtain, and spreads them out like a tent to dwell in.

- Zechariah 12:1: The burden of the word of the LORD against Israel. Thus says the LORD, who stretches out the heavens, lays the foundation of the earth, and forms the spirit of man within him.

This fulfilled prediction is exactly what we expected to find in the heavens.

Mr. Nye, 1-minute response:

First, let's begin with what Mr. Nye concluded in his one-minute response. Mr. Nye ended with:

> And the big thing I want from you, Mr. Ham, is can you come up with something that you can predict? Do you have a creation model that predicts something that will happen in nature?

Well, Mr. Ham made it clear that the biblical model predicts that the heavens are being stretched out. Mr. Ham made a number of predictions based on the Bible and the biblical creation model throughout the debate, but Mr. Nye would never acknowledge this.

- Where did we come from?

Mr. Nye also said:

> There's a question that troubles us all from the time we are absolutely youngest and first able to think. And that is, where did we come from? Where did I come from? And this question is so compelling that we've invented the science of astronomy, we've invented life science, we've invented physics, we've discovered these natural laws so that we can learn more about our origin and where we came from.

Actually Mr. Nye has it back to front. It is because the great scientists and thinkers of the past who founded these branches of science believed in God and His Word that they developed these sciences to understand and study what God had created. For example, Johannes Kepler, a creationist, developed scientific astronomy. He stated that as he was conducting his research, he was just thinking God's thoughts after him.[1] In fact, Bible-believing Christians developed most fields of science.[2]

Today many secular scientists reject God, basing their research on the false assumption that the universe came into being by natural processes. They will not find the correct answers concerning the topic of origins because they have the wrong starting point. God's Word tells us where we came from. Mr. Nye is simply suppressing this (as we noted earlier when discussing Romans 1). Because of Mr. Nye's religion of evolutionary naturalism (i.e., humanism), he will never come to the right answer and will continue to be baffled about how life and the universe came to be. If he is prepared to question his starting point, then he may begin to see the universe in a whole different way. Really, because of our sinful natures, only the work of the Holy Spirit on our hearts can change our starting point.

The Bible tells us where we came from (yes, there is a Book, as Mr. Ham quoted in the next two questions!). Even little children can understand where we came from when the Bible's account is presented to them — perhaps the wise and learned should be humbled by this (e.g., Matthew 11:25[3]).

---

1. C. Dao, "Man of Science, Man of God: Johann Kepler," *Acts & Facts*, 37, no. 3 (2008): p. 8.
2. Editors, "Which Scientists of the Past Believed in a Creator?" in Creation Scientists and Other Biographies of Interest, Answers in Genesis, https://answersingenesis.org/Home/Area/bios/#pastsci.
3. "At that time Jesus answered and said, 'I thank You, Father, Lord of heaven and earth, that You have hidden these things from the wise and prudent and have revealed them to babes.'"

Question: How did the atoms that created the Big Bang get there?

Mr. Nye, 2-minute response:

Mr. Nye's response was baffling:

> This is the great mystery; you've hit the nail on the head. No, this is, so where did — what was before the Big Bang? This is what drives us; this is what we want to know, let's keep looking, let's keep searching.

His answer was basically "I don't know." In the Big Bang models, it is just storytelling that something somehow popped into existence from nothing and exploded. But why would that "drive" anyone?

Mr. Nye then switched to talk about the universe accelerating instead of concentrating on answering the specific question. And he proclaimed:

> And the universe isn't slowing down; it's accelerating. The universe is accelerating in its expansion. And do you know why? Nobody knows why. Nobody knows why.

Of course, the Bible says why, and it says who is doing it: God, *who alone stretches out the heavens (Job 9:8a)*. Then Mr. Nye made a claim that made me think, *How close you are*. Mr. Nye said:

> And then isn't it reasonable that whatever is out there causing the universe to expand is here also, and we just haven't figured out how to detect it.

The One who stretched out the heavens is God. He is here also. He loves us and wants us to repent of our sin and receive Him as Lord. He came and sought us out. He's given us a book with the relevant and sufficient information to understand our origins. Yet it seems as though Mr. Nye wants to be left alone without that loving God who has cared for him and been patient with him. Mr. Nye has failed to realize that the Creator Himself has answered the question of origins. Why not trust God?

Mr. Ham, 1-minute response:

At this stage, Mr. Ham made a statement that has become the quote of the debate. Mr. Ham responded:

Bill, I just want to let you know that there actually is a Book out there that actually tells us where matter came from.

"There… is a Book" has gone viral! You will find out why shortly. Of course, Mr. Ham doesn't buy into the Big Bang models. The answer for the origin of matter, time, space, and the like is easy for the biblical creationist to explain: it is by the power of an infinite Creator God. Mr. Ham's response was again excellent (see the transcript in Appendix A for the full answer).

Question: The overwhelming majority of people in the scientific community have presented valid physical evidence, such as carbon dating and fossils, to support evolutionary theory. What evidence besides the literal word of the Bible supports creationism?

Mr. Ham, 2-minute response:

Mr. Ham's response is broken into three parts:

1. The majority can be wrong
2. The evidence of making predictions in creation
3. Observational and historical science

It is true that the majority can be wrong and has been in the past, so that should not play a factor in the actual truth of a matter. So Mr. Ham was right on that.

But when asked about evidence supporting creation, he specifically used a couple of examples such as one race being a prediction of the creation model that was confirmed after subsequent genetics research. He also covered this briefly in his main presentation.

Mr. Ham's main presentation also covered the Bible's discussion about created kinds. On the basis of this statement about biology, Mr. Ham showed that the science of genetics confirmed created kinds with boundaries; that is, one kind will not change into a totally different kind. Then Mr. Ham transitioned into the discussion on historical versus observational science because to understand predictions based on the Bible, one needs to understand the difference between historical and observational (or operational) science.

- Nature of evidence (semi-technical)

I would like to make a note here about one aspect of this question that Mr. Ham did not have time to cover, as it does take some discussion to fully understand it. This concerns the nature of evidence.

The question was framed as *evidence* that "supports creationism," as if evidence holds the foundational role in the debate about a worldview (biblical creation). And remember, when discussing the topic of origins (creation/evolution), we are dealing with historical science — beliefs about the past to explain the evidence of the present.

Asking what evidence supports creation is in one sense back to front. Really, the question should be about how observational science in the present confirms the interpretation of the evidence based on the creation account in God's Word!

Let's apply this to something else to properly understand the issue: if a table supports a book on the table (that is sitting on the table), is it logical to ask how the book supports the table? Allow me to elaborate here.

There is a false stance that human logic is seen as the absolute standard, and then using that human logic we look at evidence and build worldviews like Christianity (with its aspects of creation). Hence, evidence is erroneously seen as supporting or *being foundational* to that worldview. But scientists never start with evidence — they always start with presuppositions coming from their worldview that determine how they interpret the evidence!

Our starting point (God's Word or man's word) is foundational to our worldview. Then logic is built on that worldview (if it makes sense to have logic in that worldview — which, as we discussed earlier, it does within the worldview based on the Word of the Creator God). *And then* based on that worldview and using the tool of logic, we look at evidence. It is actually more correct to say that the worldview is necessary to even look at the evidence. Evidence is then interpreted within that worldview.

You see, evidence has no mind; evidence neither confirms, denies, speaks, nor supports; rather, it is people, using their worldviews to look at evidence, who confirm, speak, and so on. So when biblical creationists like Mr. Ham look at evidence, they do so in light of God's Word (in light of a creationist worldview).

218

When a materialist, like Mr. Nye, looks at evidence, he begins with his worldview founded on naturalism, presumes logic exists in that worldview (which it can't since logic isn't material), and then tries to draw conclusions (which are also not material) about evidence.

But the evidence doesn't do the *supporting* or the *denying*, as it is people who try to make an argument using their attempted interpretation of the evidence to support or deny a worldview.

So it really is *back to front* to ask someone if there is evidence to support his or her worldview. The question to ask is which worldview makes sense of the evidence. In addition, observations in the present (using observational science such as the study of genetics) can be used to confirm or otherwise deny one's interpretation. Does God's Word make sense of the evidence? Absolutely!

Mr. Nye, 1-minute response:

- Louis Pasteur

Mr. Nye never addressed the question but instead discussed how people like Professor Louis Pasteur changed the world by offering a new understanding of things like germs. Actually, Pasteur was conducting great observational science concerning germs. And Pasteur's experiments did nothing to support evolution! In fact, the opposite is true — Pasteur's work confirmed creation!

Of course, we applaud Professor Pasteur — a young-earth creationist, by the way — for thinking biblically and opposing *abiogenesis* (life came about from matter by itself), which was a common idea in his day. Professor Pasteur was a contemporary of Mr. Darwin and opposed him even though many were gravitating toward Darwinistic thought that life came about by itself through natural processes. Bucking prevailing thought, Professor Pasteur sided with God's Word that God is the author of life; furthermore, he proved the law of biogenesis: life comes from life, not nonlife. For many years, school textbooks taught this law to students. Evolutionists, though, believe life arose from inanimate matter, which contradicts the law of biogenesis.

Now keep in mind that Mr. Nye claimed to approve of Professor Pasteur's work. However, Mr. Nye believes in abiogenesis for the origin of life (life came from matter accidentally) and so in practice, he really opposes Pasteur. This is a common problem among skeptics. They praise the achievements of great scientists of the past (e.g., Pasteur, Newton, Boyle) because they just can't ignore the incredible discoveries they made. Then, in actual practice, they deny what these great men stood for in regard to their position on origins! Today, evolutionists like Mr. Nye claim that biblical creationists can't be real scientists!

- Evolutionists applaud things that go against common thought… really?

Mr. Nye also pointed out that:

> No, if you find something that changes — that disagrees with common thought, that's the greatest thing going in science; we look forward to that change, we challenge you.

But creationists have been pointing out inconsistencies, fallible assumptions (arbitrariness), and many other issues and absurdities illustrating clearly that naturalism and molecules-to-man evolution just don't work to explain life. And yet, Mr. Nye won't even listen — he just brushes them off. That's because he is already committed to his religion of naturalism/humanism, so no matter what is pointed out, he has already decided not to accept it.

For instance, creationists have shown that the bulk of the rock layers containing fossils are explained on the basis of the global Flood of Noah's day. The evidence in the present is consistent with such an explanation and clearly does not support an interpretation based on slow gradual processes over millions of years.[4]

The idea of a global Flood is opposed on nearly every front by the secularists because that does away with the notion of millions of years (of uniformitarianism), which is crucial to the molecules-to-man evolution belief! One does not observe such evolution in the present. The secularists propose millions of years of time — an incomprehensible amount of time — to indoctrinate people into believing that the small changes we observe (e.g., adaptation, speciation) will lead to the big changes necessary for evolution. This is exactly what led evolutionist Dr. Per Bak to comment:

---

4. For example, see A. Snelling, *Earth's Catastrophic Past: Geology, Creation & the Flood*, Volume II, Section Vi and X (Dallas, TX: Institute for Creation Research, 2009).

Lyell's uniformitarian view appears perfectly logical. The laws of physics are generally expressed as smooth, continuous equations. Since these laws should describe everything, it is natural to expect that the phenomena that we observe should also vary in a smooth and gradual manner. An opposing philosophy, catastrophism, claims that changes take place mostly through sudden cataclysmic events. Since catastrophism smacks of creationism, it has been largely rejected by the scientific community, despite the fact that catastrophes actually take place.[5]

Actually, we could say that the belief in millions of years is really an unquestioned tenet of the secularists' religion. It's their proposed belief attempting to account for why we don't observe the evolutionary process in the molecules-to-man sense. As the American biochemist Dr. George Wald stated in 1954:

> Time is in fact the hero of the plot...What we regard as impossible on the basis of human experience is meaningless here. Given so much time, the "impossible" becomes possible, the possible probable, and the probable virtually certain. One has only to wait: time itself performs the miracles.[6]

- Explanations are good enough

Mr. Nye made a comment that I simply couldn't let pass without further discussion. He said:

> Tell us why the universe is accelerating, tell us why these mothers were getting sick. And we found an explanation for it.

Now I want the readers to understand that just because someone has an explanation for something, that doesn't make it true. The Greeks had all sorts of explanations for things, like the moon and the sun being pulled by chariots...that doesn't make it true.

Just because evolutionists come up with an explanation (i.e., a story) for the expansion of the universe, that has little to do with the truth. Keep in mind that the evolutionists commonly do what their cousins, the Epicureans, did in ancient Greece. They come up with stories that

---

5. P. Bak, *How Nature Works* (New York, NY: Springer Publishing, Verlag, 1996), p. 212.
6. G. Wald, "The Origin of Life," *Scientific American*, 191, no. 48 (August 1954): p. 54.

they call explanations, and, like their Epicurean cousins, they limit themselves to stories that are within the bounds of materialism.

Now also keep in mind that from observation, astronomers (both evolutionist and creationist) will conclude that the universe is expanding. That's observational science. But they do not observe what happened in the past to cause this to happen — that's historical science.

However, both creationists and evolutionists can do experiments in the present (and repeat their experiments) to show that organisms like bacteria do cause disease — that's an example of observational science.

Once again, Bill Nye mixed up historical and observational science in the examples he used.

- Truth

Mr. Nye then made a comment about truth existing:

> And just the idea that the majority has sway in science is true only up to a point.

First, I heartily agree with the premise that the majority view isn't always true in science. The majority wasn't right when it came to a global Flood in Noah's day — after all, the majority perished! However, as a point of inconsistency, Mr. Nye's materialistic worldview means that truth doesn't exist, since truth isn't material. For example, you can't stub your toe on a big block of truth sitting in the living room! Famous evolutionist Professor Richard Lewontin made a very revealing claim about the evolutionary faith when he wrote:

> We take the side of science *in spite* of the patent absurdity of some of its constructs, *in spite* of its failure to fulfill many of its extravagant promises of health and life, *in spite* of the tolerance of the scientific community for unsubstantiated just-so stories, because we have a prior commitment, a commitment to materialism. It is not that the methods and institutions of science somehow compel us to accept a material explanation of the phenomenal world, but, on the contrary, that we are forced by our *a priori* adherence to material causes to create an apparatus of investigation and a set of concepts that produce material explanations, no matter how counter-intuitive, no matter how mystifying to the uninitiated.

Moreover, that materialism is an absolute, for we cannot allow a Divine Foot in the door.[7]

In a no God evolutionary worldview, the underlying assumption is that everything is material, and therefore, it must be so for all explanations. This is a faith statement. This *is* Mr. Nye's religion, and it is governed by certain rules of faith. So when Mr. Nye inconsistently appeals to the religion of Christianity by agreeing that truth exists, it needs to be pointed out.

For Mr. Nye to make this statement about truth, he must give up his worldview and borrow from God's, where God is the truth, hence truth exists — and because we are made in God's image, we can understand truth.

- Mr. Nye tried to sneak something past everyone: complexity is not order!

Then Mr. Nye stated his final point for his one-minute rebuttal [where he didn't address the question]:

> And then the other thing I just want to point out, what you may have missed in evolutionary explanations of life, is it's the mechanism by which we add complexity. The earth is getting energy from the sun all the time, and that energy is used to make life forms somewhat more complex.

Mr. Nye has confused what complexity is. Let's briefly define these:

- **Order**: succession or sequence of one thing after another (i.e., "ATHATHATHATHATH" is an example of order).

- **Complexity**: complicated or intricate arrangement of part, units, or information (i.e., "THE HAT THAT SAT NEAR THE BAT NOT BY THE MAT" is an example of a complexity).

Complexity is not order (a crystal or a snowflake has order but not complexity). Nor is complexity something that just comes about by adding sunlight (energy) to a system. Complexity, for the lay reader, is like this book. If sunlight comes down on earth, a book this complex is not just going to spontaneously come about.

---

7. R. Lewontin, "Billions and Billions of Demons," *The New York Review*, January 9, 1997, p. 31.

Now consider that the human DNA is complex (three billion base pairs that intricately code for specific information to make a person). But the single-celled organism *Valonia ventricosa* (an algae) is not going to *get more complex* and turn into a human by adding sunlight…

We can test Mr. Nye's hypothesis scientifically by applying sunlight to the algae and seeing if it turns into a person or a goat or even a tree (all of which are "somewhat more complex" by Mr. Nye's standard). Basically, Mr. Nye stated what he believes which is arbitrary and sadly, he thinks that is a good explanation. But it is merely another debate tactic to put out an idea that he believes is true and see if anyone catches him on it.

Question: How did consciousness come from matter?

Mr. Nye, 2-minute response:

- No answers

Mr. Nye's response:

> Don't know; this is a great mystery…. So we don't know where consciousness comes from, but we want to find out. Furthermore, I'll tell you it's deep within us. I claim that I have spent time with dogs that have had the joy of discovery. It's way inside us; we have one ancestor, as near as we can figure.

So Mr. Nye has no answer but thinks it came from an ancestor he has in common with a dog. At least that is what he figures. Evidently, he merely believes or guesses that this is so and is arbitrary. If he were more consistent with his materialism, Mr. Nye's response should have been:

> Consciousness doesn't exist since it is not material. But what we view as consciousness is merely chemical reactions in the brain that help us survive but are otherwise meaningless.

- Tax dollars used to support religion (Bill Nye's religion)

Then Mr. Nye made it perfectly clear that tax dollars were being used to investigate religious claims by humanists:

And by the way, if you can find what we in science call a second genesis — this is to say did life start another way on the earth — there are researchers at Astrobiology Institute, researchers supported by NASA, your tax dollars, that are looking for answers to that very question — is it possible that life could start another way? Is there some sort of life form akin to science fiction that's crystal instead of membranous? This would be a fantastic discovery that would change the world.

Tax dollars are being used to look for alien life and how life might have arisen on other planets. NASA and the Astrobiology Institute clearly can't figure out how life arose on its own on earth, so they are looking for it elsewhere! It is sad that our tax dollars are being spent on whims by this false religion. I would rather see funds put toward useful technology (like renewable oil from sewage waste[8] or fuel from algae[9]) and meaningful space exploration, than toward humanistic religious stories.

Mr. Nye summed up his answer by appealing to tax payers, "And I remind you, taxpayers and voters that might be watching, if we do not embrace the process of science — I mean in the mainstream — we will fall behind economically; this is a point I can't say enough." So his idea of getting ahead is spending tax dollars on humanistic stories and neglecting actual technological advances. But in his religion, who really cares? On the one hand, he seems to want to support developing technology (which creationists are for, by the way), but underneath it all, he is really trying to push his humanistic religion of evolutionary naturalism in the guise of what he calls "science."

People need to wake up and realize that Mr. Nye is on a mission — a campaign. He makes it sound like he really wants to help mankind by contributing to technological advances, but in reality, he is on a mission to try to eliminate Christianity and convert people to an atheistic worldview. The more you study what Mr. Nye said in the debate, the more you realize the true nature of the debate (which Mr. Ham made clear to everyone)

---

8. A. Snelling, "How Fast Can Oil Form?" Answers in Genesis, March 1, 1990, https://answersingenesis.org/geology/catastrophism/how-fast-can-oil-form/.
9. B. Thomas, "One-Hour Oil Production," Institute for Creation Research, January 13, 2014, http://www.icr.org/article/7874/.

— that it's a conflict of worldviews because it's a conflict of two religions: one based on God's Word and the other based on man's word (humanism in its broadest sense).

Mr. Ham, 1-minute response:

Mr. Ham's response once again emphasized "the Book." A portion is re-iterated here:

> Bill, I do want to say that there is a Book out there that does document where consciousness came from. And in that Book, the One who created us said that He made man in His image, and He breathed into man and he became a living being. And so the Bible does document that; that's where consciousness came from, that God gave it to us.

Mr. Ham continued, and I also echo this:

> And you know, the other thing I want to say is, I'm sort of a little — I have a mystery, and that is, you talk about the joy of discovery. But you also say that when you die, it's over, and that's the end of you. And if when you die it's over and you don't even remember you were here, what's the point of the joy of discovery anyway, I mean in an ultimate sense? I mean, you know, you won't ever know you were ever here, and no one who knew you will know they were ever here ultimately, so what's the point anyway? I love the joy of discovery because this is God's creation and I'm finding more out about that to take dominion for man's good and for God's glory.

Amen. Mr. Ham hit it on the head. From a perspective of naturalism and materialism, life is ultimately meaningless and hopeless. Mr. Nye's religion is really one of despair. He can live life in the here and now and decide what is joyful for him — but ultimately, from his perspective, he will never know he existed! That's why Mr. Ham emphasized a very special Book — God's Book.

Mr. Ham wanted Mr. Nye to know that there is a God who created us and loves us. We are *not* going to cease to exist; we will live forever either with God or separated from Him, being upheld by God in Hell with the everlasting wrath of God as punishment.[10] Mr. Ham wanted Mr. Nye and all those listening to hear the saving message of the Gospel to know that they can live forever with their Creator and all His goodness and blessings if they have received the free gift of salvation.

We are all condemned by our sin. But God has made a way in Jesus Christ, who is God and *became* a man to suffer and die to take upon Himself the infinite punishment we all deserve. Only Christ could take the infinite punishment from an infinite God to satisfy the wrath of God upon sin. Now the Lord offers the free gift of salvation through repentance of sin and reception of Jesus Christ, who is the Resurrection and the Life for all eternity, by faith through grace. Our desire is to see others saved from their sin too — including Mr. Nye.

Question: What, if anything, would ever change your mind?

I do have some preliminary comments on this question. First, I wished that this question were more specific. If I was in a debate and someone asked what would change my mind, I would respond, "Change my mind on what?" The reason is simple.

Are they asking if I am willing to change my mind about how a scientific model works? To answer that, yes; if new information arises that gives me a reason to change my mind on the specifics, I am willing to do so. Models are always subject to change. So a good argument can change an understanding of a scientific creation model. But God's Word, on which the model is built, does not change. And think about it — the Bible must be true for truth to exist.

Mr. Ham, 2-minute response:

Mr. Ham answered the question in two ways in his response. I will address his second portion first. Mr. Ham responded:

> We build models based upon the Bible, and those models are always subject to change. The fact of Noah's Flood is not subject to change; the model of how the Flood occurred is subject to

---

10. Consider that those who are unsaved have basically waged war against an infinite, eternal, and all-powerful God — they will not win, and this punishment for their high treason will endure for eternity. This is what Hell is — their eternal separation from all God's goodness.

change, because we observe in the current world, and we're able to come up with maybe different ways this could have happened or that could have happened. And that's part of that scientific discovery, that's part of what it's all about.

Mr. Ham drew out the proper connection between what can change and what can't. For example, he pointed out that in a Christian worldview (that is, that the Bible is God's Word and the revelation in that Word is true), the models that are built on God's revealed truth can change, but the Scriptures themselves are absolute and cannot change (e.g., the Flood in Noah's day did occur, but the model on exactly how the Flood occurred and what happened geologically during the time of the Flood is subject to change). I commend this answer.

• Proof and Persuasion

The first part of Mr. Ham's response was:

> And as a Christian, I can't prove it to you, but God has definitely shown me very clearly through His Word and shown Himself in the person of Jesus Christ, the Bible is the Word of God. And I admit that that's where I start from. I can challenge people that you can go and test that; you can make predictions based on that, you can check the prophecies in the Bible, you can check the statements in Genesis, you can check that. And I did a little bit of that tonight. And I can't ultimately prove that to you; all I can do is to say to someone, "Look, if the Bible really is what it claims to be, if it really is the word of God, and that's what it claims, then check it out."

Mr. Ham was explaining (in the short time he had to do this), that it is not he who *persuades* someone or *convinces* him or her about the Lord Jesus or about the Bible being true. And I heartily agree — that is the job of the Holy Spirit (e.g., 1 Corinthians 12:3[11]).

It's important to understand that there is a difference between *proof* and *persuasion*. From an engineering perspective, I can prove if a rickety-looking bridge is sound and not going to break, but persuading someone to walk over it is a different question!

---

11. "Therefore I make known to you that no one speaking by the Spirit of God calls Jesus accursed, and no one can say that Jesus is Lord except by the Holy Spirit."

Regarding God's Word, it must be true for provability to be possible (knowledge, logic, truth, and so on). So I would state that nothing is provable without God's Word being true — the ultimate level of proof by God's own standard. This *is* nothing less than the proof required since God is the absolute standard above all other standards!

Now when Mr. Ham said to go check things out, obviously, based on many other things he stated in the debate (and has stated numerous times over the years), Mr. Ham meant for *confirmation* purposes. Going back to his 30-minute presentation, he made predictions based on Scripture, then used examples in biology (genetics and dogs) and anthropology (the human race) to show that observational science confirms statements in the Bible. Such confirmation is not proof in that sense, but it does illustrate that we can check out the statements in the Bible (historical science) and see if they are confirmed by observational science.

Mr. Ham also explained earlier that all evidence is interpreted anyway! So in regard to the origins issue, it's not a battle over evidence but over how one interprets evidence, which depends on one's worldview and starting point. The question actually should have been asked this way:

> "Are you prepared to give up your starting point of God's Word and adopt Mr. Nye's starting point of naturalism?" Mr. Ham gave "no" as his correct answer.

For God and His Word to be ultimately proved, a standard on the level of God and His Word would be required; all other standards are lesser and thus not adequate for provability. So the only standard available for God to prove something is His own self-authentication. In other words, when dealing with final authority, the final authority is the only possible standard. A philosopher, Dr. Greg Bahnsen, once remarked:

> If God is God, then who or what authority could be higher than His?...There cannot be an authority higher than God's.[12]

Mr. Nye, 1-minute response:

Mr. Nye then took a stab at the question by responding:

12. G. Bahnsen, *Defending the Christian Worldview Against All Opposition*, Part 2, Circular Reasoning, American Vision, http://store.americanvision.org/products/defending-the-christian-worldview-against-all-opposition.

We would just need one piece of evidence. We would need the fossil that swam from one layer to another. We would need evidence that the universe is not expanding. We would need evidence that the stars appear to be far away but they're not. We would need evidence that rock layers can somehow form in just 4,000 years instead of the extraordinary amount. We would need evidence that somehow you can reset atomic clocks and keep neutrons from becoming protons.

First of all, I suggest that Mr. Ham's answer did show that he is totally committed to the Christian faith — with no doubt. He is secure in what he believes.

Since Mr. Nye said that he would just need *one piece of evidence*, why did he list so many? But the fact is that one piece of evidence didn't change Mr. Nye's mind. Mr. Ham gave quite a bit of evidence (examples that fulfilled at least two of Nye's suggested pieces of evidence needed), but that didn't affect Mr. Nye at all.

Also, Mr. Nye's statement "that somehow you can reset atomic clocks and keep neutrons from becoming protons" was another example of mixing historical and observational science together. It would seem with this example that Mr. Nye was referring to dating methods. Now Mr. Ham explained that dating methods are based on assumptions.

When Mr. Nye said "keep neutrons from becoming protons," he was introducing a straw man argument. He was basically saying that something you observe in chemistry (observational science) means atomic clocks can't be changed (historical science). But no one denies that neutrons can become protons — creationists don't deny the observational science. But creationists do question the many fallible assumptions in interpreting the data from radioactive decay in regard to the age of a sample. Either Mr. Nye just doesn't understand the difference between interpretation based on assumption and what one actually observes — or he is deliberately stating things to mislead people in order to try to get them to believe his worldview.

If only one piece of evidence was required to change Mr. Nye's mind, then as soon as he heard about the wood encased in lava (found only thousands of years old by carbon-14 dating but supposedly millions of years old by the potassium-argon, K-AR, method),[13] Mr. Nye should have said, "Well, that evidence illustrates that radiometric dating is inaccurate, so I have to be prepared to question whether or not my worldview is right. Mr. Ham could be right — the debate is over." Did that happen? No, of course not, because Mr. Nye (like Mr. Ham) is committed to his starting point.

So although Mr. Nye professed that evidence would change his mind...that is not true. At this point, I believe we can say that Mr. Ham was honest in admitting his total adherence to his worldview. Now Mr. Nye is also totally committed to his worldview — but he was prepared to entertain giving an answer in regard to what evidence would change his mind to give the false impression that of being "open minded." So he was really inconsistent. No matter what "evidence" Mr. Ham gave him, he would not change his mind.

Furthermore, we have animal footprints in lower geologic rock layers (as previously discussed), and we do not find their burial until higher layers. Hence, they were swimming and walking up to higher layers. Would Mr. Nye change his mind with this evidence? No — he is committed to his evolutionary worldview based on naturalism.

Furthermore, both creationists and evolutionists agree that the universe is expanding, the stars are far away, and radiometric materials can undergo radiometric decay. However, such things have no bearing on the worldview debate or on changing our minds over creation versus evolution. But I must specifically comment on Mr. Nye's statement:

> We would need evidence that rock layers can somehow form
> in just 4,000 years instead of the extraordinary amount.

There is video footage of Mt. St. Helens erupting on June 12, 1980. It laid down multiple sedimentary layers very quickly as a result of pyroclastic flows, mudflows, and ash fall.[14] Such deposits didn't take millions of years or even 4,000 years.

Observable science showed that it doesn't take long periods of time for rock layers to form! Mr. Ham has often related an event that occurred when he was speaking in a university auditorium in Spain. A student

---

13. A. Snelling, Radioactive "Dating" in Conflict!, Answers in Genesis, December 1, 1997, https://answersingenesis.org/geology/radiometric-dating/radioactive-dating-in-conflict/.
14. J. Morris and S. Austin, *Footprints in Ash* (Green Forest, AR: Master Books, 2003), pp. 19–37.

Mount St. Helens in the early 1980s — often steam, gas, or ash could be seen.

An aerial view of Mount St. Helens.

there said that everyone knows it takes millions of years to form rock. The student then asked if Mr. Ham could give an example of rock forming quickly. Mr. Ham responded, "Yes — concrete." Concrete is really just artificial rock. The same sorts of processes and chemicals that produce concrete can occur in nature. Time is not as important a factor as having the right conditions and elements present.

- Change the subject

Mr. Nye then asked a question, once again: "What can you predict?" I have already addressed the fact that Mr. Ham put up a list of six predictions and dealt with two of them in particular. However, let's consider one more creationist prediction, which will lay to rest Mr. Nye's false claim that creationists can't make scientific predictions that can be verified. Let's turn to the work of biblical creationist and professor, Dr. David DeWitt, who is the chair of the Department of Biology and Chemistry and the director for the Center for Creation Studies from Liberty University.

Dr. DeWitt, basing his model of anthropology on the Bible, predicted that Neanderthals and modern humans were closer genetically than previously touted. He also predicted that the genetic variations that are being reported that allegedly made Neanderthals unique and very different from modern humans would turn out to be in the same places (genetically) that modern humans differed from each. This prediction was confirmed after later studies and mapping of the Neanderthal genome.[15]

The skull on the left is a modern ape (gorilla), the second is an extinct ape (Australopithecine), the third is a modern human, and the last one is a Neanderthal. Clearly the differences between Neanderthal and human skulls are very slight.

---

15. D. DeWitt, "Does the Creation Model Make Predictions? Absolutely!" Answers in Genesis, February 8, 2014, https://answersingenesis.org/creation-science/does-the-creation-model-make-predictions-absolutely/.

Question: Outside of radiometric methods, what scientific evidence supports your view of the age of the earth?

Mr. Nye, 2-minute response:

Mr. Nye used much of his response time discussing radiometric dating anyway. He started by arguing that:

> …radiometric evidence is pretty compelling.

However, it isn't compelling, and this was shown clearly in the debate as Mr. Ham exposed some of the assumptions behind such methods. Mr. Ham also gave specific examples (the wood encased in lava and dating problems on the lava dome at Mt. St. Helens) that clearly illustrated that radioactive dating methods have major problems.

Furthermore, extensive research on radioactive dating methods such as the RATE project[16] and other studies[17] have shown that such methods are not absolute. Of course, Mr. Nye didn't even mention Mr. Ham's slide that stated "Hundreds of physical processes set limits on the age of the universe" and "More than 90% of these processes give an age of less than billions of years."

- Deposition rates by Lyell

Mr. Nye then used the example of deposition rates as an answer to the question and appealed to the work of Mr. Charles Lyell.[18] Mr. Nye claimed:

> It was Lyell, a geologist, who realized he — my recollection, he came up with the first use of the term deep time, when people realized that the earth had to be much, much older.

First, Mr. Lyell was first and foremost a lawyer, and he turned his hand toward geology by trying to apply strict uniformitarianism to geological

---

16. L. Vardiman, A. Snelling, and E. Chaffin, eds., *Radioisotopes and the Age of the Earth*, Vol. 2 (El Cajon, CA: Institute for Creation Research; Chino Valley, AZ: Creation Research Society, 2005).

17. J. Woormorappe, *The Mythology of Modern Dating Methods* (El Cajon, CA: Institute for Creation Research, 1999).

18. C. Lyell, *Principles of Geology: Being an Attempt to Explain the Former Changes of the Earth's Surface, By Reference to Causes Now in Operation* (London, England: John Murray Publisher, Volume 1, 1830, Volume 2, 1832, and Volume 3, 1833).

processes. Essentially, Mr. Lyell proposed that there were no catastrophes in the past that formed geological deposits, and geological processes, for the most part, always occur at the same basic rates. Of course, his long age naturalistic assumptions (worldview) determined how he interpreted the evidence he observed in the present in relation to the past (historical science).

One of the most glaring errors made by Mr. Lyell was imposing his long age uniformitarian model (historical science) on Niagara Falls in regard to erosion rates rather than taking into account the actual observations (observational science) of people who lived there. It was obvious that Mr. Lyell had an agenda and did not really want the truth.[19]

By the time Mr. Lyell published his three-volume set, *Principles of Geology*, in the 1830's, several others had already proposed long ages (see Appendix B). What Mr. Lyell did was popularize uniformitarianism and ostracize those who believed that catastrophic processes (such as those resulting from the global Flood of Noah's day) were a major factor in the formation of the geologic record. Mr. Lyell's strict uniformitarian view was dominant for many years, and it is just now, in our era of history, that people are starting to see through it. Dr. Warren D. Allmon said in 1993:

> Indeed geology appears at last to have outgrown Lyell. In an intellectual shift that may well rival that which accompanied the wide spread acceptance of plate tectonics, the last 30 years have witnessed an increasing acceptance of rapid, rare, episodic, and "catastrophic" events.[20]

Modern secular geologists have introduced multiple catastrophes into their explanation of geologic formations. As I've heard Mr. Ham put it in some of his lectures, "secular geologists once believed that the geologic record formed slowly over millions of years — now they are saying it happened quickly over millions of years."

---

19. J. Morris, "Dating Niagara Falls," *Acts & Facts*, 32, no. 5 (2003), http://www.icr.org/article/dating-niagara-falls/.
20. W. Allmon, "Post-Gradualism," review of *The New Catastrophism* by Derek V. Ager (New York: Cambridge University Press, 1993, 231 pp.), *Science*, 262 (October 1, 1993): p. 122.

As you know, Mr. Nye did not appeal to scientific evidence here. He appealed to a person's idea (Mr. Lyell) that things have always been the same. In other words, he appealed to Mr. Lyell's historical science. Again, until Mr. Nye admits the difference between historical science and observational science, he will likely not be prepared to question his belief (historical science) in long ages like "millions of years."

Actual observations (observational science) show that things can change quickly (e.g., rates and processes) depending on the event (e.g., Mt. St. Helens eruption, floods, earthquakes, tsunamis, etc.). So not only did Mr. Nye appeal to someone's idea that it took a long time, he also appealed to an idea that many now reject. The fact is that no one has been able to observe or repeat millions of years of slow sedimentation.

- We need three billion years for evolution!

Mr. Nye then tried to reverse engineer an answer when he said:

> In a related story, there was a mystery as to how the earth could be old enough to allow evolution to have taken place. How could the earth possibly be three billion years old?

First, three billion years isn't remotely enough time based on the odds of origin of life and evolution.[21] But this is not a scientific argument anyway. Mr. Nye was presuming three billion years because he incorrectly believed that was the amount of time needed for the origin and evolution of life.

- Lord Kelvin Gaffe's calculation

Next, Mr. Nye appealed to Lord Kelvin's calculation when he said:

> Lord Kelvin did a calculation; if the sun were made of coal and burning, it couldn't be more than 100,000 or so years old.

First, Lord Kelvin did not believe that the sun was made of coal; that was a previous belief held by others. Next, Lord Kelvin's calculation ranged from 20 – 100 million years, not 100,000 years. But keep in mind that this was a *calculation* based on assumptions (historical science), not observational science. No one has observed or repeated this alleged millions of years of the sun burning.

---

21. M. Riddle, "Can Natural Processes Explain the Origin of Life?" in K. Ham, gen. ed., *The New Answers Book 2* (Green Forest, AR: Master Books, 2008), pp. 63–71.

- No observational scientific arguments

Mr. Nye then wanted to bring up radiometric dating again, and he transitioned to say the universe is expanding (which we agree with and see as a great confirmation of a biblical prediction). He also arbitrarily asserted that a flood 4,000 years ago is unprovable.

Of course, floods happen virtually every year, but I'm sure Mr. Nye means the global Flood of Noah's day. Now we would say, based on genealogical data, that the date of the Flood was closer to about 4,350 years ago as opposed to 4,000 years ago. But we can be forgiving here.

Note that Mr. Nye did not present any actual observational *scientific* arguments for the long ages in terms of the age of the earth. They were merely conjectures and appeals to other people's ideas (historical science).

- Mr. Nye then changed the subject again.

Perhaps Mr. Nye knew he didn't have real observational scientific arguments for his professed age of the earth, so he changed the subject to ask a question of Mr. Ham. He asked Mr. Ham to address the issue of skulls that he had mentioned earlier in the debate:

> Furthermore, Mr. Ham, you never quite addressed this issue of the skulls. There are many, many steps in what appears to be the creation or the coming into being of you and me, and those steps are consistent with evolutionary theory.

Mr. Ham's one-minute response was actually to address the question at hand, not a different topic. Mr. Ham said (rightly) that he believed answers and responses from the two debate participants in regard to the questions asked should deal with the topic of the questions.

As I discussed earlier, Mr. Nye's slide was difficult to read, and one would need quite some time to go through each skull and understand exactly what was found, where, etc. On reviewing the slide since the debate, it is quite obvious that most of the skulls were from the human kind, and a few were from the ape kind. Here are a few big picture points to be reminded of regarding these skulls

1. These skulls are either human or ape, but do not fit the allegation of step-by-step evolution.

Petrified wood, stalactite, coal, and synthetic sapphire stone.

2. Each of these fossils was found in what creationists refer to as post-Flood (very modern) sediment, which means man (e.g., Noah and the pre-Flood people) already existed prior to any of them being fossilized.

Mr. Ham, 1-minute response:

Mr. Ham dealt with the question that was asked of Mr. Nye (and did not get sidetracked in talking about Mr. Nye's difficult-to-read slide with lots of skulls pictured); as such, he pointed out that the 4.5 billion year age of the earth was not obtained from any earth rock! Instead, it was obtained from meteorites that were assumed to be the same age as the earth (most people don't realize that this is where the current secular age of the earth comes from). Also, secular scientists only used extremely long age dating methods so they would be sure not to get a calculation of the age of the meteorites that was very old.[22]

Next, Mr. Ham reinforced that most scientific dating methods give an age of the earth that is far less than billions of years — about 90%

---

22. Interestingly many meteorites contain cosmogenic carbon-14, which means they really can't be millions or billions of years old (some via internal sampling). The secularists assume that the C-14 became part of them after entering the atmosphere and remaining on the ground, and they try to use this for terrestrial dates. How does a meteorite take in C-14? They are not plants and animals that use this as part of their diet. For example, see A. Snelling, "Radioisotope Dating of Meteorites: I. The Allende CV3 Carbonaceous Chondrite," *Answers Research Journal*, 7 (2014): pp. 103–145, https://cdn-assets. answersingenesis.org/doc/articles/pdf-versions/radioisotope_dating_Allende.pdf. See also Pillinger et al., "The Meteorite from Lake House," 74th Annual Meteoritical Society Meeting, 2011, http://www.lpi.usra.edu/meetings/metsoc2011/pdf/5326.pdf.

contradict the billions of years. So why are these ignored? Mr. Ham nailed the answer.

But I want to add more! I've been taught that it takes millions and billions of years for hosts of processes to occur...like the formation of coal, oil, gemstones, petrified wood, stalactites and stalagmites, or what have you. But does it?

1. Coal can be made in a lab in weeks.[23]
2. Oil forms in one hour to a few days.[24]
3. Gemstones can form when volcanoes erupt[25] or in a lab in days to weeks.[26]
4. Stalactites can form in days,[27] stalagmites in a few years.[28]
5. Petrified wood can form in hours.[29]

What evidence is there for millions of years? Perhaps vague speculations are good enough for the general public, but they should not be entertained by respected scientists.

Actually, Mr. Nye's adherence to millions of years in spite of contrary evidence illustrates clearly that evolutionists have to have millions of years to even attempt to propose that the observed changes in living things (e.g., speciation) are a part of a supposed process where one kind changes into a totally different kind.

From a perspective of genetics, molecules-to-man evolution is an incomprehensible process. So how does one try to brainwash the public into believing such an inexplicable process? One has to propose

23. R. Hayatsu, R. McBeth, R. Scott, R. Botto, Winans, R., *Organic Geochemistry*, 6 (1984): pp. 463–471.
24. A. Snelling, "The Origin of Oil," *Answers*, 2, no. 1, pp. 74–77, http://www.answersingenesis.org/articles/am/v2/n1/origin-of-oil; Thomas, B., "One-Hour Oil Production," ICR, January 13, 2014, https://www.icr.org/article/7874/.
25. Editors, "Featuring Mount St. Helens Emerald Jewelry (Obsianite, Helenite)," Mt. St. Helens Website, Accessed July 18, 2014, http://www.mt-st-helens.com/obsidianite.html.
26. A. Snelling, "Creating Opals," *Creation Ex Nihilo*, 17, no. 1 (December, 1994): pp. 14–17; G. Hunter and A. Paparella, "New Diamond Age?" (Editor's note, it is now titled: "Lab-Made Diamonds Just Like Natural Ones"), ABC News website, September 9, 2003, http://abcnews.go.com/GMA/story?id=124787.
27. M. Taylor, "Descent," *Arizona Highways*, January, 1993, p. 11.
28. Editors, "Bottle Stalagmite," *Creation*, 17, no. 2 (March 1995): p. 6.
29. A. Snelling, "Instant Petrified Wood," Answers in Genesis, Sept. 1, 1995, http://www.answersingenesis.org/articles/cm/v17/n4/wood; "Instant Petrified Wood," Physics.org, http://www.physorg.com/news2801.html (accessed Nov. 1, 2006).

an unfathomable amount of time (millions of years). As Mr. Ham has stated in his lectures, "millions of years is really the god (religion) of the secularists to try to explain life without God (the one Creator God of the Bible)."

Question: Can you reconcile the change in the rate [*at which*] continents are now drifting versus how quickly they must have traveled at creation 6,000 years ago?

Mr. Ham, 2-minute response:

First of all, the Genesis account tells us that the dry land was created on the third day of creation, and God gathered the waters into one place. The implication is that there may have been only one continent. So, on the basis of the creation account in the Bible, creationists believe there was probably only one continent originally. The first hints of a mechanism that could break the earth's one continent came 1,656 years later with the global Flood of Noah's day.[30]

The *springs of the great deep* burst forth violently and were not restrained until the 150th day (Genesis 7:24–8:3[31]). The mountains rose and the valleys sank to the place which God had established for them in Psalm 104:8–9.[32] So essentially, any plate movement shouldn't have occurred until the Flood.

Mr. Ham related this rate of continental movement to historical science to affirm his running theme in the debate about historical science. We can't observe the past rate, nor can we repeat it, so it falls into the realm of the past (not observational/operational science). In short, Mr.

---

30. One might argue that sin and the curse in Genesis 3 could have been responsible for beginning a continental breakup, but there is just little to confirm this from the text. Though I would agree that this is the earliest point in Bible history for such a thing to be possible, the more logical place is at the breakup of the Flood, and the text gives us strong clues to catastrophic occurrences in Genesis 6–8.

31. "And the waters prevailed on the earth one hundred and fifty days. Then God remembered Noah, and every living thing, and all the animals that were with him in the ark. And God made a wind to pass over the earth, and the waters subsided. The fountains of the deep and the windows of heaven were also stopped, and the rain from heaven was restrained. And the waters receded continually from the earth. At the end of the hundred and fifty days the waters decreased."

32. "The mountains rose; the valleys sank down To the place which You established for them. You set a boundary that they may not pass over, So that they will not return to cover the earth" (NAS).

Ham answered correctly when said that the Flood catastrophically broke up the plates, they moved quickly initially, and what we observe today is "a remnant of that movement."

Then Mr. Ham referred to other people who have more expertise in this subject such as Dr. John Baumgardner and Dr. Andrew Snelling. They have published extensively on this subject, as have others, but perhaps the most succinct chapter for laymen on the subject is referenced here.[33]

Mr. Nye, 1-minute response:

- Mr. Ham lived a century ago?

Mr. Nye's response was directed back toward Mr. Ham and he claimed:

It must have been easier for you to explain this a century ago, before the existence of tectonic plates was proven.

Once again, as happened over and over again in the debate, Mr. Nye absolutely refused to acknowledge the difference between what we observe in the present and interpretations about the past. Throughout the debate, Mr. Ham dealt in different ways with this difference. Mr. Nye totally ignored this. Otherwise he would have to admit his beliefs about the past were just that — beliefs!

Now in response to Mr. Nye's comment about a century ago, he seemed to not know that it was actually a creationist who came up with the idea of the continents splitting apart (based on the biblical record). Mr. Antonio Snider-Pellegrini published this in 1859 in French in his book *La création et ses mystères dévoilés*.

Even though Dr. Alfred Wegener acknowledged the drift of continents in 1915,[34] it still took about 50 years for geologists to finally succumb to the idea that they did move! So a creationist was finally vindicated. But people need to understand that when secular geologists look at the slow movement of continents today (observational science), it is an assumption on their part that this is the rate at which continents have been moving in the past (historical science). The point Mr. Ham was

---

33. A. Snelling, "Can Catastrophic Plate Tectonics Explain Flood Geology?" in K. Ham, gen. ed., *The New Answers Book 1* (Green Forest, AR: Master Books, 2006), pp. 186–197.
34. A. Wegener, "Die Entstehung der Kontinente und Ozeane," 1915, http://www.gutenberg.org/ebooks/45460.

making is that there was a time in the past (the time of the global Flood) when rates of continental break up were different. Again, it all has to do with different interpretations of what happened in the past because of different assumptions.

- Magnetic field reversals (semi-technical)

Mr. Nye transitioned to appeal to magnetic field reversals to argue that the continental drift rates have remained the same in the past. Mr. Nye assumed naturalism for magnetic field reversals to argue for naturalism for the continental plate movements. In other words, he used naturalism to prove naturalism, which is assuming the very things he was trying to prove and hence fallacious!

Allow me to explain magnetic field reversals for the reader because this can be confusing if you don't know what we are talking about in this context. When the plates moved apart, the ocean floor spread out and was replaced by molten rock that cooled. This cooling lava at the ocean floor contains grains of iron that orient themselves to the magnetic field of the earth as they rapidly cool — just like a compass needle.

So researchers began researching the ocean floor and found that there have been several times when the ocean floor had different magnetic orientations — some facing north and others facing south. So the conclusion is that the magnetic field has been reversed in the past. It has been estimated that the magnetic field has reversed as many as 170 times.

So the question is, was this occurring slowly and gradually over long periods of time as Mr. Nye assumed, or was it rapidly reversing due to catastrophism from the Flood? If it was rapid, then it was predicted by creationists that continental lava flows should also have some signs of rapid reversals if these flows occurred at the same time. And this prediction was shown accurate.[35]

So it makes much more sense that these were rapid reversals at the time of the Flood. This makes sense since the earth's magnetic field is

---

35. D. Humphreys, "Reversals of the Earth's Magnetic Field During the Genesis Flood," *Proceedings of the First International Conference on Creationism, Vol. II* (Pittsburgh, PA: Creation Science Fellowship, 1986), pp. 113–126; A. Snelling, The "Principle of Least Astonishment"! *CEN Technical Journal*, 9, no. 2 (1995): pp. 138–139; R. Coe and M. Prévot, "Evidence Suggesting Extremely Rapid Field Variation During a Geomagnetic Reversal," *Earth and Planetary Science Letters*, 92 (1989): pp. 292–298; R. Coe, M. Prévot, and P. Camps, "New Evidence for Extraordinary Rapid Change of the Geomagnetic Field During a Reversal," *Nature*, 374 (1995): pp. 687–692.

continually decreasing, being about 40% greater 1,000 years ago.[36] If this were wound backward, the maximum age of the earth would only be about 10,000 years via this method.[37] Furthermore, if you were to assume this uniform rate of decay as secularists do and extrapolate backward into the past for millions of years, the geomagnetic field of the earth would have been so strong that life would have been impossible![38]

- Continental plate movements lead to catastrophic effects

Mr. Nye summed up with a strange twist that undercut his arguments for slow, gradual processes of millions of years. He claimed:

> As I said, I lived in Washington State when Mount St. Helens exploded. That's a result of a continental plate going under another continental plate and cracking, and this water-laden rock led to a steam explosion; that's how we do it on the outside.

But catastrophic effects destroy the idea of uniformitarianism (long ages of slow gradual time). Mr. Nye wants uniformitarianism, but then appeals to catastrophes! However, that undercuts the idea of uniformitarianism's millions of years that assumes no significant catastrophes changed things.

Question: And this is a question for you, Mr. Nye, but I guess I can put it to both of you. One word answer, please: favorite color?

Okay, a lighthearted question! In fact, for the debate response, I thought I could skip over this question, but Mr. Nye did say I should question everything. So at the last moment, I decided to look at this question — and good thing I did!

First, Mr. Nye's one-word response was not one word. In fact, the moderator, Tom Foreman, had to cut Mr. Nye off and Mr. Nye still continued! But here is one thing that Mr. Nye said:

> I will go along with most people and say green.

---

36. The magnetic field reduces about 5 percent each century.
37. D. Humphreys, "The Earth's Magnetic Field Is Young," *Acts & Facts*, 22, no. 8 (1993), http://www.icr.org/article/earths-magnetic-field-young/.
38. J. Lisle, *Taking Back Astronomy* (Green Forest, AR: Master Books, 2006), pp. 58–60, https://answersingenesis.org/answers/books/taking-back-astronomy/the-age-of-the-universe-part-2/.

I don't dispute that green is Mr. Nye's favorite color. But I decided to check what most people's favorite color was to verify that it was green. The answer turned out to be blue, not green, according to *ColorMatters.com* and the *The Top Tens* website.[39]

Interestingly, Mr. Ham's favorite color was blue, the most popular color. But this was a nice break in the debate — time to have a little fun! Actually, Mr. Ham used this lighthearted question to turn it into a teaching point to emphasize something he had been communicating over and over again — the difference between observational and historical science. Mr. Ham motioned to his blue tie and stated:

> Okay, observational science, blue.

Question: How do you balance the theory of evolution with the second law of thermodynamics?

Mr. Nye, 2-minute response:

For the reader, the second law of thermodynamics, or law of entropy, states in laymen's terms that in a closed system, things go from a position of order to disorder as heat is used. This is why the universe cannot be infinite, as all the usable energy/heat would have been used up, and yet stars still shine and we can digest food — both utilize the second law of thermodynamics.

There are two parts to this question: dealing with the *general theory of evolution* (that is the whole materialistic worldview that the universe and life arose by natural processes, and specifically, molecules-to-man evolution [biological evolution]). Mr. Nye didn't really address this in his response. The closest he came was when he stated:

> But the fundamental thing that this questioner has missed is the earth is not a closed system. So there's energy pouring in here from the sun, if I may, day and night — ha-ha — because the night, it's pouring in on the other side. And so that energy is what drives living things on earth, especially for, in our case, plants.

39. Editors, "The Most Popular Color in the World is ..." accessed July 29, 2014, http://webcenters.netscape.compuserve.com/homerealestate/package.jsp?name=fte/popularcolor/popularcolor; Editors, "Top Ten Favorite Colors," accessed July 29, 2014, http://www.the-toptens.com/top-ten-favorite-colors/.

Regardless of whether the questioner missed this or not, adding energy doesn't drive biological evolution. For biological evolution to occur, one needs to add complexity, not just energy. For example, adding sunlight to a plant or a lump of coal isn't going to cause it to have a brain and nervous system — it won't increase in complexity!

The second law of thermodynamics states that things go from an ordered state to a disordered state in a closed system (i.e., entropy increases). Mr. Nye was basically saying that the earth is not a closed system. But just the fact that the earth is not a closed system is not going to help him much. Many open systems, even if energy is added to them, are not fighting against entropy — e.g., a dead animal is an open system, yet it is not moving to a more ordered state by fighting against entropy and becoming more complex.

But Mr. Nye has failed to realize something significant — the universe *is* a closed system. Because of this, where did order come from in the universe? How did this supposed infinitely dense (super-ordered) and infinitely hot singularity (that allegedly exploded to cause rapid expansion for the Big Bang) come about? In other words, how did the second law of thermodynamics fail to work within this closed system?

The second law is rather devastating to an evolutionary worldview as a whole. In fact, my thermodynamics textbooks from university actually state in the section about the second law:

> The final point to be made is that the second law of thermodynamics and the principle of the increase of entropy have philosophical implications. Does the second law of thermodynamics apply to the universe as a whole? Are there processes unknown to us that occur somewhere in the universe, such as "continual creation," that have a decrease in entropy associated with them, and thus offset the continual increase of entropy that is associated with the natural processes that are known to us?... Quite obviously it is impossible to give conclusive answers to these questions on the basis of the second law of thermodynamics alone. However, we see the second law of thermodynamics as a description of the prior and continuing work of a creator,

who also holds the answer to our future destiny and that of the universe.[40]

These experts who wrote the textbook on the second law of thermodynamics (literally) dismiss the atheistic worldview that Mr. Nye has been arguing for based on their understanding of this law.

Mr. Ham, 1-minute response:

Mr. Ham nailed the response with one sentence:

> You can have all the energy that you want, but energy or matter will never produce life.

Mr. Ham affirmed the law of biogenesis (life only comes from life, not nonlife), whereas Mr. Nye's worldview must violate the law of biogenesis and the law of entropy (second law of thermodynamics). Christians can make sense of these laws, but naturalists, though they pay "lip service" to them, must violate them.

Question: Hypothetically, if evidence existed that caused you to have to admit that the earth was older than 10,000 years and creation did not occur over six days, would you still believe in God and the historical Jesus of Nazareth and that Jesus was the Son of God?

First, evidence doesn't exist for long ages. Mr. Ham made it very clear that no one can prove the age of the earth, and all dating methods are based on fallible assumptions.

I do want to address the last portion of the question. Actually, Mr. Ham dealt with this in his first rebuttal when he discussed the topic of death. He explained that when Christians believe in millions of years, they are accepting that death, disease, carnivory, and thorns existed for long ages before sin.

There *are* people who do not believe in biblical creation, yet they openly claim to be Christians — whether or not they are is between them and Christ. A person can be saved as long as they repent (e.g.,

---

40. G. Wylen, R. Sonntag, and C. Borgnakke, *Fundamentals of Classical Thermodynamics,* 4th Edition (New York: John Wiley and Sons, Inc., 1994), p. 272.

2 Corinthians 7:10[41]), believe in the Jesus Christ of Scripture (i.e., the triune God; e.g., Acts 16:31[42]), and hold firmly to the resurrection of Christ (e.g., Romans 10:9;[43] 1 Corinthians 15:17[44]).

Mr. Ham has made it clear many times (as can be documented on the *Answers in Genesis* website) that salvation is not conditional upon what one believes about the age of the earth but upon faith in Christ. See his article entitled "Does the Gospel Depend on a Young Earth?"[45] Mr. Ham has also explained that when Christians do hold to the belief in millions of years, they are really undermining the authority of the Word.

So the answer is that some people may feel like they can dismiss one part of the Bible (e.g., Genesis 1–11) and yet hold strongly to another part of it (e.g., reception of Christ or the Gospels). However, the obvious answer is that they are being inconsistent; they are trying to mix two different worldviews or religions.

Research has shown that the next generation abandon the faith when they see the inconsistency of Christians (particularly Christian leaders) accepting some parts of the Bible and rejecting others.[46] The kids of the next generation rightly see through this and say, if I can't trust one part, why trust the rest?

So the parents and many Christian leaders are leading the kids of the next generation down a path of inconsistency. We want to call people back to God's Word from the very first verse in Genesis (i.e., the path of consistency). I am shocked at how many Christians want to give up Genesis and yet hold to Christ when the whole reason for holding to Christ is founded in Genesis. If you get rid of Genesis, there is no fall into sin and no need for a Savior.

---

41. "For godly sorrow produces repentance leading to salvation, not to be regretted; but the sorrow of the world produces death."
42. "So they said, 'Believe on the Lord Jesus Christ, and you will be saved, you and your household.'"
43. "That if you confess with your mouth the Lord Jesus and believe in your heart that God has raised Him from the dead, you will be saved."
44. "And if Christ is not risen, your faith is futile; you are still in your sins!"
45. K. Ham, "Does the Gospel Depend on a Young Earth?" Answers in Genesis, December 8, 2013, https://answersingenesis.org/creationism/young-earth/does-the-gospel-depend-on-a-young-earth/.
46. See, for example, Ken Ham, *Already Gone* (Green Forest, AR: Master Books, 2009).

Mr. Ham, 2-minute response:

Mr. Ham pointed out that scientifically one couldn't prove the age of the earth — any attempts to do so are at best calculated guesses. In fact, most scientific age-dating methods give different ages! Most give an age of the earth far less than the billions of years proposed by evolutionists today.

He also pointed out that any age given in a scientific setting is merely hypothetical! Only God's Word is in a position to point to an absolute date, as the very nature of God is absolute.[47] Mr. Ham reaffirmed this when he said:

> Now, I've said to you before and I admit again that the reason I believe in a young universe is because of the Bible's account of origins. I believe that God, who has always been there, the infinite creator God, revealed in His Word what He did for us. And when we add up those dates, we get thousands of years. But there's nothing in observational science that contradicts that.

The conclusion for Mr. Ham was that:

> …You can't prove scientifically the age of the earth or the universe, bottom line.

Mr. Nye, 1-minute response:

Mr. Nye's response:

> Well, of course this is where we disagree. You can prove the age of the earth with great robustness by observing the universe around us.

But Mr. Nye never proved it. Mr. Ham made it very clear that the issue of the earth's age is one of historical science. Mr. Ham stated in his main presentation that we can observe radioactive decay and that this is an example of observational science. However, using radioactive decay to try to determine the age of the rock is historical science, as many assumptions are involved to come up with a particular interpretation. It's

---

47. Dates for creation based on God's absolute Word that are calculated are called standard dates that use a standard chronology. These calculations are not absolute, but God's Word is. For a discussion on standard chronologies please see F. Jones, *The Chronology of the Old Testament*, 16ᵗʰ Edition (Green Forest, AR: Master Books, 2005), pp. 21–22.

such a shame that Mr. Nye, said to be the "science guy," would never acknowledge this difference and get down to the real nature of the origins debate.

Mr. Bill Nye claimed you could "prove the age of the earth" through observation. But that is simply not true — as Mr. Ham made clear. Mr. Nye could not point to a rock with a label stating its age! We know he believes in millions of years, but that doesn't help. Mr. Nye never proved the age of the earth in the debate by observation. This is a blind faith statement. He simply wanted us to take his word for it. Then Mr. Nye had the audacity to say:

> And I get the feeling, Mr. Ham, that you want us to take your word for it.

Really now! Mr. Ham admitted his beliefs and correctly explained that the age of the earth is based on the plain reading of God's Word — the ultimate authority on all things! Yet Mr. Nye is the one who wants us to take his word for it that the earth is millions of years old!

But the real issue, as Mr. Ham challenged, is trusting God's Word for it. This is in opposition to taking man's word for it.

• Anything can be interpreted to mean anything?

Mr. Nye then attacked the Bible but in an interesting way. He reiterated:

> This is to say, your interpretation of a book written thousands of years ago, as translated into American English, is more compelling for you than everything that I can observe in the world around me.

Godly men have held to biblical creation for thousands of years before Mr. Ham. Mr. Ham isn't saying anything new. Mr. Ham's "interpretation" is to take the Bible "naturally" (as he explained in the debate) — according to the type of literature — the grammatical-historical method.

However, if, as Mr. Nye was proposing here, words don't mean what they say, and can be interpreted to mean anything...well then...does that mean Mr. Nye's words here could be interpreted to say that he believes evolution is false? Seriously!

Mr. Nye was implying that it is okay to interpret the Bible to mean exactly the opposite of what it says. If Mr. Nye really holds to this standard, then any person should be able to interpret Mr. Nye as being a young-earth creationist — by his own standard! This should be enough to show that Mr. Nye's standard is not adequate.

Genesis is written as a typical historical narrative. I'm sure both Mr. Ham and Mr. Nye would read an historical account of Julius Caesar and have the same interpretation — reading it as history. But according to Mr. Nye, when Mr. Ham (like millions of Christians) reads Genesis as history, it is *his* interpretation!

This was again an attempt by Mr. Nye to claim that Mr. Ham's stand on Scripture is somehow his own. The truth of the matter is that millions of Christians past and present have taken the same view!

- Mr. Nye attacked the law of biogenesis

Mr. Nye then attacked a scientific law. He said to Mr. Ham:

> You asserted that life cannot come from something that's not alive. Are you sure? Are you sure enough to say that we should not continue to look for signs of water and life on Mars, that that's a waste? You're sure enough to claim that? That is an extraordinary claim that we want to investigate.

Mr. Ham is not the one who formulated the law of biogenesis — that was Dr. Louis Pasteur. This law has repeatedly been confirmed. Never once has life been observed to come from nonlife. It is purely blind faith for someone to ascribe to abiogenesis (life from nonlife).

The onus is on the believer in abiogenesis to observe life coming from nonlife by purely natural means (i.e., no intelligence involved). Mr. Nye here was also alluding to the search for life on other planets. Because he believes life somehow came from nonlife, in a way he was admitting there is no evidence for this on earth, so one has to look elsewhere in the universe to try to find such evidence. In a way, Bill Nye didn't answer the problem; he just moved it from earth to another planet!

Mr. Nye then asked (again), "What is it you can predict?" Mr. Ham (and I) had already answered this many times (Mr. Ham listed and confirmed predictions in his debate presentation), and creationists like Isaac Newton, Gregor Mendel, Raymond Damadian, Louis Pasteur, and so on made predictions that have been confirmed. Recall the debate tactic by Mr. Nye — even if it was wrong or refuted, he would keep saying it.

Question: Is there room for God in science?

Mr. Nye, 2-minute response:

- I agree with Bill Nye

Here we agree:

> There are billions of people around the world who are religious and who accept science and embrace it, and especially all the technology that it brings us. Is there anyone here who doesn't have a mobile phone that has a camera? Is there anyone here whose family members have not benefited from modern medicine? Is there anyone here who doesn't use e-mail? Is there anybody here who doesn't eat? Because we use information sent from satellites in space to plant seeds on our farms; that's how we're able to feed 7.1 billion people where we used to barely be able to feed a billion. So that's what I see, that's what — we have used science or the process. Science for me is two things. It's the body of knowledge, the atomic number of rubidium, and it's the process, the means by which we make these discoveries.

Yes, I agree with Mr. Nye in regard to the above statements. But the debate question was about the viability of the creation model of origins — historical science. Mr. Nye in the above quote was using example after example of technology based on observational science. Not one of the examples Mr. Nye used in this series of statements has anything to do with believing in evolution! Mr. Nye was once again attempting to equate observational science with historical science. The underlying statement he was making is, "I believe in evolution and millions of years, and without this, one can never develop this wonderful technology." But this is absurd.

Mr. Ham gave specific examples of biblical creationists who have developed leading technology. Actually, I assert that Mr. Ham is the real

251

"science guy," as he teaches the true meaning of the word "science," and he teaches people how to think correctly about the origins issue.

• Now I disagree with Bill Nye

Then Mr. Nye claimed that Mr. Ham didn't believe in science. He asserted:

> So for me, that's not really that connected with your belief in a spiritual being or a higher power. If you reconcile those two, scientists — the head of the National Institutes of Health is a devout Christian. There are billions of people in the world who are devoutly religious. They have to be compatible, because those same people embrace science.

Mr. Nye wants to disconnect science from belief in God. Here Mr. Nye used a great scientist involved in employing observational science in the human genome project and the fact that he believes in God (but not biblical creation as Mr. Ham does) to justify claiming that there is no connection between one's beliefs about origins and observational science.

Actually, Mr. Nye was in a sense admitting that his belief in origins has nothing to do with empirical science that develops technology — the opposite of what Mr. Nye had been claiming! But this point is what Mr. Ham had been saying — that Mr. Nye's belief in evolution has nothing to do with technology.

But Mr. Nye once again failed to realize that science is predicated on the Bible being true.[48] Observable science is predicated on our senses and memory being basically reliable, which is a biblical construct. Repeatable and operational science is due to God upholding the creation in a particular fashion, so we can know that the laws of science are going to remain constant. God promised these laws would be in place so long as the earth endures (e.g., Genesis 8:22[49], Jeremiah 33:25[50]). These things are *Christian* based. If others hold to them, they must borrow these from God's Word.

---

48. J. Lisle, "Evolution: The Anti-science," Answers in Genesis, February 13, 2008, https://answersingenesis.org/theory-of-evolution/evolution-the-anti-science/.
49. "While the earth remains, seedtime and harvest, cold and heat, winter and summer, and day and night shall not cease."
50. "Thus says the LORD: 'If My covenant is not with day and night, and if I have not appointed the ordinances of heaven and earth.'"

In a secular understanding, where things pop into existence from nothing (like the Big Bang, which is actually inconsistent within its origin), the notion that life came from nonlife (which violates the law of biogenesis) destroys the idea of predictability in science — after all, one has no way of knowing what will happen tomorrow!

An evolutionary worldview not only violates the laws of science, but also has no *basis* to do science; in contrast, Christians standing on the authority of God's Word do have a basis for it and can logically defend these scientific laws. It sounds like Mr. Nye actually opposes the very things he claims to embrace — empirical science.

- Mr. Nye committed a bait-and-switch fallacy

Mr. Nye attacked Mr. Ham's embrace of empirical science when he said:

> The exception is you, Mr. Ham; that's the problem for me.

I've known Mr. Ham for over a decade, and I can readily affirm that he loves empirical science as well as the technology that can be produced from it, and embraces it. So have other young-earth creationists like Isaac Newton, Robert Boyle, Michael Faraday, Raymond Damadian, the scientists employed at Answers in Genesis, and many others.

So in reality, Mr. Nye shouldn't have a problem with Mr. Ham, since Mr. Ham embraces science. So what is the hang-up with Mr. Nye — why does he have an issue and claim that Mr. Ham doesn't embrace science? It is a bait and switch fallacy (a type of equivocation fallacy).

Because Mr. Nye disagreed with Mr. Ham's historical science, he then made the false claim that Mr. Ham is against science — implying Mr. Ham is against the observational science that builds technology. It's the same bait and switch fallacy that Mr. Nye used through the entire debate. Actually, Mr. Nye was guilty of what Mr. Ham revealed is happening in the government school system when he stated in his debate presentation:

> Public school textbooks are using the **same word** *science* for **observational** and **historical** science. They **arbitrarily define** *science* as **naturalism** and outlaw the supernatural. They present molecules-to-man evolution as fact. They are **imposing the religion of naturalism**/atheism on generations of students.

Let me re-write this paragraph to reflect what was happening in the debate:

> Mr. Bill Nye used the **same word** *science* for **observational** and **historical** science. He **arbitrarily defined** *science* as **naturalism** and outlawed the supernatural. He presented molecules-to-man evolution as fact. He was **imposing the religion of naturalism**/atheism on generations of people.

This fallacy changes the meaning of a word to mean something else. For example, I could say that because Billy Joe created a piece of artwork, when God created everything, it really wasn't that special. Now you would be able to recognize that I baited you with the word "created," which often means develop or make something from preexisting materials. But created was switched with the meaning of creation *ex nihilo* (that is, creation from nothing when calling space, time, and matter into existence).

Mr. Nye did the same thing with the word "science." He was talking about the good, observable, repeatable operational science (which all agree on by the way), but then he switched it another (new) definition that means the religion of *naturalism* or *evolutionism*. This is what Mr. Nye doesn't like about Mr. Ham — it has nothing to do with cell phones and GPS but instead has to do with the fact that Mr. Ham doesn't embrace Mr. Nye's naturalistic religion. In doing do, Mr. Nye baited the audience to think that Mr. Ham opposes email, cell phones, and so on, but that simply isn't the case. Beware of the bait and switch in regard to the word "science" and the word "evolution."

I suggest people need to be on the lookout for this fallacy from evolutionists. Other words are often used to bait and switch as well. A common one is the word "evolution." You are baited with "evolution," meaning simply change (e.g., your hair evolves to gray when you get older or this car evolved from a two-wheel drive to an all-wheel drive[51]), and then they switch to say "evolution" is true (meaning molecules-to-man religion) since we see things evolving (meaning *changing*) all the time. Mr. Ham warned about this in his debate presentation:

---

51. In reality, this occurred because cars were intelligently designed from one model to the next.

The word evolution has been hijacked using a bait and switch to indoctrinate students to accept evolutionary belief as observational science.

- Attacking God's Word again

Once again, Mr. Nye attacked God's Word. He asserted:

> You want us to take your word for what's written in this ancient text to be more compelling than what we see around us.

Note the big picture here. The question is: is there room for God in science (observational science)? Of course without God, such science wouldn't be possible as observations couldn't be trustworthy if God hadn't made us in His image and permitted our memory to be reliable.

However, Mr. Nye gave approval for those who are religious and use such science at the outset of his response — but at this point, he attacked Christianity as being against observational science. In other words, Mr. Nye evidenced a double standard. He even finished his response by claiming "But right now, I see no incompatibility between religions and science." So really Mr. Nye was saying yes and no about the same thing — an obvious contradiction.

The issue is really between Mr. Nye and God. God has commanded Mr. Nye (and also all of us) to be submissive to His Word, repent of his sin, and be saved for eternity. It is God who commands people to listen to Him; He does not ask them to go against what can be observed, but as God said, even by looking at things that have been made, the reality of a Creator God can clearly be seen. The Bible also tells us in Romans 1 that those who reject God as Creator are without excuse, and they will work to suppress the truth. Mr. Nye is guilty of attempting to suppress the truth of the Creator God to advance his own religion of naturalism. One of the ways Mr. Nye did this was by lashing out at Mr. Ham.

Romans 1 states,

> 18 For the wrath of God is revealed from heaven against all ungodliness and unrighteousness of men, who suppress the truth in unrighteousness,
> 19 because what may be known of God is manifest in them, for God has shown it to them.

20 For since the creation of the world His invisible attributes are clearly seen, being understood by the things that are made, even His eternal power and Godhead, so that they are without excuse,

21 because, although they knew God, they did not glorify Him as God, nor were thankful, but became futile in their thoughts, and their foolish hearts were darkened.

22 Professing to be wise, they became fools,

23 and changed the glory of the incorruptible God into an image made like corruptible man — and birds and four-footed animals and creeping things.

24 Therefore God also gave them up to uncleanness, in the lusts of their hearts, to dishonor their bodies among themselves,

25 who exchanged the truth of God for the lie, and wor-shiped and served the creature rather than the Creator, who is blessed forever. Amen.

When Mr. Nye denies that the creation should be separated from the question of God, he is trying to worship the creation rather than God, who created those things. Romans 1 also tells us that God has given each of us the ability to know that He is the Creator. This is why those who don't believe are without excuse. So Mr. Nye is suppressing that knowl-edge. He has no excuse before God. Please be praying for Mr. Nye to repent of his rebellion and receive the free gift of salvation in Christ.

- More debate tactics

Mr. Nye then began closing out his response with his debate tactic, as he outlined in a letter from the NCSE (the *skeptical method*, using what was referred to as the "Gish Gallop").[52] He asked Mr. Ham to NOT answer the question at hand in the next minute but instead address things like fossils, ice layers, trees, and Noah's Ark.

Mr. Ham had already addressed those very issues as much as could be done in this limited time debate format, so there was no need to do so again. But this was a debate tactic to try to convince a listener that Mr.

---

52. K. Ham, "Secularists Use Ham-Nye Debate for Fundraising," Answers in Genesis, July 28, 2014, https://answersingenesis.org/ministry-news/core-ministry/secularists-use-ham-nye-debate-for-fundraising/.

Ham hadn't addressed those listed issues. Throughout this volume, I too have addressed them in more detail.

Mr. Ham, 1-minute response:

Clearly Mr. Ham saw through Mr. Nye's debate tactic when he began with:

> "...I actually want to take the minute to address *the question*" (emphasis mine).

As I said earlier, Mr. Ham believed it was important to honor the agreed-to debate format and devote the time given for answering questions from the audience to do just that — and not to use this time to deal with other issues.

• God is predicated for science to be possible

Mr. Ham responded directly to the question, just as I had mentioned. As such, Mr. Ham appealed to the fact that God is *necessary* for operational science. In doing so, he transitioned to other biblical creationists like Dr. Stuart Burgess who, like Mr. Ham, embrace empirical science and technology. Mr. Ham again repeated a powerful mantra:

> But see, I say God is necessary because you have to assume the laws of logic, you have to assume the laws of nature, you have to assume the uniformity of nature. And there's a question I had for you. Where does that come from if the universe is here by natural processes?

Mr. Ham had already challenged Mr. Nye about the origin of the laws of logic. Recall that Mr. Ham had asked Mr. Nye this question in his debate presentation:

> How do you account for the laws of logic and laws of nature from a naturalistic worldview that excludes the existence of God?

This question destroys all other worldviews as all scientists (Christian or secular) have to ultimately borrow from God's Word to make sense of science or logic and the laws of nature (whether they acknowledge that or not). These are Christian principles, and the world is trying to "hijack" them — but they simply do not comport to their respective religions — especially Mr. Bill Nye's naturalism.

Consider this — Mr. Nye had to borrow from the biblical worldview just to argue against it. In other words, the fact that Mr. Nye showed up for the debate (which precludes that the laws of logic and debate exist — a Christian principle) means he had to give up his view of naturalism just to debate. Thus, Mr. Nye lost the debate…by showing up. So Mr. Ham could confidently state:

> You know, Christianity and science, the Bible and science, go hand in hand; we love science!

Question: Do you believe the entire Bible is to be taken literally? For example, should people who touch pigskin — I think it says here — be stoned? Can men marry multiple women?

Mr. Ham, 2-minute response:

Well, this question is easy to respond to: Mr. Ham's response was excellent (I refer you to the transcript in Appendix A). I heartily agree. I also addressed this question as it came up in the debate in the Ham 30-minute case. So it makes more sense to refer you there as well.

Keep in mind that these questions were written and handed in prior to the debate's onset, so the questioner may not have realized this was going to be discussed in the debate.

Mr. Nye, 1-minute response:

- Mr. Nye was close to understanding Mr. Ham's point

Mr. Nye almost understood it when he responded:

> So it sounds to me, just listening to you over the last two minutes, that there are certain parts of this document — of the Bible — that you embrace literally and other parts you consider poetry. So it sounds to me in those last two minutes like you're going to take what you like and interpret literally and other passages you're going to interpret as poetic or descriptions of human events.

What Mr. Nye failed to catch was that it is actually the Bible that reveals the nature of the literary style, not Mr. Ham. Mr. Ham mentioned this when he mentioned "interpreting Scripture with Scripture." This is common phraseology in churches, seminaries, Christian colleges, and so on that means if there is a question about any piece of Scripture, one should interpret it using other passages of Scripture. Then the onus is on God to interpret it correctly, not on the fallible ideas of man.

Consider, for example, if the question arises, did the Flood of Noah's day (or for that matter Noah himself) really exist in history (i.e., Genesis 6–7 is literal history) or was it allegorical/poetic? You turn to other passages of Scripture to see how God's Word views that passage. First Chronicles 1:4[53] mentions Noah in a genealogical list, so it clearly saw him as real. In Isaiah 54:9,[54] Noah is seen as real, as was the Flood. Ezekiel 14:20[55] views Noah as person who really lived; there, he is listed alongside other people who lived in the past. Jesus and Peter both viewed Noah and the Flood as real (several passages). So the issue is settled. Scripture interprets Scripture, not fallible people.

But this is a key point. When someone interprets Scripture based on their own ideas *outside of* Scripture, they can — and in many cases will — be wrong. In such a situation, the opinion of fallible man is elevated to be greater than God's Word, which comes with the authority of God Himself. When people's ideas are thus elevated, false teachings generally result.

This is why when fallible Christians take ideas like evolution or millions of years (*not* interpreting Scripture with Scripture) and impose them on Genesis, then man's ideas are being elevated to be superior to God's revelation, leading to false views.

- But in the end, Mr. Nye didn't understand

Mr. Nye then failed to get the point when he said:

All that aside, I'll just say scientifically, or as a reasonable man, it doesn't seem possible that all these things that contradict your literal interpretation of those first few passages, all those things that contradict that, I find unsettling when you want me to embrace the rest of it as literal.

---

53. Noah, Shem, Ham, and Japheth.
54. "For this is like the waters of Noah to Me; for as I have sworn that the waters of Noah would no longer cover the earth, so have I sworn that I would not be angry with you, nor rebuke you."
55. "Even though Noah, Daniel, and Job were in it, as I live," says the Lord God, "they would deliver neither son nor daughter; they would deliver only themselves by their righteousness."

First, reason doesn't exist in Mr. Nye's materialistic worldview. Reason is from God and not material. Since we are made in His image, we can reason, but due to sin and the curse, we don't always do it right, which is all the more reason to rely on God's Word to set us straight!

But Mr. Nye did not show anything that contradicts a literal historical rendering of the early pages of Genesis. Nor did Mr. Ham, or any other Christian, state that they want Mr. Nye to embrace the rest of the Bible as literal! Mr. Ham just told Mr. Nye in the debate that much of the Bible is not written as literal history!

In fact, Mr. Ham explained that when someone asks if he takes the Bible literally, he affirms that provided the person understands that by literally, he means "naturally." This has already been discussed in detail. In other words, take what is written in the Bible according to the literature, context, etc. Genesis is written as typical historical narrative, but the Psalms are written as poetry. There is symbolism used in the Bible (just as we use in our everyday speaking).

In the Bible, there are also parables (and we are usually told it is a parable, or the context makes it clear it's a parable), and phenomenological language is used in places (such as when the sun stood still in the sky). But if Mr. Nye had really researched what Christians like Mr. Ham believe, he would have known this. It seems that he was just regurgitating the same old false accusations secularists have been coming up with for years.

So just when Mr. Nye started to get the point that not all the Bible is to be taken as literal history, he immediately reverted and totally ignored this point! But for the reader, when studying the Bible, it is quite simple: literal history is literal history, poetry is poetry, metaphors are metaphors, genealogies are genealogies, letters are letters, prophecy is prophecy, and so on. Is this too hard?

- Mr. Nye failed to realize what debate he was at

Once again, Mr. Nye failed to get the debate topic correct. He stated:

> Now, I, as I say, am not a theologian, but we started this debate, is Ken Ham's Creation model viable, does it hold water, can it fly, does it describe anything? And I'm still looking for an answer.

Instead the debate topic was: *"Is creation a viable model of origins in today's modern, scientific era?"* So Mr. Nye was looking for an answer to the wrong question! But Mr. Ham adequately defended the position that creation is a viable model as creationists are doing science, and it is the Bible that must be predicated or presupposed for science to be possible in the first place. Mr. Ham made predictions based on the creation model and then illustrated how observational science confirmed those predictions. Mr. Nye was not able to show otherwise, nor would he be able to without borrowing from the Bible and giving up his professed worldview.

And just as an aside, Mr. Nye said he is "not a theologian," but then acted as a theologian in attempting to critique how Mr. Ham interprets the Scriptures! This is a double standard.

Question: Have you ever believed that evolution was accomplished through way of a higher power? I think that's what they're trying to ask here; this is the intelligent design question, I think. If so, why or why not? Why could not the evolutionary process be accomplished in this way? (Actual question: *have you ever believed that evolution partook through way of evolution?*)

Mr. Nye, 2-minute response:

- Agnosticism

Mr. Nye began:

> The idea that there's a higher power that has driven the course of events in the universe and our own existence is one that you cannot prove or disprove. And this gets into this expression agnostic; you can't know. I'll grant you that.

Mr. Nye affirmed in the debate that we are a product of the universe/nature, i.e., naturalism (no God). He did this when he claimed, "You and I are a product of the universe." This is consistent with many other statements he made in the debate. His argument therefore stated that humans are the product of nature, and yet, now he stated that you can't know if a God was involved! This was inconsistent. He claims to be an agnostic, but he spoke like an atheist throughout the debate.

How can Mr. Nye say that one can't know if God exists (and hence can't know if God was involved), and yet hold to naturalism that excludes God? An agnostic, if they were consistent with their religion, would say:

> One can't know if God exists, nor can we really know if we can't know if God exists or not, because we can't know if knowledge exists or if logic exists — so we can't even know if what we are saying is true or not…that is…if truth exists or not since we can't know that either!

That sounds confusing doesn't it? When it comes down to it, one theoretically can't know anything at all in agnosticism. Is this how Mr. Nye debated? No — he acted like an atheist, which goes to show that his humanistic bias is really not agnosticism but naturalism (atheism). Excluding supernaturalism is his *a priori* assumption, as clearly shown throughout the debate.

- Intelligent design

Mr. Nye then discussed the topic of *Intelligent Design*. Now this is actually a more complicated topic than Mr. Nye understood. One needs first of all to distinguish between intelligent design arguments and the Intelligent Design Movement. Mr. Ham agrees with intelligent arguments, but does not agree with the philosophy of the Intelligent Design Movement.

The movement is against naturalism, but does not take a stand on what intelligence is responsible for life and the universe. Not all those in the Intelligent Design Movement are Christians — some are — but it is definitely not a Christian movement. In fact, there are evolutionists in the Intelligent Design Movement who would propose that intelligent aliens designed the first life here on earth.

Biblical creationists like Mr. Ham make no apology about the fact that they point to the Creator God of the Bible as the intelligent designer, and they won't divorce intelligent design arguments from the words of Christ, our Designer. After all, as Mr. Ham has stated in his lectures, "Romans 10 verse 17 tells us that Faith comes by hearing and hearing by the Word of God." That's why Mr. Ham made sure that God's Word and the saving Gospel message were clearly presented during the debate.

Now it is important to say that there are many qualified scientists in the Intelligent Design Movement who are adamant that the evidence in the present concerning life and the universe does not fit with a worldview of naturalism. So obviously, Mr. Nye would not agree with the Intelligent Design Movement or the Biblical Creation movement.

- Reification fallacy

Perhaps one of the most common fallacies by evolutionists…and creationists… is the fallacy of reification (personification is a specific form of it). Such a device is acceptable in poetic, metaphorical, or allegorical uses, but in debate it is strictly taboo because it is fallacious. Untrained debaters tend to use reification. Many times (sometimes even in this debate), I skipped over it and did not comment. But I have opted not to skip over it in this instance, as a teaching point. Mr. Nye claimed:

> This is the fundamental insight in the explanation for living things that's provided by evolution.

Evolution doesn't provide insight or explanation. People do. As I've heard Mr. Ham say many times, "Science doesn't say anything; it's scientists who say something."

This fallacy of trying to give humanlike qualities to a concept was employed here by Mr. Nye in his use of the word evolution. Mr. Nye's tendency to reify or personify evolution ("This is the fundamental insight…provided by evolution) was shown when he imposed human image qualities upon something inanimate. Other examples to help us understand this concept are when someone says "science says…," "the evidence speaks for itself," "evolution thought of an answer," "life found a way," or as Mr. Nye commented a couple of sentences later — "nature has its mediocre designs eaten by its good designs."

Science doesn't speak — scientists do. Evidence doesn't speak…if it speaks to you, seek counseling! Evolution doesn't think, life doesn't find things, and nature doesn't direct designs to eat! Interesting that Mr. Nye believes things are *designed ("mediocre designs…good designs")*, as that requires intelligence, not blind processes.

But the point is that these notions are fallacious. It is fascinating, though, that God created us in His image to be creative, to speak, and to think abstractly, and yet many people, reflecting the image that is stamped upon them, don't even realize it; thus, they try to make inanimate evidence and concepts like science and evolution in *our (man's)* image.

- Mr. Nye disagrees with most evolutionists

I recall in the debate when Mr. Nye made a particular statement. I was shocked! He said:

> Evolution is a process that adds complexity through natural selection.

Now here is why I was shocked — no evolutionists, I thought, believe this today. This is called traditional Darwinism. Let's have a brief history lesson to explain this situation.

Epicureanism

Epicureans (atheists in the Greek culture) were really the first evolutionists we know of. Darwin didn't invent the idea of evolution; he just popularized a particular form of it to attempt to explain life without God. When variant forms of Epicureanism began to revive in the late 1700s and early 1800s with men such as Mr. Erasmus Darwin and Professor Jean-Baptiste Lamarck, evolutionists needed a way to explain new features. It is not a new idea, but merely one form of Greek mythology.[56] The Epicureans believed in no gods, unlike the many gods of the Greek culture. They believed everything evolved from very tiny things they called "atoms." This is from where we get our modern term "atom."

As you can see, evolutionists today basically adhere to this same religious mythology that Paul argued against in the first century in Acts 17. But it has changed. Today, instead of a tiny particle as the Greeks proposed, secularists propose that a cosmic egg or an almost infinitely dense hot particle somehow popped into existence from nothing to begin the universe in accordance with the Big Bang.

---

56. B. Hodge, "If Paul Were Around Today, Would He Argue Against Evolutionists?" Answers in Genesis, June 14, 2010, https://answersingenesis.org/apologetics/if-paul-were-around-today-would-he-argue-against-evolutionists/.

In Lamarckian evolution, animals change due to environmental factors and the use or disuse of a feature. For example, a giraffe's neck will get longer over time as it continually stretches it to reach higher leaves on trees.

Lamarckian Evolution

When Epicureanism was rehashed, the leading view was called Lamarckian evolution. This view was promoted and popularized by Professor Jean Lamarck in France[57] and Dr. Erasmus Darwin (Charles Darwin's grandfather) in England.[58] Lamarckian evolution is famous for its teaching that the giraffe's neck became longer because it kept reaching for leaves that were higher and higher. Then, supposedly, this feature of a longer stretched neck was passed onto the next generation of giraffes.

Mr. Charles Darwin's grandfatᵒher Erasmus even wrote a book on Lamarckian evolution called *Zoonomia*.[59] Most people don't know that Mr. Charles Darwin used a form of Lamarck's ideas in his book to give his own explanation for new characteristics appearing in new generations. Modern evolutionists would, of course, reject this idea today even though they hold Darwin's book *On the Origin of Species* as the "Bible" of the evolution movement.

But anyone can test Lamarck's ideas of acquired inheritance. For instance, as a farmer (my background prior to engineering), I can tell you that if you cut the tail off of a sheep (docking) generation after generation, the baby lambs will still grow a tail! So the evolutionists still needed a different mechanism to try to make evolution work.

---

57. For his collective works, see Jean-Baptiste Lamarck, http://www.lamarck.cnrs.fr/index.php?lang=en.
58. E. Darwin, *Zoonomia; or, The Laws of Organic Life*, Volume I (London, England: J. Johnson Publisher, 1796).
59. Ibid.

Traditional Darwinism

A Christian named Mr. Ed Blyth published a number of papers on variations within the kinds of creatures that God created and how the environment influences why such variations succeed or not. He did this about 25 years before Mr. Darwin. Mr. Darwin, a theologian, read these papers and thought, *Maybe this is the mechanism that will lead to evolution.* He called this process "natural selection."

Creationists, by and large, believe in this observable process (often referred to as "adaptation," "variation," or what is called "natural selection"). Such a process, though, only operates on the information already contained in the genome of a particular kind. No new information is generated — just different combinations of already existing information; this is why we have variations within the dog kind, for example.

Also, sometimes information is corrupted by mutations (e.g., cancer, deformations, or extra copies of something such as extra fingers or toes are mutations). These things (selection and mutations) help explain variations in animals (and the formation of different species within a kind — remember the example of dogs that Mr. Ham related in his debate presentation) as they spread around the globe. But Mr. Darwin thought this process would lead to evolution in the sense of the production of brand new characteristics that weren't previously possible.

Of course, Mr. Darwin was emphatic about natural selection (and some Lamarckian process too) being the mechanism for this in the first edition of *Origin of Species by Means of Natural Selection, or the Preservation of Favored Races*. But by the sixth edition, Mr. Darwin had backed off of this significantly in his wording, knowing that natural selection wasn't turning out to be the mechanism he desired.[60] But Mr. Darwin had by then popularized naturalistic evolution (one kind changing into a different kind — molecules-to-man evolution), and it had started to become a mainstream idea in the population even though it still lacked a viable mechanism and had no directly observed evidence. Keep in mind, as Mr. Ham made clear in his debate presentation, that speciation is not evolution in the molecules-to-man sense.

---

60. R. Hedtke, *Secrets of the Sixth Edition* (Green Forest, AR: Master Books, 2010).

Darwin originally proposed that natural selection would be the primary mechanism acting to change organisms over millions of years. He was not aware of the role of mutations in heredity.

So basically traditional Darwinism was natural selection (with aspects of the Lamarckian process of passing along these newly acquired traits, e.g., Darwin's proposed "gemmules"), plus the notion that long periods of time will somehow lead to the evolution of new kinds of living things (amoeba-to-man).

Neo-Darwinism

Later evolutionists (called neo-Darwinists) postulated that *mutations* were mechanisms to increase complexity by generating new information into the genome. Neo-Darwinists differ from traditional Darwinists, who appeal to natural selection alone as that mechanism. Neo-Darwinists also appeal to natural selection as part of the mechanism but not the process for originating complexity from new information. They see natural selection as a means of filtering out organisms to allow a more complex (or "better") one to take its place.

This is what shows like *X-Men*, *Spiderman*, *Heroes*, and so on appeal to as well. So basically, neo-Darwinism could be described this way:

> Natural selection, plus mutation, plus long periods of time lead to evolution.

Many learned evolutionists and creationists alike recognize what mutations really do, and by and large they are rather detrimental. In some cases, they are nearly neutral or do not affect function too much;[61] but

---

61. See for, example, J. Sanford, *Genetic Entropy & the Mystery of the Genome* (Waterloo, New NY: FMS Publications, 2005); L. Spetner, *Not By Chance* (Brooklyn, NY: Judaica Press, Inc., 1997).

Natural Selection + Mutations

+ Millions of Years

After the discovery of DNA and its role in inheritance, evolutionists pointed to mutations in the DNA as a source for new traits. These accidental mutations provide differences in the offspring that can be selected for. This selection is believed to lead to new kinds of life.

they simply do not result in brand new information being generated and added into the genes, despite evolutionists' claims to the contrary.[62] So a new mechanism is still required for evolutionists to attempt an explanation for the complexities of life!

The reason is that we do not observe mutations (the billions that we should be seeing if evolution were true) moving in a positive direction. Cancer, for example, is a mutation. Furthermore, after years of experiments on fruit flies, for instance, bombarding them with radiation to cause mutations, they never improve with brand new characteristics (generated by new information) not previously possible! Dr. Lee Spetner states:

> No mutations have ever been observed that have converted an animal to a markedly different species, say from a fly (sic) to a wasp (sic)."[63]

Punctuated Equilibrium

Furthermore, the problem of mutations gets worse since we do not find the gradual changing of creatures in the fossil record from one to another that evolutionary scientists predicted. This was particularly troubling to evolutionist Dr. Stephen J. Gould from Harvard University, who became

---

62. The best example to date that I've seen evolutionists propose for new information is the nylon bug. However, this was only based on preprogrammed design changes in the plasmids, which are extrachomosomal segments that are autonomous to the bacterial DNA, so with a proper understanding, it doesn't support evolutionary changes at all. Please see G. Purdom and K. Anderson, "A Creationist's Perspective of Beneficial Mutations in Bacteria," *Answers in Depth,* May 27, 2009, https://answersingenesis.org/genetics/mutations/a-creationist-perspective-of-beneficial-mutations-in-bacteria/.
63. L. Spetner, *Not By Chance* (Brooklyn, NY; Judaica Press, Inc., 1997), p. 177.

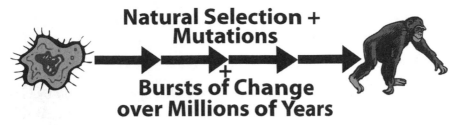

Natural Selection + Mutations
+
Bursts of Change over Millions of Years

Contrary to Neo-Darwinism, punctuated equilibrium tries to account for the lack of fossil intermediates by appealing to rapid bursts of change interspersed in the millions of years. They still rely on mutations and natural selection, but at a much faster rate.

the popular advocate of the Punctuated Equilibrium idea; however, not all evolutionists jumped on board his particular evolutionary view.

Essentially, Dr. Gould argued that things didn't change much over long periods of time, but rather, the change happened in short spurts or bursts for evolution in isolated populations. This was proposed to eliminate the problem of no undisputed transitional forms in the fossil record.

The idea was that these changes happened so fast, you don't see the results in the fossil layers. Basically, they weren't finding evidence for molecules-to-man evolution in the fossil layers (it's nice that Dr. Gould was honest about that), so it was proposed that they didn't need any because they could explain this away using the Punctuated Equilibrium idea.

In essence, Punctuated Equilibrium is the idea that mutations plus natural selection produced short bursts of evolution over long ages. I've heard creationists facetiously explain it this way — "It used to be that the reason for no transitional forms in the fossil record and the reason why we don't see molecules-to-man evolution happening is because it happens slowly over a long time. Now it is proposed that the reason we don't see evolution happening or find transitional forms is because it happened so fast we missed it!"

In retrospect, Mr. Nye appealed to traditional Darwinism, which most evolutionists reject in favor of more modern ideas. But in the end, the evolutionist still doesn't have an observable and repeatable process to change one kind of organism like algae into a totally different kind such as a dog. The only mechanisms they propose are what they call natural selection and mutations. But both of these are actually working in the wrong direction for evolution.[64]

Mr. Ham, 1-minute response:

Mr. Ham doesn't believe in evolution but rather special creation by God as revealed in the Bible in Genesis. Mr. Ham had already covered why Christians can't be consistent and believe in the Bible as well as the idea of evolution and/or millions of years.

Mr. Ham challenged Mr. Nye to give an example of "function that arose that was not previously possible from the genetic information that was there."

For evolution to be a possibility, considering the enormous (really incomprehensible) amount of information in living things, where is just one example of matter producing new information? Where do we observe matter generating the code for a brand new characteristic that was not previously possible? Mr. Ham asked only for one such example. Given the immense amount of information in nature, surely there must be a law of nature that results in matter generating information.

Let's consider an example — if humans were to theoretically evolve to the next level, where are the mutations to make new organs to receive radio waves or to be able to tell the future? What new (nascent) organ has shown up to do something like that? None.

What new complexity has mutated on a dog to make, say, feathers? We see misplaced copies of information, like extra toes or extra fingers (polydactyl, which are actually detrimental), but we don't see totally new characteristics arising like hair on a fish. We observe the result of genes that turn on and off, but that information was already there, and turning these on and off has nothing to do with molecules-to-man evolution (i.e., eventually turning microbes into turkeys).

Mr. Ham's point is that we observe variation within kinds, which is what the Bible predicts, but not new characteristics that weren't previously coded for in the genes.

---

64. For more on these views of evolution, please see T. Mortenson and R. Patterson, "Do Evolutionists Believe Darwin's Ideas about Evolution?" in K. Ham, gen. ed., *The New Answers Book 3* (Green Forest, AR: Master Books, 2010), pp. 271–282; Also, I understand that there are variations within these models like neo-Lamarckianism or Hopeful Monster (an even faster model of Punctuated Equilibrium), but none offer a viable mechanism for evolution.

Question: Mr. Ham, name one institution, business, or organization other than a church, amusement park, or the Creation Museum that is using any aspect of Creationism to produce its product.

Mr. Ham, 2-minute response:

Mr. Ham's response on this point was excellent. To quote it:

> Any scientist out there, Christian or non-Christian, that is involved in inventing things, involved in scientific method, is using creation. They are, because they are borrowing from a Christian worldview. They're using the laws of logic; I keep emphasizing that. I want Bill to tell me in a view of the universe that's a result of natural processes, explain where the laws of logic came from. Why should we trust the laws of nature? I mean, are they going to be the same tomorrow as they were yesterday?

In other words, Mr. Ham's response was that anyone doing empirical science is borrowing from a Christian/creationist worldview. It is this worldview that predicated for science to produce our technology.

I will go one step further. Mr. Bill Nye was borrowing from our biblical worldview just to do this debate. In an agnostic worldview like Mr. Nye professes, for example, science would be impossible because you can't know if the laws of nature will change tomorrow! We know since God promised this in His Word as previously discussed. So Mr. Nye's presentation was resting on Christian laurels even though he was arguing against it.

Mr. Nye, 1-minute response:

- Mr. Nye avoided the question

Mr. Nye never even attempted to address the question. Instead he wanted to talk about things that had already been refuted in the debate, like once again falsely claiming a lack of predictability by creationists. Remember, Mr. Ham actually used slides listing some predictions! And the onus was on Mr. Nye to prove how the work of creationists such as Mr. Isaac Newton, Dr. Louis Pasteur, or Dr. Raymond Damadian was not empirical science that advanced our technology and understanding of the universe.

- Attacking the Gospel

Mr. Nye then moved to attack the Gospel when he said:

> Well, what became of all those people who never heard of it, never heard of you? What became of all those people in Asia? What became of all those First Nations people in North America? Were they condemned and doomed?… to have you tell them that they are inherently lost or misguided. It's very troubling.

Mr. Ham has often told people that when one is debating with those who oppose biblical creationists, if the opponent ends up attacking the Bible by bringing up supposed contradictions or impugning unjust accusations on God — then that person has moved the debate to its real subject matter. The real debate is over God's Word versus man's word.

Personally, I think Mr. Ham's continued insistence on explaining the difference between historical science and observational science, and his challenging Mr. Nye concerning the origin of the laws of nature and logic, pushed Mr. Nye to this point. Once Mr. Nye started attacking God and the Bible as he did here, it clearly illustrated that Mr. Ham's persistence in a focused message was very successful.

So is Mr. Nye troubled by the fact that he is saying we are lost and misguided as creationists? Note his double standard. He wants to be able to tell Bible-believing creationists they are misguided, but he doesn't want Christians to tell people they are misguided and must understand their sin and their need for a Savior in Jesus Christ.

Actually, the Christian is giving people good news because Jesus Christ has made a way of escape from the eternal consequences of our sin (eternal punishment). And why does it matter to Mr. Nye anyway? If from his perspective a human being ceases to exist once they die, why does it matter what anyone tells anyone? The fact that Mr. Nye was so emphatic about wanting to stop the message of man's sin and need for repentance being proclaimed to people illustrates that this is a spiritual issue. If it weren't, why would he bother?

In actuality, Mr. Nye (by his own philosophy), would rather that lost people sit in darkness and never know the truth until they are condemned for all eternity. It is sad that Mr. Nye doesn't think people are lost and in need of a Savior. Would it be wrong to tell a person that they are in a burning building, in need of rescue, and the time is short? Would it be misguided and troubling to tell them that there is a way out? Not at all — this good news would be welcome to someone who wanted to live.

Besides the fact that Romans 1 makes it clear that no one has an excuse before God, the Bible speaks on this issue. Jesus said:

> And I, if I am lifted up from the earth, will draw all peoples to Myself (John 12:32).

> No one can come to Me unless the Father who sent Me draws him; and I will raise him up at the last day (John 6:44).

All people are drawn by God regardless of where they are. At the first preaching of the Gospel after the resurrection of Christ, there were people representing every nation under heaven (Acts 2:5[65]) who took the message of the Gospel back to their homelands after Pentecost. Many Christians were scattered among the nations due to Jewish persecution (Acts 8:1–8), taking the Gospel with them where they went.

The apostles, not just Peter and Paul, took the message to many places. For instance, Philip took the Gospel message to the South, even converting a leading Cushite (Ethiopian) who surely took the Gospel back to Africa (Acts 8:26–40). Acts 10–11 shows the speed at which the Gospel was spreading in the apostolic age. There were already Christians in Rome awaiting Paul when he arrived (Acts 28:11–15). There were even Christians in Nero Caesar's own household (Philippians 4:22[66]).

Without a doubt, Paul could rightly state that the message of the Gospel had been preached to all the nations by the time of his letters to Colossi and Rome (Colossians 1:6,[67] 1:23;[68] Romans 1:8,[69] 16:26[70]); and many believe that this fulfills the prediction of Christ that the Gospel would be preached to all nations prior to the destruction of the Temple

---

65. "And there were dwelling in Jerusalem Jews, devout men, from every nation under heaven."
66. "All the saints greet you, but especially those who are of Caesar's household."
67. "Which has come to you, as it has also in all the world, and is bringing forth fruit, as it is also among you since the day you heard and knew the grace of God in truth."
68. "If indeed you continue in the faith, grounded and steadfast, and are not moved away from the hope of the gospel which you heard, which was preached to every creature under heaven, of which I, Paul, became a minister."
69. "First, I thank my God through Jesus Christ for you all, that your faith is spoken of throughout the whole world."
70. "But now made manifest, and by the prophetic Scriptures made known to all nations, according to the commandment of the everlasting God, for obedience to the faith."

in Mark 13:10[71] and Matthew 24:14.[72] Any restriction of this Gospel since then has been by the hands of men fighting against the Good News (Gospel).

But from a big picture, those in the past who were saved looked *forward* to the finished work of Christ on the Cross — just as those after Christ look *back* to his finished work on the Cross. It is the same Gospel (salvation through faith) and always has been since an all-knowing God can rightly proclaim that Christ, the Lamb of God, was slain from the foundation of the world (Revelation 13:8[73]).

Question: Mr. Nye, since evolution teaches that man is evolving and growing smarter over time, how can you explain the numerous evidences of man's high intelligence in the past?

Mr. Nye, 2-minute response:

- Two parts to the question

There are two aspects to this question. The first is dealing with man's intelligence in the distant past, when man was supposed to be more primitive, and thus less intelligent than the present. Mr. Nye never addressed this, which is a powerful argument against an evolutionary worldview; and I suspect this is what the questioner was actually asking. There is considerable evidence that people in past cultures were highly intelligent — even developing technology we do not understand today. Books have been written on this subject.[74] From a biblical perspective, man has always been highly intelligent and inventive — in fact, probably more so in the past as one gets closer to the first man created — Adam. Because of sin and the curse, if anything, man's intellect may have degenerated somewhat.

The other aspect of this question was to ask if man is really getting smarter (because of evolution). By the way, inherent to this, would also

---

71. "And the gospel must first be preached to all the nations."
72. "And this gospel of the kingdom will be preached in all the world as a witness to all the nations, and then the end will come."
73. "All who dwell on the earth will worship him, whose names have not been written in the Book of Life of the Lamb slain from the foundation of the world."
74. For example, please see B. Hodge, *The Tower of Babel* (Green Forest, AR: Master Books, 2013); D. Chittick, *The Puzzle of Ancient Man* (Newburg OR: Creation Compass Publishers, 2006); D. Landis, ed., *The Genius of Ancient Man* (Green Forest, AR: Master Books, 2012).

be the question as to whether the smarter ones survive more than others! Mr. Nye selected this aspect to respond to. Mr. Nye rightly corrected the mistake here by pointing out that evolutionists wouldn't necessarily say that the smartest are the ones who survive.

Instead, Mr. Nye argued that it was the fittest who survive, and they may not be the smartest, but simply those who survive in a particular situation. Of course, so-called "survival of the fittest" doesn't explain nascent features (newly evolved organs or new information-based features). "Survival of the fittest" only explains why certain creatures were able to survive in a particular environment, but it isn't valid to use for explaining the origin of these creatures. In other words, "survival of the fittest" explains why polar bears survive in the arctic but not crocodiles. But survival of the fittest doesn't explain where warm-bloodedness comes from or where the origin of hair comes from. Really, "survival of the fittest" means "survival of those who survive!"

- I agree with Mr. Nye

Mr. Nye said:

> Our intellect, such as it is, has enabled us to dominate the world.

I agree, largely because we are made in the image of a ruling God who has intellect. Also, God instructed man to have "dominion over the fish of the sea, over the birds of the air, and over the cattle, over all the earth and over every creeping thing that creeps on the earth" (Genesis 1:26). Intellect, by the way, is not material, hence shouldn't be a viable possibility within the materialistic worldview; rather, it only makes sense in a Christian worldview.

Also consider that fact that God gave man dominion over the world (e.g., Genesis 1:26,[75] 1:28,[76] and 9:2[77]). Now Christ, who is fully God

---

75. "Then God said, 'Let Us make man in Our image, according to Our likeness; let them have dominion over the fish of the sea, over the birds of the air, and over the cattle, over all the earth and over every creeping thing that creeps on the earth.'"
76. "Then God blessed them, and God said to them, 'Be fruitful and multiply; fill the earth and subdue it; have dominion over the fish of the sea, over the birds of the air, and over every living thing that moves on the earth.'"
77. "And the fear of you and the dread of you shall be on every beast of the earth, on every bird of the air, on all that move on the earth, and on all the fish of the sea. They are given into your hand."

and yet fully man, has that ultimate dominion (e.g., Numbers 24:19 [as prophesied]; Matthew 28:18;[78] 1 Peter 5:11[79] and 4:11[80]).

- Mr. Nye and dinosaur extinction

Mr. Nye flew the banner for dinosaurs dying out from "a worldwide fireball" by an impact (by a comet, asteroid, etc.) when he claimed:

> So as the world changed, as it did, for example, the ancient dinosaurs, they were taken out by a worldwide fireball apparently caused by an impactor; that's the best theory we have.

By the way, he is comfortable suggesting a worldwide catastrophe in the past — as long as it's not a catastrophe like Noah's Flood that is found in the Bible!

I find it fascinating that the dinosaur fossils are not charred (from a fireball) but have evidence of burial by flood sediment (e.g., waterborne sediments, buried with marine fossils, etc.). Furthermore, why would this impactor and fireball kill all the dinosaurs and not too many other things?

Biblical creationists do believe most of the dinosaur fossils were formed at the time of the global Flood of Noah's day — but representatives of each kind of dinosaur (probably about 50 kinds representing the approximately 50 families of dinosaurs) were on board Noah's Ark. Thus dinosaur extinction, like that of several other animals that became extinct, occurred in the post-Flood world.

Most evolutionists today take the position that dinosaurs evolved into birds[81] and thus aren't really extinct in the sense that they purportedly became these feathered creatures.

However, secularists tend to call certain creatures that are obviously birds "dinosaurs" (e.g., Archaeopteryx, Confuciousornis, Microraptor). They also call certain dinosaurs birds using debated evidence of

---

78. "And Jesus came and spoke to them, saying, 'All authority has been given to Me in heaven and on earth.'"
79. "To Him be the glory and the dominion forever and ever. Amen."
80. "If anyone speaks, let him speak as the oracles of God. If anyone ministers, let him do it as with the ability which God supplies, that in all things God may be glorified through Jesus Christ, to whom belong the glory and the dominion forever and ever. Amen."
81. D. Menton, "Did Dinosaurs Turn into Birds?" in K. Ham, gen. ed., *The New Answers Book 1* (Green Forest, AR: Master Books, 2006), pp. 296–305.

feathers.[82] There is also the case of the Theropod dinosaur that had eaten three birds,[83] a parrot beak found in Cretaceous rock,[84] and fossilized feathers found in rock layers prior to dinosaurs existing (from an evolutionist perspective). The evolutionists tried to tie these fossilized feathers to a reptile in the same rock layer![85]

Biblical creationists certainly don't believe dinosaurs evolved into birds, as birds were actually created one day (Day 5) before dinosaurs (land animals), which were created on Day 6 of the creation week as recorded in Genesis. Creationists believe the fossils of dinosaurs and birds are in Flood or post-Flood sediment.

Mr. Ham, 1-minute response:

Since the question was directed to Mr. Nye, Mr. Ham's answer is obvious — that man has been intelligent since God created Adam and Eve in the Garden of Eden as previously explained.

Mr. Ham then opted to respond to the claim of survival of the fittest. For example, Mr. Ham used a popular example of alleged evolutionary change: blind cave fish. They lost the ability to see. This may have been a beneficial outcome for fish living in a dark environment, but this is not an example of onward and upward evolution. This illustrates a loss of function because of a loss of information (or information switched off). In other words, it was a change in the *wrong direction* for evolution!

For evolution to be a possibility, a single-celled organism needs to increase its complexity because of new information being generated. Eventually, information for constructing a heart, circulatory system, nervous system, hair, lungs, kidneys, and numerous other features has to be

---

82. The evolutionists are using collagen fibers found fossilized with some dinosaurs to say they are "proto-feathers," which are supposedly the beginnings of feathers! But this is clearly not so. Collagen is like the glue that holds our tissues — e.g., our skin or ligaments — together.
83. L. Xing, P.R. Bell, W.S. Persons, S. Ji, et al., "Abdominal Contents from Two Large Early Cretaceous Compsognathids (Dinosauria: Theropoda) Demonstrate Feeding on Confuciusornithids and Dromaeosaurids," *PLoS ONE*, 7, no. 8 (2012): e44012. doi:10.1371/journal. pone.0044012, http://www.plosone.org/article/info:doi/10.1371/journal.pone.0044012.
84. T. Stidham, "A Lower Jaw From a Cretaceous Parrot," *Nature* magazine, November 5, 1998, pp. 29–30; see also H. Gee, "I Wish to Register a Complaint," *Nature* magazine online, May 27, 1999, http://www.nature.com/news/1999/990527/full/news990527-3. html.
85. J. Hecht, "Reptile Grew Feather-like Structures Before Dinosaurs," *NewScientist*, March 24, 2012, p. 8.

generated. Losing eyesight is definitely going in the wrong direction for molecules-to-man evolution.

Final Question: The question is, what is the one thing more than anything else upon which you base your belief?

With this last question, both debaters were permitted a 2-minute response that commenced with Mr. Ham. Instead of analyzing both responses separately in detail, I am going to discuss them together.

Both debaters answered as expected. And this is really the question of the debate — to paraphrase: *what is your absolute authority?* For Mr. Ham, God and His Word is the absolute authority. For Mr. Nye, it is man's opinions. For example, Mr. Nye proclaimed:

> So the process of science, the way *we* know nature, is the most compelling thing to me (emphasis mine).

His adherence to man's word (we) is his absolute authority and where his faith begins. It is with man and man's opinions, which is secular humanism. And this is the crux of the debate — God's Word versus man's word. Actually, this is the battle that began in Genesis 3 when Adam and Eve followed after their own beliefs instead of God's Word and ate of the forbidden fruit. Since then, man's battle has been over trusting the Creator God's Word or being his own "god!" This battle has gone on ever since the Fall of man. It is the same battle before us today. The historic debate between Mr. Nye and Mr. Ham was over the same battle — God's Word versus man's word.

Do we submit to God or do we submit to man's whims? Man's fallible ideas have been changing ever since sin was introduced into the Garden of Eden. Man's opinions vary so rapidly and in so many directions that one should be thankful to an all-knowing God who reveals things to us in His Word to get us back to the correct thinking.

But from a big picture of history, the debate is really over God versus man. It has always been that way once sin entered into the world, when man's ideas were elevated to be greater than God's Word. God said *not to eat* (Genesis 2:17[86]) from the fruit of the tree of the knowledge of good

---

86. "But of the tree of the knowledge of good and evil you shall not eat, for in the day that you eat of it you shall surely die."

and evil.[87] Eve was deceived into believing that she could determine the truth on her own apart from God's Word. She elevated her thoughts to be greater than those of God and ate. Eve was essentially the first humanist (at least her thoughts were the first form of autonomous humanistic thinking).

Adam fared no better! He also elevated his thoughts and ate willingly! And since this time, mankind has been plunged into sin permeated with continual wrong thinking, in need of a Savior, in need of a new creation (this one has been cursed and is degenerating), and in need of the ability to think correctly about the origin of life, the universe, and the purpose and meaning of it all.

God's Word enables us to have the ability to think properly by thinking God's thoughts after Him. God's Word also reveals how Jesus Christ made salvation possible through His blood shed for our sin on the cross, with His resurrection showing how He alone has conquered sin and death. God also promises a time when Christians will enjoy a new heaven and a new earth, and the curse will be removed (e.g., Revelation 21:1,[88] 22:3[89]).

What do man's opinions say will happen in the end? You die, you cease to exist, and thus nothing really ultimately matters. Finally, there will supposedly be a heat death to the universe and no one will know they ever even existed. As we read in Ecclesiastes:

> I have seen all the works that are done under the sun; and indeed, all is vanity and grasping for the wind (Ecclesiastes 1:14).

So the conclusion to man's religion is simple: death and utter meaninglessness and purposelessness! Man's opinions led to death in the Garden of Eden, and sadly man's opinions today now tell us to worship that death as the hero in an evolutionary world. Man's opinions lead only to death (Proverbs 16:25[90]).

---

87. Simply the name of the tree, not where knowledge literally comes from, by the way. But the name does have special significance in that when man sinned, man was thrust into an *experiential* knowledge of good and evil; that is, we were subjected to it.
88. "Now I saw a new heaven and a new earth, for the first heaven and the first earth had passed away. Also there was no more sea."
89. "And there shall be no more curse, but the throne of God and of the Lamb shall be in it, and His servants shall serve Him."
90. "There is a way that seems right to a man, but its end is the way of death."

There is a battle over a *god of death* (man's opinions) and the *God of life* (God and His Word — God is the author of life and the giver of eternal life for those who will receive His free gift of salvation). What is fallible and sinful man next to an infallible and sinless God? Man would be next to nothing (Isaiah 2:22[91]), and yet this same loving God stepped into history to become a man — Jesus Christ — to take the penalty that we all deserve for our sin. That is not just a God worth serving but a God worth loving. That's the message Mr. Ham wanted all those watching — and Mr. Nye — to glean from the debate.

Final Comments

Debate topic

First, when dealing with the debate topic, "Is creation a viable model of origins in today's modern, scientific era?" Mr. Nye never addressed it. He inadvertently attacked it a few times when he tried refuting a warped version of Mr. Ham's position (changing the topic), but that was not the debate question that was up for discussion. So in retrospect, Mr. Nye never really dealt with the debate topic. By avoiding the actual issue, he lost the debate out of hand.

Was creation disproved as a viable option?

On the contrary, the debate showed that creationists do observational science and even excel at it in today's modern scientific and technological age, being innovative and creative. Furthermore, operational science is possible due to the Bible (which is where biblical creation emanates), on which it must be predicated.

Consider this implication. All other worldviews must borrow from the Bible, whether intentionally or inadvertently, for science to be a possibility. In other words, science is based on the Bible being true, hence creation is true. Therefore, when evolutionists do science, they are giving up their worldview and latching onto a biblical worldview. In light of this, evolution is not viable in today's modern scientific age.

Returning to the spark

The reason for the debate was Mr. Nye attacking creationists, who teach the truth of creation to children. Of course, the Bible commands this

---

91. "Stop regarding man, whose breath of life is in his nostrils; for why should he be esteemed?" (NASB).

(e.g., Proverbs 22:6;[92] Colossians 2:8[93]). Yet Mr. Nye's view has no basis for truth to exist in his materialistic religion; nor does Mr. Nye's religion have any basis for teaching the next generation. This is another biblical doctrine being hijacked by secularists.

Ken Ham's after-the-debate perspective

Quite a number of people asked Mr. Ham after the debate which of the statements he'd made during the debate that he would like to go back and change if he could.

Mr. Ham responded with this:

> I would change nothing, I said. The reason I say this is because I, along with many people around the world, were earnestly praying for myself and my preparation and every aspect of this debate. Before the debate I did receive many emails, letters, phone calls, and even registered letters from well-meaning people wanting to tell me what I should present during the debate. Then after the debate, I received emails, letters, and phone calls from people telling me what I should have presented.
>
> However, I worked hard to research and prepare for the debate — including many hours in the Bible. I sought the counsel of scientists, theologians, and others concerning what I believe God laid on my heart to present. I listened to advice, used the experience, wisdom, and knowledge the Lord had enabled me to obtain through over 35 years in the creation apologetic ministry. I presented my debate presentation to a select group of people to critique and give feedback. I explained the philosophy behind the material I included in my presentation. At the debate itself, I did the best I could to present the information I had prepared for so diligently.
>
> Therefore, having done all this, I do not consider that I should think about going back and changing anything. With God's help, and knowing I had been very conscientious about preparing for this debate, I did the best I could. I gave my

---

92. "Train up a child in the way he should go, and when he is old he will not depart from it."
93. "Beware lest anyone cheat you through philosophy and empty deceit, according to the tradition of men, according to the basic principles of the world, and not according to Christ."

presentation, responded to questions, and then left it in God's hands. I also had promised the Lord that I would honor his Word and His Gospel — and I believe I did that. I stood unashamedly as a Christian before a world audience, and before the world's media.

Mr. Ham has been asked by many people who he thinks won the debate. Here is Mr. Ham's answer:

Before the debate, when the secular media asked if I thought I could win the debate, I told them I wasn't looking to win or lose. I was looking to do my best to defend the Christian faith and the biblical creation position. I know there are formal rules for debates, and debate judges can judge debaters using certain agreed-upon rules. But the winner of a debate in such circumstances is not necessarily the person who is correct in their position, but who is the most articulate presenter who kept to the rules of the debate.

I told the secular media that if as a result of this debate, the conversation about creation vs. evolution and God's Word is opened up with people who normally wouldn't discuss such issues — then it would be a great success. And that certainly has happened. Also, when I realized that this debate was to become a worldwide sensation (our conservative estimate is that upwards of 15 million people worldwide have now seen the debate in one way or another), I was greatly burdened to ensure I honored God's Word and presented the Gospel.

Knowing the platform the Lord was giving me, I understand the incredible responsibility to ensure the message of the truth of God's Word and the message of salvation came through clearly. If the Lord used the debate to save one person for eternity, there would be rejoicing in Heaven ("Likewise, I say to you, there is joy in the presence of the angels of God over one sinner who repents," Luke 15:10).

Actually, I've heard quite a number of testimonies from people saved as a result of the debate — and numerous instances of skeptics who were prepared to discuss the creation topic with their Christian friends, whereas previously they would not do so.

Mr. Ham also stated:

> To me it's not a matter of who won or lost the debate. It really is a matter of knowing I did my best to give answers for what I believe and know to be true, and unashamedly stood on the authority of God's Word and shared the saving Gospel. I know Bill Nye prepared for the debate and I'm sure did his best. Now people can consider what was said, and continue the discussion and conduct further research and I trust, be challenged to look more into the claims of Scripture.

I asked Mr. Ham how he and Bill Nye parted for the evening. He said:

> I asked Bill Nye for his autograph — which he gave me. I then autographed one of our *Answers* books and presented it to him. Bill Nye said he didn't have room in his luggage to take it, so we shipped it to him. I pray he opens it and reads it. I do know that before the debate, Bill Nye made comments that indicated he didn't think I was sincere in what I believed. After the debate he made comments that I do obviously sincerely believe what I presented — and of course I do!

A Final Admonition

For those Christians reading this, please be in prayer about Mr. Nye and his salvation. He has been going down the wrong path, the wide gate of destruction (Matthew 7:13–15[94]), and he is adamantly trying to take other people down that path.

We sometimes forget that Paul was once in opposition to the Gospel of Jesus Christ to a point of approving murder toward Christians (e.g., Galatians 1:13[95]). And yet you can see what God can do. When Paul was saved, the Lord used him to write nearly two-thirds of the New Testament.

---

94. "Enter by the narrow gate; for wide is the gate and broad is the way that leads to destruction, and there are many who go in by it. Because narrow is the gate and difficult is the way which leads to life, and there are few who find it. Beware of false prophets, who come to you in sheep's clothing, but inwardly they are ravenous wolves."

95. "For you have heard of my former conduct in Judaism, how I persecuted the church of God beyond measure and tried to destroy it."

Be praying for Mr. Nye to repent and receive Christ as Lord. Also be praying that people who read this book will not be ashamed of the Gospel or of creation, which is the very foundation for the Gospel, but will be emboldened to spread the truth of God's Word and the saving Gospel message.

And be praying for those who are not saved reading this book that they will be able, by the power of the Holy Spirit, to see through the false religion of evolutionary humanism in its various forms. There are two religions in the world…God's and not God's (that is *man's* religion/man's word). Choose this day whom you will serve (echoing Joshua 24:15[96]). I commend Mr. Ham for standing up for the truth before millions to profess the name of Jesus Christ and the authority of God's Word.

---

96. "And if it seems evil to you to serve the LORD, choose for yourselves this day whom you will serve, whether the gods which your fathers served that were on the other side of the River, or the gods of the Amorites, in whose land you dwell. But as for me and my house, we will serve the LORD."

Appendix A

Ham-Nye Debate Transcript

Legacy Hall at the Creation Museum, Petersburg, KY, February 4, 2014
Moderated by Tom Foreman, CNN
Debate Topic: Is Creation a viable model in today's modern Scientific era?

Format: Each debater had a 5-minute opening statement, a 30-minute presentation of argument supported by visuals, and then two, 5-minute rebuttals in alternating order, Mr. Ham going first after a coin toss. The arguments and rebuttal were followed by a 45-minute period of questions and answers taken from the audience and asked by the moderator. Questions were alternated between the debaters with two minutes to respond followed by a 1-minute response from the opponent. Mr. Ham was asked the first question and the moderator alternated the questions from that point on. The final question was asked to both men, two minutes given to each to respond. There was no formal cross examination during the debate.

Note: This transcript has been produced from an original document provided by a professional transcription service and edited to match the words of the speakers as closely as possible. Word stumbles and choppy sentences have been minimally edited to preserve the integrity of this transcript (often noted by an en dash, –), though partial words have been omitted or completed for clarity.

The reader is invited to check this transcript against the video to verify any statements. Due to the nature of directly recording what has been spoken, you will notice grammatical errors that reflect the speakers' actual words. Brackets,[for example], were used to make editorial notes for clarity where speakers change or visuals were used in the presentations.

Estimated time markers based on the total time of the debate have been included in the margin. These markers will be given at five-minute intervals from the moderators opening comments, though these markers will vary depending on the version of the video you view (e.g., DVD, digital download, YouTube, etc.).

This transcript has been annotated with the references used by the speakers to give the reader access to the source material used. Additionally, a few explanatory notes will be added to help the reader understand several comments made.

Initial transcription provided by Maverick Captioning Service, Cincinnati, OH, www.maverickcaptioning.com

Transcript Outline

Origin of Consciousness

Change Your Mind

Evidence for the Age of the Earth

Continental Drift

Favorite Color

Second Law of Thermodynamics

Hypothetical Evidence of the Age of the Earth

God and Science

Literal Interpretation of the Bible

Intelligent Designer

Creationism in Commerce

Evolving Intelligence

Basis of Belief

Moderator Closing Remarks

Moderator's Introduction

Tom Foreman: Good evening I'm pleased to welcome you to Legacy Hall at the Creation Museum in Northern Kentucky in the metropolitan area of Cincinnati.

I'm Tom Foreman from CNN, and I'm pleased to be tonight's moderator for this evolution versus creation debate.

This is a very old question: Where did we come from?

My answer is, "From Washington this morning by airplane," but there is a more profound, longer answer that people have sought after for a long time.

So tonight's question to be debated is the following: Is creation a viable model of origins in today's modern scientific era?

Our welcome extends to hundreds of thousands people who are watching on the internet at debatelive.org, we're glad you have joined us.

Of course, to our auditorium here, all of the folks who have joined us here as well.

We're joined by 70 media representatives from many of the world's great news organizations, we're glad to have them here as well.

And now let's welcome our debaters Mr. Bill Nye and Mr. Ken Ham.

We had a coin toss earlier to determine who would go first of these two men. The only thing missing was Joe Namath in a fur coat.[1] But it went very well. Mr. Ham won the coin toss and he opted to speak first. But first let me tell you a little bit about both of these gentlemen.

Mr. Nye's website describes him as a scientist, engineer, comedian, author, and inventor. Mr. Nye as you may know produced a number of award-winning TV shows including the program he became so well known for, "Bill Nye the Science Guy." While working on the "Science Guy" show, Mr. Nye won seven national Emmy awards for writing, performing, and producing the show; won 18 Emmys in 5 years. In between creating the shows he wrote five kids' books about science including his latest title, *Bill Nye's Great Big Book of Tiny Germs.*

Bill Nye is the host of three television series; his program "The 100 Greatest Discoveries" airs on The Science Channel, "The Eyes of Nye" airs on PBS stations across the country.

---

1. Mr. Foreman was referring to the Superbowl XLVII coin flip a few days before the debate where Joe Namath was wearing a fur coat for the coin toss.

He frequently appears on interview programs to discuss a variety of science topics. Mr. Nye serves as Executive Director of the Planetary Society, the world's largest space interest group. He's a graduate of Cornell with a bachelor's of science degree in mechanical engineering.

Mr. Ken Ham is the President and co-founder of Answers in Genesis, a Bible-defending organization that upholds the authority of the Scriptures from the very first verse. Mr. Ham is the man behind the popular high-tech Creation Museum where we're holding this debate. The museum has had 2 million visitors in six years and has attracted much of the world's media.

The Answers in Genesis website is well trafficked with two million visitors alone last month. Mr. Ham is also a best-selling author, a much-in-demand speaker, and the host of a daily radio feature carried on 700-plus stations.

This is his second public debate on evolution and creation. The first was at Harvard in the 1990s.

Mr. Ham is a native of Australia. He earned a bachelor's degree in applied science with an emphasis in environmental biology from the Queensland Institute of Technology, as well as a diploma of education at the University of Queensland in Brisbane, Australia.

Now, Mr. Ham, you opted to go first so you will be first with your 5-minute opening statement.

5-minute Opening Remarks — Ken Ham

Mr. Ham: Good evening, I know that not everyone watching this debate will necessarily agree with what I have to say, but I'm an Aussie and live over here in America and they tell me I have an accent and so it doesn't matter what I say, some people tell me, "We just like to hear you saying it." So, I hope you enjoy me saying it anyway.

Well, the debate topic is this: Is creation a viable model of origins in today's modern scientific era?

You know, when this was first announced on the internet there were lots of statements like this one from the Richard Dawkins Foundation: Scientists should not debate creationists. Period.[2]

---

2. Dan Arel, "Why Bill Nye Shouldn't Debate Ken Ham," Richard Dawkins Foundation, https://richarddawkins.net/2014/01/why-bill-nye-shouldnt-debate-ken-ham/.

Ken Ham

And this one from one of the discovery.com websites: Should Scientists Debate Creationists?[3]

You know, right here I believe there's a gross misrepresentation in our culture. We're seeing people being indoctrinated to believe that creationists can't be scientists. I believe it's all a part of secularists hijacking the word "science."

I want you to meet a modern day scientist who is a biblical creationist.

5:00

[Video clip] "My name is Stuart Burgess. I'm a professor of engineering design at Bristol University in the UK. I have published over 130 scientific papers on the science of design and engineering and biological systems. For my research work I find that the scientific evidence fully supports creationism as the best explanation to origins. I've also designed major parts of spacecraft, launched by ESA and NASA."[4]

Mr. Ham: So here's a biblical creationist who's a scientist who's also an inventor, and I want young people to understand that. You know, the problem I believe is this: we need to define terms correctly. We need to define creation, evolution in regard to origins, and we need to define science.

In this opening statement I want to concentrate on dealing with the word "science." I believe the word science has been hijacked by secularists.

Now, what is science? Well, the origin of the word comes from classical Latin *scientia* which means "to know."[5]

And if you look up a dictionary it'll say: the state of knowing : knowledge as distinguished from ignorance or misunderstanding.[6]

But there's different types of knowledge and I believe this is where the confusion lies. There's experimental or observational science as we call it. That's using the scientific method: observation, measurement, experiment, testing.[7]

3. Benjamin Radford, "Should Scientists Debate Creationists?" Discovery News, http://news.discovery.com/earth/should-scientists-debate-creationists-140105.htm.
4. Video clip available at http://www.youtube.com/watch?v=4nMRZuPcOtc
5. American Heritage Science Dictionary, s.v. "science," http://www.yourdictionary.com/science#science.
6. Merriam-Webster Online Dictionary, s.v. "science," http://www.merriam-webster.com/dictionary/science.
7. Oxford English Dictionary, s.v. "scientific method."

That's what produces our technology; computers, spacecraft, jet planes, smoke detectors, looking at DNA, antibiotics, medicines, and vaccines.

You see, all scientists, whether creationists or evolutionists, actually have the same observational or experimental science. And it doesn't matter whether you're a creationist or an evolutionist, you can be a great scientist.

For instance, here's an atheist who is a great scientist, Craig Venter, one of the first researchers to sequence the human genome.[8]

Or Dr. Raymond Damadian, he is a man who invented the MRI scanner and revolutionized medicine. He's a biblical creationist.

But I want us to also understand molecules-to-man evolution belief has nothing to do with developing technology. You see, when we're talking about origins we're talking the past, we're talking about origin. We weren't there, you can't observe that whether it's molecules-to-man evolution or whether it's the creation account. I mean, you're talking about the past. We like to call that origins or historical science, knowledge concerning the past.

Here at the Creation Museum we make no apology about the fact to our origins or historical science actually is based upon the biblical account of origins.

Now when you research science textbooks being used in public schools what we found is this: By and large the origins or historical science is based upon man's ideas about the past, for instance the ideas of Darwin.

And our research has found that: Public school textbooks are using the same word science for observational science and historical science. They arbitrarily define science as naturalism and outlaw the supernatural. They present molecules-to-man evolution as fact. They are imposing, I believe, the religion of naturalism/atheism on generations of students.

You see I assert that the word "science" has been hijacked by secularists in teaching evolution to force the religion of naturalism on generations of kids. Secular evolutionists teach that all life developed by natural processes from some primordial form, that man is just an evolved animal which has a great bearing on how we view life and death.

8. Craig Venter, Wikipedia, http://en.wikipedia.org/wiki/Craig_Venter.

For instance, as Bill states: [video clip] "It's very hard to accept for many of us that when you die it's over."[9]

But you see, the Bible gives a totally different account of origins, of who we were, where we came from, the meaning of life, and our future:

> "From the beginning of the creation, God 'made them male and female.' 'For this reason a man shall leave his father and mother and be joined to his wife.'" (Mark 10:6–7, NKJV)

> Through one man sin entered the world, and death through sin. (Romans 5:12, NKJV)

> For God so loved the world that He gave His only begotten Son, that whoever believes in Him should not perish but have everlasting life. (John 3:16, NKJV)

So, is creation a viable model of origins in today's modern scientific era?

I say: The creation/evolution debate is [really] a conflict between two philosophical worldviews based on two different accounts of origins or [historical] science beliefs. Creation is the only viable model of historical science confirmed by observational science in today's modern scientific era.

Moderator Comments

Tom Foreman: And that is time. I have the unenviable job of being the timekeeper here. So, I'm like the referee in football that you don't like, but I will periodically if either one of our debaters runs over on anything I will stop them in the name of keeping it fair for all. Mr. Ham, thank you for your comments. Now it's Mr. Nye's turn for a 5-minute opening statement, Mr. Nye.

5-minute Opening Remarks — Bill Nye

Mr. Nye: Thank you, it's a pleasure to be here. I very much appreciate you including me in your facility here. Now, looking around the room I think I see just one bowtie; is that right? Just one. I'm telling you once you try it — Oh, there's yes, two, that's great! I started wearing bow ties when I was young in high school.

---

9. LeVar Burton and Bill Nye, interview with Larry King, "LeVar Burton & Bill Nye," *Larry King Now*, April 1, 2013, http://www.hulu.com/watch/473418.

Bill Nye

My father showed me how, his father showed him, and there's a story associated with this which I find remarkable. My grandfather was in The Rotary and he attended a convention in Philadelphia. And even in those days, at the turn of last century, people rented tuxedos. And the tuxedo came with a bowtie, untied bowtie. So he didn't know how to tie it so he wasn't sure what to do so he took a chance.

10:00

He went to the hotel room next door, knocked on the door, "Excuse me, can you help me tie my tie?" And the guy said, "Sure, lie down on the bed." So, my grandfather, he wanted to have the tie on; wasn't sure what he was getting into. So, he is said to have lain on the bed and the guy tied a perfect bowtie knot. And quite reasonably my grandfather said, "Thank you. Why did I have to lie down on the bed?" The guy said, "I'm an undertaker. It's really the only way I know how to do it."

Now, that story was presented to me as a true story; it may or may not be. But it gives you something to think about and it certainly is something to remember.

So here tonight we're going to have two stories, and we can compare Mr. Ham's story to the story from what I will call the outside, from mainstream science.

The question tonight is: Does Ken Ham's creation model hold up? Is it viable?

So let me ask you all, what would you be doing if you weren't here tonight? That's right, you'd be home watching "CSI," "CSI: Petersburg." Is it coming? I think it's coming.

And on "CSI" there is no distinction made between historical science and observational science. These are constructs unique to Mr. Ham. We don't normally have these anywhere in the world except here.

Natural laws that applied in the past apply now. That's why they're natural laws. That's why we embrace them. That's how we made all these discoveries that enabled all this remarkable technology.

So "CSI" is a fictional show, but it's based absolutely on real people doing real work. When you go to a crime scene and find evidence, you have clues about the past and you trust those clues and you embrace them and you move forward to convict somebody.

Mr. Ham and his followers have this remarkable view of a worldwide flood that somehow influenced everything that we observe in nature — a 500-foot wooden boat, 8 zookeepers for 14,000 individual animals, every land plant in the world under water for a full year.

I ask us all is that really reasonable?

You'll hear about the Grand Canyon I imagine also, which is a remarkable place, and it has fossils. And the fossils in the Grand Canyon are found in layers. There is not a single place in the Grand Canyon where the fossils of one type of animal cross over into the fossils of another.

In other words, when there was a big flood on the earth you would expect drowning animals to swim up to a higher level. Not any one of them did. Not a single one. If you could find evidence of that, my friends, you could change the world.

Now, I just want to remind us all there are billions of people in the world who are deeply religious, who get enriched, who have a wonderful sense of community from their religion. They worship together, they eat together, they live in their communities, and enjoy each other's company. Billions of people, but these same people do not embrace the extraordinary view that the earth is somehow only 6,000 years old; that is unique.

And here's my concern: What keeps the United States ahead, what makes the United States a world leader is our technology, our new ideas, our innovations.

If we continue to eschew science, eschew the process, and try to divide science into observational science and historic science we are not going to move forward, we will not embrace natural laws, we will not make discoveries, we will not invent and innovate and stay ahead.

So if you ask me if Ken Ham's creation model is viable I say no, it is absolutely not viable.

So, stay with us over the next period and you can compare my evidence to his.

Thank you all very much.

Moderator Comments

Tom Foreman: Very nice start by both of our debaters here.

And now each one will offer a 30-minute illustrated presentation to fully offer their case for us to consider.

Mr. Ham, you're up.

30-minute Presentation — Ken Ham

Mr. Ham: Well the debate topic was this: Is creation a viable model of origins in today's modern scientific era?

And I made this statement at the end of my opening statement: Creation is the only viable model of historical science confirmed by observational science in today's modern scientific era.

15:00

And I said what we need to be doing is actually defining our terms, and particularly three terms: science, creation, and evolution.

Now, I discussed the meaning of the word "science" and what is meant by experimental or observational science briefly, and that both creationists and evolutionists can be great scientists. For instance, I mentioned Craig Venter a biologist, he's an atheist, and he's a great scientist. He was one of the first researchers to sequence the human genome.

I also mentioned Dr. Raymond Damadian who actually invented the MRI scanner. I want you to meet a biblical creationist who is a scientist and inventor.

> [Video clip] "Hi, my name is Dr. Raymond Damadian. I am a young earth creation scientist and believe that God created world in six, 24-hour days, just as recorded in the Book of Genesis. By God's grace and the devoted prayers of my godly mother-in-law I invented the MRI scanner in 1969. The idea that scientists who believe the earth is 6,000 years old cannot do real science is simply wrong."[10]

Mr. Ham: Well, he's most adamant about that, and actually he revolutionized medicine, he's a biblical creationist. And I encourage children to follow people like that and make them their heroes.

Let me introduce you to another biblical creation scientist.

> [Video clip] "My name is Danny Faulkner. I received my PhD in astronomy from Indiana University. For 26 and a half years I was professor at the University of South Carolina Lancaster where

---

10. Video clip available at http://www.youtube.com/watch?v=fOM0v0dQnjI.

I hold the rank of Distinguished Professor Emeritus. Upon my retirement from the university in January 2013, I joined the research staff at Answers in Genesis. I'm a stellar astronomer. That means my primary interest is stars, but I'm particularly interested in the study of eclipsing binary stars. And I've published many articles in the astronomy literature, places such as *The Astrophysical Journal, The Astronomical Journal,* and *The Observatory.* There is nothing in observational astronomy that contradicts a recent creation."

Mr. Ham: I also mentioned Dr. Stuart Burgess, Professor of Engineering Design at Bristol University in England.

Now he invented, designed, a double action worm gear set for the three hinges of the robotic arm on a very expensive satellite. And if that had not worked, if that gear set had not worked, that whole satellite would have been useless. Yet Dr. Burgess is a biblical creationist who believes just as I believe.

Now, think about this for a moment. A scientist like Dr. Burgess who believes in creation just as I do, a small minority in the scientific world, but let's see what he says about scientists believing in creation.

[Video clip] "I find that many of my colleagues in academia are sympathetic to the creationist viewpoint, including biologists. However they are often afraid to speak out because of the criticisms they would get from the media and atheist lobby."

Mr. Ham: I agree, that's a real problem today. We need to have freedom to be able to speak on these topics.

You know, I just want to say by the way that creation — Christian — non-Christian scientists I should say. Non-Christian scientists are really borrowing from the Christian worldview anyway to carry out their experimental or observational science.

Think about it. When they're doing observational science using the scientific method they have to assume the laws of logic, they have to assume the laws of nature, they have to assume the uniformity of nature.

I mean think about it. If the universe came about by natural process where did the laws of logic come from? Did they just pop into existence? Are we in a stage now where we have only half logic?

So you see, I have a question for Bill Nye: How do you account for the laws of logic and laws of nature from a naturalistic worldview that excludes the existence of God?

Now, in my opening statement I also discussed a different type of science or knowledge, origins or historical science. See again, there's a confusion here, there's a misunderstanding here.

People by and large have not been taught to look at, you know, what you believe about the past as different to what you're observing in the present. You don't observe the past directly, even, you know, when you think about the creation account, I mean we can't observe God creating, we can't observe the creation of Adam and Eve. We admit that; we're willing to admit our beliefs about the past.

But see, what you see in the present is very different. Even some public school textbooks actually, well, they sort of acknowledge the difference between historical and observational science.

Here is an earth science textbook that is used in public schools and we read this: "In contrast to physical geology, the aim of historical geology is to understand Earth's long history."

Then they make the statement: "Historical geology," so we're talking about historical science, "tries to establish a timeline of the vast number of physical and biological changes that have occurred in the past. . . . We study physical geology before historical geology because we first must understand how earth works before we try to unravel its past."[11]

In other words, we observe things in the present and then, okay, we're assuming that that's always happened in the past, and we're going to try and figure out how this happened. See there is a difference between what you observe and what happened in the past.

20:00

Let me illustrate it this way. If bill Nye and I went to the Grand Canyon we could agree that that's Coconino Sandstone and the Hermit Shale and there's the boundary, they're sitting one on top of the other. We could agree on that, but do you know what we would disagree on? I mean we could even analyze the minerals and agree on that, but we would disagree on how long it took to get there.

---

11. E. Tarbuck and F.K. Lutgens, *Earth Science,* Indiana Teacher's Edition (Upper Saddle River, NJ: Pearson Prentice Hall, 2006), pp. 2–3.

But see none of us saw the sandstone or the shale being laid down. There's a supposed 10-million-year gap there, but I don't see a gap, but that might be different to what Bill Nye would see. But see there's a difference between what you actually observe directly and then your interpretation in regard to the past.

When I was at the Goddard Space Center a number of years ago I met creationists and evolutionists who were both working on the Hubble Telescope. They agreed on how to build the Hubble Telescope. You know what they disagreed on? Well, they disagreed on how to interpret the data that telescope obtained in regard to the age of universe.

And, you know, we could go on and talk about lots of other similar sorts of things.

For instance, I've heard Bill Nye talk about how a smoke detector works using the radioactive element Americium. And you know what? I totally agree with him on that. We agree how it works. We agree how radioactivity enables that to work.

But if you're then going to use radioactive elements and talk about the age of the earth you've got a problem because you weren't there. We've got to understand parent elements, daughter elements, and so on.

We could agree, whether you're creationist or evolutionist, on the technology to put the rover on Mars, but we're going to disagree on how to interpret the origin of Mars. I mean there are some people that believe there was even a global flood on Mars and there's no liquid water on Mars.

But you know we're going on disagree maybe on our interpretation of origins and you can't prove either way because, not from an observational science perspective, because we've only got the present.

Creationists and evolutionists both work on medicines and vaccines.

You see it doesn't matter whether you're creationist or an evolutionist, all scientists have the same experimental or observational science.

I have a question for Bill Nye: Can you name one piece of technology that could only have been developed starting with a belief in molecules-to-man evolution?

Now here's another important fact: Creationists and evolutionist all have the same evidence.

Bill Nye and I have the same Grand Canyon, we don't disagree on that.

We all have the same fish fossil; this is one from the Creation Museum.

The same dinosaur skeletons, the same animals, the same humans, the same DNA, the same radioactive decay elements that we see, we have the same universe.

Actually we all have the same evidences. It is not the evidences that are different; it's a battle over the same evidence in regard to how we interpret the past.

You know why that is? Because it's really a battle over worldviews and starting points. It's a battle over philosophical worldviews and starting points, but the same evidence.

Now I admit my starting point is that God is the ultimate authority. If someone doesn't accept that, then man has to be the ultimate authority. And that's really the difference when it comes down to it.

You see, I've been emphasizing the difference between historical origin science, knowledge about the past when you weren't there, and we need to understand that we weren't there.

Or experimental observational science; using our five senses in the present, the scientific method, what you can directly observe, test, repeat. There's a big difference between those two, and that's not what's being taught in our public schools and that's why kids aren't being taught to think critically and correctly about the origins issue.

But you know, it's also important to understand when talking about creation/evolution both involve historical science and observational science.

You see, the role of observational science is this: It can be used to confirm other otherwise one's historical science based on one's starting point.

Now, when you think about the debate topic and what I affirmed concerning creation, if our origins or historical science based on the Bible's account of origins is true, then there should be predictions from this that we can test using observational science, and there are.

For instance, based on the Bible we'd expect to find evidence confirming an intelligence produced life.

We'd expect to find evidence confirming "after their kind." The Bible says God made kinds of animals and plants after their kind implying each kind produces its own, not that one kind changes into another.

You'd expect to find evidence confirming a global Flood of Noah's day.

Evidence confirming one race of humans because we all go back to Adam and Eve; biologically that would mean there's one race.

Evidence confirming the Tower of Babel, that God gave different languages.

Evidence confirming a young universe.

Now I can't go through all of those, but a couple of them we'll look at briefly.

After their kind, evidence confirming that.

25:00

In the Creation Museum we have a display featuring, replicas actually, of Darwin's finches. They're called Darwin's finches. Darwin collected finches from the Galapagos and took them back to England, and we see the different species, the different beak sizes here. And you know, from the specimens that Darwin obtained in the Galapagos he actually pondered these things and how do you explain this? [Images of finch beaks and Darwin's notebook]

And in his notes actually he came up with this diagram here, a tree, and he actually said, "I think." So he was talking about different species, and maybe those species came from some common ancestor.

Actually, when it comes to finches, we actually would agree as creationists that different finch species came from a common ancestor, but a finch is what that would have to come from.

You see, Darwin wasn't just thinking about species; Darwin had a much bigger picture in mind. When you look at the *Origin of Species* and read that book you'll find he made this statement: ". . . from such low and intermediate form, both animals and plants may have been developed; and, if we admit this, we must likewise admit that all organic beings which have ever lived on this earth may be descended from some one primordial form."[12]

So he had in mind what we today know as an evolutionary tree of life; that all life has arisen from some primordial form.

Now, when you consider the classification system — kingdom, phylum, class, order, family, genus, species — we would say as creationists, and we have many scientists who have researched this, and for lots of reasons, I would say the "kind" in Genesis 1 really is more at the family level of classification.

---

12. Charles Darwin, *The Origin of Species By Means of Natural Selection or the Preservation of Favored Races in the Struggle for Life* (New York: The Modern Library, 1993), p. 643.

For instance, there's one dog kind, there's one cat kind; even though you have different genera or different species. That would mean, by the way, you didn't need anywhere near the number of animals on the Ark as people think. You wouldn't need all the species of dogs, just two. Not all the species of cats, just two.

And you see based on the biblical account there in Genesis 1, creationists have drawn up what they believe is a creation orchard. In other words they're saying, "Look, there is great variation in the genetics of dogs and finches and so on."

And so over time, particularly after Noah's Flood you'd expect, if there were two dogs for instance, you could end up with different species of dogs because there's an incredible amount of variability in the genes of any creature.

And so you'd expect these different species up here, but there's limits. Dogs will always be dogs; finches will always be finches.

As a creationist I maintain that observational science actually confirms this model based on the Bible.

For instance, take dogs, okay? In a scientific paper dated January 2014, that's this year, scientists working at the University of California stated this: "We provide several lines of evidence supporting a single origin for dogs, and disfavoring alternative models in which dog lineages arise separately from geographically distinct wolf populations (Figures 4–5, Table S10)."[13]

And they put this diagram in the paper. By the way, that diagram is very, very similar to this diagram that creationists propose based upon the creation account in Genesis. [Visuals displayed]

In other words, you have a common dog ancestor that gives rise to the different species of dogs, and that's exactly what we're saying here.

Now in the Creation Museum, we actually show the finches here, and you see the finches with their different beaks, beside dogs skulls, different species of dogs. By the way, there's more variation in the dog skulls here than there are in these finches. Yet the dogs, well that's never used as an example of evolution, but the finches are, particularly in the public school textbooks.

---

13. Adam H. Freedman et al., "Genome Sequencing Highlights the Dynamic Early History of Dogs," *PLoS Genetics* 10, no. 1 (2014): 8.

Students are taught, "Ah, see the changes that are occurring here?"

And here's another problem that we've got. Not only has the word "science" been hijacked by secularists, I believe the word "evolution" has been hijacked by secularists.

The word "evolution" has been hijacked using what I call a bait and switch. Let me explain to you.

The word "evolution" is being used in public school textbooks and we often see it documentaries and so on. It's used for observable changes, that we would agree with, and then used for unobservable changes, such as molecules-to-man.

Let me explain to you what's really going on because I was a science teacher in the public schools and I know what the students there were taught and I check the public school textbooks anyway to know what they're taught. You see, students are taught today, "Look, there's all these different animals, plants, but they're all part of this great big tree of life that goes back to some primordial form. And look, we see changes, changes in finches, changes in dogs, and so on."

Now, we don't deny the changes; you see that, you see different species of finches, different species of dogs. But then they put it all together in this evolutionary tree, but that's what you don't observe. You don't observe that. That's belief there. That's the historical science I would say is wrong. [Visuals displayed comparing the creationist orchard to the evolutionary tree of life]

But you know what you do observe? You do observe different species of dogs, different species finches, but then there are limits and you don't see one kind changing into another.

Actually, we're told that if you teach creation in the public schools, that's teaching religion; if you teach evolution, that's science. And I'm going to say, "Wait a minute. Actually, the creation model here based upon the Bible, observational science confirms this."

30:00

This is what you observe. You don't observe this tree. [Visuals displayed[14]]

---

14. Mr. Ham uses an illustration that contrasts the creationist orchard of life with the evolutionary tree of life. Examples of these diagrams and the contrast can be found in: Georgia Purdom, "Is Natural Selection the Same Thing as Evolution?" http://www.answersingenesis.org/articles/nab/is-natural-selection-evolution.

Actually, it's the public school textbooks that are teaching a belief, imposing it on students and they need to be teaching them observational science to understand the reality of what's happening.

Now, what we found is that: Public school textbooks present the evolutionary "tree" as "science," but reject the creation "orchard" as religion. But observational science confirms the creation orchard — so public school textbooks are rejecting observational science and imposing a naturalistic religion on students.

The word "evolution" has been hijacked using a bait and switch to indoctrinate students to accept evolutionary belief as observational science.

Let me introduce you to another scientist, Richard Lenski of Michigan State University. He's a great scientist. He's known for culturing *E. coli* in the lab. And he found there were some *E. coli* that actually seemed to develop the ability to grow on substrate — or on citrate in substrate. But Richard Lenski is here mentioned in this book and it's called "Evolution in the Lab."[15]

So, the ability to grow on citrate is said to be evolution. And there are those that say, "Hey, this is against the creationists."

For instance: "Lenski's experiment is also yet another poke in the eye for anti-evolutionists," notes Jerry Coyne, an evolutionary biologist at the University of Chicago. "The thing I like most is it says you can get these complex traits evolving by a combination of unlikely events," he says. "That's just what creationists say can't happen."[16] [Text from slide]

But is it a poke in the eye for anti-evolutionists? Is it really seeing complex traits evolving? What does it mean that some of these bacteria are able to grow on citrate?

Let me introduce you to another biblical creationists who is a scientist.

[Video clip] "Hi, my name is Dr. Andrew Fabich. I got my PhD from the University of Oklahoma in microbiology. I teach at Liberty University and I do research on *E. coli* in the intestine. I have published in secular journals from the American Society for Microbiology including *Infection and Immunity*, and *Applied and*

---

15. Joan L. Slonczewski and John W. Foster, *Microbiology: An Evolving Science*, 3rd ed. (New York: W.W. Norton and Co., 2014), p. 2.
16. Bob Holmes, "Bacteria make major evolutionary shift in the lab," June 9, 2008, http://www.newscientist.com/article/dn14094-bacteria-make-major-evolutionary-shift-in-the-lab.html.

Environmental Microbiology, as well as several others. My work has been cited even in the past year in the journals *Nature, Science: Translational Medicine, Public Library of Science, Public Library of Science: Genetics*. It is cited regularly in those journals. And while I was taught nothing but evolution, I don't accept that position. I do my research from a creation perspective. When I look at the evidence that people cite of *E. coli* supposedly evolving over 30 years, over 30,000 generations in the lab, and people say that it is now able to grow on citrate, I don't deny that it grows on citrate, but it's not any kind of new information. The information's already there and it's just a switch that gets turned on and off. And that's what they reported in there, there's nothing new."

Mr. Ham: See, students need to be told what's really going on here. Certainly there's change, but it's not change necessary for molecules-to-man.

Now, we could look at other predictions. What about evidence confirming one race.

Well, when we look at the human population we see lots of differences, but based on Darwin's ideas of human evolution as presented in *The Descent of Man*, I mean Darwin did teach in *The Descent of Man* there were lower races and higher races.

Would you believe that back in the 1900s one of the most popular biology textbooks used in the public schools in America taught this: "At the present time there exists upon earth five races or varieties of man... and finally the highest type of all, the Caucasians, represented by the civilized white inhabitants of Europe and America."[17]

Can you imagine if in it was in the public schools today? And yet that's what was taught, but it was based on Darwin's ideas that are wrong. You have a wrong foundation; you are going to have a wrong worldview.

Now, had they started from the Bible and from the creation account in the Bible, what does it teach?

We're all descendants of Adam and Eve, we go through the Tower of Babel, different languages so different people groups formed distinct characteristics, but we'd expect, we'd say, "You know what? That means there's biologically only one race of humans."

---

17. George William Hunter, *A Civic Biology: Presented in Problems* (New York: American Book Company, 1914), p. 196. This textbook was used in Dayton, TN, sparking the Scopes Trial.

Well, I mentioned Dr. Venter before and he was a researcher with the human genome project. And you'll remember in the year 2000 this was headline news, and what we read was this: ". . . they had put together a draft of the entire sequence of human genome and unanimously declared there is only one race, the human race."[18]

Wow! Who would have guessed?

But you see, there we have observational science confirming the creation account, not confirming at all Darwin's ideas.

Now, there's much more that could be said on each of these topics, obviously you can't do that in a short time like this and you could do a lot more research. I suggest you visit our website at Answers in Genesis for a lot more information.

So, the debate topic: Is creation a viable model of origins in today's modern scientific era?

35:00

I said we need to define the terms, particularly the terms science and evolution. And, I believe we need to understand how they are being used to impose an anti-God religion on generations of unsuspecting students.

You see I keep emphasizing we do need to understand the difference between experimental or observational science and historical science.

And you know what? The secularists don't like me doing this because they don't want to admit that there's a belief aspect to what they're saying, and there is, and they can't get away from it.

Let me illustrate this with a statement from Bill Nye.

> [Video clip: Bill Nye] "You can show the earth is not flat. You can show the earth is not 10,000 years old."[19]

Mr. Ham: By the way, I agree you can show the earth is not flat. There's a video from the Galileo spacecraft showing the earth and speeded up, of course, but spinning. You can see it's a sphere. You can observe that. You can't observe the age of the earth; you don't see that.

---

18. Natalie Angier, "Do Races Differ? Not Really, DNA Shows," *New York Times*, Aug. 22, 2000, http://partners.nytimes.com/library/national/science/082200sci-genetics-race.html.

19. LeVar Burton and Bill Nye, interview with Larry King, "LeVar Burton & Bill Nye," *Larry King Now*, April 1, 2013, http://www.hulu.com/watch/473418.

You see, again, I emphasize there's a big difference between historical science, talking about the past, and observational science, talking about the present.

And I believe what's happening is this: That students are being indoctrinated by the confusion of terms. The hijacking of the word "science" and the hijacking of the word "evolution" in a bait and switch.

Let me illustrate further with this video clip, because here I assert that Bill Nye is equating observational science with historical science. And I also say it's not a mystery when you understand the difference.

> [Video clip: Bill Nye] "Apparently people with these deeply held religious beliefs, they embrace that whole literal interpretation of Bible as written in English as a worldview, and at the same time they accept aspirin, antibiotic drugs, airplanes, but they're able to hold these two worldviews. And this is a mystery."[20]

Mr. Ham: Actually I suggest to you it's not a mystery. You see when I'm talking about antibiotics, aspirin, smoke detectors, jet planes, that's Ken Ham the Observational Science Bloke. I'm an Australian, we call guys blokes, okay?

But when you're talking about creation and thousands of years or the age of the earth, that's Ken Ham the Historical Science Bloke. I'm willing to admit that.

Now, when Bill Nye is talking about aspirin, antibiotics, jet planes, smoke detectors, he does a great job at that, I used to enjoy watching him on TV too, that's Bill Nye the Observational Science Guy. But when he's talking about evolution and millions of years, I'm challenging him that that's Bill Nye the Historical Science Guy.

And I challenge the evolutionists to admit the belief aspects of their particular worldview.

Now, at the Creation Museum we're only too willing to admit our beliefs based upon the Bible, but we also teach people the difference between beliefs and what one can actually observe and experiment with in the present.

I believe we're teaching people to think critically and to think in the right terms about science. I believe it's the creationists that should

20. Ibid.

be educating the kids out there because we're teaching them the right way to think. You know, we admit our origins or historical science is based upon the Bible, but I'm just challenging evolutionists to admit the belief aspects of evolution and be upfront about the difference here. As I said, I'm only too willing to admit my historical science based on the Bible.

And let me further go on and define the term "creation" as we use it.

By "creation" we mean, here at Answers in Genesis and the Creation Museum, we mean the account based on the Bible. Yes, I take Genesis as literal history, as Jesus did.

And here at the Creation Museum we walk people through that history.

We walk them through Creation, a perfect Creation, God made Adam and Eve, land animal kinds, sea creatures, and so on. And then sin and death entered the world, so there was no death before sin. That means; how can you have billions of dead things before man sinned? [Visuals depicting the Seven C's of History displayed]

And then the Catastrophe of Noah's Flood. If there was a global flood you'd expect to find billions of dead things buried in rock layers laid down by water all over the earth. I had to say that because a lot of our supports would want me to. And what do you find? Billions of dead things buried in rock layers laid down by water all over the earth.

Confusion, the Tower of Babel, God gave different languages so you get different people groups. So this is the geological, astronomical, anthropological, biological history as recorded in the Bible. So this is concerning what happened in the past that explains the present.

And then of course, that God's Son stepped into history to be Jesus Christ, the God-man, to die on the Cross, be raised from the dead, and one day there's going to be a new heavens and a new earth to come [Consummation visual displayed].[21]

And you know, not only is this an understanding of history to explain the geology, biology, astronomy, and so on to connect the present to the past, but it's also a foundation for our whole worldview.

For instance, in Matthew 19 when Jesus was asked about marriage He said, "Have you not read that He who made them at the beginning 'made them male and female,' and said, 'For this reason a man shall leave

21. For more information see Ken Ham and Stacia McKeever, "Seven C's of History," Answers in Genesis, http://www.answersingenesis.org/articles/2004/05/20/seven-cs-of-history.

his father and mother and be joined to his wife, and the two shall become one flesh'?" (Matthew 19:4–5, NKJV).

He quoted from Genesis as literal history — Genesis 1 and 2. God invented marriage, by the way, that's where marriage comes from, and it's to be a man and woman. And not only marriage, ultimately every single biblical doctrine of theology, directly or indirectly, is founded in Genesis.

40:00

Why is there sin in the word? Genesis.
Why is there death? Genesis.
Why do we wear clothes? Genesis.
Why did Jesus die on a cross? Genesis.

It's a very important book; it's foundational to all Christian doctrine.

And you see, when we look at what I call the Seven C's of History that we walk people through here at the museum, think about how it all connects together; a perfect Creation, it'll be perfect again in the future. [Visuals depicting the Seven C's of History displayed]

Sin and death entered the world; that's why God's Son died on the Cross and to conquer death and offer a free gift of salvation.

The Flood of Noah's day; a reminder that the Flood was a judgment because of man's wickedness, but at the same time a message of God's grace and salvation. As Noah and his family had to go through a door to be saved, so we need to go through a door to be saved.

Jesus Christ said, "I am the door, by me if any man enter in he will be saved." [John 10:9]

We make no apology about the fact that what we're on about is this: "That if you confess with your mouth the Lord Jesus and believe in your heart that God has raised Him from the dead, you will be saved." (Romans 10:9, NKJV)

Now, as soon as I say that people say, "See, if you allow creation in schools for instance, if you allow students to even hear about it, ahh, this is religion."

You know let me illustrate this talking about a recent battle in Texas over textbooks in the public school.

The newspaper report said this: "Textbook and classroom curriculum battles have long raged in Texas pitting creationists — those who

Bill Nye and Ken Ham

see God's hand in the creation of the universe — against academics who worry about religious and political ideology trumping scientific fact."[22]

Stop right there, notice "creationists; academics." Creationists can't be academics, creationists can't be scientists. See it's the way things are worded out there. It's an indoctrination that's going on.

"... who worry about religious and political ideology trumping scientific fact."

Wait a minute; what do they mean by "science"? Are you talking about what you observe, or are you talking about your beliefs about the past.

Now, Kathy Miller is the President of the Texas Freedom Network and she has vocally spoken out, she's spoken out about this textbook battle there in Texas. And the mission statement of the organization she is president of says: "The Texas Freedom Network advances a mainstream

---

22. Will Weissert, "Evolution Edits Unlikely in Texas Science Books," *Texas News*, http://www.nbcdfw.com/news/local/Texas-Science-Textbook-Battle-Reignites-232640031.html. [It has come to our attention after the debate that the quote we used

agenda of religious freedom and individual liberties to counter the religious right."[23]

Religious freedom, individual liberties, hmmm.

And then she makes this statement: "Science education should be based on mainstream established science, not on the personal ideological beliefs of unqualified reviewers."[24]

Wait a minute, they want religious liberty and not personal ideological beliefs?

I assert this: Public school textbooks are using the same word science for observational and historical science. They arbitrarily define science as naturalism and outlaw the supernatural. They present molecules-to-man evolution as fact. They are imposing the religion of naturalism/atheism on generations of students.

They are imposing their ideology on the students, that everything is explained by natural processes. That is a religion.

What does she mean by religious liberty? They tolerate their religion.

You see, the battle is really about authority. It's more than just science or evolution or creation. It's about who is the authority in this world — man or God?

If you start with naturalism then what about morals? Who decides right and wrong? Well, it's subjective.

Marriage? Well, whatever you want it to be.

Get rid of old people, I mean why not. I mean, they're just animals, they're costing us a lot of money.

Abortion? Get rid of spare cats, get rid of spare kids. We're all animals.

But if you start from God's Word there are moral absolutes. God decides right from wrong.

Marriage: One man and one women.

The sanctity of life: We care for old people; they're made in the image of God.

Life begins at fertilization: So abortion is killing a human being.

23. Texas Freedom Network, "Mission Statement," http://www.tfn.org/site/PageServer?pagename=about_mission.

24. "Reviewers are pushing for creationism in Texas biology textbooks," KHOU News, http://www.khou.com/news/texas-news/Reviewers-are-pushing-for-creationism-in-Texas-biology-textbooks-223404951.html. [It has come to our attention after the debate that the quote we used had a minor error. The transcript reflects her actual words.]

We do see the collapse of Christian morality in our culture and increasing moral relativism because generations of kids are being taught the religion of naturalism and that the Bible can't be trusted.

And so again I say, creation is the only viable model of historical science confirmed by observational science in today's modern scientific era.

You know what? I'm a science teacher. I want to see kids taught science. I love science. I want to see more Dr. Damadians in the world. You know if we teach them the whole universe is a result of natural processes and not designed by a Creator God, they might be looking in the wrong places or have the wrong idea when they're looking at the creation in regard to how you develop technology.

Because if they look it as just random processes, that could totally influence the way they think. If they understand it was a perfect world marred by sin that could have a great effect on how they then look for overcoming diseases and problems in the world.

I want children to be taught the right foundation, that there's a God who created them, who loves them, who died on the Cross for them, and that they're special, they're made in the image of God.

Moderator Comments

Tom Foreman: Thank you, Mr. Ham. We can applaud Mr. Ham's presentation.

45:00

And you know it did occur to me when you had my old friend Larry King up there, you could have just asked him. He's been around a long time and he's a smart guy. He could probably answer for all of us.

Now, let's all be attentive to Mr. Nye as he gives us his 30-minute presentation.

30-minute Presentation — Bill Nye

Bill Nye: Thank you very much, and Mr. Ham, I learned something, thank you.

But let's take it back around to the question at hand: Does Ken Ham's creation model hold up? Is it viable?

So, for me, of course, well take a look. We're here in Kentucky on layer upon layer upon layer of limestone. I stopped at the side of the road

314

today and picked up this piece of limestone that has a fossil right there. Now, in these many, many layers in this vicinity of Kentucky there are coral animals, fossil: zooxanthellae.

And when you look at it closely you can see that they live their entire lives, they lived typically 20 years, sometimes more than that if the water conditions are correct. And so we are standing on millions of layers of ancient life. How could those animals have lived their entire life and formed these layers in just 4,000 years? There isn't enough time since Mr. Ham's flood for this limestone that we're standing on to have come into existence.

My scientific colleagues go to places like Greenland, the Arctic, they go to Antarctica and they drill into the ice with hollow drill bits. It's not that extraordinary, many of you have probably done it yourselves drilling other things; hole saws to put locks in doors, for example. And we pull out long cylinders of ice, long ice rods, and these are made of snow. And by long tradition it's called snow ice, and snow ice forms over the winter as snowflakes fall and are crushed down by subsequent layers, they're crushed together entrapping the little bubbles. And the little bubbles must needs be ancient atmosphere. There's nobody running around with a hypodermic needle squirting ancient atmosphere into the bubbles.

And we find certain of these cylinders to have 680,000 layers. 680,000 snow winter-summer cycles. How could it be that just 4,000 years ago all of this ice formed?

Let's just run some numbers. This is some scenes from lovely Antarctic.

Let's say we have 680,000 layers of snow ice and 4,000 years since the Great Flood, that would mean we would need 170 winter-summer cycles every year for the last 4,000 years. I mean wouldn't someone have noticed that? Wow! Wouldn't someone have noticed that there's been winter, summer, winter, summer 170 times one year?

If we go to California we find enormous stands of bristlecone pines, some of them are over 6,000 years old — 6,800 years old. There is a famous tree in Sweden — Old Tjikko is 9,550 years old. How could these trees be there if there was an enormous flood just 4,000 years ago?

You can try this yourself, everybody, get — I mean, I don't mean to be mean to trees, but get a sapling and put it under water for a year. It will not survive in general nor will its seeds, they just won't make it. So how could these trees be that old if the earth is only 4,000 years old?

Now when we go to the Grand Canyon, which is an astonishing place and I recommend to everybody in the world to someday visit the Grand Canyon, you find layer upon layer of ancient rocks. And if there was this enormous flood that you speak of, wouldn't there have been churning and bubbling and roiling? How would these things have settled out?

Your claim that they settled out in an extraordinary short amount of time is, for me, not satisfactory. You can look at these rocks, you can look at rocks that are younger, you can go to seashores where there's sand.

This is what geologists on the outside do, study the rate at which soil is deposited at the end of rivers and deltas, and we can see that it takes a long, long time for sediments to turn to stone.

Also, in this picture you can see where one type of sediment has intruded on another type. Now, if that was uniform wouldn't we expect it all to be even without intrusion?

50:00

Furthermore you can find places in the Grand Canyon where you see an ancient riverbed on that side going to an ancient riverbed on that side and Colorado River has cut through it.

And by the way, if this great flood drained through the Grand Canyon, wouldn't there have been a Grand Canyon on every continent? How can we not have Grand Canyons everywhere if this water drained away in this extraordinary short amount of time, 4,000 years?

Now when you look at these layers carefully you find these beautiful fossils. And when I say beautiful, I am inspired by them, they're remarkable because we are looking at the past. You find, down low, you'll find what you might consider as rudimentary sea animals, up above you'll find the famous trilobites, above that you might find some clams, some oysters, and above that you'll find some mammals.

You never ever find a higher animal mixed in with a lower one. You never find a lower one trying to swim its way to the higher one.

If all happened in such an extraordinary short amount of time, if this water drained away just like that, wouldn't we expect to see some turbulence?

And by the way, anyone here, really, if you can find one example of that, one example of that anywhere in the world, the scientists of the world challenge you, they would embrace you, you would be a hero, you would change the world if you could find one example of that anywhere. People have looked and looked and looked; they have not found a single one.

Now here's an interesting thing. These are fossil skulls[25] that people have found all around the world. It's by no means representative of all of the fossil skulls that have been found, but these are all over the place. Now, if you were to look at these I can assure you not any of them is a gorilla. Right?

If, as Mr. Ham and his associates claim, there was just man and then everybody else, there were just humans and all other species, where would you put modern humans among these skulls?

How did all of these skulls get all over the earth in these extraordinary fashion, where would you put us? I can tell you we are on there, and I encourage you when you go home to look it up.

Now, one of the extraordinary claims associated with Mr. Ham's worldview is that this giant boat, very large wooden ship, went aground safely on a mountain in the Middle East — what we now call the Middle East. And so places like Australia are populated, then, by animals who somehow managed to get from the Middle East all the way to Australia in the last 4,000 years. Now that to me is an extraordinary claim.

We would expect then somewhere between the Middle East and Australia we would expect to find evidence of kangaroos. We would expect to find some fossils, some bones. In the last 4,000 years somebody would have been hopping along there and died along the way and we'd find them.

And furthermore there is a claim that there was a land bridge that allowed these animals to get from Asia all the way to the continent of Australia. And that land bridge has disappeared, has disappeared in the last 4,000 years. No navigator, no divers, no U.S. Navy submarine, no one's ever detected any evidence of this, let alone any fossils of kangaroos. So your expectation is not met, it doesn't seem to hold up.

So, let's see, if there are 4,000 years since Ken Ham's flood. And let's say, as he said many times, there are 7,000 kinds, today the very, very lowest estimate is that there are about 8.7 million species, but a much

---

25. An image of skulls and skull fragments is shown and credited to Matt Cartmill, but no source is given.

more reasonable estimate is it is 50 million or even a 100 million when you start counting the viruses and the bacteria and all the beetles that must be extant in the tropical rainforest that we haven't found.

So we'll take a number which I think is pretty reasonable, 16 million species today. Okay?

If these came from 7,000 kinds, that's let's say we have 7,000 subtracted from 15 million, that's 15,993, we have 4,000 years, we 365 and a quarter days a year. We would expect to find 11 new species every day.

55:00

So you'd go out into your yard, you wouldn't just find a different bird, a new bird, you'd find a different kind of bird, a whole new species of bird every day, a new species of fish, a new species of organism you can't see, and so on. I mean this would be enormous news. The last 4,000 years people would have seen these changes among us. So the Cincinnati Enquirer I imagine would carry a column right next to the weather report: "Today's new species." And they would list these 11 every day, but we see no evidence of that. There's no evidence of these species, there just simply isn't enough time.

Now as you may know, I was graduated from engineering school and I was, I got a job at Boeing. I worked on 747s.

Okay, everybody, relax, I was very well supervised, everything's fine. There is a tube in the 747 I kind of think of as my tube, but that aside.

I traveled the highways of Washington state quite a bit. I was a young guy, I had a motorcycle. I used to go mountain climbing in Washington state, Oregon. And you can drive along and find these enormous boulders on top of the ground, enormous rocks, huge, sitting on top of the ground.

Now out there in regular academic pursuits, regular geology, people have discovered there was — used to be a lake in what is now Montana which we charmingly refer to as Lake Missoula. It's not there now, but the evidence for it of course is, if I may, overwhelming. And so an ice dam would form at Lake Missoula and once in a while it would break, it would build up and break. And there were multiple floods in my old state of Washington state.

Before we go on let me just say, "Go Seahawks!" That was very gratifying, very gratifying for me.[26]

Anyway, you drive along the road and there are these rocks. So if as
is asserted here at this facility that the heavier rocks would sink to the
bottom during a flood event, the big rocks and especially their shape,
instead of aerodynamic, the hydrodynamic, the water changing shape as
water flows past, you'd expect them to sink to the bottom.

But here are these enormous rocks right on the surface and there's no
shortage of them. If you go driving in Washington state or Oregon there
are readily available. So how could those be there if the earth is just 4,000
years old? How could they be there if this one flood caused that?

Another remarkable thing I'd like everybody to consider, along — inherent in this worldview is that somehow Noah and his family were able
to build a wooden ship that would house 14,000 individuals, there were
7,000 kinds and there's a boy and girl for each one of those.

So it's about 14,000, 8 people, and these people were unskilled. As far
as anybody knows, they never built a wooden ship before. Furthermore
they had to get all of these animals on there, and they had to feed them.
And I understand that Mr. Ham has some explanations for that, which I
frankly find extraordinary, but this is the premise of the bit.

And we can then run a test, a scientific test. People in the early
1900s build an extraordinarily large wooden ship, the *Wyoming*. It was
a six-masted schooner, the largest ever built. It had a motor on it for
winching cables and stuff, but this boat had a great difficulty. It was not
a big as the *Titanic*, but it was a very long ship.

60:00

It would twist in the sea. It would twist this way, this way, and this
way. [Motioning] And in all that twisting it leaked; it leaked like crazy.
The crew could not keep the ship dry, and indeed it eventually foundered
and sank; loss of all 14 hands. So there were 14 crewmen aboard a ship
built by very, very skilled shipwrights in New England. These guys were
the best in the world at wooden ship building, and they couldn't build a
boat as big as the Ark is claimed to have been.

---

26. This was a reference to the Seattle Seahawks win in Superbowl XLVII on the Sunday before the debate.

Is that reasonable? Is that possible that the best the in world couldn't do what 8 unskilled people, men and their wives, were able to do?

If you visit the National Zoo in Washington D.C., it is 163 acres, and they have 400 species.

By the way, this picture[27] that you're seeing was taken by spacecraft in space orbiting the earth. If you told my grandfather, let alone my father, that we had that capability they would have been amazed. That capability comes from our fundamental understanding of gravity, of material science, of physics, and life science, where you go look looking.

This place is often, as any zoo, is often deeply concerned and criticized for how it treats its animals. They have 400 species on 163 acres, 66 hectares. Is it reasonable that Noah and his colleagues, his family, were able to maintain 14,000 animals and themselves, and feed them aboard a ship that was bigger than anyone has ever been able to build?

Now here is the thing, what we want in science, science as practiced on the outside, is an ability to predict. We want to have a natural law that is so obvious and clear, so well understood, that we can make predictions about what will happen. We can predict that we can put a spacecraft in orbit and take a picture of Washington, D.C. We can predict that if we provide this much room for an elephant it will live healthfully for a certain amount of time.

So I'll give you an example. In the explanation provided by traditional science of how we came to be, we find, as Mr. Ham alluded to many times in his recent remarks, we find a sequence of animals in what generally is called the fossil record.

This would be to say, when we look at the layers that you would find in Kentucky, you look at them carefully, you find a sequence of animals, a succession. And, as one might expect, when you're looking at old records there are — some pieces seem to be missing, a gap. So scientists got to thinking about this. There are lung fish that jump from pond to pond in Florida and end up in people's swimming pools. And there are amphibians, frogs and toads, croaking and carrying on.

And so people wondered if there wasn't a fossil or an organism, an animal, that had lived that had characteristics of both. People over the

27. A satellite photograph of the National Zoo is shown on the screen along with images of animals there.

years had found that in Canada there was clearly a fossil marsh, a place that used to be a swamp that dried out. And they found all kinds of happy swamp fossils there, ferns, so on, and organisms, animals, fish that were recognized.

And people realized that if this — with the age of the rocks there, as computed by traditional scientists, with the age of the rocks there, this would be a reasonable place to look for an animal, a fossil of animal that lived there. And indeed, scientists found it, *Tiktaalik*, this fish-lizard guy. And they found several specimens; this wasn't one individual.

In other words they made a prediction that this animal would be found and it was found.

So far, Mr. Ham and his worldview, the Ken Ham creation model, does not have this capability. It cannot make predictions and show results.

Here's an extraordinary one that I find remarkable. There are certain fish, the topminnows, that have the remarkable ability to have sex with other fish, traditional fish sex, and they can have sex with themselves.

Now, one of the old questions in life science, everybody, one of the old sort of chin-strokers, is why does any organism, whether you're an ash tree, a sea jelly, a squid, a marmot, why does anybody have sex?

I mean there are more bacteria in your tummy right now than there are humans on earth. And bacteria, they don't bother with that, man. They just like split themselves in half, they get new bacteria like, "Let's get 'er done, let's go."

But why does any — think of all the trouble a rose bush goes through to make a flower and the thorns and the bees with swimming — flying around, interacting.

Why does anybody bother with all of that? And the answer seems to be: your enemies. And your enemies are not lions and tigers and bears, oh, my. No, your enemies are germs and parasites. That's what's going to get you: germs and parasites.

My first cousin's son died tragically from essentially the flu. This is not some story heard about, it is my first cousin once removed, because apparently the virus had the right genes to attack his genes.

1:05:00

So when you have sex you have a new set of genes, you have a new mixture. So people studied these topminnows and they found that the ones who reproduce sexually had fewer parasites than the ones that reproduced on their own, this black spot disease. Wait, wait, there's more.

In these populations, with flooding and so on with river ponds get isolated and they dry up and the river flows again, in between some of the fish will have sex with other fish sometimes and they'll have sex on their own, what's called asexually. And those fish, the ones that are in between, sometimes, sometimes that, they have an intermediate number of infections. In other words, the explanation provided by evolution made a prediction, and the prediction's extraordinary and subtle, but there it is. How else would you explain it?

And to Mr. Ham and his followers, I say this is something that we in science want, we want the ability to predict. And your assertion that there's some difference between the natural laws that I use to observe the world today and the natural laws that existed 4,000 years ago is extraordinary and unsettling.

I travel around, I have a great many family members in Danville, Virginia, one of the world — one of the U.S.'s most livable cities, it's lovely. And I was driving along and there was a sign in front of a church: "Big Bang Theory, you got to be kidding me, God."

Now, everybody, why would someone at the church, a pastor for example, put that sign up unless he or she didn't believe that the Big Bang was a real thing? I just want to review briefly with everybody why we accept, in the outside world, why we accept the Big Bang.

Edwin Hubble, oh, sorry there you go. "You got to be kidding me, God."

Edwin Hubble was sitting at Mt. Wilson which is up from Pasadena, California. On a clear day you can look down and see where the Rose Parade goes, it is that close to civilization. But even in the early 1900s, the people who selected this site for astronomy picked an excellent site; the clouds and smog are below you. And Edwin Hubble sat there at this very big telescope night after night studying the heavens. And he found that the stars are moving apart.

The stars are moving apart. And he wasn't sure why but it was clear that the stars are moving farther and farther apart all of the time.

So people talked about it for a couple decades. And then eventually another astronomer — almost a couple decades — another astronomer,

Fred Hoyle, just remarked, "Well, it was like there was a big bang," there was an explosion.

This is to say, since everything's moving apart, it's very reasonable that at one time they were all together, and there's a place from whence, or rather, whence these things expanded. And it was a remarkable insight. But people went, still, questioning it for decades, science and conventional scientists, questioning it for decades.

These two researchers wanted to listen for radio signals from space, radio astronomy. And this is why we have visible light for our eyes, there is a whole 'nother bunch of waves of light that are much longer.

The microwaves in your oven are about that long. The radar at the airport is about that long. Your FM radio signal is about like this. [Making motions] AM radio signals are, kill me, they're several soccer fields.

They went out listening and there was this hiss, this [hissing sound] all the time that wouldn't go away.

And they thought, "Oh, dog gone it, there's some loose connector." They plugged in the connector. They rescrewed it, they made it tight. They turned it this way, the hiss was still there, they heard it that way, it was still there. They thought it was pigeon droppings that had affected the reception of this horn, it's called. This thing is still there, it's in Basking Ridge, New Jersey. It's a national historic site.

And Arno Penzias and Robert Wilson had found this cosmic background sound that was predicted by astronomers. Astronomers running the numbers, doing math, predicted that in the cosmos would be left over, this echo, this energy from the Big Bang that would be detectable, and they detected it.

We built the Cosmic Observatory for Background Emissions, the COBE Spacecraft, and it matched exactly, exactly the astronomer's predictions. You've got to respect that. It's a wonderful thing.

1:10:00

Now, along that line is some interest in the age of the earth. Right now it's generally agreed that the Big Bang happened 13.7 billion years ago. What we can do on earth, these elements that we all know on the periodic table of chemicals, even ones we don't know, are created when stars explode.

And I look like nobody, but I attended a lecture by Hans Bethe who won a Nobel Prize for discovering the process by which stars create all of these elements. The one that interests me especially is our good friend rubidium and strontium.

Rubidium become strontium spontaneously. It's an interesting thing to me, a neutron becomes a proton and it goes up the periodic table.

When lava comes out of the ground, molten lava, and it freezes, it turns to rock, when the melt solidifies or crystallizes, it locks the rubidium and strontium in place.

And so by careful assay, by careful — by being diligent, you can tell how — when the rock froze. You can tell how old the rubidium and strontium are and you can get an age for the earth. When that stuff falls on fossils you can get a very good idea of how old the fossils are.

I encourage you all to go to Nebraska, go to Ash Fall State Park and see the astonishing fossils. It looks like a Hollywood movie. There are rhinoceroses, there are three-toed horses in Nebraska.

None of those animals are extant today and they were buried catastrophically by a volcano in what is now Idaho, is now Yellowstone National Park. It's called a hot spot, people call it the super volcano.

And it's a remarkable thing, apparently, as I can tell you as a northwesterner around for Mount St. Helens, I'm — full disclosure, I'm on the Mount St Helens Board.

When it [explosion sound effect] when it goes off it gives out a great deal of gas that's toxic and knocked these animals out. Looking for relief they go to a watering hole and then when the ash comes they were all buried, also. It's an extraordinary place.

Now if in the bad old days you had heart problems they would right away cut you open. Now, we use a drug based on rubidium to look at the inside of your heart without cutting you open.

Now, my Kentucky friends, I want you to consider this. Right now there is no place in the Commonwealth of Kentucky to get a degree in this kind of nuclear medicine, this kind of drugs associated with that. I hope you find that troubling. I hope you're concerned about that.

You want scientifically literate students in your commonwealth for a better tomorrow for everybody. You can — you can't get this here; you have to go out of state.

Now as far as the distance to stars, understand, this is very well understood. We — it's February. We look at a star in February, we measure an angle to it, we wait six months, we look at that same star again and we measure that angle. It's the same way carpenters built this building. It's the same way surveyors surveyed the land that we're standing on.

And so by measuring the distance to a star you can figure out how far away it is, that star, and then the stars beyond it, and the stars beyond that.

There are billions of stars, billions of stars, more than 6,000 light years from here. A light year is a unit of distance, not a unit of time. There are billions of stars.

Mr. Ham, how could there be billions of stars, more distant than 6,000 years, if the world's only 6,000 years old? It's an extraordinary claim.

There's another astronomer, Adolphe Quetele, who remarked first about the "reasonable man." Is it reasonable that we have ice older by a factor of a hundred than you claim the earth is?

We have trees that have more tree rings than the earth is old? That we have rocks with rubidium and strontium and uranium-uranium and potassium-argon dating that are far, far, far older than you claim the earth is?

Could anybody have built an ark that would sustain the better than any ark anybody was able to build on the earth?

So if you're asking me, and I got the impression you were, is Ken Ham's creation model viable?

I say, no, absolutely not!

One last thing, you may not know that in the U.S. Constitution, from the founding fathers, is the sentence: " . . . to promote the progress of science and useful arts."

Kentucky voters — voters who might be watching online in places like Texas, Tennessee, Oklahoma, Kansas — please, you don't want to raise a generation of science students who don't understand how we know our place in the cosmos, our place in space, who don't understand natural law.

1:15:00

We need to innovate to keep the United States where it is in the world.

Thank you very much.

Moderator Comments

Tom Foreman: That's a lot to take in. I hope everybody's holding up well. That's a lot of information.

What we're going to have now is a 5-minute rebuttal time for each gentleman to address the other one's comments. And then there will be a 5-minute counter rebuttal after that.

Things are going to start moving a little more quickly now, so at this point in particular I want to make sure we don't have applauding or anything else going on that slows it down.

So, Mr. Ham, if you'd like to begin with your 5-minute rebuttal first.

First 5-minute Rebuttal — Ken Ham

Ken Ham: Well, first of all, Bill, if I was to answer all the points that you brought up the moderator would think I was going on for millions of years. So I can only deal with some of them.

And you mentioned the age of the earth a couple of times, so let me deal with that.

As I said in my presentation, you can't observe the age of the earth. And I would say that comes under what we call historical or origins science.

Now just to understand, just so you understand where I'm coming from, yes, we admit we build our origins from historical science on the Bible. The Bible says God created in six days.

Hebrew word "yom" as it's used in Genesis 1 with evening, morning, number means an ordinary day. Adam was made on Day Six.

So when you add up all those genealogies specifically given in the Bible from Adam to Abraham, you've got 2,000 years from Abraham to Christ, 2,000 years, from Christ to the present, 2,000 years. That's how we get 6,000 years. So that's where it comes from, just so you know.

Now, a lot of people say, "Now by the way, the earth's age is 4.5 billion years old. And we have radioactive decay dating methods that found that."

You see, we certainly observe radioactive decay, whether it's rubidium-strontium, whether it's uranium-lead, potassium-argon. But when you're talking about the past we have a problem.

I'll give you a practical example. In Australia there were engineers that were trying to search out about a coal mine. So they drilled down and found a basalt layer, a lava flow, that had woody material in it, branches and twigs, and so on. And when Dr. Andrew Snelling, a PhD geologist, sent that to a lab in Massachusetts in 1994, they used potassium-argon dating and dated it to 45 million years old.

Well, he also sent the wood to the radiocarbon section of the same lab and that dated it at 45,000 years old. 45,000-year-old wood in 45-million-year-old rock. The point is, there's a problem.[28]

Let me give you another example of a problem. There was a lava dome that started to form in the '80s after Mount Saint Helens erupted. And in 1994, Dr. Steve Austin, another PhD geologist, actually sampled the rock there. He took whole rock, crushed it, sent it to the same lab actually, I believe, and got a date of 0.35 million years. When he separated out the minerals amphibole and pyroxene and used potassium-argon dating he got 0.9 million, 2.8 million.[29]

My point is all these dating methods actually give all sorts of different dates. In fact, different dating methods on the same rock , we can show, give all sorts of different dates.

See there's lots of assumptions in regard to radioactive dating.

Number one, for instance, the amounts of the parent and daughter isotopes at the beginning when the rock formed. You have to know them, but you weren't there. See that's historical science.

Assumption two, that all daughter atoms measured today must have only been derived *in situ* radioactive decay of parent atoms. In other words, it's a closed system, but you don't know that and that's a lot of evidence that that's not so.

Assumption number three, that the decay rates have remained constant. That's just some of them, there are others as well.

The point is there's lots of assumptions in regard to the dating methods. So there is no dating method you can use that you can absolutely age date a rock. There's all sorts of differences out there.

And I do want to address the bit you brought up about Christians believing millions of years. Yeah, there's a lot of Christians out there that believe in millions of years, but I'd say they have a problem.

28. Andrew Snelling, "Geological Conflict: Young Radiocarbon Date for Ancient Fossil Wood Challenges Fossil Dating," http://www.answersingenesis.org/articles/cm/v22/n2/geology.
29. Keith Swenson, "Radio-dating in Rubble: The Lava Dome at Mount. St. Helens Debunks Dating Methods," http://www.answersingenesis.org/articles/cm/v23/n3/radiodating.

I'm not saying they're not Christians, but — because salvation is conditioned upon faith in Christ, not the age of the earth. But there's an inconsistency with what the Bible teaches. If you believe in millions of years you've got death and bloodshed, suffering, disease, over millions of years leading to man because that's what you see in the fossil record. The Bible makes it very clear death is a result of man's sin.

In fact the first death was in the Garden when God killed an animal, clothed Adam and Eve, first blood sacrifice pointing towards what would happen with Jesus Christ.[30] He would be the one who would die once and for all.

Now if you believe in millions of years as a Christian, in the fossil record there's evidence of animals eating each other. The Bible says originally all the animals and man were vegetarian.[31] We weren't told we could eat meat until after the Flood.[32]

There's diseases represented in the fossil record like brain tumors, but the Bible says when God made everything it was "very good." God doesn't call brain tumors very good.

There's fossilized thorns in the fossil record said to be hundreds of millions of years old. The Bible says thorns came after the curse.

So these two things can't be true at the same time.

You know what, there's hundreds of dating methods out there, hundreds of them. Actually 90% of them contradict billions of years. And the point is, all such dating methods are fallible.

And I claim there's only one infallible dating method, it's the Witness who was there, who knows everything, who told us, and that's from the Word of God.

And that's why I would say that the earth is only 6,000 years, and as Dr. Faulkner said, there's nothing in astronomy, and certainly Dr. Snelling would say there's nothing in geology to contradict a belief in a young age for the earth and the universe.

Moderator Comments

Tom Foreman: Thank you, Mr. Ham. Mr. Nye, your 5-minute rebuttal, please.

---

30. Genesis 3:21.
31. Genesis 1:29–30.
32. Genesis 9:3.

First 5-minute Rebuttal — Bill Nye

Bill Nye: Thank you very much.

Let me start with the beginning, if you find 45 million year old rock on top of 45,000 year old trees, maybe the rock slid on top. Maybe that's it. That seems a much more reasonable explanation than it's impossible.

Then as far as dating goes, actually the methods are very reliable.

One of the mysteries or interesting things that people in my business, especially at the Planetary Society, are interested in, is why all the asteroids seem to be so close to the same date in age, 4.5–4.6 billion years. It's a remarkable thing. People at first expected a little more of a spread.

So I understand that you take the Bible as written in English, translated countless — oh, not countless, but many, many times over the last three millennia, as to be a more accurate, more reasonable assessment of the natural laws we see around us than what I and everybody in here can observe.

That to me is unsettling, troubling.

And then about the disease thing where the — are the fish sinners? Have they done something wrong to get diseases? That's sort of an extraordinary claim that takes me just a little past what I'm comfortable with.

And then as far as you can't observe the past, I just have to stop you right there. That's what we do in astronomy. All we can do in astronomy is look at the past.

By the way, you're looking at the past right now because the speed of light bounces off of me and then gets to your eyes. And I'm delighted to see that the people in the back of the room appear just that much younger than the people in the front.

So this idea that you can separate the natural laws of the past from the natural laws that we have now I think at the heart of our disagreement. I don't see how we're ever going to agree with that if you insist that natural laws have changed.

It's, for lack of a better word, it's magical. And I have appreciated magic since I was a kid, but it's not really what we want in conventional mainstream science.

So, your assertion that all of the animals were vegetarians before they got on the Ark, that's really remarkable. I have not been — spent a lot of time with lions, but I can tell they have got teeth that really aren't set up for broccoli. That these animals were vegetarians until this flood is something that I would ask you to provide a little more proof for.

I give you the lion's teeth, you give me verses as translated into English over, what, 30 centuries? So, that is not enough evidence for me.

If you've ever played telephone, I did, I remember very well in kindergarten, where you have a secret and you whisper it to the next person, to the next person, to the next person. Things often go wrong.

So it's very reasonable to me that instead of lions being vegetarians on the Ark, lions are lions, and the information that you use to create your worldview is not consistent with what I as a reasonable man would expect.

So, I want everybody to consider the implications of this. If we accept Mr. Ham's point of view, that — Mr. Ham's point of view that the Bible as translated into American English serves as a science text, and that he and his followers will interpret that for you, just, I want you to consider what that means.

It means that Mr. Ham's word, or his interpretation of these other words, is somehow to be more respected than what you can observe in nature, what you can find literally in your back yard in Kentucky.

It's a troubling and unsettling point of view, and it's one I very much like you to address when you come back.

As far as the five races that you mentioned, it's kind of the same thing. The five races were claimed by people who were of European descent and they said, "Hey, we're the best. Check us out." And that turns out to be if you've ever traveled anywhere or done anything, not to be that way. People are much more alike than they are different.

So, are we supposed to take your word for English words translated over the last 30 centuries instead of what we can observe in the universe around us?

Moderator Comments

Tom Foreman: Very good. Mr. Ham, would you like to offer your 5-minute counter rebuttal?

Second 5-minute Rebuttal — Ken Ham

Ken Ham: First of all, Bill, I just don't want a misunderstanding here and that is the 45,000 year old wood, or supposedly 45,000 was inside the basalt. So it was encased in the basalt and that's why I was making that particular point.

And I would also say that natural law hasn't changed.

As I talked about, you know, I said we have the laws of logic, the uniformity of nature and that only makes sense within a biblical worldview anyway, of a creator God who set up those laws. And that's why we can do good experimental science because we assume those laws are true and that will be true tomorrow.

I do want to say this: That you said a few times, you know, "Ken Ham's view," or "Ken Ham's model." It is not just Ken Ham's model. We have a number of PhD scientists on our own staff. I quoted — had video quotes from some scientists.

It is Dr. Damadian's model, it's Dr. Fabich's model, it's Dr. Faulkner's model, it's Dr. Snelling's model, it's Dr. Purdom's model, and so it goes on.

In other words, and you go on our website and there are lots of creation scientists who agree with exactly what we're saying concerning the Bible, concerning the Bible's account of creation. So it's not just my model in that sense.

There's so much that I could say that — as I listen to you, I believe you're confusing terms in regard to species and kinds. Because we're not saying God created all those species, we're saying God created kinds, and we're not saying species got on the Ark, we're saying kinds. In fact we've had researchers working on what is a kind.

For instance, there's a number of papers published on our website where, for instance, they look at dogs and they say well this one breeds with this one, with this one with this one, with this one, this one. And you can look at all the papers around the world and you can connect them all together and say, "That obviously represents one kind."

If fact as they have been doing that research they have predicted probably less than actually a thousand kinds were on Noah's Ark, which means just over 2,000 animals. And the average size of a land animal is not that big, so, you know, there was plenty of room on the Ark.

I also believe that a lot of what you were saying was really illustrating my point.

You were talking about tree rings and ice layers and talking about kangaroos getting to Australia and all sorts of things like that. But see, we're talking about the past when we weren't there. We didn't see those tree rings actually forming. We didn't see those layers being laid down.

You know in 1942 for instance, there was some planes that were landed on the ice in Greenland. And they found them what 46 years later, I think it was, three miles away from the original location with 250 feet of ice buried on top of them. So, ice can build up catastrophically. If you assume one layer a year or something like that, it's like the dating methods; you are assuming things in regard to the past that aren't necessarily true.

In regard to lions and teeth. Bears, most bears, have teeth very much like a lion or tiger and, yet, most bears are primarily vegetarian. The panda if you look at its teeth you'd say, "Maybe it should be a savage carnivore." It eats mainly bamboo. The little fruit bat in Australia has really sharp teeth, looks like a savage little creature and it rips into fruit.

So just because an animal has sharp teeth doesn't mean it is a meat eater, it means it has sharp teeth.

And so again, it really comes down to our interpretation of these things. I think too, in regard to the Missoula example that you gave, you know creationists do believe there's been post-Flood catastrophism. Noah's Flood certainly was a catastrophic event, but then there's been post-Flood catastrophism since that time as well.

1:30:00

And again, in regard to historical science, why would you say Noah was unskilled? I mean, I didn't meet Noah, and neither did you. And you know, really, it's an evolutionary view of origins, I believe, because you're thinking in terms of people before us aren't as good as us.

Hey, there are civilizations that existed in the past and we look at their technology and we can't even understand today how they did some of the things that they did. Who says Noah couldn't build a big boat? By the way, the Chinese and the Egyptians built boats. In fact some of our research indicates that some of the wooden boats that were built had three layers interlocking so they wouldn't twist like that and leak. Which is why here at the Creation Museum we have an exhibit on the Ark where we have rebuilt 1% of the Ark to scale and showed three interlocking layers like that.

And one last thing, concerning the speed of light, and that is, I'm sure you're aware of the horizon problem, and that is, from a Big Bang perspective, even the secularists have a problem of getting light and radiation out to the universe to be able to exchange with the rest of the universe to get that even microwave background radiation. On their model, 15 billion years or so, they can only get it about halfway, and that's why they have inflation theories. Which means everyone has a problem regarding the light issue, there's things people don't understand.

And we have some models on our website by some of our scientists to help explain those sorts of things.

Moderator Comments

Tom Foreman: Mr. Nye, your counter rebuttal.

Second 5-minute Rebuttal — Bill Nye

Bill Nye: Thank you, Mr. Ham, but I'm completely unsatisfied. You did not, in my view, address the fundamental questions.

680,000 years of snow ice layers which require winter-summer cycle, let's say you have 2,000 kinds instead of 7, that makes the problem even more extraordinary.

Multiplying 11 by what's — by 3 and a half? We get to 35, 40 species every day that we don't see. They're not extant. In fact you probably know we're losing species due to mostly human activity and the loss of habitat.

Then as far as Noah being an extraordinary shipwright, I'm very skeptical. The shipwrights, my ancestors, the Nye family in New England, spent their whole life learning to make ships. I mean, it's very reasonable perhaps to you that Noah had super powers and was able to build this extraordinary craft with seven family members. But to me it's just not reasonable.

Then, by the way, the fundamental thing we disagree on, Mr. Ham, is this nature of what you can prove to yourself. This is to say, when people make assumptions based on radiometric data, when they make assumptions about the expanding universe, when they make assumptions about the rate at which genes change in populations of bacteria in laboratory growth media, they're making assumptions based on previous experience.

They're not coming out of whole cloth.

So next time you have a chance to speak, I encourage you to explain to us why we should accept your word for it, that natural law changed just 4,000 years ago, completely, and there's no record of it.

You know, there are pyramids that are older than that.

There are — there are human populations that are far older than that with traditions that go back further than that.

And it's just not reasonable to me that everything changed 4,000 years ago. By everything I mean the species, the surface of the earth, the stars in the sky, and the relationship of all the other living things on earth to humans. It's just not reasonable to me that everything changed like that.

And another thing I would very much appreciate you addressing: There are billions of people in the world who are deeply religious, and I respect that. People get tremendous community and comfort and nurture and support from their religious fellows in their communities, in their faiths, in their churches, and yet they don't accept your point of view. There are Christians who don't accept that the earth could somehow be this extraordinarily young age because of all of the evidence around them.

And so, what is to become of them in your view?

And by the way, this thing started, as I understand it, Ken Ham's creation model is based on the Old Testament. So when you bring in — I'm not a theologian — when you bring in the New Testament, isn't that a little out of the box?

I'm looking for explanations of the creation of the world as we know it based on what I'm going to call science, not historical science, not observational science — science. Things that each of us can do, akin to what we do, we're trying to outguess the characters on murder mystery shows, on crime scene investigation, especially.

What is to become of all of those people who don't see it your way?

For us in the scientific community I remind you that when we find an idea that's not tenable, that doesn't work, that doesn't fly, doesn't hold water, whatever idiom you'd like to embrace, we throw it away, we're delighted.

That's why I say, if you can find a fossil that has swum between the layers, bring it on. You would change the world.

If could you show that somehow the microwave background radiation is not a result of the Big Bang, come on, write your paper, tear it up.

So your view that we're supposed to take your word for this book written centuries ago, translated into American English, is somehow more important than what I can see with my own eyes is an extraordinary claim.

And for those watching online especially, I want to remind you that we need scientists and especially engineers for the future. Engineers use science to solve problems and make things. We need these people so that the United States can continue to innovate and continue to be a world leader. We need innovation and that needs science education.

Thank you.

Moderator Comments

Tom Foreman: All right. Thank you both.

Now we're going to get to the — things moving a little bit faster, and I think they may be quite interesting here. It's 40 to 45 minutes — maybe a little bit more, actually, we'll have a little more — for questions and answers submitted by our audience here in the Creation Museum.

Beforehand, we handed out these cards to everyone. I shuffled them here in the back, and in fact I dropped a lot of them and then I scooped them up again. And if you saw me sorting through them here, it was to get a pile for Mr. Nye and a pile for Mr. Ham so that we can alternate reasonably between them.

Other than that, the only reason I will skip over one is if I can't read it or if it's a question that I don't know how to read because it doesn't seem to make any sense, which sometimes happens just because of the way people write.

What's going to happen is we're going to go back and forth between Mr. Nye and Mr. Ham. Each debater will have two minutes to answer the question addressed to him, and then the other will have one minute to also answer the question, even though it was addressed to the other man.

And I did pull one card aside here because I noticed it was to both men, so we may be able to get to that at some point.

Mr. Ham, you've been up first. If you'll hop up first this time, and Mr. Nye, you can stand by for your responses.

Audience Questions

Expansion of the Universe

Tom Foreman: Two minutes — how does creationism account for the celestial bodies — planets, stars, moons — moving further and further apart, and what function does that serve in the grand design?

Mr. Ham: Well, when it comes to looking at the universe, of course we believe that in the beginning God created the heavens and the earth. And I believe our creationist astronomers would say, yes, you can observe the universe expanding.

Why God is doing that, in fact, in the Bible it even says He stretches out the heavens and seems to indicate that there is an expansion of the universe. And so we would say, yes, you can observe that; that fits with what we call observational science.

Exactly why God did it that way, I can't answer that question, of course, because the Bible says that God made the heavens for His glory, and that's why He made the stars that we see out there, and it's to tell us how great He is and how big He is. And in fact, I think that's the thing about the universe; the universe is so large, so big out there.

One of our planetarium programs looks at this, where we go in and show you how large the universe is. And I think it shows us how great God is, how big He is, that He's an all-powerful God, He's an infinite God, an infinite, all-knowing God who created the universe to show us His power.

I mean, can you imagine that? And the thing that's remarkable, in the Bible, for instance it says, on the fourth day of creation, and oh, "He made the stars also." It's almost like, "Oh, by the way, I made the stars." And just to show us, He's an all-powerful God, He's an infinite God. So, "I made the stars," and He made them to show us how great He is. And He is; He's an infinite creator God.

And the more that you understand what that means, that God is all-powerful, infinite, you stand back in awe, you realize how small we are. You realize, wow, that God would consider this planet is so significant that He created human beings here knowing they would sin, and yet stepped into history to die for us and be raised from the dead and offer us the free gift of salvation — wow, what a God.

And that's what I would say when I see the universe as it is.

Tom Foreman: Mr. Nye, one minute. Any response?

Mr. Nye: There's a question that troubles us all from the time we are absolutely youngest and first able to think. And that is, where did we come from? Where did I come from?

And this question is so compelling that we've invented the science of astronomy, we've invented life science, we've invented physics, we've discovered these natural laws so that we can learn more about our origin and where we came from.

To you, when it says He invented the stars also, that's satisfying, you're done, oh good. Okay, to me, when I look at the night sky, I want to know what's out there, I'm driven. I want to know if what's out there is any part of me, and indeed it is. The "oh, by the way" I find compelling, you are satisfied.

And the big thing I want from you, Mr. Ham, is can you come up with something that you can predict?

Do you have a creation model that predicts something that will happen in nature?

Origin of Matter

Tom Foreman: And that's time. Mr. Nye, the next question is for you.
How did the atoms that created the Big Bang get there?

Mr. Nye: This is the great mystery; you've hit the nail on the head. No, this is, so where did — what was before the Big Bang? This is what drives us; this is what we want to know, let's keep looking, let's keep searching.

When I was young, it was presumed that the universe was slowing down. There's a Big Bang, except it's in outer space, there's no air, so it goes out like that. [Motions]

And so people presumed that it would slow down, that the universe, that gravity especially, would hold everything together, and maybe it's going to come back and explode again. And people went out — and the mathematical expression is "Is the universe flat?" — this is a mathematical expression. Will the universe slow down, slow down, slow down asymptotically without ever stopping?

Well, in 2004, Saul Perlmutter and his colleagues went looking for the rate at which the universe was slowing down. Let's go out and measure it, and we're doing it with this extraordinary system of telescopes around the world, looking at the night sky, looking for super novae; these are a standard brightness that you can infer distances with. And the universe isn't slowing down; it's accelerating. The universe is accelerating in its expansion.

And do you know why? Nobody knows why. Nobody knows why.

And you'll hear the expression nowadays "dark energy," "dark matter," which are mathematical ideas that seem to reckon well with what seems to be the gravitational attraction of clusters of stars, galaxies, and their expansion. And then isn't it reasonable that whatever is out there causing the universe to expand is here also, and we just haven't figured out how to detect it.

My friends, suppose a science student from the Commonwealth of Kentucky pursues a career in science and finds out the answer to that deep question — where did we come from? What was before the Big Bang? To us, this is wonderful and charming and compelling. This is what makes us get up and go to work every day, is to try to solve the mysteries of the universe.

Tom Foreman: And that's time. Mr. Ham, a response?

Mr. Ham: Bill, I just want to let you know that there actually is a book out there that actually tells us where matter came from.

And the very first sentence in that book says, "In the beginning, God created the heavens and the earth." And really that's the only thing that makes sense; it's the only thing that makes sense of why not just matter is here and where it came from, but why matter — when you look at it, we have information and language systems that build life, not just matter.

And where did that come from, because matter can never produce information? Matter can never produce a language system. Languages only come from an intelligence; information only comes from information.

The Bible tells us that the things we see, like in the Book of Hebrews, are made from things that are unseen. An infinite creator God who created the universe, created matter, the energy, space-mass-time universe, and created the information for life. It's the only thing that makes logical sense.

Evidence Supporting Creationism

Tom Foreman: All right, Mr. Ham, a new question here.

The overwhelming majority of people in the scientific community have presented valid physical evidence, such as carbon dating and fossils, to support evolutionary theory. What evidence besides the literal word of the Bible supports creationism?

Mr. Ham: Well, first of all, I often hear people talking about the majority. I would agree that the majority of scientists would believe in millions of years, the majority would believe in evolution. But there's a large group out there that certainly don't.

But first thing I want to say is that it's not the majority that's a judge of truth. There have been many times in the past when the majority have got it wrong.

The majority of doctors in England once thought after you cut up bodies you could go and deliver babies and wonder why the death rate was high in hospitals until they found out about diseases caused by bacteria and so on.

The majority once thought the appendix was a leftover organ from our evolutionary ancestry, so when it's okay, rip it out, when it's diseased, rip it out anyway. But these days we know that it's for the immune system and it's very, very important.

So, you know, first it's important to understand that just because a majority believes something doesn't mean that it's true.

1:45:00

And then I'm sorry — I missed the last part of the question there.

Tom Foreman: What was the — make sure I have the right question here.

Mr. Ham: About carbon-dating.

Tom Foreman: So what evidence besides the literal word of the Bible supports creationism?

Mr. Ham: Okay, one of the things I was doing was I was making predictions, I made some predictions, there's a whole list of predictions. And I was saying if the Bible's right and we're all descendants of Adam and Eve, there's one race; and I went through and talked about that. If the Bible's right and God made kinds, I went through and talked about that.

And so really that question comes down to the fact that we're again dealing with the fact there's aspects about the past that you can't scientifically prove because you weren't there, but observational science in the present.

Bill and I all have the same observational science; we're here in the present, we can see radioactivity. But when it comes to them talking about the past, you're not going to be scientifically able to prove that, and that's what we need to admit.

But we can be great scientists in the present, as the examples I gave you of Dr. Damadian or Dr. Stuart Burgess or Dr. Fabich, and we can be investigating the present. Understanding the past is a whole different matter.

Tom Foreman: Mr. Nye, a one-minute response.

Mr. Nye: Thank you, Mr. Ham. I have to disabuse you of a fundamental idea. If a scientist — if anybody makes a discovery that changes the way people view natural law, scientists embrace him or her; this person's fantastic.

Louis Pasteur — you made reference to germs. No, if you find something that changes — that disagrees with common thought, that's the greatest thing going in science; we look forward to that change, we challenge you.

Tell us why the universe is accelerating, tell us why these mothers were getting sick. And we found an explanation for it.

And just the idea that the majority has sway in science is true only up to a point.

And then the other thing I just want to point out, what you may have missed in evolutionary explanations of life, is it's the mechanism by which we add complexity. The earth is getting energy from the sun all the time, and that energy is used to make life forms somewhat more complex.

Origin of Consciousness

Tom Foreman: And that's time.

New question for you, Mr. Nye. How did consciousness come from matter?

Mr. Nye: Don't know; this is a great mystery.

A dear friend of mine is a neurologist; she studies the nature of consciousness.

Now I will say I used to embrace a joke about dogs; I love dogs — I mean who doesn't?

And you can say — this guy remarked, "I've never seen a dog paralyzed by self-doubt." Actually, I have.

Furthermore, the thing that we celebrate — there are three sun dials on the planet Mars that bear an inscription to the future, "To those who visit here, we wish you safe journey and the joy of discovery." It's inherently optimistic about the future of humankind that we will one day walk on Mars.

But the joy of discovery, that's what drives us, the joy of finding out what's going on.

So we don't know where consciousness comes from, but we want to find out. Furthermore, I'll tell you it's deep within us. I claim that I have spent time with dogs that have had the joy of discovery. It's way inside us; we have one ancestor, as near as we can figure.

And by the way, if you can find what we in science call a second genesis — this is to say, did life start another way on the earth — there are researchers at Astrobiology Institute, researchers supported by NASA, your tax dollars, that are looking for answers to that very question. Is it possible that life could start another way? Is there some sort of life form akin to science fiction that's crystal instead of membranous? This would be a fantastic discovery that would change the world.

The nature of consciousness is a mystery; I challenge the young people here to investigate that very question. And I remind you, taxpayers and voters that might be watching, if we do not embrace the process of science — I mean in the mainstream — we will fall behind economically; this is a point I can't say enough.

Tom Foreman: Mr. Ham, a one-minute response.

Mr. Ham: Bill, I do want to say that there is a book out there that does document where consciousness came from. And in that book, the One who created us said that He made man in His image, and He breathed into man and he became a living being.

And so the Bible does document that; that's where consciousness came from, that God gave it to us.

And you know, the other thing I want to say is, I'm sort of a little — I have a mystery, and that is, you talk about the joy of discovery. But you also say that when you die it's over, and that's the end of you. And if when you die it's over and you don't even remember you were here, what's the point of the joy of discovery anyway, I mean in an ultimate sense? I mean, you know, you won't ever know you were ever here, and no one who knew you will know they were ever here ultimately, so what's the point anyway?

I love the joy of discovery because this is God's creation and I'm finding more out about that to take dominion for man's good and for God's glory.

Change Your Mind

Tom Foreman: And that's time.

Mr. Ham, a new question. This is a simple question, I suppose but one that actually is fairly profound for all of us in our lives. What, if anything, would ever change your mind?

Mr. Ham: Well, the answer to that question is, I'm a Christian. And as a Christian, I can't prove it to you, but God has definitely shown me very clearly through His Word and shown Himself in the person of Jesus Christ, the Bible is the Word of God. And I admit that that's where I start from.

I can challenge people that you can go and test that; you can make predictions based on that, you can check the prophecies in the Bible, you can check the statements in Genesis, you can check that. And I did a little bit of that tonight.

And I can't ultimately prove that to you; all I can do is to say to someone, "Look, if the Bible really is what it claims to be, if it really is the word of God, and that's what it claims, then check it out."

And the Bible says, "If you come to God believing that He is, He will reveal Himself to you," and you will know. As Christians, we can say we know. And so as far as the Word of God is concerned, no, no one is ever going to convince me that the Word of God is not true.

But I do want to make a distinction here and for Bill's sake. We build models based upon the Bible, and those models are always subject to change. The fact of Noah's Flood is not subject to change; the model of how the Flood occurred is subject to change, because we observe in the current world, and we're able to come up with maybe different ways this could have happened or that could have happened.

And that's part of that scientific discovery, that's part of what it's all about.

So the bottom line is that as a Christian, I have a foundation. But as a Christian, I would ask Bill the question, what would change your mind?

I mean, you said even if you came to faith, you'd never give up believing in billions of years. I think I quoted you correctly; you said something like that recently.

So that would be also my question to Bill.

Tom Foreman: Time. Mr. Nye?

Mr. Nye: We would just need one piece of evidence. We would need the fossil that swam from one layer to another.

We would need evidence that the universe is not expanding.

We would need evidence that the stars appear to be far away but they're not.

We would need evidence that rock layers can somehow form in just 4,000 years instead of the extraordinary amount.

We would need evidence that somehow you can reset atomic clocks and keep neutrons from becoming protons.

You could bring on any of those things and you would change me immediately. The question I have for you, though, fundamentally, and for everybody watching — Mr. Ham, what can you prove?

What you have done tonight is spent most of the — all of the time coming up with explanations about the past. What can you really predict, what can you really prove in a conventional scientific — or in a conventional "I have an idea that makes a prediction and it comes out the way I see it"?

This is very troubling to me.

Evidence for the Age of the Earth

Tom Foreman: Mr. Nye, a new question.

Outside of radiometric methods, what scientific evidence supports your view of the age of the earth?

Mr. Nye: The age of the earth. Well, the age of stars.

Let's see — radiometric evidence is pretty compelling. Also, the deposition rates. It was Lyell, a geologist, who realized, he — my recollection, he came up with the first use of the term deep time, when people realized that the earth had to be much, much older.

In a related story, there was a mystery as to how the earth could be old enough to allow evolution to have taken place. How could the earth possibly be 3 billion years old?

Lord Kelvin did a calculation; if the sun were made of coal and burning, it couldn't be more than 100,000 or so years old.

But radioactivity was discovered; radioactivity is why the earth is still as warm as it is, it's why the earth has been able to sustain its internal heat all these millennia.

And this discovery, it's something like — this question, "Without radiometric dating how would you view the age of the earth?" to me, it's akin to the expression, "Well, if things were any other way, things would be different." This is to say, that's not how the world is.

Radiometric dating does exist, neutrons do become protons, and that's our level of understanding today.

The universe is accelerating; these are all provable facts. That there was a flood 4,000 years ago is not provable.

In fact, the evidence, for me at least, as a reasonable man, is overwhelming that it couldn't possibly have happened; there's no evidence for it.

Furthermore, Mr. Ham, you never quite addressed this issue of the skulls. There are many, many steps in what appears to be the creation or the coming into being of you and me, and those steps are consistent with evolutionary theory.

Tom Foreman: And that's time. Mr. Ham, your response.

Mr. Ham: By the way, I just want people to understand too, in regard to the age of the earth being about 4.5 billion years, no earth rock was

Bill Nye and Ken Ham

dated to get that date. They dated meteorites, and because they assumed meteorites were the same age as the earth left over from the formation of the solar system, that's where that comes from. People think they dated rocks on the earth to get the 4.5 billion years; that's just not true.

And the other point that I was just making — and I just put this slide back up because I happen to just have it here — and that is I said at the end of my first rebuttal time that there are hundreds of physical processes that set limits on the age of the earth.

Here's the point — every dating method involves a change with time, and there are hundreds of them.

And if you assume what was there to start with and you assume something about the rate and you know about the rate, you make lots of those assumptions. Every dating method has those assumptions; most of the dating methods — 90% of them — contradict the billions of years.

There's no absolute age-dating method from scientific method because you can't prove, scientifically, young or old.

Continental Drift

Tom Foreman: And here is a new question; it starts with you, Mr. Ham.

Can you reconcile the change in the rate continents are now drifting versus how quickly they must have traveled at creation 6,000 years ago?

Mr. Ham: The rate — sorry, I missed that word.

Tom Foreman: Can you reconcile the speed at which continents are now drifting today to the rate they would have had to have traveled 6,000 years ago to reach where we are now? I think that's the question.

Mr. Ham: Okay, I think I understand the question.

Actually, this again illustrates exactly what I'm talking about in regard to historical science and observational science. We can look at continents today — and we have scientists who have written papers about this on our website. I'm definitely not an expert in this area, and don't claim to be — but there are scientists, even Dr. Andrew Snelling, our PhD geologist, has done a lot of research here too as well, and there are others out there, into plate tectonics and continental drift.

And certainly we can see movements of plates today. And if you look at those movements, and if you assume the way it's moving today, the rate it's moving, that it's always been that way in the past, see, that's an assumption. That's the problem when it comes to understanding these things.

You can observe movement, but then to assume that it's always been like that in the past, that's historical science. And in fact we would believe basically in catastrophic plate tectonics that as a result of the Flood, at the time of the Flood, there was catastrophic breakup of the earth's surface. And what we're seeing now is sort of, if you like, a remnant of that movement.

And so we do not deny the movement, we do not deny the plates; what we would deny is that you can use what you see today as a basis for just extrapolating into the past.

It's the same with the Flood; you can say, well, layers today only get laid down slowly in places. But if there was a global Flood, that would have changed all of that. Again, it's this emphasis on historical science and observational science.

And I would encourage people to go to our website at Answers in Genesis because we do have a number of papers — in fact very technical papers — Dr. John Baumgartner is one who has written some very extensive work dealing with this very issue.

On the basis of the Bible, of course, we believe there's one continent to start with, because the waters were gathered together into one place. So we do believe that the continent has split up, but particularly the Flood had a lot to do with that.

Tom Foreman: And time on that. Mr. Nye, a response.

Mr. Nye: It must have been easier for you to explain this a century ago, before the existence of tectonic plates was proven. If you go into a clock store and there's a bunch of clocks, they're not all going to say exactly the same thing. Do you think that they're all wrong?

2:00:00

The reason that we acknowledge the rate at which continents are drifting apart — one of the reasons — is we see what's called sea floor spreading in the Mid-Atlantic. The earth's magnetic field has reversed over the millennia, and as it does, it leaves a signature in the rocks, as the continental plates drift apart. So you can measure how fast the continents were spreading; that's how we do it on the outside.

As I said, I lived in Washington state when Mount St. Helens exploded. That's a result of a continental plate going under another continental plate and cracking, and this water-laden rock led to a steam explosion; that's how we do it on the outside.

Favorite Color

Tom Foreman: Time. And this is a question for you, Mr. Nye, but I guess I can put it to both of you.

One word answer, please: favorite color?

Mr. Nye: I will go along with most people and say green. And it's an irony that green plants reflect green light.

Tom Foreman: Did I not say a one-word answer? I said one-word answer.

Mr. Nye: Most of the light from [multiple speakers].

Tom Foreman: Mr. Ham, favorite color?

Mr. Nye: It's a mystery.

Mr. Ham: Well, can I have three words since he had 300?

Tom Foreman: You can have three.

Mr. Ham: Okay, observational science, blue. [Motions to shirt]

Second Law of Thermodynamics

Tom Foreman: All right. We're back to you, Mr. Nye.

How do you balance the theory of evolution with the second law of thermodynamics?

And I'd like to add a question here; what is the second law of thermodynamics?

Mr. Nye: The second law of thermodynamics is fantastic, and I call the words of Eddington, who said, "If you have a theory that disagrees with Isaac Newton, that's a great theory; if you have a theory that disagrees with relativity, wow, you've changed the world, that's great. "But if your theory disagrees with the second law of thermodynamics, I can offer you no hope, I can't help you."[33]

And the second law of thermodynamics basically is where you lose energy to heat. This is why car engines are about 30% efficient, that's it, thermodynamically; that's why you want the hottest explosion you can get in the coldest outside environment. You have to have a difference between hot and cold, and that difference can be assessed scientifically or mathematically with this word entropy, this disorder of molecules.

But the fundamental thing that this questioner has missed is the earth is not a closed system. So there's energy pouring in here from the sun, if I may, day and night — ha-ha — because the night, it's pouring in on the other side. And so that energy is what drives living things on earth, especially for, in our case, plants.

By the way, if you're here in Kentucky, about a third and maybe a half of the oxygen you breathe is made in the ocean by phytoplankton, and they get their energy from the sun.

So the second law of thermodynamics is a wonderful thing; it has allowed us to have everything you see in this room. Because our power generation depends on the robust and extremely precise computation of how much energy is in burning fuel.

Whether it's nuclear fuel or fossil fuel or some extraordinary fuel to be discovered in the future, the second law of thermodynamics will govern any turbine that makes electricity that we all depend on and allowed all these shapes to exist.

Tom Foreman: Any response, Mr. Ham?

Mr. Ham: Let me just say two things, if I can — if a minute goes that fast — or long.

One is, you know what? Here's a point we need to understand. You can have all the energy that you want, but energy or matter will never produce life. God imposed information, a language system, and that's

---

33. The actual quote: " The law that entropy always increases holds, I think, the supreme position among the laws of Nature. If someone points out to you that your pet theory of the universe is in disagreement with Maxwell's equations — then so much the worse for Maxwell's equations. If it is found to be contradicted by observation — well, these experimentalists do bungle things sometimes. But if your theory is found to be against the second law of thermodynamics I can give you no hope; there is nothing for it but to collapse in deepest humiliation." Sir Arthur Stanley Eddington, *The Nature of the Physical World* (1927).

how we have life. Matter by itself could never product life no matter what energy you have.

And even if you've got a dead stick; you can have all the energy in the world in the dead stick, it's going to decay, and it's not going to produce life. From a creationist perspective, we certainly agree. I mean, before man sinned, there was digestion and so on. But because of the Fall, now things are running down; God doesn't hold everything together as He did back then.

So now we see in regard to the second law of thermodynamics, we'd say it's sort of, in a sense, a bit out of control now compared to what it was originally, which is why we have a running down universe.

Hypothetical Evidence of the Age of the Earth

Tom Foreman: And that's time. A new question for you, Mr. Ham. Hypothetically, if evidence existed that caused you to have to admit that the earth was older than 10,000 years and creation did not occur over six days, would you still believe in God and the historical Jesus of Nazareth and that Jesus was the Son of God?

Mr. Ham: Well, I've been emphasizing all night, you cannot ever prove — using the scientific method in the present, you can't prove the age of the earth. So you can never prove it's old, so there is no hypothetical, because you can't do that.

Now, we can certainly use methods in the present and making assumptions. I mean, creationists use methods that change over time, as I said, there's hundreds of physical processes that you can use, but they set limits on the age of the universe, but you can't ultimately prove the age of the earth, not using the scientific method. You can't ultimately prove the age of the universe.

Now, you can look at methods and you can see that there are many methods that contradict billions of years, many methods that seem to support thousands of years. As Dr. Faulkner said in the little video clip I showed, there is nothing in observational astronomy that contradicts a young universe.

Now, I've said to you before and I admit again that the reason I believe in a young universe is because of the Bible's account of origins. I believe that God, who has always been there, the infinite creator God, revealed in His Word what He did for us. And when we add up those dates, we get thousands of years. But there's nothing in observational science that contradicts that.

But there — as far as the age of the earth, the age of the universe, even when it comes to the fossil record — that's why I really challenge Christians. If you're going to believe in millions of years for the fossil record, you got a problem with the Bible, and that is that then you've got have death and disease and suffering before sin.

So there is no hypothetical in regard to that; you can't prove scientifically the age of the earth or the universe, bottom line.

Tom Foreman: Mr. Nye.

Mr. Nye: Well, of course this is where we disagree. You can prove the age of the earth with great robustness by observing the universe around us.

And I get the feeling, Mr. Ham, that you want us to take your word for it. This is to say, your interpretation of a book written thousands of years ago, as translated into American English, is more compelling for you than everything that I can observe in the world around me. This is where you and I, I think, are not going to see eye-to-eye.

You asserted that life cannot come from something that's not alive. Are you sure? Are you sure enough to say that we should not continue to look for signs of water and life on Mars, that that's a waste? You're sure enough to claim that? That is an extraordinary claim that we want to investigate.

Once again, what is it you can predict? What do you provide us that can tell us something about the future, not just about your vision of the past?

God and Science

Tom Foreman: Time. New question, Mr. Nye.

Is there room for God in science?

Mr. Nye: Well, we remind us, there are billions of people around the world who are religious and who accept science and embrace it, and especially all the technology that it brings us.

Is there anyone here who doesn't have a mobile phone that has a camera? Is there anyone here whose family members have not benefited from modern medicine? Is there anyone here who doesn't use email? Is

351

there anybody here who doesn't eat? Because we use information sent from satellites in space to plant seeds on our farms; that's how we're able to feed 7.1 billion people where we used to barely be able to feed a billion.

So that's what I see, that's what — we have used science or the process. Science for me is two things.

It's the body of knowledge, the atomic number of rubidium, and it's the process, the means by which we make these discoveries.

So for me, that's not really that connected with your belief in a spiritual being or a higher power. If you reconcile those two, scientists — the head of the National Institutes of Health is a devout Christian. There are billions of people in the world who are devoutly religious. They have to be compatible, because those same people embrace science.

The exception is you, Mr. Ham; that's the problem for me. You want us to take your word for what's written in this ancient text to be more compelling than what we see around us.

The evidence for a higher power and spirituality is for me separate.

I encourage you to take the next minute and address this problem of the fossils, this problem of the ice layers, this problem of the ancient trees, this problem of the Ark — I mean really address it. And so then we could move forward.

But right now, I see no incompatibility between religions and science.

Tom Foreman: Mr. Ham, response?

Mr. Ham: Yes, I actually want to take the minute to address the question.

And let me just say this — my answer would be God is necessary for science. In fact, you know, you talked about cell phones; yes, I have a cell phone. I love technology, we love technology here at Answers in Genesis. And I have e-mail; probably had millions of them while I have been speaking up here.

And satellites and what you said about the information we get, I agree with all that.

See, they're the things that can be done in the present. And that's just like I showed you.

Dr. Stuart Burgess, who invented that gear set for the satellite; creationists can be great scientists.

But see, I say God is necessary because you have to assume the laws of logic, you have to assume the laws of nature, you have to assume the uniformity of nature.

And there's a question I had for you. Where does that come from if the universe is here by natural processes?

You know, Christianity and science, the Bible and science, go hand in hand; we love science! But again, you've got to understand, inventing things, that's very different than talking about our origins, two very different things.

Literal Interpretation of the Bible

Tom Foreman: Mr. Ham, a new question. Do you believe the entire Bible is to be taken literally?

For example, should people who touch pigskin — I think it says here — be stoned? Can men marry multiple women?

Mr. Ham: Do I believe the entire Bible should be taken literally? Well, remember in my opening address I said we have to define our terms. So when people ask that question and say "literally," I have to know what that person meant by literally.

Now, I would say this — if you say "naturally," and that's what you mean by literally, I would say yes, I take the Bible naturally. What do I mean by that? Well, if it's history, as Genesis is, it's written as typical historical narrative, you take it as history. If it's poetry, as we find in the Psalms, then you take it as poetry. It doesn't mean it doesn't teach truth, but it's not a cosmological account in the sense that Genesis is.

There's prophecy in the Bible, and there's literature in the Bible concerning future events and so on.

So if you take it as written naturally, according to type of literature, and you let it speak to you in that way, that's how I take the Bible.

It's God's revelation to man. He used different people — the Bible says that all Scripture is inspired by God, so God moved people by His Spirit to write His words.

And also there's a lot of misunderstanding in regard to Scripture and in regard to the Israelites. I mean, we have laws in our civil government here in America that the government sets. Well, there were certain laws for Israel. And you know, some people take all that out of context and then they try to impose it on us today as Christians and say, "You should be obeying those laws." It's a misunderstanding of the Old Testament; it's a misunderstanding of the New Testament.

And you know, again, it's important to take the Bible as a whole, interpreting Scripture with Scripture. If it really is the Word of God, then there's not going to be any contradiction, which there's not.

And by the way, when men were married to multiple women, there were lots of problems. And the Bible condemns that for what it is and the Bible is very clear. You know, the Bible is a real book; there were people that did things that were not in accord with Scripture, and it records this for us. Helps you understand it's a real book. But marriage was one man for one woman. Jesus reiterated that in Matthew 19, as I had in my talk. And so those that did marry multiple women were wrong.

Tom Foreman: Time there. Mr. Nye, a response.

Mr. Nye: So it sounds to me, just listening to you over the last two minutes, that there are certain parts of this document — of the Bible — that you embrace literally and other parts you consider poetry. So it sounds to me in those last two minutes like you're going to take what you like and interpret literally and other passages you're going to interpret as poetic or descriptions of human events.

All that aside, I'll just say, scientifically, or as a reasonable man, it doesn't seem possible that all these things that contradict your literal interpretation of those first few passages, all those things that contradict that, I find unsettling when you want me to embrace the rest of it as literal.

Now, I, as I say, am not a theologian, but we started this debate, is Ken Ham's creation model viable, does it hold water, can it fly, does it describe anything? And I'm still looking for an answer.

Intelligent Designer

Tom Foreman: And time on that. Mr. Nye, here's a new question.

I believe this was miswritten here because they've repeated a word, but I think I know what they were trying to ask. Have you ever believed that evolution was accomplished through way of a higher power?

I think that's what they're trying to ask here; this is the intelligent design question, I think. If so, why or why not? Why could not the evolutionary process be accomplished in this way?

Mr. Nye: I think you may have changed the question just a little, but no, it's all good.

Tom Foreman: The word-for-word question is, have you ever believed that evolution partook through way of evolution? [Multiple speakers]

2:15:00

Mr. Nye: Let me introduce these ideas for Mr. Ham to comment.

The idea that there's a higher power that has driven the course of events in the universe and our own existence is one that you cannot prove or disprove. And this gets into this expression agnostic; you can't know. I'll grant you that.

When it comes to intelligent design, which is, if I understand your interpretation of the question, intelligent design has a fundamental misunderstanding of the nature of nature. This is to say the old expression is if you were to find a watch in the field and you'd pick it up, you would realize that it was created by somebody who was thinking ahead, something with an organization chart with somebody at the top, and you'd order screws from screw manufacturers and springs from spring manufacturers and glass crystals from crystal manufacturers. But that's not how nature works.

This is the fundamental insight in the explanation for living things that's provided by evolution. Evolution is a process that adds complexity through natural selection. This is to say nature has its mediocre designs eaten by its good designs. And so the perception that there's a designer that created all this is not necessarily true because we have an explanation that is far more compelling and provides predictions and things are repeatable.

I'm sure, Mr. Ham, here at the facility you have an organization chart. I imagine you're at the top, and it's a top-down structure. Nature is not that way. Nature is bottom-up; this was the discovery. Things merge up, whatever makes it keeps going, whatever doesn't make it falls away. And this is compelling and wonderful and fills me with joy, and is inconsistent with a top-down view.

Tom Foreman: And that's time. Mr. Ham.

Mr. Ham: What Bill Nye needs to do for me is to show me an example of something — some new function that arose that was not previously possible from the genetic information that was there. And I would claim and challenge you that there is no such example that you can give. That's why I brought up the example in my presentation of Lenski's experiments in regard to *E. coli*, and there were some that seemed to develop the ability to exist on citrate.

But as Dr. Fabich said, from looking at his research, he's found that that information was already there; it's just the gene that switched on and off. And so there is no example, because information that's there in the genetic information of different animals, plants, and so on, there's no new function that can be added.

Certainly great variation within a kind, and that's what we look at. But you'd have to show an example of brand-new function that never previously was possible; there is no such example that you can give anywhere in the world.

Creationism in Commerce

Tom Foreman: Fresh question here.

Mr. Ham, name one institution, business, or organization other than a church, amusement park or the Creation Museum, that is using any aspect of Creationism to produce its product.

Mr. Ham: Any scientist out there, Christian or non-Christian, that is involved in inventing things, involved in scientific method, is using creation. They are, because they are borrowing from a Christian worldview. They're using the laws of logic; I keep emphasizing that.

I want Bill to tell me in a view of the universe that's a result of natural processes, explain where the laws of logic came from. Why should we trust the laws of nature? I mean, are they going to be the same tomorrow as they were yesterday?

In fact, some of the greatest scientists that ever lived — Isaac Newton, James Clerk Maxell, Michael Faraday — were creationists. And as one of them said, you know, he's thinking God's thoughts after Him.[34]

---

34. This quote is from Johannes Kepler who described the process of studying creation as "merely striving to think God's thoughts after Him."

And that's really — modern science really came out of that thinking, that we can do experiments today and we can do the same tomorrow, we can trust the laws of logic, we can trust the laws of nature. And if we don't teach our children correctly about this, they're not going to be innovative and they're not going to be able to come up with inventions to advance in our culture.

And so I think the person was trying to get out that, see, there are lots of secularists out there doing work and they don't believe in creation and they come up with great inventions. Yes, but my point is they are borrowing from the Christian worldview to do so.

And, as you saw from the video quotes I gave, people like Andrew Fabich and also Dr. Faulkner have published in the secular journals. There's lots of creationists out there who publish, people might not know they're creationists because the topic doesn't specifically pertain to creation versus evolution, but there's lots of them out there. If I go to our website, there's a whole list there of scientists who are creationists who are out there doing great work in this world and helping to advance technology.

Tom Foreman: Mr. Nye.

Mr. Nye: There's a reason that I don't accept the Ken Ham model of creation; it's that it has no predictive quality, as you touched on.

And something that I've always found troubling — it sounds as though — and next time around you can correct me — it sounds as though you believe your world view, which is a literal interpretation of most parts of the Bible, is correct. Well, what became of all those people who never heard of it, never heard of you? What became of all those people in Asia? What became of all those First Nations people in North America? Were they condemned and doomed?

I mean, I don't know how much time you've spent talking to strangers, but they are not sanguine about that, to have you tell them that they are inherently lost or misguided. It's very troubling.

And you say there are no examples in nature; there are countless examples of how the process of science makes predictions.

Evolving Intelligence

Tom Foreman: Mr. Nye, since evolution teaches that man is evolving and growing smarter over time, how can you explain the numerous evidences of man's high intelligence in the past?

Mr. Nye: Hang on. There's no evidence that men — or humans are getting smarter.

Now — especially if you ever met my old boss, heh, heh, heh.

No, it's that what happens in evolution — and it's a British word that was used in the middle 1800s — it's survival of the fittest. And in this usage, it doesn't mean the most pushups or the highest scores on standardized tests. It means those that fit in the best.

Our intellect, such as it is, has enabled us to dominate the world. I mean, the evidence of humans is everywhere. James Cameron just made another trip to the bottom of the ocean, the deepest part of the ocean, the first time since 1960. And when they made the first trip, they found a beer can. Humans are everywhere. And so it is our capacity to reason that has taken us to where we are now.

If a germ shows up, as it did for example in World War I, where more people were killed by the flu than were killed by the combatants in World War I — that is a troubling and remarkable fact — if the right germ shows up, we'll be taken out, we'll be eliminated. Being smarter is not a necessary consequence of evolution. So far, it seems to be the way things are going because of the remarkable advantage it gives to us over — we can control our environment and even change it, as we're doing today, apparently by accident.

So everybody just take a little while and grasp this fundamental idea — it's how you fit in with nature around you. So as the world changed, as it did, for example, the ancient dinosaurs, they were taken out by a worldwide fireball apparently caused by an impactor; that's the best theory we have. And we are the result of organisms that lived through that catastrophe. It's not necessarily smarter; it's how you fit in with your environment.

Tom Foreman: Mr. Ham, a response.

Mr. Ham: I remember at university one of my professors was very excited to give us some evidence for evolution, and he said, "Look at this, here's an example, these fish have evolved the ability not to see." And he was going to give an example of blind cave fish, and he said, "See, in this cave, they're evolving, because now the ones that are living there, their ancestors had eyes and now these ones are blind." And I remember this, telling my professor, "But wait a minute; now they can't do something that they could do before." They might have an advantage in this sense; in a situation that's dark like that, those with eyes might have got diseases and died out. Those that had mutations for no eyes are the ones that survived. It's not survival of the fittest; it's survival of those who survive. And it's survival of those that have the information in their circumstance to survive.

But it's not — you're not getting new information, you're not getting new function. There's no example of that at all. So we need to correctly understand these things.

Basis of Belief

Tom Foreman: All right. We're down to our final question here, which I'll give to both of you.

And in the interest of fairness here, because it is a question to both of you, let's give each man two minutes on this if we can, please. And also in the interest of you having started first, Mr. Ham, I will have you start it first here. You had the first word; Mr. Nye will have the last word.

The question is, what is the one thing more than anything else upon which you base your belief?

Mr. Ham: What is the one thing upon anything else which I base my belief? Well, again, to summarize the things that I've been saying, there is a book called the Bible. It's a very unique book, it's very different to any other book out there.

In fact, I don't know of any other religion that has a book that starts off by telling you that there's an infinite God and talks about the origin of the universe and the origin of matter and the origin of light and the origin of darkness and the origin of day and night and the origin of the earth and the origin of dry land and the origin of plants and the origin of the sun, moon and stars, the origin of sea creatures, the origin of flying creatures, the origin of land creatures, the origin of man, the origin of woman, the origin of death, the origin of sin, the origin of marriage, the origin of different languages, the origin of clothing, the origin of nations.

I mean, it's a very, very specific book, and it gives us an account of a global Flood and the history and the Tower of Babel. And if that history is true, then what about the rest of the book? Well, that history also says man is a sinner and it says that man is separated from God. And it gives us a message that we call the gospel, the message of salvation, that God's Son stepped into history to die on a cross, be raised from the dead and offers a free gift of salvation.

Because the history is true, that's why the message based in history is true.

I actually went through some predictions and listed others, and there's a lot more that you can look at, and you can go and test it for yourself.

If this book really is true, it is so specific, it should explain the world, it should make sense of what we see. The Flood, yes, we have fossils all over the world. The Tower of Babel, yes, different people groups, different languages. They have flood legends, very similar to the Bible, creation legends similar to the Bible. There's so much you can look at, and prophecy and so on.

And most of all, as I said to you, the Bible says if you come to God believing that He is, He'll reveal himself to you, you will know. If you search out the truth you really want God to show you as you would search after silver and gold, He will show you, He will reveal Himself to you.

Tom Foreman: Mr. Nye.

Mr. Nye: Would you repeat the question?

Tom Foreman: The question is, what is the one thing more than anything else upon which you base your belief?

Mr. Nye: As my old professor Carl Sagan said so often, "When you're in love, you want to tell the world!" And I base my beliefs on the information and the process that we call science. It fills me with joy to make discoveries every day of things I had never seen before. It fills me to joy to know that we can pursue these answers. It is a wonderful and astonishing thing to me that we are — you and I are somehow at least one of the ways that the universe knows itself. You and I are a product of the universe.

It's astonishing, I admit — I see your faces — that we have come to be because of the universe's existence. And we are driven to pursue that, to find out where we came from.

And the second question we all want to know — are we alone? Are we alone in the universe?

And these questions are deep within us, and they drive us. So the process of science, the way we know nature, is the most compelling thing to me.

And I just want to close by reminding everybody what's at stake here. If we abandon all that we've learned, our ancestors, what they've learned about nature and our place in it, if we abandon the process by which we know it, if we eschew — if we let go of everything that people have learned before us, if we stop driving forward, stop looking for the next answer to the next question, we in the United States will be out-competed by other countries, other economies.

Now, that would be okay, I guess, but I was born here, I'm a patriot. And so we have to embrace science education. To the voters and taxpayers that are watching, please keep that in mind. We have to keep science education in science — science classes.

Thank you.

Moderator Closing Remarks

Tom Foreman: One tiny bit of important housekeeping for everyone here. The county is now under a Level II snow emergency; drive home carefully. You'll have a lot to talk about, but drive carefully.

This debate will be archived at debatelive.org — that's debatelive.org, one word. It will be found at that site for several days so you can encourage friends and family to watch and talk it over.

Thanks so much to Mr. Nye and to Mr. Ham for an excellent discussion.

I'm Tom Foreman. Thank you. Goodnight from Petersburg, Kentucky, and the Creation Museum.

Appendix B

How Old Is the Earth?

The question of the age of the earth has produced heated discussions on Internet debate boards, TV, radio, in classrooms, and in many churches, Christian colleges, and seminaries. The primary sides are

- Young-earth proponents (biblical age of the earth and universe of about 6,000 years)[1]
- Old-earth proponents (secular age of the earth of about 4.5 billion years and a universe about 14 billion years old)[2]

The difference is immense! Let's give a little history of where these two basic calculations came from and which worldview is more reasonable.

Where Did a Young-earth Worldview Come From?

Simply put, it came from the Bible. Of course, the Bible doesn't say explicitly anywhere, "The earth is 6,000 years old." Good thing it doesn't; otherwise it would be out of date the following year. But we wouldn't expect an all-knowing God to make that kind of a mistake.

God gave us something better. In essence, He gave us a "birth certificate." For example, using a personal birth certificate, a person can calculate

---

1. Not all young-earth creationists agree on this age. Some believe that there may be small gaps in the genealogies of Genesis 5 and 11 and put the maximum age of the earth at about 10,000–12,000 years. However, see chapter 5, "Are There Gaps in the Genesis Geologies?"
2. Some of these old-earth proponents accept molecules-to-man biological evolution and so are called theistic evolutionists. Others reject neo-Darwinian evolution but accept the evolutionary timescale for stellar and geological evolution, and hence agree with the evolutionary order of events in history.

how old he is at any point. It is similar with the earth. Genesis 1 says that the earth was created on the first day of creation (Genesis 1:1–5). From there, we can begin to calculate the age of the earth.

Let's do a rough calculation to show how this works. The age of the earth can be estimated by taking the first five days of creation (from earth's creation to Adam), then following the genealogies from Adam to Abraham in Genesis 5 and 11, then adding in the time from Abraham to today.

Adam was created on day 6, so there were five days before him. If we add up the dates from Adam to Abraham, we get about 2,000 years, using the Masoretic Hebrew text of Genesis 5 and 11.[3] Whether Christian or secular, most scholars would agree that Abraham lived about 2,000 B.C. (4,000 years ago). So a simple calculation is:

$$
\begin{array}{r}
5 \text{ days} \\
+ \sim 2{,}000 \text{ years} \\
+ \sim 4{,}000 \text{ years} \\
\hline
\sim 6{,}000 \text{ years}
\end{array}
$$

At this point, the first five days are negligible. Quite a few people have done this calculation using the Masoretic text (which is what most English translations are based on) and with careful attention to the biblical details, they have arrived at the same time frame of about 6,000 years, or about 4000 B.C. Two of the most popular, and perhaps best, are a recent work by Dr. Floyd Jones[4] and a much earlier book by Archbishop James Ussher[5] (1581–1656). See table 1.

Table 1. Jones and Ussher

Name	Age Calculated	Reference and Date
Archbishop James Ussher	4004 B.C.	*The Annals of the World*, A.D. 1658
Dr. Floyd Nolan Jones	4004 B.C.	*The Chronology of the Old Testament*, A.D. 1993

3. Bodie Hodge, "Ancient Patriarchs in Genesis," Answers in Genesis, www.answersingenesis.org/articles/2009/01/20/ancient-patriarchs-in-genesis.
4. Floyd Nolan Jones, *Chronology of the Old Testament* (Green Forest, AR: Master Books, 2005).
5. James Ussher, *The Annals of the World,* transl. Larry and Marion Pierce (Green Forest, AR: Master Books, 2003).

The misconception exists that Ussher and Jones were the only ones to arrive at a date of 4000 B.C.; however, this is not the case at all. Jones[6] lists several chronologists who have undertaken the task of calculating the age of the earth based on the Bible, and their calculations range from 5501 to 3836 B.C. A few are listed in table 2.

Table 2. Chronologists' Calculations According to Dr. Jones

	Chronologist	When Calculated?	Date B.C.
1	Julius Africanus	c. 240	5501
2	George Syncellus	c. 810	5492
3	John Jackson	1752	5426
4	Dr William Hales	c. 1830	5411
5	Eusebius	c. 330	5199
6	Marianus Scotus	c. 1070	4192
7	L. Condomanus	n/a	4141
8	Thomas Lydiat	c. 1600	4103
9	M. Michael Maestlinus	c. 1600	4079
10	J. Ricciolus	n/a	4062
11	Jacob Salianus	c. 1600	4053
12	H. Spondanus	c. 1600	4051
13	Martin Anstey	1913	4042
14	W. Lange	n/a	4041
15	E. Reinholt	n/a	4021
16	J. Cappellus	c. 1600	4005
17	E. Greswell	1830	4004
18	E. Faulstich	1986	4001
19	D. Petavius	c. 1627	3983
20	Frank Klassen	1975	3975
21	Becke	n/a	3974
22	Krentzeim	n/a	3971
23	W. Dolen	2003	3971
24	E. Reusnerus	n/a	3970
25	J. Claverius	n/a	3968
26	C. Longomontanus	c. 1600	3966
27	P. Melanchthon	c. 1550	3964
28	J. Haynlinus	n/a	3963
29	A. Salmeron	d. 1585	3958
30	J. Scaliger	d. 1609	3949
31	M. Beroaldus	c. 1575	3927
32	A. Helwigius	c. 1630	3836

6. Jones, *Chronology of the Old Testament*, p. 26.

As you will likely note from table 2, the dates are not all 4004 B.C. There are several reasons chronologists have different dates,[7] but two primary reasons:

1. Some used the Septuagint or another early translation instead of the Hebrew Masoretic text. The Septuagint is a Greek translation of the Hebrew Old Testament, done about 250 B.C. by about 70 Jewish scholars (hence it is often cited as the LXX, which is the Roman numeral for 70). It is good in most places, but appears to have a number of inaccuracies. For example, one relates to the Genesis chronologies where the LXX indicates that Methuselah would have lived past the Flood, without being on the ark!

2. Several points in the biblical timeline are not straightforward to calculate. They require very careful study of more than one passage. These include exactly how much time the Israelites were in Egypt and what Terah's age was when Abraham was born. (See Jones's and Ussher's books for a detailed discussion of these difficulties.)

The first four in table 2 (bolded) are calculated from the Septuagint, which gives ages for the patriarchs' firstborn much higher than the Masoretic text or the Samarian Pentateuch (a version of the Old Testament from the Jews in Samaria just before Christ). Because of this, the Septuagint adds in extra time. Though the Samarian and Masoretic texts are much closer, they still have a few differences. See table 3.

Using data from table 2 (excluding the Septuagint calculations and including Jones and Ussher), the average date of the creation of the earth is 4045 B.C. This still yields an average of about 6,000 years for the age of the earth.

Extra-biblical Calculations for the Age of the Earth

Cultures throughout the world have kept track of history as well. From a biblical perspective, we would expect the dates given for creation of the earth to align more closely to the biblical date than billions of years.

This is expected since everyone was descended from Noah and scattered from the Tower of Babel. Another expectation is that there should be

---

7. Others would include gaps in the chronology based on the presence of an extra Cainan in Luke 3:36. But there are good reasons this should be left out. See Ken Ham, gen. ed., *The New Answers Book 2* (Green Forest, AR: Master Books, 2008), chapter 5, "Are There Gaps in the Genesis Genealogies?" and chapter 27, "Isn't the Bible Full of Contradictions?"

Table 3. Septuagint, Masoretic, and Samarian Early Patriarchal Ages at the Birth of the Following Son

Name	Masoretic	Samarian Pentateuch	Septuagint
Adam	130	130	230
Seth	105	105	205
Enosh	90	90	190
Cainan	70	70	170
Mahalaleel	65	65	165
Jared	162	62	162
Enoch	65	65	165
Methuselah	187	67	167
Lamech	182	53	188
Noah	500	500	500

some discrepancies about the age of the earth among people as they scattered throughout the world, taking their uninspired records or oral history to different parts of the globe.

Under the entry "creation," *Young's Analytical Concordance of the Bible*[8] lists William Hales's accumulation of dates of creation from many cultures, and in most cases Hales says which authority gave the date. See table 4.

Historian Bill Cooper's research in *After the Flood* provides intriguing dates from several ancient cultures.[9] The first is that of the Anglo-Saxons, whose history has 5,200 years from creation to Christ, according to the Laud and Parker Chronicles. Cooper's research also indicated that Nennius's record of the ancient British history has 5,228 years from creation to Christ. The Irish chronology has a date of about 4000 B.C. for creation, which is surprisingly close to Ussher and Jones! Even the Mayans had a date for the Flood of 3113 B.C.

This meticulous work of many historians should not be ignored. Their dates of only thousands of years are good support for the biblical date of about 6,000 years, but not for billions of years.

8. Robert Young, *Young's Analytical Concordance to the Bible* (Peadoby, MA: Hendrickson, 1996), referring to William Hales, *A New Analysis of Chronology and Geography, History and Prophecy,* 1 (1830): p. 210.
9. Bill Cooper, *After the Flood* (UK: New Wine Press, 1995), p. 122–129.

The Origin of the Old-earth Worldview

Prior to the 1700s, few believed in an old earth. The approximate 6,000-year age for the earth was challenged only rather recently, beginning in the late 18th century. These opponents of the biblical chronology essentially left God out of the picture. Three of the old-earth advocates included Comte de Buffon, who thought the earth was at least 75,000 years old. Pièrre LaPlace imagined an indefinite but very long history. And Jean Lamarck also proposed long ages.[10]

However, the idea of millions of years really took hold in geology when men like Abraham Werner, James Hutton, William Smith, Georges Cuvier, and Charles Lyell used their interpretations of geology as the standard, rather than the Bible. Werner estimated the age of the earth at about one million years. Smith and Cuvier believed untold ages were needed for the formation of rock layers. Hutton said he could see no geological evidence of a beginning of the earth; and building on Hutton's thinking, Lyell advocated "millions of years."

From these men and others came the consensus view that the geologic layers were laid down slowly over long periods of time based on the rates at which we see them accumulating today. Hutton said:

> The past history of our globe must be explained by what can be seen to be happening now. . . . No powers are to be employed that are not natural to the globe, no action to be admitted except those of which we know the principle.[11]

This viewpoint is called naturalistic uniformitarianism, and it excludes any major catastrophes such as Noah's Flood. Though some, such as Cuvier and Smith, believed in multiple catastrophes separated by long periods of time, the uniformitarian concept became the ruling dogma in geology.

Thinking biblically, we can see that the global Flood in Genesis 6–8 would wipe away the concept of millions of years, for this Flood would explain massive amounts of fossil layers. Most Christians fail to realize

---

10. Terry Mortenson, "The Origin of Old-earth Geology and its Ramifications for Life in the 21st Century," *TJ* 18, no. 1 (2004): 22–26, online at www.answersingenesis.org/tj/v18/i1/oldearth.asp.

11. James Hutton, *Theory of the Earth* (Trans. of Roy. Soc. of Edinburgh, 1785); quoted in A. Holmes, *Principles of Physical Geology* (UK: Thomas Nelson & Sons Ltd., 1965), p. 43–44.

that a global flood could rip up many of the previous rock layers and redeposit them elsewhere, destroying the previous fragile contents. This would destroy any evidence of alleged millions of years anyway. So the rock layers can theoretically represent the evidence of either millions of years or a global flood, but not both. Sadly, by about 1840, even most of the Church had accepted the dogmatic claims of the secular geologists and rejected the global Flood and the biblical age of the earth.

After Lyell, in 1899, Lord Kelvin (William Thomson) calculated the age of the earth, based on the cooling rate of a molten sphere, at a maximum of about 20–40 million years (this was revised from his earlier calculation of 100 million years in 1862).[12] With the development of radiometric dating in the early 20th century, the age of the earth expanded radically. In 1913, Arthur Holmes's book, *The Age of the Earth,* gave an age of 1.6 billion years.[13] Since then, the supposed age of the earth has expanded to its present estimate of about 4.5 billion years (and about 14 billion years for the universe).

12. Mark McCartney, "William Thompson: King of Victorian Physics," *Physics World,* December 2002, physicsweb.org/articles/world/15/12/6.
13. Terry Mortenson, "The History of the Development of the Geological Column," in *The Geologic Column,* eds. Michael Oard and John Reed (Chino Valley, AZ: Creation Research Society, 2006).

Table 5. Summary of the Old-earth Proponents for Long Ages

Who?	Age of the Earth	When Was This?
Comte de Buffon	78 thousand years old	1779
Abraham Werner	1 million years	1786
James Hutton	Perhaps eternal, long ages	1795
Pièrre LaPlace	Long ages	1796
Jean Lamarck	Long ages	1809
William Smith	Long ages	1835
Georges Cuvier	Long ages	1812
Charles Lyell	Millions of years	1830–1833
Lord Kelvin	20–100 million years	1862–1899
Arthur Holmes	1.6 billion years	1913
Clair Patterson	4.5 billion years	1956

But there is growing scientific evidence that radiometric dating methods are completely unreliable.[14]

Christians who have felt compelled to accept the millions of years as fact and try to fit them into the Bible need to become aware of this evidence. It confirms that the Bible's history is giving us the true age of the creation.

Today, secular geologists will allow some catastrophic events into their thinking as an explanation for what they see in the rocks. But uniformitarian thinking is still widespread, and secular geologists will seemingly never entertain the idea of the global, catastrophic Flood of Noah's day.

The age of the earth debate ultimately comes down to this foundational question: Are we trusting man's imperfect and changing ideas and assumptions about the past? Or are we trusting God's perfectly accurate eyewitness account of the past, including the creation of the world, Noah's global Flood, and the age of the earth?

---

14. For articles at the layman's level, see www.answersingenesis.org/home/area/faq/dating.asp. For a technical discussion, see Larry Vardiman, Andrew Snelling, and Eugene Chaffin, eds., *Radioisotopes and the Age of the Earth,* vol. 1 and 2 (El Cajon, CA: Institute for Creation Research; Chino Valley, AZ: Creation Research Society, 2000 and 2005). See also "Half-Life Heresy," *New Scientist*, October, 21 2006, pp. 36–39, abstract online at www.newscientist.com/channel/fundamentals/mg19225741.100-halflife-heresy-accelerating-radioactive-decay.html.

Other Uniformitarian Methods for Dating the Age of the Earth

Radiometric dating was the culminating factor that led to the belief in billions of years for earth history. However, radiometric dating methods are not the only uniformitarian methods. Any radiometric dating model or other uniformitarian dating method can and does have problems, as referenced before. All uniformitarian dating methods require assumptions for extrapolating present-day processes back into the past. The assumptions related to radiometric dating can be seen in these questions:

- Initial amounts?
- Was any parent amount added?
- Was any daughter amount added?
- Was any parent amount removed?
- Was any daughter amount removed?
- Has the rate of decay changed?

If the assumptions are truly accurate, then uniformitarian dates should agree with radiometric dating across the board for the same event. However, radiometric dates often disagree with one another and with dates obtained from other uniformitarian dating methods for the age of the earth, such as the influx of salts into the ocean, the rate of decay of the earth's magnetic field, and the growth rate of human population.[15]

The late Dr. Henry Morris compiled a list of 68 uniformitarian estimates for the age of the earth by Christian and secular sources.[16] The current accepted age of the earth is about 4.54 billion years based on radiometric dating of a group of meteorites,[17] so keep this in mind when viewing table 6.

As you can see from table 6, uniformitarian maximum ages for the earth obtained from other methods are nowhere near the 4.5 billion years estimated by radiometric dating; of the other methods, only two calculated dates were as much as 500 million years.

The results from some radiometric dating methods completely undermine those from the other radiometric methods. One such example

---

15. For many more examples see www.answersingenesis.org/go/young.
16. Henry M. Morris, *The New Defender's Study Bible* (Nashville, TN: World Publishing, 2006), p. 2076–2079.
17. C.C. Patterson, "Age of Meteorites and the Age of the Earth," *Geochemica et Cosmochemica Acta*, 10 (1956): 230–237.

Table 6. Uniformitarian Estimates Other than Radiometric Dating Estimates for Earth's Age Compiled by Morris

	0 – 10,000 years	>10,000 – 100,000 years	>100,000 – 1 million years	>1 million – 500 million years	>500 million – 4 billion years	>4 billion – 5 billion years
Number of uniformitarian methods*	23	10	11	23	0	0

* When a range of ages is given, the maximum age was used to be generous to the evolutionists. In one case, the date was uncertain so it was not used in this tally, so the total estimates used were 67. A few on the list had reference to Saturn, the sun, etc., but since biblically the earth is older than these, dates related to them were used.

is carbon-14 (^{14}C) dating. As long as an organism is alive, it takes in ^{14}C and ^{12}C from the atmosphere; however, when it dies, the carbon intake stops. Since ^{14}C is radioactive (decays into ^{14}N), the amount of ^{14}C in a dead organism gets less and less over time. Carbon-14 dates are determined from the measured ratio of radioactive carbon-14 to normal carbon-12 ($^{14}C/^{12}C$). Used on samples that were once alive, such as wood or bone, the measured $^{14}C/^{12}C$ ratio is compared with the ratio in living things today.

Now, ^{14}C has a derived half-life of 5,730 years, so the ^{14}C in organic material supposedly 100,000 years old should all essentially have decayed into nitrogen.[18] Some things, such as wood trapped in lava flows, said to be millions of years old by other radiometric dating methods, still have ^{14}C in them.[19] If the items were really millions of years old, then they shouldn't have any traces of ^{14}C. Coal and diamonds, which are found in or sandwiched between rock layers allegedly millions of years old, have been shown to have ^{14}C ages of only tens of thousands of years.[20] So

18. This does not mean that a ^{14}C date of 50,000 or 100,000 would be entirely trustworthy. I am only using this to highlight the mistaken assumptions behind uniformitarian dating methods.
19. Andrew Snelling, "Conflicting 'Ages' of Tertiary Basalt and Contained Fossilized Wood, Crinum, Central Queensland Australia," *Technical Journal* 14, no. 2 (2005): p. 99–122.
20. John Baumgardner, "^{14}C Evidence for a Recent Global Flood and a Young Earth," in *Radioisotopes and the Age of the Earth: Results of a Young-Earth Creationist Research Initiative*, ed. Vardiman et al. (Santee, CA: Institute for Creation Research; Chino Valley, AZ: Creation Research Society, 2005), p. 587–630.

which date, if any, is correct? The diamonds or coal can't be millions of years old if they have any traces of ^{14}C still in them. This shows that these dating methods are completely unreliable and indicates that the presumed assumptions in the methods are erroneous.

Similar kinds of problems are seen in the case of potassium-argon dating, which has been considered one of the most reliable methods. Dr. Andrew Snelling, a geologist, points out several of these problems with potassium-argon, as seen in table 7.[21]

These and other examples raise a critical question. If radiometric dating fails to give an accurate date on something of which we *do* know the true age, then how can it be trusted to give us the correct age for rocks that had no human observers to record when they formed? If the methods don't work on rocks of known age, it is most unreasonable to trust that they work on rocks of unknown age. It is far more rational to trust the Word of the God who created the world, knows its history perfectly, and has revealed sufficient information in the Bible for us to understand that history and the age of the creation.

Conclusion

When we start our thinking with God's Word, we see that the world is about 6,000 years old. When we rely on man's fallible (and often demonstrably false) dating methods, we can get a confusing range of ages from a few thousand to billions of years, though the vast majority of methods do not give dates even close to billions.

Cultures around the world give an age of the earth that confirms what the Bible teaches. Radiometric dates, on the other hand, have been shown to be wildly in error.

The age of the earth ultimately comes down to a matter of trust — it's a worldview issue. Will you trust what an all-knowing God says on the subject or will you trust imperfect man's assumptions and imaginations about the past that regularly are changing?

> Thus says the LORD: "Heaven is My throne, and earth is My footstool. Where is the house that you will build Me? And where is the place of My rest? For all those things My hand has made,

21. Andrew Snelling, "Excess Argon: The 'Achilles' Heel' of Potassium-Argon and Argon-Argon Dating of Volcanic Rocks," *Impact,* January 1999, online at www.icr.org/article/436.

and all those things exist," says the LORD. "But on this one will I look: On him who is poor and of a contrite spirit, and who trembles at My word" (Isaiah 66:1–2).

Appendix C

The Triune God

There are numerous passages that teach that God the Father, God the Son, and God the Holy Spirit are distinct persons and yet each hold the attributes of deity.

But the Bible also emphatically and unambiguously declares that there is only one God (Isaiah 44:8, 45:18; Deuteronomy 6:4; Malachi 2:10; James 2:19; Mark 12:29). Hence, taking all the Scriptures into account, orthodox Christian theology has always affirmed that the one true God is triune in nature — three co-equal and co-eternal persons in the Godhead.

This triune God (or Trinity) began to allude to this aspect of His nature right in Genesis 1:26–27. There we read that "God said, 'Let us make man in Our image' . . . God created man in His own image." Here God is a plural noun, *said* is in the third-person singular verb form, and we see both the plural pronoun *our* and the singular *His* referring to the same thing (God's image). This is not horribly confused grammar. Rather, we are being taught, in a limited way, that God is a plurality in unity. We can't say from this verse that He is a trinity, but God progressively reveals more about Himself in later Scriptures to bring us to that conclusion.

In Isaiah 48:12–16 we find the speaker in the passage describing himself as the Creator and yet saying that "the Lord God and His Spirit have sent Me." This is further hinting at the doctrine of the trinity, which becomes very clear in the New Testament. There are many other Old Testament Scriptures that hint at the same idea.

In Matthew 28:18–20 Jesus commanded His disciples to baptize His followers in the name (singular) of the Father, Son, and Holy Spirit. John's Gospel tells us that "the Word" is God who became man in Jesus Christ (John 1:1–3, 14). Jesus was fully man and fully God. Many other verses combine together to teach that God is triune.

The following chart is an accumulation of many of the passages that show the deity of the Father, the Son, and the Holy Spirit.

	God, the Father	God, the Son	God, the Holy Spirit
is the Creator	Genesis 1:1, 2:4, 14:19–22; Deuteronomy 32:6; Psalm 102:25; Isaiah 42:5, 45:18; Mark 13:19; 1 Corinthians 8:6; Ephesians 3:9; Hebrews 2:10; Revelation 4:11	John 1:1–3; Colossians 1:16–17; 1 Corinthians 8:6; Hebrews 1:2, 8–12	Genesis 1:2; Job 33:4; Psalm 104:30
is unchanging and eternal	Psalm 90:2, 102:25–27; Isaiah 43:10; Malachi 3:6	Micah 5:2; Colossians 1:17; Hebrews 1:8–12, 13:8; John 8:58	Hebrews 9:14
has a distinct will	Luke 22:42	Luke 22:42	Acts 13:2; 1 Corinthians 12:11
accepts worship	Too many to list	Matthew 14:33; Hebrews 1:6	—
accepts prayer	Too many to list	John 14:14; Romans 10:9–13; 2 Corinthians 12:8–9	—
is the only savior	Isaiah 43:11, 45:21; Hosea 13:4; 1 Timothy 1:1	John 4:42; Acts 4:12, 13:23; Philippians 3:20; 2 Timothy 1:10; Titus 1:4, 2:13, 3:6; 2 Peter 1:11, 2:20, 3:18; 1 John 4:14	John 3:5; 1 Corinthians 12:3

has the power to resurrect	1 Thessalonians 1:8–10	John 2:19, 10:17	Romans 8:11
is called God	John 1:18, 6:27; Philippians 1:2, 2:11; Ephesians 4:6; 2 Thessalonians 1:2	John 1:1–5, 1:14, 1:18, 20:28; Colossians 2:9; Hebrews 1:8; Titus 2:13	Acts 5:3–4; 2 Corinthians 3:15–17
is called Mighty God	Isaiah 10:21; Luke 22:69	Isaiah 9:6	—
is omnipresent/ everywhere	1 Kings 8:27; Isaiah 46:10	Matthew 28:18–20	Psalm 139:7–10
is omnipotent/ has power and authority	2 Chronicles 20:6, 25:8; Job 12:13; Romans 1:20; 1 Corinthians 6:14; Jude 1:25	John 3:31, 3:35, 14:6, 16:15; Philippians 2:9–11	1 Samuel 11:6; Luke 1:35
is all-knowing	Psalm 139:2; Isaiah 46:10; 1 John 3:20; Acts 15:8	John 16:3, 21:17	1 Corinthians 2:10–11
has the fullness of God in him (not just "a part of God")	N/A	Colossians 2:9	—
gives life	Genesis 1:21, 1:24, 2:7; Psalm 49:15; John 3:16, 5:21; 1 Timothy 6:13	John 5:21, 14:6, 20:31; Romans 5:21	2 Corinthians 3:6; Romans 8:11
loves	John 3:16; Romans 8:39; Ephesians 6:23; 1 John 4:6, 4:16	Mark 10:21; John 15:9; Ephesians 5:25, 6:23	Romans 15:30
has ownership of believers	Psalm 24:1; John 8:47	Romans 7:4, 8:9	—
is distinct	Matthew 3:16–17, 28:19; John 17:1	Matthew 3:16–17, 4:1, 28:19; John 17:1	1 Samuel 19:20; Matthew 3:16–17, 4:1, 28:19
is judge	Genesis 18:25; Psalm 7:11, 50:6, 94:1–2, 96:13, 98:9; John 8:50; Romans 2:16	John 5:21–27; Acts 17:31; 2 Corinthians 5:10; 2 Timothy 4:1	—

forgives sin	Micah 7:18	Luke 7:47–50	—
claimed divinity	Exodus 20:2	Matthew 26:63–64	—
is uncreated, the First and the Last, the Beginning and the End	Isaiah 44:6	Revelation 1:17–18, 22:13	—
lives in the believer	John 14:23; 2 Corinthians 6:16; 1 John 3:24	John 14:20–23; Galatians 2:20; Colossians 1:27	John 14:16–17; Romans 8:11; 1 Peter 1:11
has the godly title "I Am," pointing to the eternality of God	Exodus 3:14	John 8:58	—
is personal and has fellowship with other persons	1 John 1:3	1 Corinthians 1:9; 1 John 1:3	Acts 13:2; 2 Corinthians 13:14; Ephesians 4:30; Philippians 2:1
makes believers holy (sanctifies them)	1 Thessalonians 5:23	Colossians 1:22	1 Peter 1:2
knows the future	Isaiah 46:10; Jeremiah 29:11	Matthew 24:1–51, 26:64; John 16:32, 18:4	1 Samuel 10:10, 19:20; Luke 1:67; 2 Peter 1:21
is called "Lord of Lords"	Deuteronomy 10:17; Psalm 136:3	Revelation 17:14, 19:16	—

Appendix D

Topical Links to Subject Matter

For more information on subjects covered in the debate, go to the following website: https://answersingenesis.org/countering-the-culture/bill-nye-debates-ken-ham/answers/. The following subjects are listed there with links to each item.

Animal Migration
How Did Animals Spread All Over the World from Where the Ark
    Landed?
Feedback: Animal Migrations
Church Leader "Aghast" at Belief in a Worldwide Flood?

Animals and Carnivory
Creation's Original Diet and the Changes at the Fall
How Did Defense/Attack Structures Come About?
Odd Saber-Toothed Beast Discovered — Preyed on . . . Plants?

Astronomy
Straight Answers to Common Questions
Universe by Design
What Does the Bible Say about Astronomy?
Just Right for Life

Feedback: Assuming the Origin of Comets
Discussing Recent Developments in Astronomy
The Big Bang and Evidence for the "Inflation Theory" — A Preliminary
Comment

Bad Evolutionary Arguments
Peppered Moths — Back on the agenda?
An Examination of Error: Trends in Science Teaching and Textbooks
Error in the UK Classroom
Recapitulation Repackaged and Re-Applied
Something Fishy about Gill Slits!
The Human Vermiform Appendix: A General Surgeon's Reflections
Appendix

Bible
How Do We Know That the Bible Is True?
How Did We Get the Bible in English?
Dead Sea Scrolls — Timeless Treasures
How Should We Interpret the Bible, Part 1: Principles for
Understanding God's Word
How Should We Interpret the Bible, Part 2: Is Genesis 1–11 Historical
Narrative?
Is the Old Testament Reliable?
Is the New Testament Reliable?
Contradictions: Introduction
Why Don't Christians Follow All the Old Testament Laws?
How Should We Understand the Literary Genre of the Creation
Account? (audio)
Why Do We Regard the Creation Account as Historical Narrative?
(audio)

Big Bang
Universe by Design: Misconceptions about General Relativity,
Cosmology, and the Big Bang
Galaxies — Unexplained Spirals
Science Still in the Dark about Dark Energy
Do We Live in a Giant Cosmic Bubble?
Have Cosmologists Discovered Evidence of Inflation?

The Big Bust
Universe by Design: Non-Biblical Alternatives to the Big Bang
The Hubble Law
The Origin of the Universe
Universe by Design: Introduction
The Bible and Modern Astronomy, Part 1
Big Bang — The Evolution of a Theory

Canyon Creation
Canyon Creation: Faster Than Most People Would Think Possible,
    Beauty Was Born from Devastation
Feedback: What Is Unique about the Colorado River?
Durham's Grand Canyon: A Canyon in an Instant
Mount St. Helens — Evidence for Genesis!
Mount St. Helens in Washington State
Why Is Grand Canyon So Significant for Geology? (audio)

Climate Change
Should We Be Concerned about Climate Change?
Global Warming: Examine the Issue Carefully
Human-Caused Global Warming Slight So Far
How Much Global Warming Is Natural?

Consciousness from Matter
Apes Are Our Brothers — Just Ask the Post Office
What Makes Us Human, and Why It Is Not the Brain: A Creationist
    Defense of the Soul
Evolutionary Psychology: Why It Fails as a Science and Is Dangerous
The Essential Nature of Man

Coral Reefs
Ancient "Fossil Reefs" — Formed in the Flood?
Massive Modern Reefs — Finding Time to Grow
Creation, Flood, and Babel Legends
Genesis — The Original Myth Buster
Is Genesis 1–11a Derivation from Ancient Myths?
The Genesis Flood — Not Just Another Legend
Was the Dispersion at Babel a Real Event?

Creation Account
Could God Really Have Created Everything in Six Days?
The Days of Creation: A Semantic Approach

Creation Scientists
Do Creationists Reject Science?
Can Creationists Be "Real" Scientists?
Real Scientists, Really?
NASA Creationists!
Creation Scientists and Other Biographies of Interest
Read online: In Six Days: Why Fifty Scientists Choose to Believe in
    Creation
Don't Creationists Deny the Laws of Nature?
God and Natural Law
Never Assume: 3 Assumptions Evolutionists Make
God and Natural Law
3 Assumptions Evolutionists Make
Are We Anti-Science?
Testimony of a Professional Geologist
In Six Days: Why Fifty Scientists Choose to Believe in Creation
Creation Scientists and Other Biographies of Interest
Joseph Lister: Father of Modern Surgery
Antony van Leeuwenhoek: Creation "Magnified" Through His
    Magnificent Microscopes
Biography of Prof. Andy McIntosh
Super-Scientist Slams Society's Spiritual Sickness!
Renowned Scientist Visits Creation Museum
Science or the Bible?
Def Ear to Toleration?
Is Science Secular?
Atheism: An Irrational Worldview
Evolution: The Anti-science
Why Would an Evolutionist Become a Doctor?
Modern Medicine and Ancient Authority (video)
Revolutionary Atmospheric Invention by Victim of Anti-creationist
    Discrimination
Biography of Prof. Stuart Burgess

Biography of Dr. Danny Faulkner
Can Creation Models Be Wrong?

Dinosaur Extinction
The Extinction of the Dinosaurs
Origin of Dinosaur-killing Asteroid Remains a Mystery
What Really Happened to the Dinosaurs?
What Does the Bible Teach about Dinosaurs? (audio)

Distant Starlight
A Proposal for a New Solution to the Light Travel Time Problem
Distant Starlight: The Anisotropic Synchrony Convention
Anisotropic Synchrony Convention — A Solution to the Distant
    Starlight Problem

Dominion Mandate
Can an Evolutionist Celebrate Earth Day?
Feedback: Does the Bible Prohibit Space Travel?
Are They Teaching the Truth in Biology Class?

Evidence Is Subject to Interpretation
Cosmologists Can't Agree and Are Still In Doubt!
The Pigs Took It All
How Shall We Refute the "Evidence" Evolutionists Present? (audio)
What Can We Learn from the Scriptures about Astronomy? (audio)

Evolution
Can Natural Processes Explain the Origin of Life?
Why the Miller–Urey Research Argues Against Abiogenesis
Information in Living Organisms
Bottom-Up Science
The Origin of Microorganisms
Genetic "Crossing-over" Is No Help to Evolution
A House Divided
Is Evolution a Religion?
Leading Anti-creationist Philosopher Admits That Evolution Is a
    Religion
Feedback: Evidence of New Genetic Information?
Is Evolution a Religion?
Feedback: Evidence of New Genetic Information?

Gene Duplication: Evolution Shooting Itself in the Foot
In the Beginning Was Information

Fossils
Do Fossils Show Signs of Rapid Burial?
Doesn't the Order of Fossils in the Rock Record Favor Long Ages?
Order in the Fossil Record
How Fast?
Feedback: Where Are All the Bunny Fossils?
Where Are All the Human Fossils?
Why Don't We Find Human & Dinosaur Fossils Together?
Geologic Column
Unlocking the Geologic Record

Genetics
Professor of Genetics Says "No!" to Evolution
Genetics and Biblical Demographic Events
Feedback: "The Search for the Historical Adam" and Population
      Genomics
How Genomes are Sequenced and Why It Matters: Implications for
      Studies in Comparative Genomics of Humans and Chimpanzees

God
How Do We Know There Is a God?
Is There Really a God? How Would You Answer?
Is There Really a God?

Gospel
The Gospel of Jesus Christ
The Biggest Question of All
Seven C's of History
What's the Core Message of the Answers in Genesis Ministry?
Man: The Image of God
Biblically, Could Death Have Existed before Sin?
Did Death of any Kind Exist before the Fall?
Twenty Reasons Why Genesis and Evolution Do Not Mix
Beauty and the Curse
Our Cursed World

Human Evolution

Did Humans Really Evolve from Apelike Creatures?

Making Man Out of Monkeys

It's an Ape… It's a Human… It's… It's… a Missing Link!

What Proof Do We Have of a Literal Adam and Eve? (audio)

Human History and the Flood

The Pyramids of Ancient Egypt

Were the Pyramids Built before the Flood?

Doesn't Egyptian Chronology Prove That the Bible Is Unreliable?

Feedback: How Does Man's History Fit with the Biblical Timeline?

Dating the Pyramids

Evidentialism — The Bible and Assyrian Chronology

Are There Gaps in the Genesis Genealogies?

Why the Electric Battery Was Forgotten

Ancient Civilizations and Modern Man

A Comparison from Secular Historical Records

Farming Frustrations?

Selling Science to the Public

Billions of People in Thousands of Years?

Ice Cores

Do Greenland Ice Cores Show over One Hundred Thousand Years of Annual Layers?

Do Ice Cores Show Many Tens of Thousands of Years?

Rapid Changes in Oxygen Isotope Content of Ice Cores

Deep Layers

Lake Missoula

Aren't Millions of Years Required for Geological Processes?

The Story That Won't Be Told: The Planned Lake Missoula Flood Interpretive Pathway

The Mystery of the Megaflood

The Ice Age

Where Does the Ice Age Fit?

Catastrophic Melting

Continuing Catastrophes

Mars
Water on Mars: A Creationist Response
Was Noah a Martian?
Mars, a Testament to Catastrophe

Morality, Sanctity of Life
Morality and the Irrationality of an Evolutionary Worldview
Morality — The Secular Response?
When Does Life Begin?
Euthanasia: Hospital Humanism

Natural Selection
Does Natural Selection Exist?
Conquering Cockroaches
Is Natural Selection the Same Thing as Evolution?
The Effect of Mutations down on the Farm
Finding God in Galapagos
"Evolution" of Finch Beaks — Again
Natural Selection vs. Evolution
A Poke in the Eye? Lenski and the Adaptive Acrobatics of E. coli

Noah's Ark
Was There Really a Noah's Ark & Flood?
What Did Noah's Ark Look Like?
Genuine Ark, Part 6: Large Construction Crew
Feedback: Was Noah's Ark Seaworthy, or Is That Impossible?
The Large Ships of Antiquity
Thinking Outside the Box

Noah's Care of the Animals
How Could Noah Fit the Animals on the Ark and Care for Them?
Caring for the Animals on the Ark

Nuclear Medical Technologist Schools in Kentucky
Mr. Nye criticized the lack of undergraduate programs in nuclear medicine in Kentucky. The Joint Review Committee on Educational Programs in Nuclear Medicine Technology (JRCN-MT) currently lists one accredited program in the state.

Joint Review Committee on Educational Programs in Nuclear

Medicine Technology (JRCNMT)

Answering Bill Nye — Rebutting Nye's Argument That Kentucky Is Backward Technologically

One Human Race

Are There Really Different Races?

One Blood

OneHumanRace.com

Origin of Life

The Elusive Origin of Life

Life: Designed to Inspire Awe and Aid Learning

Plants and the Flood

How Did Plants Survive the Flood?

What Happened to Land Plants During the Flood?

Plate Tectonics

Can Catastrophic Plate Tectonics Explain Flood Geology?

Plate Tectonics

World Under Water

Time for an Upgrade?

Does the Catastrophic Plate Tectonics Model Assume Too Much Uniformitarianism?

Polystrate Fossils

How Fast?

Collective Portrait

Feedback: What Is the Most Compelling Scientific Evidence of a Young Earth?

Predictions

Successful Predictions by Creation Scientists

Scientists for Creation

The Creation of Planetary Magnetic Fields

Completeness of the Fossil Record

Do Creationists Believe in "Weird" Physics like Relativity, Quantum Mechanics, and String Theory?

Weird Physics

The Hubble Law

Does the Creation Model Make Predictions? Absolutely!

Clipped Fins Hamper Hatchery Salmon, UVic Biologist's Study Finds (evolutionists made an incorrect prediction)

Back Problems: How Darwinism Misled Researchers

Radio Astronomy

The Big Bang and Evidence for the "Inflation Theory" — A Preliminary Comment

Discussing Recent Developments in Astronomy

Universe by Design: Appendix

Echoes of the Big Bang ... or Noise?

Universe by Design: Problems with the Big Bang

Big Bang Explanations Fall Flat

Radiometric Dating

Feedback: Radiometric Dating and Proof

Billion-Fold Acceleration of Radioactivity Demonstrated in Laboratory

The Fallacies of Radioactive Dating of Rocks

Discordant Potassium-Argon Model and Isochron "Ages" for Cardenas Basalt (Middle Proterozoic) and Associated Diabase of Eastern Grand Canyon, Arizona

Radioisotopes and the Age of the Earth

Radioactive "Dating" Failure

More and More Wrong Dates

Reason 8: Radioactivity

Radioisotopes in the Diabase Sill (Upper Precambrian) at Bass Rapids, Grand Canyon, Arizona

Carbon-14 Dating — Understanding the Basics

Carbon-14 in Fossils and Diamonds

A Creationist Puzzle: 50,000-Year-Old Fossils

Radiometric Dating: Back to Basics

Radiometric Dating: Problems with the Assumptions

Radiometric Dating: Making Sense of the Patterns

Does Radiometric Dating Prove the Earth Is Old?

Dating Methods

Radioactive "Dating" in Conflict!

Radio-Dating in Rubble

Stumping Old-Age Dogma
Field Studies in the Columbia River Basalt, Northwest USA
Radioactive and Radiocarbon Dating
Thousands ... Not Billions
Earth's Catastrophic Past
Dating Fossils and Rocks

Religious People Who Do Not Accept Evolution
Feedback: The God of an Old Earth
Feedback: Deeply Saddened over Old-Earth Compromise
Jewish Scientists Who Oppose Darwinism
Muslims — Creationists' Friend?
Building Bridges with Muslims
Evolution, the Election and the "Enlightened"
Council of Europe Proposes Creation Motion Again
A Young Earth — It's Not the Issue!

Reversal of Earth's Magnetic Field
Fossil Magnetism Reveals Rapid Reversals of the Earth's Magnetic Field
The Earth's Magnetic Field and the Age of the Earth
#5 Rapidly Decaying Magnetic Field
The "Principle of Least Astonishment"!
The Earth's Magnetic Field
The Earth's Magnetic Field
Still Trying to Make Ice Cores Old
Evidence for a Young World

Science — The Process of Science (discovery of new ideas, especially those that challenge prevailing opinion)
The Story That Won't Be Told: The Planned Lake Missoula Flood
    Interpretive Pathway
JPL Worker Sues over Intelligent Design Demotion
No Country For Ol' Creationists
Job Candidate Sues UK, Claiming Religion Cost Him the Post
Do Creationists Publish in Notable Refereed Journals?
The Smithsonian/Sternberg Controversy: Cast Doubt on Darwin, Get
    Cast Out
Slaughter of the Dissidents: The Shocking Truth about Killing the

Careers of Darwin Doubters

Science — What Is It?
What Is Science?
Two Kinds of Science?
De-Nyeing Science
Is Science Secular?
Feedback: Evolutionary Call to Arms

Scopes Trial
Why Is the Scopes Trial Significant?
The Scopes "Monkey Trial" — 80 Years Later

Sea Floor Spreading
A Catastrophic Breakup: A Scientific Look at Catastrophic Plate Tectonics
Catastrophic Plate Tectonics: the Geophysical Context of the Genesis Flood

Search for Extraterrestrial Intelligence
Should We Search for Extraterrestrial Intelligence?
Further Comments on the PBS-TV Series "Origins"
Any Little Green Men Out There?
The Bible and Modern Astronomy, Part 2
Secrets of the Universe: What Happens When People Look in the Wrong Place for Signs of Intelligence Outside Earth?
The Search for Alien Life

Second Law of Thermodynamics
The Search for a Cursed Cosmos
Just Add Energy …
The Second Law of Thermodynamics and the Curse
Arguments Christians Shouldn't Use: The Second Law of Thermodynamics Began at the Fall
Thoughts on the Goodness of Creation: In What Sense was Creation "Perfect"?
The Search for a Cursed Cosmos
The Mystery of Life's Origin: Reassessing Current Theories
The Scientific Case Against Evolution

Spacetime: Virtual Particles, Time . . . and the Trinity
Big Bang — The Evolution of a Theory
Light-Travel Time: A Problem for the Big Bang
Universe by Design: Conclusions and Recommendations
How Do Current Astronomical Observations Relate to the Bible?
   (audio)

Speciation After the Flood
No Kind Left Behind: Recounting the Animals on the Ark
Human Evolution — Faster than a Speeding Bullet
Do Species Change?
Zonkeys, Ligers, and Wolphins, Oh My!
What Are "Kinds" in Genesis?
Rapid Speciation (video)
Rapid Speciation (video)

Survival of the Fittest
Misreading Earth's Groanings: Why Evolutionists and Intelligent
   Design Proponents Fail Ecology 101
A Fin with a Function
Persuaded by the Evidence

Tiktaalik
Tiktaalik and the Fishy Story of Walking Fish
Tiktaalik and the Fishy Story of Walking Fish, Part 2
Did Tiktaalik's Pelvis Prepare Fish to Walk on Land?
Fish Fins Are Not Fingers That Failed

Tree Rings
Tree Rings and Biblical Chronology
Living Tree "8,000 Years Older Than Christ"(?)
Biblical Chronology and the 8,000-Year-Long Bristlecone Pine Tree-
   Ring Chronology
Feedback: Revisiting Bristlecone Pines and the Bible
Much-Inflated Carbon-14 Dates from Subfossil Trees: A New
   Mechanism

Worldviews
What's Your Worldview?
Evolutionism — Is There Such a Word?

Critical Thinking Questions

Examples of Critical Thinking: Scientific Application

Examples of Critical Thinking: Biblical Application

Why Is It Impossible to Understand Our World Without a Proper View of God and His Word? (audio)

Young Earth/Universe

Feedback: Radiometric Dating and Proof

Evidence for a Young World

Feedback: What Is the Most Compelling Scientific Evidence of a Young Earth?

Feedback: Lunar Recession

Aren't Millions of Years Required for Geological Processes?

Geological Conflict: Young Radiocarbon Date for Ancient Fossil Wood Challenges Fossil Dating

How Old Is the Earth?

Photo Credits

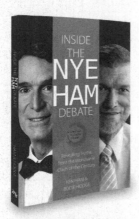
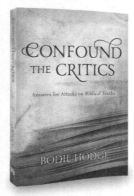

Ken Ham 6 *classics*

The Lie (revised)
How Could a Loving God
Raising Godly Children in an Ungodly World
Already Gone
One Race One Blood
Six Days

978-0-89051-720-8

$74.99

Master Books®
A Division of New Leaf Publishing Group
www.masterbooks.net

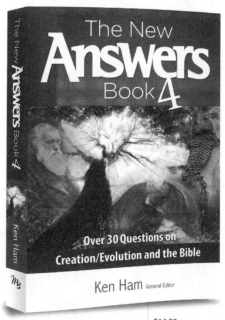
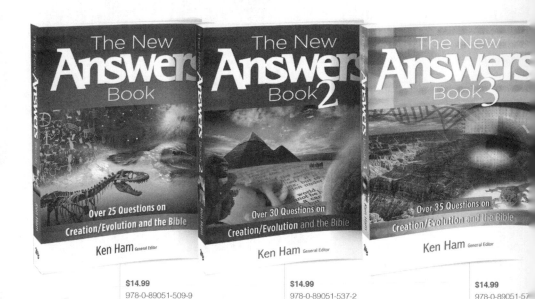

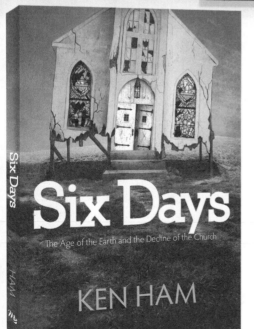

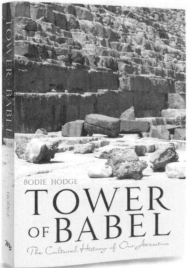